ROBERT MORRIS—PATRIOT AND FINANCIER
AMERICA'S FOREMOST LAND BOOMER

The
GREAT AMERICAN
LAND BUBBLE

The Amazing Story of
Land-Grabbing, Speculations, and Booms
from Colonial Days to
the Present Time

by

A. M. SAKOLSKI
ASSISTANT PROFESSOR OF FINANCE
COLLEGE OF THE CITY OF NEW YORK

Martino Publishing
Mansfield Centre, CT
2011

Martino Publishing
P.O. Box 373,
Mansfield Centre, CT 06250 USA

www.martinopublishing.com

ISBN-13: 978-1-57898-778-8 (softcover: alk. paper)
ISBN-10: 1-57898-778-4 (softcover: alk. paper)

Library of Congress Cataloging-in-Publication Data

Sakolski, Aaron M. (Aaron Morton), 1880-1955.
The great American land bubble: the amazing story of land-
grabbing, speculations, and booms from colonial days to the
present time / A. M. Sakolski.
      p. cm.
Originally published: New York: Harper & Brothers, 1932.
Includes bibliographical references and index.

ISBN-13: 978-1-57898-778-8 (softcover: alk. paper)

ISBN-10: 1-57898-778-4 (softcover: alk. paper)

1.   Land use--United States. 2. Real property--United States--
History. 3. Real estate business--United States. 4. Speculation--
History. 5. Swindlers and swindling. I. Title.

HD191.S3 2009
333.00973--dc22   2009026362

Cover design by T. Matarazzo

Printed in the United States of America On 100% Acid-Free Paper

The
GREAT AMERICAN
LAND BUBBLE

The Amazing Story of
Land-Grabbing, Speculations, and Booms
from Colonial Days to
the Present Time

by

A. M. SAKOLSKI
ASSISTANT PROFESSOR OF FINANCE
COLLEGE OF THE CITY OF NEW YORK

HARPER & BROTHERS PUBLISHERS
NEW YORK AND LONDON
1932

PREFACE

LAND speculation in the United States has been a national business. Yet no history of it has hitherto been written—and small wonder! Pecuniary speculation has ever been looked upon as a dubious business. It therefore has been conducted largely in secret and without enduring records. Arduous research is required by those who delve into its intricate dealings. From time to time, however, an historian or research student has given to the public intimate or fragmentary accounts of isolated episodes relating directly or indirectly to American land speculation. To these authors I wish to convey my acknowledgment of valuable assistance. In the present volume no attempt has been made to give a detailed account of all important speculative land transactions. Moreover the story is restricted to *speculation* and is not directly concerned with the loss or growth of great fortunes from real estate investment.

In the preparation of the manuscript, credit is due to Miss Alice Strass. To Professor H. S. Commager of New York University I owe a debt of gratitude for valuable suggestions, and to Professor John Hastings of the College of the City of New York for the preparation of the maps. Mr. Myron L. Hoch of the Department of Economics at the City College gave valuable assistance in the preparation of the work for publication.

A. M. SAKOLSKI

May, 1932

Contents

Illustrations

THE
GREAT AMERICAN
LAND BUBBLE

CHAPTER I

PRE-REVOLUTIONARY PRECEDENTS

AMERICA, from its inception, was a speculation. It was a speculation to Columbus. It was considered a speculation by the kings of Spain, France and England. They looked upon it as a source of riches in gold, silver and pelts. It was from the land that these precious goods were produced, and the ownership of the land was as essential to them as the political jurisdiction over it. Royal favorites were accordingly given vast territories, and land was distributed to individuals and companies as royal rewards.

The colonial charters granted in England to individuals and companies gave proprietorship of the soil, but the king reserved political jurisdiction and control, as well as the mineral rights. Thus, Penn and Calvert and Oglethorpe received merely grants of land. The governing and feudal rights which they assumed were revocable at the royal will, and as the colonies became more densely settled and advanced in political status, the king appointed governors to rule over them. When the proprietary right to the soil had been given, the possessors of these rights or their assigns continued to hold the land originally allotted to them. James, Duke of York, to whom his affectionate brother had presented the whole Dutch province of New Amsterdam, and more besides, began to sell or otherwise dispose of his vast domain. He granted to Lords Carteret and Berkeley most of the province of New Jersey. These sold out to two companies, —the "Proprietors of East Jersey" and the "Proprietors of West Jersey" respectively,—companies which continued in existence during the eighteenth century, though they lost their feudal rights as early as 1702. James also made other lavish grants. Some of these were revived in later years, causing serious trepidation to property owners whose titles were threatened by new claimants.

Thus, the conveyance of unoccupied lands to private individuals or companies, which undertook the management, settlement and resale, was a common practice in colonial times. In fact, much of the early English settlement of America was conducted on this plan. The London and Plymouth companies were ostensibly trading companies, but the motive of land speculation, though not openly expressed, was an important factor in the settlement of the colonies. As population began to fill up the accessible regions within colonial charter grants, the acquisition of large unsettled tracts for pecuniary gain came more and more into vogue.

During the first hundred years of North American colonization, economic conditions gave little encouragement to private land schemes. Land was too plentiful. A few such enterprises were undertaken, however. Thus, as early as 1661, the Colony of Massachusetts sold to a few individuals for £400 a large tract on the Kennebec River in Maine. This became known as the "Kennebec Purchase." The heirs held it for nearly a century without doing anything with it. In 1753, they incorporated as the "Proprietors of the Kennebec Purchase" and proceeded to dispose of their holdings. The corporation continued in existence until 1816.[1] "The Pejebscot Company" was another Maine land deal. None of these held out promise of profit to proprietors until about a quarter century before the Revolution.

About this time, wealth had accumulated in the colonies. Free land, obtained under crown grants, or "head rights," had ceased. Cities and channels of trade were established and population gradually pushed forward to the Alleghany foothills. The vast unoccupied tracts beyond became a lure. Few dared to settle in the region. Actual ownership was held by the Indians, and claimed by the French. This was not a discouragement, however. Did not the territories occupied by the flourishing colonies once belong to the Indians? And was it not bought from them for mere trifles? Why not, then, establish similar colonies to the west,

[1] *Maine Historical Collections,* Vol. II, pp. 268-294.

and start anew in building up land values. To the descendants of the pioneer colonials, the backwoods, Indians, and hostile Frenchmen presented no serious obstacles.

Proprietorship of large landed estates, moreover, was highly regarded by the colonials. It was an emblem of nobility. It carried with it political as well as pecuniary preferment. This was particularly characteristic of the South. There, during the colonial days the presence of large landed estates, engrossed in comparatively few hands, fostered a landed aristocracy. Land ownership, therefore, was desirable for social and political, as well as for pecuniary reasons. The Virginian was not much of a "gentleman" unless he lived in the midst of countless acres. If he was a non-resident owner, or a large "patentee" of the crown, he employed land agents on the spot to look after his estates or to sell and lease his holdings. Grants of land in the southern colonies were a source of continual political intrigues. In fact, land grabbing in the South began before the importance of either negroes or tobacco was recognized.

As the areas east of the Alleghany Mountains were gradually engrossed, and as towns and plantations spread out to the Piedmont sections, covetous eyes were pointed toward the vast unsettled domain to the westward. The political sovereignty and administrative control of the territory were in doubt. Various colonies claimed a share of the westward area as part of their original charter grants. The charter limits were not fixed, so that the conflicting claims overlapped. This brought about disputes regarding ownership and right to the control of the soil. Intercolonial jealousy and territorial greed led the rival claimants to take measures, secretly and openly, to assert their rights by actual occupation or by royal conveyances.

· · · · ·

The first definite move to obtain a large grant of western land was made in 1748, when a group of Virginians, styling themselves the "Ohio Company," obtained a crown grant of 500,000 acres west of the Alleghanies adjacent to Virginia. The next year another group of forty-six Virginia gentlemen styling themselves "The Loyal Company" received an additional 800,000 acres near by. Both grants were made by the Governor and Council of Virginia. The locations were not surveyed nor definitely marked out. That of the Ohio Company was to be located "south of the Ohio River," and the Loyal Company's grant was to be "in one or more surveys beginning on the bounds between Virginia and South Carolina and running westward to the North Seas." The companies were to locate their lands, and make return of surveys within four years' time.

Both set about to secure their grants. Christopher Gist, one of the noted surveyors of Virginia, was sent in October, 1750, to "search out" and to discover the Ohio Company's lands. He went down the Ohio as far south as the present site of Louisville. During his journey he made strong overtures of friendship with the Indians. He was enthusiastic about the project. "Nothing," he said, "is wanting but cultivation to make it a most delightful country."

In the meantime, the "Loyal Company" group was not idle; its proprietors sent Dr. Thomas Walker, of Albermarle, Va., to make a reconnaissance, and to discover a proper place of settlement. The two "companies" then became engaged in a controversy, and neither made a survey or fixed the bounds of their grants. The apparent ease with which they obtained land donations led to other schemes, and aroused an epidemic of interest in distant western wild lands. Not only was the land ownership eagerly sought after, but the establishment of new colonies, with separate and distinct governments, was planned. Favoritism and collusion infested the Virginian colonial government, due in large part to the persistence of speculators in western land grants. Lobbyists were sent to London to obtain the crown's sanction to land-grabbing schemes and the question of the disposal of the vast western domain won from the French infested British politics. "One half of England is now land mad," wrote George Croghan, of Philadelphia, one of the land schemers, to Sir William Johnson, on March 30, 1766, "and everybody there has their eyes fixed on this country."[2]

George Washington and his half-brothers, Augustine and Lawrence Washington, were concerned in the Ohio Company.

[2] *The Sir William Johnson Papers*, Vol. V, p. 129. See also, C. W. Alvord, *The Mississippi Valley in British Politics*, Cleveland, 1917.

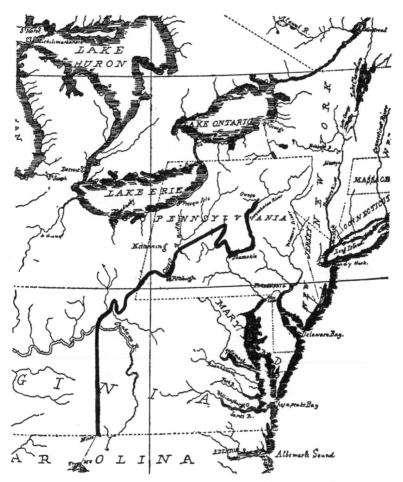

THE BLACK LINE MARKS THE "INDIAN BOUNDARY" BEYOND WHICH THE
COLONISTS WERE ORDERED NOT TO GO

Thus, Washington, early in his political career, was brought into contact with land grabbing. From this time on, until the outbreak of the Revolution, his interest in western lands was supreme. He was one of the most active land speculators of colonial times. He was, moreover, a surveyor by profession. As a "land agent" of Lord Fairfax, whose estates comprised over 5,000,000 acres, he became infected with the "wild land" virus. Besides taking an active part in pressing the claims of the Ohio Company, he, together with his neighbors, the Lees, formed "The Mississippi Company" and petitioned, in 1768, for an additional large grant.

The French and Indian War interrupted for a while Washington's land schemes, but following the peace treaty in 1763, he entered whole-heartedly into western land acquisitions. Virginia had set aside a large section of territory west of the Alleghanies as bounties for its soldiers in the war, and Washington eagerly set about to secure the claims of the veterans. While thus garnering the means of acquiring lands, he secretly employed an agent, his old frontier friend, Captain William Crawford, to seek out and preëmpt the best locations. He had even entered upon plans of colonization and thought of importing Germans from the Palatinate as settlers.

Nor was he dismayed or discouraged, when, in 1763, a royal proclamation arrived from London, forbidding the colonial governors from granting patents for land beyond the sources of any of the rivers which flow into the Atlantic from the west and northwest. This he scornfully treated as a "scrap of paper." In writing to his friend and agent, Crawford, who had taken up his residence in the back country on the Youghiogheny River, the future Father of his Country set forth definitely his speculation aims:

I offered in my last to join you in attempting to secure some of the most valuable lands in the King's part, which I think may be accomplished after awhile, notwithstanding the proclamation that restrains it at present and prohibits the settlement of them at all; for I can never look upon that proclamation in any other light (but this I say between ourselves) than as a temporary expedient to quiet the minds of the Indians. It must fall, of course, in a few years, especially when those Indians consent to our occupying the lands. *Any person, therefore who neglects the present opportunity of hunting out good lands, and in some measure marking and distinguishing them, for his own, in order to keep others from settling them, will never regain it.*[3]

"If you will be at the trouble," he adds, "of seeking out the lands, I will take upon me the part of securing them, as soon as there is a possibility of doing it, and will, moreover, be at all the cost and charges of surveying and patenting the same."

George Washington had an eye for business. Had he not become a great general and the Father of his Country, he probably would have been a foremost colonial financier and landlord. "It may be easy for you to discover," he wrote Crawford, "that my plan is to secure a good deal of land. You will consequently come in for a very handsome quantity; and as you will obtain it without any cost or expenses, I hope you will be encouraged to begin your search in time." He directed that "if it were practical, to get large tracts together," and suggested the neighborhood of Fort Pitt (Pittsburgh) but "not to neglect others of a greater distance, if fine bodies of it lie in one place." In fact, he had "no objection to a grant of land upon the Ohio, a good way below Pittsburgh, but would first willingly secure some valuable tracts nearer at hand."

Washington had some apprehension of conflict with the Ohio Company, but he promised Crawford to make inquiries "so we may know what to apprehend from them." Above all, he cautions the utmost secrecy: "I recommend," he added, as a final admonition, "that you keep the whole matter a secret, or trust it only to those in whom you can confide, and who can assist you in bringing it to bear by their discoveries of land. This advice proceeds from several very good reasons, and in the first place, because I might be censured for the opinion I have given in respect to the King's proclamation, and then, if the scheme I am now proposing to you were known, it might give the alarm to others, and by putting them upon a plan of the same nature before we could lay a proper foundation for success ourselves, set the dif-

[3] Herbert B. Adams, "Washington's Interest in Western Lands," *Johns Hopkins University Studies,* Third Series, No. 1, January, 1885. Italics are mine.— A. M. S.

ferent interests clashing, and probably, in the end, overturn the whole."

Crawford "heartily embraced" the colonel's offer. He promised shortly to set out in search of lands. "This may be done," he said, "under a hunting scheme." He acknowledged that other land seekers had approached him, with similar offers, "but have not agreed to any; nor will I with any but yourself or whom you think proper."[4]

In view of the caution required in carrying out the location of lands, the matter proceeded slowly. It was not until October 5, 1770, that Washington left his comfortable country seat at Mount Vernon ostensibly on a hunting trip in the western wilderness. In his diary he carefully noted the physical features of the terrain over which he passed. He was not lacking in a knowledge of land values. On October 15 he wrote:

Went to view some land, which Captain Crawford had taken up for me near the Youghiogheny. . . . This tract, which contains about one thousand six hundred acres, includes some as fine land as ever I saw, and a great deal of rich meadow. . . . The lands, which I passed over today, were generally hilly, and the growth chiefly white oak, but very good notwithstanding; and, what is extraordinary, and contrary to the property of all other lands I ever saw before, the hills are the richest land; the soil upon the sides and summits of them being as black as coal and the growth walnut and cherry. The flats are not so rich, and a good deal more mixed with stone.

He next took a trip down the Ohio, with a small company of white men and Indians, to view some tracts along the Great Kanawha River, which had been set aside by Virginia as bounty land to officers and soldiers. Here again he carefully noted the qualities of the soil:

The land on both sides this [the Great Kanawha] river, just at the mouth, is very fine, but on the east side, when you get towards the hills, it appears wet, and better adapted for meadow than tillage.

Returning to the confluence of the Kanawha and Ohio rivers, he "marked two maples, an elm and hoop-wood tree, as a corner

⁴ Adams, op. cit., p. 58.

of the soldiers' land (if we can get it), intending to make all the bottom from hence to the rapids in the Great Bend into one survey." "I also marked, at the mouth of another river," he added, "an ash and hoop-wood for the beginning of another of the soldier's surveys."

Part of these "soldiers' lands" not long afterwards came into Washington's possession. On August 20, 1773, less than three years after his exploration, there appeared the following advertisement in the *Maryland Journal and Baltimore Advertiser*:

Mount Vernon in Virginia, July 15, 1773.

The subscriber having obtained patents for upwards of twenty thousand acres of land on the Ohio and Great Kanawha (ten thousand of which are situated on the banks of the first-mentioned river, between the mouths of the two Kanawhas, and the remainder on the Great Kanawha, or New River, from the mouth or near it, upwards, in one continued survey) proposes to divide the same into any sized tenements that may be desired, and lease them upon moderate terms, allowing a reasonable number of years rent free, provided, within the space of two years from next October, three acres for every fifty contained in each lot, and proportionably for a lesser quantity, shall be cleared, fenced, and tilled; and that, by or before the time limited for the commencement of the first rent, five acres of every hundred, and proportionably, as above, shall be enclosed and laid down in good grass for meadow; and moreover, that at least fifty fruit trees for every like quantity of land shall be planted on the Premises. Any person inclinable to settle on these lands may be more fully informed, of the terms by applying to the subscriber, near Alexandria, or in his absence to Mr. Lund Washington; and would do well in communicating their intentions before the 1st of October next, in order that a sufficient number of lots may be laid off to answer the demand.

As these lands are among the first which have been surveyed in the part of the country they lie in, it is almost needless to premise that none can exceed them in luxuriance of soil, or convenience of situation, all of them lying upon the banks either of the Ohio or Kanawha, and abounding with fine fish and wild fowl of various kinds, as also in most excellent meadows, many of which (by the bountiful hand of nature) are, in their present state, almost fit for the scythe. From every part of these lands water carriage is now had to Fort Pitt, by an easy communication; and from Fort Pitt, up the Monongahela, to Redstone, vessels of convenient burthen, may and do pass continually; from whence by means of Cheat River, and other navigable branches of the Monongahela, it is thought the portage to Potowmack may, and will, be reduced within the compass of a few miles, to the great ease and convenience of the settlers in transporting the produce of their lands to market. To which may be added, that as patents have now actually passed the seals for the several tracts here offered to be leased, settlers on them may cultivate and enjoy the lands in peace and safety, notwithstanding the unsettled counsels respecting a new colony on the Ohio; and as no right money is to be paid for these lands, and quitrent of two shillings sterling a hundred, demandable some years hence only, it is highly presumable that they will always be held upon a more desirable footing than where both these are laid on with a very heavy hand. And it may not be amiss further to observe, that if the scheme for establishing a new government on the Ohio, in the manner talked of, should ever be effected, these must be among the most valuable lands in it, not only on account of the goodness of soil, and the other advantages above enumerated, but from their contiguity to the seat of government, which more than probable will be fixed at the mouth of the Great Kanawha.

GEORGE WASHINGTON.

It appears from the foregoing announcement, that Washington proposed to settle the lands and not to sell them. He wished settlers to "clear, fence and till the tenements," and make other improvements, for which a period of free rental would be granted. How like the English practice! And how much opposed to democratic principles! But Washington, until he set out to lead the embattled farmers in the struggle for political freedom, was a Virginian landlord. These gentry were fast assuming all the traits, characteristics and privileges of the landed aristocracy of the mother country. Land was not only the badge of wealth. It was the emblem of nobility. The first families of Virginia not only sought land, but they sought to retain it. When the King's proclamation restricted the settlement of the western wild lands, and forbade all land purchases from the Indians, it not only created resentment against the British Government, but it gave an opportunity to the common folk, the landless yeomanry, to assert themselves and take a hand in the determination of the popular will. The Revolutionary War eventually resulted in abolishing land ownership as a basis of political prestige. To this movement, Washington and his landed associates of Virginia slowly and calmly yielded. True patriot that he was, he ungrudgingly sacrificed his personal interests in the common cause.

While engaged in war and in politics, Washington's western lands remained much as he had obtained them. His interest in the western country, however, did not abate. When peace released him from his commission, and he returned to his Mount Vernon estate, he revived his dreams of western settlements. He had become "land-poor" and possibly, with the hope of bringing value to his distant holdings, he fostered schemes of public improvements. The Potomac Company, which sought to improve navigation to the heights of the Alleghanies, and by a canal or portage open up water communication with the region beyond, was a child of his brain. But his western lands brought him little satisfaction, though at the time of his death he still owned about seventy-one thousand acres, more than half of which were wild lands lying west of the Alleghanies. Some of this he had received as bounty for his military services. Robert Morris and other land jobbers, subsequent to the Revolution, sought in vain to interest the "General" in their various deals, but he refused.

Judging by his correspondence and his diaries, Washington had incurred a strong dislike of "land jobbing," both for political and for pecuniary reasons. "From a long experience of many years," he wrote Presley Neville, in 1794, "I have found distant property in land more pregnant of perplexities than profit. I have therefore resolved to sell all I hold on the western waters, if I can obtain the prices which I conceive their quality, their situation, and other advantages would authorize me to expect."

Washington, while President, however, on advice of George Clinton, of New York, did purchase 3,000 acres in the Mohawk Valley for £1,800. He borrowed the money from Clinton. Subsequently, he sold about two-thirds of the property at a profit of

£1,500 and repaid the debt. He also bought lots in the City of Washington. At his death these were valued at $19,132.

.   .   .   .   .

Washington and his brothers, in their land deals, had many rivals and associates among prominent Virginians. These banded together, either in groups or in "companies." There were the Lees, the Nicholsons, the Carters, the Masons and the Byrds. Patrick Henry, as well as Peter Jefferson, a surveyor and the father of Thomas Jefferson, were deeply concerned in it. Further south, in the Carolinas, there were also men who eagerly grasped for the fertile regions sloping towards the Mississippi.

Judge Richard Henderson of North Carolina, the employer and backer of Daniel Boone, promoted the settlement of the Kentucky region and claimed ownership to a vast unsettled tract there. He organized a group of land grabbers under the name of "The Transylvania Company." Ignoring the British interdiction against Indian land purchases, he obtained from the Cherokees in 1773 about one-half of the present State of Kentucky, and immediately began settling the land. He advertised widely for pioneers and "shareholders." In his announcements, Henderson waxed enthusiastic. "The country [Transylvania] might invite a prince from his palace, merely for the pleasure of contemplating its beauty and excellence, but only add the rapturous idea of property, and what allurements can the world offer for the loss of so glorious a prospect?"[5]

Henderson and his associates ran into a noose of intercolonial conflict. They endeavored, during the Revolution, to get the Continental Congress to erect their territory into another state, but Patrick Henry and Thomas Jefferson, in the interests of Virginia, had their Indian purchase declared illegal. The Kentuckians, however, threatened to fight, and to appease the irate speculators, Virginia granted land to actual settlers, and finally closed out the Transylvania claim by giving Henderson's company 200,000 acres.

Though small tracts were granted freely to Kentucky settlers,

[5] See A. Henderson, "A Pre-Revolutionary Revolt in the Old Southwest" in *Mississippi Valley Historical Review*, Vol. 27, p. 198 *et seq.*

land jobbing soon became general in this new territory. The widespread tendency towards engrossment resulted in large importations of slaves into Kentucky, the redundant descendants of which, in later years, had to be sold "down the river."

As Kentucky was settled by zeal for land ownership and by the greed of land grabbers, so, also, was Tennessee. John Sevier, a hero of King's Mountain, the colonizer and first governor of the new "State of Franklin" (which later became Tennessee), held title to immense tracts in that region, and, still unsatisfied, continuously grasped for more.

Patrick Henry is generally held to have been one of the most violent of the Revolutionary Fathers in his denunciation of British tyranny. Every schoolboy knows his slogan "Give me Liberty or give me Death." But was there a selfish personal motive in this defiance? Could he not have said, "Give me Liberty or give me Death"—(and then, under his breath)—"let me have western lands." Jefferson described Henry as being "insatiable in money" —and his participation in the Georgia land frauds described in Chapter VI may bear this out.

Aside from this cupidity, however, there is strong historical proof that Henry was actively engaged in western land deals when the British proclamation against western settlement, as well as other "acts of tyranny," materialized. With Dr. Thomas Walker, agent of the "Loyal Company," also a notorious colonial land grabber, he became identified, beginning in 1767, in speculations in western lands. And in conjunction with William Byrd, a member of the Virginia Governor's Council, he conducted secret negotiations with the Cherokee tribes for land in the forbidden area. Moreover, he was the personal counsel of the Earl of Dunmore, colonial governor of Virginia, when the latter became a participant in the Illinois land schemes, described below. Following the Revolution, Henry continued to be active in land deals and died possessed of a large landed estate.

Patrick Henry, like Washington, was a man of business as well as a patriot. He was said to be "peculiarly a judge of the value of lands." When the Revolutionary War broke out, he realized that the Indian purchases were likely to be nullified. In a deposition made by him in 1777, and now contained in the Virginia Calendar of State Papers, he states that on becoming a member of the first Continental Congress he determined "to disclaim all concern and connection with Indian purchases, although shares were frequently offered him." The reasons given for this resolution were the enormous extent of the purchases, the probability of being called upon to settle disputes over such claims, and, in the event of war, the likelihood of the soil being claimed by the American states. Because of this attitude, Henry, together with Jefferson, during the Revolution vigorously opposed the private claims to western lands. The land fever, however, again took hold of him when peace was restored.

When the British Government began to take active measures to break up land "bootlegging," and to put a stop to dreams of riches in western territory, Virginia's political resentment was naturally aroused. Even Thomas Jefferson, who, in later life, frowned upon speculation and land grabbing, held the view in 1774 that the land did not belong to the British king, and that it was time for the colonies "to declare that he has no right to grant lands of himself." So he boldly wrote in the Declaration of Independence, as one of the British king's usurpations: "He has endeavored to prevent the Population of these States; for that purpose obstructing the Laws for Naturalization of Foreigners; refusing to pass others to encourage their migrations hither, *and raising the conditions of new Appropriation of Lands.*"[6]

There is nothing reprehensible in the land hunger of the southern patriots. The British laws discouraged manufacture in America, and hampered colonial trade. Virginian capitalists were restricted in their private enterprises chiefly to raising tobacco and corn, or trading in negroes. Tobacco frequently furnished little or no profit, and slave driving was distasteful to the best families of the landed aristocracy. Speculation in lands was the chief source of rapid rise to wealth, and it was considered an honorable and respectable occupation. "It does not detract from Washington's true greatness for the world to know the material side of his character," wrote Professor Herbert Adams, of Johns Hopkins

* Italics are not in the original.

University, in 1885. "To be sure, it brings Washington nearer to the level of humanity to know that he was endowed with the passions common to men, and that he was as diligent in business as he was fervent in his devotion to country. It may seem less ideal to view Washington as a man rather than as a hero or statesman, but it is the duty of history to deal with great men as they actually are." And let us accept this judgment in considering the participation of Washington and his compatriots in colonial land-jobbing schemes.

.   .   .   .   .

Another great American—the "First Civilized American," a biographer calls him—also contracted the western land fever. Benjamin Franklin's many-sided occupations—printer, philosopher, diplomat, postmaster, statesman—did not keep his mind from gainful pursuits or desires for gain. Be it said of him, however, that he was induced by his son to participate in one of the largest western land deals ever concocted in the American continent. He was not a prime mover of the proposition. But he willingly and eagerly promoted it.

During Franklin's second visit to England in 1766, as agent of Pennsylvania, his enterprising son, William Franklin, then Governor of New Jersey, in association with Sir William Johnson, the British Government's Indian Agent in the northern colonies, together with several wealthy Philadelphians, conceived the idea of buying the claims of French settlers to land in Illinois. They later expanded their proposed purchase to an immense tract west of the Ohio River. They wrote Benjamin Franklin, requesting him to use his influence to get the British Government's permission.

He was for it at once. "I like the project of a colony in the Illinois Country," he wrote his son, "and will forward it to my utmost here." He thought that Sir William Johnson's "approbation will go a great way in recommending it, as he is much relied upon in all affairs that may have any relationships with the Indians." But Johnson had an eye on the Indian lands himself, and besides advising others about purchases in the outlying sections, personally through gifts from the Indians engrossed large tracts, particularly in the Mohawk Valley. The town of Johns-town, N. Y., still marks the seat of his domain.[7]

Franklin's reward for his services was a share in the deal. "I thank the company for their willingness to take me in, and one or two others that I may nominate," he wrote his son, on September 12, 1766. "I wish," he added, "you had allowed me more [nominees], as there will be in the proposed country, by my reckoning, nearly sixty-three million acres, and, therefore, enough to content a great number of reasonable people, and by numbers we might increase the weight of our interest here."

Franklin thus knew the frailties of politicians, or else he knew human nature. Like John Law, in his "Mississippi Bubble," he sought to gain political approbation by distributing "shares" to the powers that be. He interested a prominent London banker, one Thomas Walpole, who became the nominal head of the affair. The deal thus became known as the Walpole Grant. In Philadelphia, it was called the "Vandalia Company." The members included, besides William Franklin and Sir William Johnson, Colonel George Croghan, his assistant, and Joseph Galloway, the richest merchant of Philadelphia, who, as a Tory, escaped to England at the outbreak of the Revolution. Other prominent members were John Sargent, and Samuel and Joseph Wharton of Philadelphia. The Whartons were influential Indian traders in the Illinois country. Colonel Croghan, like his superior, Sir William Johnson, was an active land grabber, and engrossed large tracts of wild land south of the Mohawk Valley. A part of his lands in this section was acquired from him by William Cooper, progenitor of James Fenimore Cooper, and founder of Cooperstown, N. Y.

The shares in the Vandalia Company were distributed in all to about thirty-two persons, some of whom were in England. Shares were privately offered to selected persons. Writing to John Foxcroft, February 4, 1772, Franklin stated "that he had

[7] In a letter to William Franklin, dated May 3, 1776, Johnson asserted "it has always been my practice to avoid engaging in lands to the great loss of my family, neither have I a foot of land from the Indians." (*Sir William Johnson Papers*, Vol. IV, p. 197.) The large tract north of the Mohawk Valley given him by the Canajoharie Indians in 1760 was confirmed by royal grant in 1769.

advanced for your share [i.e., Foxcroft's share], what has been paid by others, . . . and I shall in the whole affair, take the same care of your interest as my own."

Franklin's proposal for "a new colony" dragged along for six years without definite results. The matter was referred by the British Cabinet to the Board of Trade. The president of this board was Lord Hillsborough. He was secretly opposed to it, but deluded Franklin in pretending that it met his approval. It was he who suggested that the originally proposed tract of 2,500,000 acres be expanded into "enough to make a province." When he finally disapproved it and received the support of the board in this decision, Franklin's resentment was bitter. "Witness his [Hillsborough's] duplicity," he wrote his son, "in encouraging us to ask for more land, pretending to befriend our application."

But Franklin won out, notwithstanding Hillsborough's objection. It may have been due to the remarkable arguments he employed in his printed reply to the Board of Trade's decision; or it may have been the belief of the British Cabinet that, by acceding to the petition for a new colony, the outraged and revolting colonists might be appeased.

The grant came too late. On March 2, 1775, Franklin departed for America, never again to set foot in England. When he arrived in Philadelphia, the colonists had already revolted, and land schemes were temporarily set aside. The Vandalia Company never thereafter pressed its claims, and nothing is known regarding the disposition of its shares. The region of the proposed "new colony" was, after the Revolution, formed into the Northwest Territory, and this section, as shall be shown later, became the favorite field of the post-Revolutionary land gamblers.

Some of the members of the Vandalia Company were concerned in other western land schemes. One of these was organized in 1775 as the "Indiana Land Company," probably the first application of the name "Indiana" to the Northwest Territory. The claim to land was based on a grant of a large tract, made November 3, 1768, in what is now West Virginia, by the Six Nations at Fort Stanwix to "Chief" William Trent in liquidation of depredations. Among the shareholders were Samuel Wharton, Joseph Galloway, Robert Callender, Levi Andrew Levi, and

David Franks, all wealthy and prominent Philadelphians.[8] The Revolutionary War did not put an end to the "claim." Wharton in 1776 published a pamphlet, entitled *View of the Title to Indiana*, in which he defended the company's rights to the lands. In 1781, he republished this in enlarged form, under the title *Plain Facts; being an examination into the Rights of the Indian Nations of America to their respective Countries and a Vindication of the Grant from the Six United Nations to Proprietors of Indiana, etc.* Although Wharton pressed the validity of the "proprietors" claims, Congress then and thereafter gave little heed thereto.

.   .   .   .   .

Another alleged "purchase from the Indians," on a still more elaborate scale, which was effected just prior to the Revolution, was the basis of a larger and more enduring western "land claim." It was destined to worry Congress for more than a generation.

Notwithstanding the British Government's edict, forbidding the private purchase of lands from the Indian tribes, William Murray, an Indian trader, and several of his business associates, in 1773 formed a plan to buy from the aborigines an immense tract of country between the Mississippi, Illinois and Ohio rivers. After a "pow-wow" lasting a month, the sale was consummated. According to the land claimants, it was attended by "many persons of both descriptions and the Indians were carefully prevented from obtaining any spiritous liquors during the whole continuation of the negotiation."[9] On July 5, 1773, "for a very large and valuable consideration," the deed was delivered to the "Illinois Land Company."[10]

There is some evidence that the "purchasers" when they secured the "deed" from the Indians knew of the British Government's opposition to the acquisition of Indian lands. But they endeavored to obtain political influence to support their title.

[8] See *Pennsylvania Magazine of History*, Vol. XIV, pp. 218, 219.
[9] See *Memorial of the United Illinois and Wabash Land Companies*, Baltimore, 1816.
[10] A copy of the deed is contained in *American State Papers*, "Public Lands." Vol. I. The original copy was acquired by Cyrus H. McCormick.

Patrick Henry

BENJAMIN FRANKLIN

Thus, William Murray wrote Bernard Graetz, his associate, soon after the purchase, that he was assured by Colonel George Croghan, the British Deputy Indian Agent, "that Lords Camden and York personally confirmed to him the opinion of Lord Mansfield respecting the Indian title." "So courage, my boys!" he added. "I hope we shall yet be satisfied for our past vexations attending our concern in Illinois."

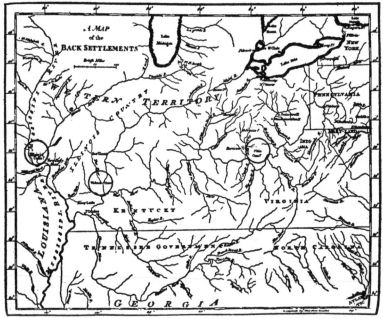

TAKEN FROM JEDIDIAH MORSE'S, *The American Geography*, PUBLISHED IN LONDON, 1794. CIRCLES SHOW CLAIMS OF THE OHIO, ILLINOIS AND WABASH COMPANIES. INDIANA IS PLACED JUST WEST OF MARYLAND.

Not content with the large purchase in the Illinois country, Murray commenced another negotiation. This time it concerned a tract on the Wabash River. Everything connected with the transaction, it was asserted, "was conducted openly and fairly," and the contract concluded October 8, 1775, by the "Wabash Land Company," "for a very large and valuable consideration."

The Revolutionary War prevented the purchasers from "taking possession." In the meantime, the two companies were combined into "The United Illinois and Wabash Land Companies," and under this high-sounding name the proprietors sold their shares during and subsequent to the period of hostilities.

In reading through the reputed Indian deeds assigned to the United Illinois and Wabash Land Companies, we come upon some familiar Philadelphia names of Revolutionary times. Among them are the Franks, the Graetzes, and the Levis, all prominent Jewish merchants and Indian traders, and staunch supporters of the Revolution—patriots who are today a pride to their descendants. Several of these were members of the Indiana Company referred to above. In addition, there were Robert Callender, William Murray, Alexander Ross and David Sproat, James Milligan, John Ingles, and Andrew and William Hamilton of Philadelphia, Thomas Minshall of York, Pa., and Joseph Campbell of Pittsburgh. The purchasers of the Wabash lands included, in addition to the above, several prominent personages. There were, first, "the Right Honorable John Earl of Dunmore, Governor of the colony and dominion of Virginia," and "the Honorable John Murray, son of the said Earl." Like Washington, these colonial officials treated the king's proclamation against purchasing lands from the Indians as a "scrap of paper."

Maryland citizens also were participants, as were also several from "the Illinois country." Other prominent persons, who were not direct purchasers, became shareholders in the "United" companies. Among these were James Wilson, learned Philadelphia jurist, and subsequent Justice of the United States Supreme Court; Robert Morris, financier of the Revolution; and Silas Deane, merchant of Wethersfield, for a time the confidential agent of the Continental Congress in France. Both Wilson and Morris, as shown in the following chapters, became immersed in land-grabbing deals after the Revolution. Morris' participation in the Illinois and Wabash Companies, however, was not large. He held an 84th share of the purchase in 1781, and he did not take an active part in pressing the claims of "the companies." But Wilson became its head. As late as 1797, he was president of the "United" companies. The extent of his holdings is not revealed, but it may be assumed that it was quite large. Silas Deane's correspondence with him, when the former was in London, following his dismissal from his French mission by Congress, shows that Wilson was very desirous of selling "shares." On April 1, 1783, Deane wrote Wilson, "I could not do anything with the Illinois lands during the War, and now, when much might be done with them, if a tolerable chance for a title appeared, I dare not venture to attempt anything." He later (July 24, 1783) inquired of Wilson regarding the affairs of the company, since the lack of information has "prevented my doing anything either with my own interest or with the shares put into my hands for sale in Europe."

Deane's previous efforts to unload "shares" in France were equally unsuccessful. Writing from Paris, September 4, 1780, to John Shee, a shareholder, he said, "I have a prospect of doing something with the shares of the Illinois and Wabash lands, but I fear your limits are rather higher than they will go at"; and he added, "I shall from time to time acquaint you, through our mutual friends, Messrs. Morris and Wilson, of my proceeding in this affair," thus showing that these two "land jobbers" were backing his merchandising efforts.

Before hostilities with the British had ceased, the "proprietors" of the Illinois and Wabash Companies petitioned Congress for a recognition of their title. It received meager consideration, and was thrown out on the ground that the Indians who sold the land never owned it. In 1791, after the establishment of the federal government, Congress was again memorialized. And again, in 1797, in 1804, in 1810 and in 1811. Each time the petitioners comprised new and prominent names. Thus, in 1810, the name of Robert Goodloe Harper, former Congressman, Senator and eminent jurist, and an associate of Robert Morris and others in post-Revolutionary land speculations, appears as one of the "proprietors and agents." Solomon Etting, a prominent Jewish merchant of Baltimore, also became a "proprietor" and signed the petitions.

Finally, on January 30, 1811, a committee of the House of Representatives definitely reported against recognition of the grant on the ground that the deed from the Indians was without the sanction of the government and that "any recognition of the claim would encroach upon the great system of policy wisely introduced to regulate intercourse with the Indians." Thus ended the "Illinois and Wabash" speculation.

. . . . .

It must not be assumed that the New Englanders, as a group, were not concerned in the pre-Revolutionary land-grabbing schemes. Yankee land greed is proverbial. Unlike the southern speculators, however, they did not, in colonial days, seek out immense regions west of the Alleghanies, though in later times they were caught in the maelstrom of western land speculation. Before the colonists took up arms against the authority of George III, the settled portions of New England were already overcrowded, and modest fortunes had been accumulated as a result of rising land values. Connecticut, in particular, felt the need of an outlet for surplus population. Packed within narrow limits and confined to rocky hills, the sturdy Yankee farmers looked with envious eyes upon the rich unoccupied lands to the westward. Silas Deane, who, as a young man, collected material for a history of his native state, Connecticut, repeatedly urged the need of an outlet for her people, and pointed out to Robert Morris and others that the western unoccupied lands would thus become the most valuable to speculators.

The desire of possession was strengthened by the belief that these lands came within the charter limits of the Connecticut colony. Did not their royal grant read, "westward to the South Sea"? Then why wait before moving westward for the sanction of the other colonies, who also claimed an endless extension of their boundaries into unknown regions? By the middle of the eighteenth century, Connecticut farmers and merchants were already emigrating into New York, Pennsylvania, Nova Scotia and even into the Floridas. The urge for new soil was strong in them even at this early period.

The adventuresome spirit of the Connecticut pioneers was fostered by the fever of speculation, as well as by desire for new land. In one colonial "land settlement" episode, at least, speculation played an important rôle. This was the "Susquehannah Company" project, a bold attempt to possess a strip in western Pennsylvania lying in what was then known as the Wyoming country.

In May, 1753, a group of 150 persons petitioned the Connecticut Legislature for a tract on the Susquehanna River, sixteen miles square, and containing 163,840 acres. The legislature refused the grant, but this did not dishearten the petitioners. They formed, on July 18, 1753, at Windham, Conn., an association "to spread Christianity as also to promote their own Temporal Interest." And they distributed "shares" among themselves.

The proposition then took on a business aspect. The number of "shares" was increased, and rights to subscribe offered at from $2 to $5 per share.[11] It attracted speculators. The shares soon rose in value. Lawyers, clergymen and politicians began buying shares. The Reverend Ezra Stiles, President of Yale College, grandfather of the poet-physician Oliver Wendell Holmes, took 2¾ shares. The Governor of Connecticut, Roger Walcott, who had become rich through local land deals, supported the project.

Without legal sanction, the promoters boldly declared that they would form a new western state. They, accordingly, hired John Henry Lydius, a Dutch trader, to buy the tract from the Indians. Lydius invited some chiefs of the Six Nations to his home in Albany, got them gloriously drunk, and got a "deed" for the land. In the meantime, two rival companies, called the "Delaware Companies," also claimed to have acquired land on the Susquehanna. Like rival banks in modern days, they were soon merged. Some settlers were quietly sent to take possession of the claim. But before they could be ordered away by the Pennsylvania proprietors, they were massacred or dispersed by the hostile Indians.

Governor Penn, of Pennsylvania, endeavored to forestall another "squatting" attempt, by leasing the Susquehanna lands to Indian traders and local land jobbers. But still the Yankees were not discouraged. The next batch of "settlers" sent out were well supplied with arms and ammunition. Open warfare ensued between "the Company" and the "Penemites." Under these disturbing circumstances, it was difficult to sell the lands for profit. Whole townships had to be offered free to get actual settlers.

[11] See J. P. Boyd, "Connecticut's Experiment in Expansion, The Susquehannah Company, 1753-1803," in *Journal of Economic and Business History*, November, 1931.

"Shares" had to be given away in order to obtain political support. The Connecticut governor, Jonathan Trumbull, as well as Pelatiah Webster, and Joseph Galloway, the wealthy Philadelphian, were granted shares "for their kind services." Moreover, the Connecticut Legislature finally validated the company's land claims. This helped some, for, in spite of the military opposition of Pennsylvania, there were already settled in the region about two thousand of the company's adherents at the outbreak of the Revolution.

The warfare did not cease when Pennsylvania and Connecticut were united by the bond of political union. It was, however, more literary than military in character. Various pamphlets, broadsides and newspaper articles for and against the "Connecticut Claims" appeared. Pennsylvania, in 1786, formed Luzerne County of the region and appointed Timothy Pickering, a venturesome land speculator, to treat with the Connecticut settlers. Their squatters' titles were confirmed, but nothing was allowed "shareholders" for unoccupied lands. Incidentally, Pickering acquired a large share of the lands for himself.

The Connecticut speculators did not accede to this arrangement. A group of the "shareholders" threatened actual revolt. They selected "General" Ethan Allen—this time inspired not by "the Great Jehovah" or "the authority of the Continental Congress," but by a liberal gift of "shares"—to fight the "Penemitish land thieves." Allen was to bring down his Green Mountain boys to chase away the "Penemites." But he merely issued a fiery proclamation of advice to the settlers. "Crowd your settlements," he wrote; "add to your numbers and strength; procure firearms and ammunition; be united among yourselves . . . Nor will I give up my interest to usurpers without trying it out by force of arms. . . . If we have not fortitude enough to face danger in a good cause, we are cowards indeed, and must in consequence of it be slaves, and our posterity, to Penemitish land thieves. Liberty and Property, or slavery and poverty are now before us, and our wisdom and fortitude, or Timidity and folly must terminate the matter."

It was a judicial decision, and not fortitude nor folly, that terminated the matter. Both Congress and the United States courts denied the validity of the Connecticut claims. Whatever may have been the wisdom of the outcome, it is certain that the "Susquehannah Company" speculators lost out. Yet, in after years, the lands they defended so courageously in relentless border warfare were engrossed by anthracite coal concerns, who reaped fortunes by extracting the precious mineral underlying the soil.

· · · · · ·

The colonial New Yorkers were conspicuously absent from participation in the early western land-grabbing schemes. This was due, however, primarily to the geographical location of the colony, wedged in between New England and the controversial territory lying westward, rather than to freedom from the manias that affected the rest of the colonies. The lack of definite boundaries, the presence of strong Indian tribes in the wild and unallotted regions, and the reluctance of the New York colonial governors to make "crown grants," in a large measure, prevented a westward movement of New York's colonial population.

However, the wild mountainous region which lay directly north of the Hudson was an attraction to the land grabbers, particularly after its liberation from the menace of the French invaders. Sir William Johnson, as already noted, preëmpted large and valuable tracts north of the Mohawk River, and divided it up among his half-breed children. As the Indian Agent of the British Government, however, he jealously guarded the Indian lands in the province against encroachment by the speculators. He, nevertheless, as we have already seen, was one of the promoters of the Vandalia project. He died in 1774 on the eve of the Revolution —a bitter foe of the colonists' cause for freedom. His lands, though divided among his large progeny, reverted to the state, because of his heirs' disloyalty to the Revolutionary cause.

Shortly before Sir William Johnson's death, Joseph Totten and Stephen Crossfield, ship carpenters in New York, under a probable pretense of seeking a source of fine shipmasts, petitioned the governor of the province for the right to buy the Indian title to a tract of about 800,000 acres, lying north of Sir William Johnson's lands, and comprising a large part of the present Warren and Hamilton counties.

The petition was granted and the purchase made at "Johnson

Hall" with the solemnity usual when Indian chiefs were present. It was soon discovered, however, that Totten and Crossfield were merely a screen for land jobbers. This displeased the crown's officers, and the patent to the grant was withheld, though preliminary fees, estimated at $10,000, had been paid by the petitioners. The "proprietors" (some thirty in number), however, did not delay in making surveys in the tract, and divided the "townships" among themselves. These proprietors included Joseph and Ebenezer Jessup, already large landowners in the same region, Philip Livingston, Jacob Watson, Christopher Duyckink, and Peter Van B. Livingston, prominent business men of colonial New York.

Most of the land in the Totten and Crossfield grant reverted to the state, following the Revolutionary War. Several of the proprietors, notably the Jessups, were Tories and escaped to Canada and England. Their property was confiscated. The claims of the Tory "proprietors" who had remained in the state during hostilities were subsequently upheld. Robert and Philip Livingston, scions of Livingston Manor, were each granted a township of 24,000 acres. Effingham Lawrence received a township in 1786, as did John Thurman and Jacob Watson. Alexander Macomb, whose "Great Purchase" of Adirondack lands is described in Chapter III, acquired five townships in 1787, through assignment of other claims. A half million acres that had reverted to the state was sold to the Saratoga and Sacketts Harbor Railroad as late as 1855, at five cents an acre. Even at this low price, the railroad company, which endeavored to construct a rail highway over the mountains to Lake Ontario, could not "make a go" of it, and much of the land was later sold under foreclosure proceedings or for taxes. A part is today comprised in the Adirondack State Park.

. . . . .

New York, before the Revolution, also had her "land" quarrels with the other colonies. The ill-defined boundaries of the Dutch province led to constant conflicts and legal controversies with her neighbors. There was a bitter dispute with New Hampshire regarding the political jurisdiction of Vermont. New York claimed the section, but New Hampshire, in 1749, acting on the principle that possession is nine points of the law, began to make free grants to both New Hampshire and Massachusetts citizens. Whole "towns" of 23,000 acres, more or less, were granted to selected groups of individuals. It is estimated that between 1749 and 1764, Governor Benning Wentworth granted 131 townships to more than six thousand persons. Among the grantees appear the names of many prominent colonial New Englanders, who had no intention of ever settling on the lands. Samuel Adams was among them. He was known as a speculator in both Maine and New Hampshire lands in this period. The governor granted himself, in all, about 65,000 acres, and is reported to have accumulated considerable wealth from the heavy fees exacted by him for grants.[12]

New York's protest against this high-handed business was brought before a British commission and received a favorable decision. Vermont was allotted to the future Empire State. The attorney for New York in the case was James Duane, a young politician, whose father owned an estate of 6,000 acres of wild land lying just west of Albany, in the present town of Duanesburg. Duane, possibly because of his connection with the Vermont controversy, contracted the wild land mania. He not only bought out his brother's interest in Duanesburg, but also acquired other large tracts in the Mohawk Valley and elsewhere. He proceeded to settle his lands with Germans from Pennsylvania. He also bought heavily of Vermont "grants" after 1764, when the territory was allotted to New York. Altogether he is said to have acquired more than 65,000 acres, at a cost of about $100,000.

His speculations, however, were highly unsuccessful. When Vermont was granted its "independence," following the Revolutionary War, and became the fourteenth state, Duane's title to the lands was not upheld. All that his heirs received was a sum of $2,621.29 from the total amount of $30,000 which the "Vermonters" paid to New York for a quit claim of all rights of the latter's citizens in the Green Mountain State.

Because of his land deals, while acting as the state's attorney, Duane was the butt of political criticism. He was led to appear in

[12] See *Publications of the Colonial Society of Massachusetts*, Vol. XXV, pp. 33-38.

person in his own defense before the state legislature in 1781. He was charged with receiving Vermont grants "under immoderate quit-rents, and excessive fees of office," and he was also accused of "holding many thousand acres of land which had never before been granted by the Crown." To this he merely answered that he "had never made a purchase or obtained a grant of land with any view to its sale." He was therefore not a "land jobber." This cleared him politically of all corruption.[13]

Duane, who had married a daughter of Colonel Robert Livingston, a "lord" of Livingston Manor and a participant in the Totten and Crossfield Purchase, gave up land grabbing as a business, after the failure of his Vermont deals. He was successful in other fields, however. He was the first Mayor of the City of New York, and the first United States Circuit Court Judge appointed by President Washington.

. . . . .

Colonial land grabbing, as a whole, was merely an advance chapter in the epic of American land speculation. The fever abated during the Revolution, but was not eradicated. It broke out with more violent and more sustained fury almost immediately after hostilities with the mother country had ceased. It is to this new phase of land speculation to which we now turn.

[13] Samuel W. Jones, *Memoir of James Duane,* 1852.

CHAPTER II

THE POST-REVOLUTIONARY WILD LAND MANIA

LORD CORNWALLIS surrendered on October 19, 1781, and the British troops sailed away from New York shortly thereafter. This left the struggling colonists free from enemy armed forces on their soil and relieved the strain on their master business minds of the successful conduct of the war. Their thoughts accordingly turned again to gainful ventures. Trade and shipping projects had almost ceased during the hostilities. Aside from privateering, little profit and much risk were involved in overseas trading. Accordingly new fields for material gain must be opened up. Before the Revolution, the colonists had been kept free from the unsavory stockjobbing schemes that beset England in the early part of the eighteenth century. Corporations, as a form of business enterprise, were practically unknown on American soil, and joint stock associations were few, and usually frowned upon. There were no securities in America, except possibly the state and federal debts—which for the most part were not interest bearing and were of little present or prospective value. The bulk of permanent wealth was in ships and land. Due to the ravages of war, ships were relatively few. Land there was in plenty.

Colonial experience also gave proof of the profitableness of land ownership. Many early settlers who had taken up tracts of land for development and resale had become rich. On July 24, 1783, Silas Deane wrote from London to James Wilson:

It clearly appears to me that the two great objects of America must be the settlement and cultivation of good lands and the establishment of manufactures. If we review the rise and progress of private fortunes in America, we shall find that a very small proportion of them has arisen or been acquired by commerce, compared with those made by prudent purchases and management of lands.

There was, therefore, a revival of land speculation schemes. These multiplied with renewed and intensified energy, particularly after the nation was established under the Constitution. In fact, the new machinery of government gained strong adherents from the capitalist classes, because of the belief that the value of lands "must be greatly increased by an efficient Federal Government."[1] The early land lust, which the colonists inherited from their European forebears, was not diminished by the democratic spirit of the Revolutionary fathers. Large estates, indeed, could no longer be a badge of nobility, but the growth of colonial fortunes through land acquisitions and sales led to the belief that this would continue to be an important means toward affluence as well as political and social prestige.

The spirit of speculation seemed to pervade the whole population. Foreigners then traveling in America took note of it. "Were I to characterize the United States," wrote William Priest in 1796, "it would be by the appellation of the land of speculations." The French nobleman and scholar, La Rochefoucauld, in his monumental work on the social and political life in the newly created states, gives detailed and vivid descriptions of some of the vast land schemes of the time. He concluded that, "though land speculations have given rise to great fortunes in America, they have also been the cause of total financial ruin and disastrous bankruptcy."

Theodore Dwight, Richard Parkinson, Isaac Weld and others give similar accounts of the widespread land mania. "You are concerned about my land speculations," wrote Timothy Pickering, a soldier of the Revolution, to his sister in 1796. "All I am now worth was gained by speculations in land. In 1785 I purchased about twelve thousand acres in Pennsylvania which cost me about one shilling in lawful money an acre . . . The lowest value of the worst tract is now not below two dollars an acre."[2]

[1] See Charles A. Beard, *An Economic Interpretation of the Constitution of the United States*, p. 50.
[2] Pickering, *The Life of Timothy Pickering*, Vol. III, p. 296.

Others as eagerly counted their prospective profits. It was thought that half or more of the Europeans would eventually remove to the United States to enjoy the blessings of liberty and independence. "There is at this time," Silas Deane wrote to James Wilson in 1783, "a general spirit for emigration from Europe to America, which I think ought to be improved by the Wabash and Illinois proprietors to settle their lands."[3] This impending immigration would tend to increase land values. The population of the states must soon double.

As the settled areas along the Atlantic seaboard were already occupied, the new immigrants would be forced to take up the wild lands at constantly increasing prices. "It clearly appears," wrote Robert Goodloe Harper, "that the population of the United States doubles in about twenty years, but to show there is no desire to exaggerate any favorable circumstances, suppose it takes twenty-five years to effect this. Now of these states, many are full of inhabitants who occupy all lands, and of the others it is supposed that they are half settled; but supposing half of each state to be unoccupied, it follows that in twenty-five years there would be an increase of inhabitants sufficient to settle this vacant half. The average price of the lands in the settled half of the United States uncultivated, cannot be at less than eight dollars an acre—sixteen times the price at which the lands of the [North American Land] company are sold for its shareholders."

But it was not land greed alone that led to the wild speculative deals following the establishment of our national government. Several of the individual states, after their separation from the mother country, became the proprietors of vast unsettled domains, the limits of which in some cases they themselves could not ascertain. These same states had become heavily involved in debt through maintaining their troops and answering the calls for funds from the Continental Congress. They had issued "debt certificates" and other "scrip," which they could neither redeem nor meet the interest payments thereon. In this impoverished condition they sought to relieve themselves of their obligations by offering lands in settlement of their debts. Thus, private land

[3] *The Deane Papers*, Vol. V, p. 164, published in *Collections of the New York Historical Society*, 1890.

speculation grew out of public poverty. It furnished a lever to the general optimism regarding the need for additional territories to provide for the expected rapid increase in population.

The post-Revolutionary land speculation was further fostered by the floating supply of military land warrants. Several of the states, particularly New York, Pennsylvania and Virginia, rewarded their soldiers with allotments of their public domains. Virginia issued warrants covering sections now comprised in Kentucky, West Virginia and Ohio. Pennsylvania issued two classes of warrants, reserving separate areas for each. One, given for losses due to currency depreciation, was designated as the "Depreciation Lands." The other, granted to Pennsylvania soldiers, were known as "Donation Lands." New York and Georgia likewise set aside "military tracts." The warrants representing these land claims were eagerly bought up by speculators and, in some cases, such warrants formed the basis of large land development schemes.

Philadelphia appears to have been the center of the land warrant business. The large land holdings of Robert Morris, John Nicholson, James Wilson, William Bingham and Timothy Pickering arose chiefly through the wholesale purchase of warrants. Henry Lee, the father of Robert E. Lee, Wilson Cary Nicholas, a Virginia governor, and George Keith Taylor, brother-in-law of John Marshall, obtained tracts in a similar manner, which they marketed among Philadelphia and New England speculators. These land-hungry individuals, living far from the regions to which they endeavored to acquire title, employed local agents, called "discoverers," to select and survey lands purchased by means of military warrants. Naturally, the system fostered fraud, villainy and deceit. As stated by a shrewd contemporary observer, Timothy Dwight, in speaking of the gamble in Virginia military warrants, "several patents were often placed successively on the same tracts. These patents were sold again and again in other states, where the nature of the measures pursued were perfectly unknown. When the purchaser went to look for his land, he found it already occupied . . . and himself the purchaser of a mere bit of paper."[4]

[4] Dwight, *Travels*, Vol. IV, p. 185.

Then there was the vast national domain! When the states agreed to settle their conflicting claims to the immense territory lying west of the Alleghanies by ceding this region to the newly created government, they made the young federal republic perhaps the largest possessor of landed property in the civilized world.

Yet it was a bankrupt national government. Its notes, "scrip," "certificates," "indents" and other forms of floating indebtedness were overdue and unpaid. The public land was proposed as a means of debt liquidation. Jefferson in 1782 estimated that 5,000,000 acres could readily be sold at a dollar per acre in government debt certificates and the whole national debt soon paid with the proceeds from additional sales. Hamilton, more astute in business affairs, however, had a better idea of values. He opposed the issue of currency based on land as security, and held firmly to the belief that wild lands in the immense tracts could afford little relief from the national debt burden. He was satisfied to pledge the lands as security for national obligations, but desired to withhold their wholesale disposal until conditions created sound values and a genuine demand for them. Indeed, Hamilton, as we shall see later, was one of the few outstanding statesmen of his time who was not lured into the maelstrom of wild land speculation.

After the Ordinance of 1787, when Congress provided a government organization for the Northwest Territory—then a howling wilderness overrun by Indian tribes—speculators or "land jobbers," as they were then called, again cast their eyes on the back country beyond the Alleghanies. Petitions for grants of vast tracts at nominal prices poured into Congress. But, despite the feebleness and poverty of the national government at the time, only two large grants—those to the Ohio Company, and the Symmes Purchase—were actually made. The establishment of a new government under the Constitution, in 1790, together with the success of Alexander Hamilton's scheme for funding the national debt, relieved the nation from the necessity of sacrificing its domain to the "land jobbers."

These land jobbers, as a group, were men of large caliber. Many had been prominent in public affairs during the war—as soldiers, as statesmen, as diplomats. Many were men of business who had engaged actively in trading and shipping before the war, and who were eager to regain the wealth the war had denied them. They possessed a spirit of boldness inherited from their pioneer ancestors. They feared not to assume risks in the hope of large gains. The very atmosphere about them seemed to favor their speculations. Although "speculation" was a term of contempt, and popular hatred was nourished against the "jobber," the "get-rich-quick" fever was engendered. It spread throughout the length and breadth of the thirteen states. As stated by Timothy Dwight, "The splendor of the object fascinated the eye of every rich adventurer and vast purchases were made by various individuals."

The principal centers of the wild land mania were in the large towns, notably Philadelphia, New York, Hartford and Boston. Each town had its own "deals," but the big operators did not confine themselves to any particular territory or district. "Whatever land was offered for sale," again comments Timothy Dwight, "they appeared ready to buy and actually bought quantities which outran every sober thought." Their purchases extended from the shores of Lake Erie to the Gulf of Mexico, from the woodlands of Maine to the prairies of the Mississippi. The outlying lands allotted to the new republic, as well as the less remote sections east of the Alleghanies, were comprised in their operations.

Foremost among the principal actors in the post-Revolutionary wild land mania was the patriot and financier, Robert Morris. No other business man in America was better known in his time, at home or abroad. His large commercial adventures before the colonies were separated from the mother country, and his relationships with the leading foreign financiers, peculiarly fitted him for the office of Superintendent of Finance, to which Congress appointed him in 1781. No man ever had a more difficult task than he in raising funds for the bankrupted colonies joined together in a patchwork nation. Yet he was called "Bobby, the cofferer," and the meager newspapers of the time caricatured him unmercifully.

Though Morris deserves undying homage as a public official, as a financier in private life he has little claim to greatness. He engaged in the wildest speculative adventures. He was a high

JAMES DUANE

(From *A Godchild of Washington*, by Catherine Schuyler Baxter)

SIR WILLIAM JOHNSON,
BRITISH INDIAN AGENT IN THE NORTHERN COLONIES

TWO COLONIAL NEW YORK LAND PROPRIETORS

James Greenleaf

Timothy Pickering

Two Post-Revolutionary Land Jobbers

liver, displaying his extravagance with the utmost ostentation. He caused the financial ruin of numerous friends and associates. And he spent several years in a debtors' prison. He died in 1806, at the age of seventy-two, "lean, low spirited and poor."

Like most wealthy Americans of pre-Revolutionary times, Morris invested in estates and plantations. With Thomas Willing, his partner in the shipping business, he had purchased before the Revolution an indigo plantation in Louisiana, but this was soon abandoned. Busy with public finances during the war, he had little time for schemes of personal gain. Yet even during this period, he took an occasional "flyer" in privateering or in land grabbing. Thus (as shown in the previous chapter), in 1781 he bought an interest in the United Illinois and Wabash Companies. He also acquired a tract of land at Trenton Falls on the Delaware River, which he called Morrisville. In this deal he had been accused of purchasing with a view to speculating on its selection as a site for the federal capital, but as will be shown later, there is no clear evidence of this motive.

Just how Morris began his wild schemes of land speculation may probably never be known. Undoubtedly, as one of his biographers states, he was led into these ventures by his belief in the rapid growth of the country. There is clear evidence from his correspondence with Silas Deane, the American commissioner to France, that during the Revolutionary War, land speculation was in his mind. In writing to Deane from Philadelphia, March 31, 1780, he requests him to determine "whether it is practicable to make sale [in Europe] of vacant lands in America by sending out drafts or surveys, descriptions and certificates, to ascertain the situation, qualities of land, titles, etc., and in what part of the continent lands are most desired by such persons as would be inclined to speculate, for *I am ready to join you in any operations of this kind* that would turn advantageously to ourselves."[5]

It was not until ten years later, however, when he was United States Senator from Pennsylvania, that Morris entered into the land business on a large scale. Regarding this, William Maclay, who was then Morris' senatorial colleague, wrote in his *Journal*, March 16, 1790:

[5] *Deane Papers,* Vol. IV, p. 117.

Mr. Morris, after sitting awhile, turned to me and began a familiar chat. At last, he asked me to walk to one side, from our seats, and asked me if back lands could still be taken up. I told him, yes. He immediately proposed to me to join him in a speculation in lands, which, he thought that he, from his connections in Europe, could sell at one dollar per acre. I paused a moment. Said as our waste lands were totally unproductive, such a thing ought be beneficial to the public as well as ourselves, that in these points of view I saw no objection.[6]

The hint of using his European connections to sell at a profit the Pennsylvania back lands, which could then be bought from the state at a few cents per acre, led Maclay to believe that Morris "is for what the speculators call 'dodging'—selling the land in Europe before he buys it here."

There is no proof, however, that Morris intended operating in this manner. He generally acquired his holdings before he offered to resell them and, although he solicited foreign purchasers, his European connections as an aid in his land speculations proved a keen disappointment to him and finally led to his ruin.

It seems probable that Morris became deeply interested in wild lands through the success and persuasion of a brilliant and energetic young Pennsylvanian, John Nicholson. When still a youth, with no known antecedents or family connections, Nicholson in 1785 was appointed Comptroller-General of Pennsylvania. In this office he supervised the disposal of state lands, by means of which Pennsylvania was endeavoring to repay its citizens and soldiers for losses due to currency inflation and for unpaid war services. Nicholson, through his official position, was able to make the best selections of these lands. He soon became the largest landowner in Pennsylvania, acquiring title to about four million acres. Like Morris, he extended his purchases to other states. The burden of carrying this vast acreage was undoubtedly too much for the young speculator. It was natural, therefore, that he should turn for help to Morris, reputed to be the most affluent person in Pennsylvania.

Morris became an active associate of Nicholson in 1793. Their confidence in each other lasted to the bitter end. Nicholson died

[6] *Journal of William Maclay* (1927 Edition), p. 209.

December 5, 1800, at the age of forty, while a fellow prisoner of Morris in the "Prune Street Prison" in Philadelphia—Morris called it "the hotel with the grated doors." Even while in jail, Nicholson was active. To pay his prison expenses he published for a while a paper with the appropriate title, *The Supporter or Daily Repast*. But prison life was fatal to him. At his death, his debts, it was said, aggregated twelve million dollars.[7]

Another partner of Morris, who joined with him about 1794, was James Greenleaf, contemporaneously known as the "celebrated land jobber." Greenleaf, scion of a prominent and prolific New England Huguenot family, of which the poet Whittier was also a member, had, when still young, amassed a comfortable fortune in his mercantile operations. For a time following the Revolutionary War, he was a partner in the shipping business of James Watson, a prominent capitalist of both Hartford and New York. Both partners individually speculated sporadically in "wild lands," and participated in various gigantic land schemes of the time. But the shipping business required Greenleaf's presence abroad, so in 1786 he went to Holland. Here, he cultivated close business relationships with Dutch speculators in American debts. Through the Amsterdam banking house of Daniel Crommelin & Sons, he negotiated several loans aggregating $1,300,000 on pledge of United States bonds and United States Bank shares. In 1793 he was made American consul at Amsterdam, but returning the same year to America, he was lured away from trade by the prospects of profitable land speculation, particularly in the new federal city of Washington. His partner, Watkins, refused to join him in these ventures, so Greenleaf sought a new connection. He endeavored to get Alexander Hamilton to join him but without success. In his letter to Hamilton, dated July 27, 1796, he represented himself as having a net estate, which "with ease could be liquidated and made to produce five million dollars."

Greenleaf succeeded in interesting Morris and Nicholson in his Washington speculations, and became their partner in other land deals. He left New York and took up his residence in Philadelphia and Washington where he personally attended to the affairs of the land-jobbing triumvirate. Failure of their schemes led to

[7] See Allen C. Clark, *Greenleaf and Law in the Federal City*, p. 42.

discord and litigation. All three were imprisoned in Prune Street, but Greenleaf succeeded in obtaining his release after a few months. Soon thereafter, he married Ann Allen, a descendant of the Penns. His last years were spent in Washington, on the growth of which he had staked his whole fortune, and lost. Old Washingtonians may still recall that the present site of the United States arsenal, in the southern part of the city, where the Eastern Branch runs into the Potomac, was for many years called "Greenleaf's Point"—a reminder of the city's pioneer promoter.

In accordance with the common practice of large land dealers of the time, Morris, Nicholson and Greenleaf formed "companies" to put through their land schemes. As their associations were unincorporated, the lands they owned were usually assigned to trustees. "Shares" were then issued, each representing a pro rata equity in the trusteed property. It was these "shares" or "scrip" which was generously offered to the land-hungry public.

The first company formed by Nicholson was the "Pennsylvania Population Company," which controlled about 450,000 acres lying north and west of the Alleghany River. It was years afterward discovered to be richly underlaid with coal. The "Asylum Company" of Pennsylvania, designed for purchase by French *émigrés* was another concern of Morris and Nicholson. Their greatest venture, in association with Greenleaf, was the "North American Land Company," the largest land trust ever known in America, if the railroad land grants following the Civil War are excluded from this category. Of this venture we shall speak later.

Morris and Nicholson were located in Philadelphia, where Greenleaf had joined them in 1794. In this "City of Brotherly Love" there were others almost equally prominent as land speculators, but, unlike Morris and Nicholson, several succeeded in disposing of their speculative purchases before succumbing to bankruptcy. James Wilson, Associate Justice of the United States Supreme Court, who, as already shown, was a large shareholder in the Illinois and Wabash Companies, bought up quantities of soldier warrants, took up large tracts, but happily for him, resold much of this to other speculators. He did not gain wealth from his numerous land deals, however, and died a bankrupt. Thomas

McKean, who in 1808 was Governor of Pennsylvania, also owned many tracts in western Pennsylvania. While governor, he deeded a princely estate consisting of 300,000 acres to his daughter who had married the Marques de Yrujo, minister from Spain to the United States. She could do nothing with it, so that most of her land was sold in later years for non-payment of taxes.

Perhaps the most successful of the Philadelphia capitalists of Revolutionary fame, who indulged in land purchases on a large scale, was William Bingham. Bingham, like Morris, was a wealthy shipper, trader and politician. But unlike Morris he retained his shipping business after the Revolution, and therefore did not succumb entirely to the land lure. He was a large purchaser of land in the "Erie triangle"—the northwest strip of Pennsylvania bordering on Lake Erie. He plastered New England with offers of these tracts, but without success, and finally sold them to a group of Dutch capitalists. He also purchased a large part of the southern strip of New York, known as the "ten townships" in which the city of Binghamton is now located. His largest acquisition, however, was a 2,000,000-acre tract in Maine, which he obtained for a mere pittance from William Duer and General Henry Knox, Washington's first War Secretary. This became known as "Bingham's Million Acres." It was willed to his five daughters, among whom was the wife of Alexander Baring, the English banker. The land was held almost intact until about 1828 when, through the skill of a land agent, it was sold in small lots and engendered one of the wildest wild land manias that has ever infected New England.[8]

Prominent New York and New England capitalists vied with their Philadelphia brethren in land-jobbing schemes. In 1784, just one year after American independence was acknowledged, a group of New York capitalists organized the first bank in the city, the "Bank of New York." It was originally intended that this institution should be a "land bank." The subscribers were to pay one-third of their subscriptions in cash, and for the other two-thirds land security was to be given. Alexander Hamilton, who prepared the bank's constitution, was opposed to this idea.

[8] See pages 240, 241.

He knew the dangers of issuing paper money without a specie backing. So through his influence the bank was established "on liberal principles, the stock to consist of specie only." Yet there were numbered among its organizers the leading land jobbers and manipulators of New York State. Prominent among these were William Constable, a wealthy trader and shipper, Alexander Macomb, his partner in land deals, Jeremiah Wadsworth, of Hartford, James Watson, partner of James Greenleaf, William Remsen, Aaron Burr, Nichols Low, and others. But the bank itself, under the guidance of Hamilton, kept clear of land deals and thus maintained its position as a "specie bank" to this day.

Among the prominent New Yorkers of post-Revolutionary days who were severely infected with the "wild land" virus were the brothers, David and Samuel Ogden, and Abraham and Thomas Ludlow Ogden, respectively the son and grandson of David Ogden. They were members of the numerous "Jersey Ogdens," and were related to Gouverneur Morris by marriage. The town of Ogdensburg, on the St. Lawrence River, is a reminder of the part they played in developing this section. They appear, however, not to have gone beyond their means in engrossing lands, as there is no record of their insolvency, though in 1816 a William Ogden became bankrupt and assigned to his creditors lands located in various counties of Northern New York. David Ogden became one of New York's prominent attorneys and resided in Whitestone, L. I., from 1789 until his death in 1800. A Tory during the Revolutionary War, he succeeded in having his Jersey estates, valued at $100,000, restored to him after the cessation of hostilities.

Alexander Macomb, who was associated in land deals with the Ogdens and who became a leading New York "land grabber," was born in Ireland in 1748, emigrated to America in his youth, and became a fur merchant in Detroit. His travels along the Great Lakes and the St. Lawrence River acquainted him with the vast extent of the northern New York wilderness, of which he became, in name at least, the "great purchaser." But his career as a land speculator was short-lived, for soon after his "great purchase" in 1791, he became involved with William Duer in security speculation, and landed in a debtors' prison. After his release he attempted to recoup his fortune by acquiring land on the Harlem River near Spuyten Duyvil, at a place still known as "Macomb's Dam." He died in 1832, in Georgetown, D. C., at the home of his son, General Alexander Macomb. By a queer twist of fate General Macomb defended from the British at Plattsburg, N. Y., the very territory that his father had acquired from New York State twenty-three years earlier for a shilling an acre—land for which New York State is now paying many millions of dollars to reacquire as a forest reserve.

Of William Duer, Macomb's partner in a bold attempt to corner the federal debt, we shall speak much hereafter. Like many other of the post-Revolutionary land speculators, he had been a purveyor for the American army. He was born in Devonshire, England, in 1747, the son of a rich West Indian planter, and came to New York in 1768. During the Revolution he served as a member of the Continental Congress, and in 1785 was appointed to the Board of Treasury, which was created to manage the national finances after Robert Morris resigned as Superintendent of Finance. As the husband of "Lady Kitty," the daughter of the self-styled "Lord Sterling," Duer was socially prominent in New York where he dined and wined in lavish style with the aristocratic gentry of the day. Speculative ventures appealed to him. He did not confine his operations to land, but entered boldly into security deals, buying heavily of United States Government bonds and the stock of the First Bank of the United States.

Duer borrowed heavily to further his speculative aims, and when the market for federal securities collapsed in March, 1792, he was forced into a debtors' prison. He had caused the ruin of many of his friends, and so great was the public rancor against him that a mob attacked the jail in which he was confined and threatened to hang the gambler. It was then that Duer appreciated the strength of prison walls, from which he, like Robert Morris in Philadelphia, sought in vain to escape. Although it is believed that through the influence of Alexander Hamilton he succeeded in obtaining a release temporarily, he remained in prison until his death on May 7, 1799. One of his sons, William A. Duer, became president of Columbia College, and another,

John Duer, was a judge of the New York Supreme Court and a leading authority on insurance law.

Gouverneur Morris, jovial statesman, diplomat and financier, occupied a peculiar position in the field of early American land speculation. There is no evidence that he bought heavily on his own account, though he participated in the New York wild land deals and undoubtedly sought great riches from this source. But, at the end of the Revolution, he was already land poor with his extensive Morrisania estate abutting on New York city. This he had inherited from his ancestors. He certainly knew the expense and difficulties of land development. Yet, like his friend and namesake, Robert Morris, in the latter years of his long life he was deeply engrossed in land deals. He did not own all the lands in which he was interested, however, but acted as the sales agent of others. To him was assigned the task of caring for and disposing of the many large tracts of wild land in New York State.

Gouverneur Morris undoubtedly became active in land deals through his official association and friendship with Robert Morris. As will be shown later, he is suspected of having been a silent partner of Robert when the latter entered upon his first great speculation in western New York lands, in 1789. He soon thereafter went to England and France with "lands for sale." Later Gouverneur was appointed American minister to France. Here, in the midst of his official duties, he was active in endeavors to dispose of lands. Monroe, arguing in the Senate against Morris' confirmation as minister, hinted that he (Morris) "was the agent of speculators in lands and debt certificates." Even after his resignation in 1794 as minister, Morris remained in Europe several years attending to his land business. He succeeded, however, in disposing of only a few tracts. One of his customers was the great financier, Jacques Necker, father of Madame de Staël, who bought a large parcel in northern New York. Following his return to America, in 1798, Morris continued to act as general sales agent for the owners of New York wild lands.

Concerning William Constable, who for a number of years was probably the largest individual owner of tracts of land in New York State, not a great deal is known. He was born in Dublin in 1752, the son of an English army surgeon. In the years immediately following the Revolutionary War, he was one of New York's leading merchants, doing a large shipping and trading business with Europe. He was among the first Americans to send ships to China. Unlike other large land operators of his time, he was not prominent politically, and does not appear to have held public office. He was associated with Macomb in the "Great Purchase," of northern New York lands and, after the latter's failure, he, together with Daniel McCormick, took over Macomb's contract. In 1792, he made a trip to Europe to dispose of the lands, but was only partially successful.

It is quite evident that Constable's speculations were not very profitable, for in July, 1801, he and his brother, James Constable, were compelled to convey some of their northern New York lands to creditors in payment of notes. Among these creditors were John Jacob Astor, who received 15,000 acres, but soon resold to Hezekiah B. Pierrepont, Constable's wealthy son-in-law. Later, all of Constable's lands were assigned in trust to the Bank of New York, but after his death, in 1803, his heirs appear to have recovered a considerable portion thereof. His three executors were his brother, James Constable, and his two sons-in-law, James McVickar and Hezekiah B. Pierrepont. The latter, a resident of Long Island, who became rich through buying up Revolutionary debt certificates, acquired most of the lands from the heirs. A son, William Constable, took up his residence in northern New York at a place named Constableville (in Lewis County), still to be located, but with much difficulty, on the map of New York State.

New Englanders were ever by nature bold adventurers, so that following the Revolutionary War, Hartford and Boston were hotbeds of land speculation. The fever swept through the whole population, and "land scrip" floated about almost everywhere in this section. For generations many of these certificates were stowed away in garrets or strong boxes, to be resurrected as curiosities of bygone days. The New Englanders did not confine their land greed to any one region or territory. They bought heavily in both the East and the West, in the North and the South. Many could never identify the location of their purchases—and in some cases the land acquired was fictitious. Surveys, if made at all, were made carelessly, and land frauds were as prevalent then as in later years.

A notorious case of fraud, swallowed by the gullible and land-hungry New England gentry, was brought to light in 1897 by James N. Granger, who published an account of the journey made in 1786 by Judge Erastus Granger, brother of Gideon Granger, Washington's Postmaster-General.[9] The journey was made into the wilds of western Virginia, for the purpose of locating tracts of land sold to Connecticut speculators by a group of prominent Virginian land warrant jobbers. Among the sellers were Wilson Cary Nicholas, who, in 1814, became Governor of Virginia, Henry Carter Lee ("Light Horse Harry"), the father of Robert E. Lee, General John Preston of Smithfield, and George Keith Taylor of Petersburg, a brother-in-law of John Marshall. These men conveyed deeds to a tract of 300,000 acres to Connecticut capitalists for $30,000. When the survey was made it figured out only 133,874 acres. The deception was blamed on "Harry" Lee, and this popular Virginia hero and progenitor of the Confederacy's greatest general was arrested in Boston just as he was preparing to embark for the West Indies. He soon compromised by giving up some of his Pennsylvania land holdings to his victims. His partners, Preston and Nicholas, were also prosecuted in Virginia, but there is no record of the outcome. They probably also compromised the claims of the irate Connecticut Yankee speculators.

There were other similar cases of fraud and deceit. Thus, Oliver Phelps purchased 100,000 acres near the present site of Charleston, W. Va. The land was located, however, 100 miles from the nearest settlement, and no title whatever was ever held by the sellers. As stated by James N. Granger: "Speculation of a more crazy type cannot be found. The best of New England capitalists and business men placed hundreds of thousands of dollars in schemes they had never investigated and did not take the trouble to explore."

A mere enumeration of the land speculators in New England following the Revolutionary War would fill pages. Foremost

[9] See *Connecticut Quarterly*, Vol. III (1897), p. 101.

among them, however, was Oliver Phelps of Hartford. He was
born in Windsor, Conn., in 1749, and later moved to Suffield in
the same state. During the Revolutionary War he acted as a
deputy for Jeremiah Wadsworth in procuring supplies for the
Continental and French armies. Settling for a while in Massachusetts, he became a member of the General Court, and one of
the Governor's Council. With this political influence he, in association with Nathaniel Gorham, of Cambridge, succeeded in purchasing from Massachusetts in 1788 that state's title to the western portion of New York State. Though, as we shall see later,
the partners were unable to fulfill the terms of the purchase contract, Phelps grew rich rapidly, estimating his wealth at
$1,000,000 by 1795. Land lust then intoxicated him. He bought
heavily in wild lands in Virginia, Georgia and elsewhere. He was
also the chief promoter of the Connecticut Company which acquired the Connecticut Western Reserve in Ohio. But his land
deals availed him little in the end. He took up his residence at
Canandaigua in western New York in 1802, later becoming a
Congressman and judge. He died in 1809, in comparative poverty,
and only a small village in New York State bears his name as a
reminder of the man, who had the ambition and the boldness to
purchase a territory comprising about one-sixth of the Empire
State.

Associated in deals with Phelps were the "Connecticut Wadsworths"—Jeremiah and James—who bought and held land
around Rochester and became "Lords of Geneseo." They also
reached far and wide for land holdings, acquiring land in Michigan and Ohio, as well as in the Genesee country. They were
prominent in business affairs both in Hartford and in New York.
Jeremiah Wadsworth, who during the war had been an intimate
associate of Robert Morris, Alexander Hamilton, and other financiers, was one of the founders of the Bank of New York, to
which he was elected president in 1785. He was also influential
in the establishment of the Bank of Hartford in 1781, most of
whose directors were prominent land gamblers. The Wadsworths,
like other wild land speculators, at first attempted to sell their
holdings in small tracts, but this appearing unprofitable, they fol-

lowed the English practice of granting long-term leases. Since they had paid cash for their lands, they could afford to hold on to them. To this day their heirs and descendants possess numerous acres of the richest agricultural lands in New York State.

Massachusetts post-Revolutionary politicians and capitalists, like those of Connecticut, were also infected with land greed. Among those who acquired extensive holdings for a time were Postmaster-General Gideon Granger, Jr., General Henry Knox, first Secretary of War, and Timothy Pickering of Salem, Mass.; also James Sullivan, Rufus Putnam, and Andrew Craigie, all prominent politicians and business men. Of Granger—who was deeply concerned in the Georgia land frauds, which are described in a later chapter—John Randolph, of Virginia said, "His gigantic grasp embraces with one hand the shores of Lake Erie, and stretches with the other to the Bay of Mobile." Knox was more moderate. He participated in New York purchases, and was concerned with William Duer in speculation in Maine lands, but fearing the adverse political effect arising from the popular hatred of land jobbers, he crawled out by selling his interest to William Bingham, of Philadelphia.

In their land dealings these men, almost without exception, had one object in view, viz., to dispose of their holdings at a profit in a short time. Unlike European land grabbers they did not acquire land as a badge of wealth or as an emblem of nobility. They did not seek to own large estates; to work them and thereby obtain a source of income or riches. The social prestige of landed property had begun to fade in North America even in pre-Revolutionary days. Although in the South large plantations were common and agriculture was the chief source of income for rich and poor alike, in the northern regions, particularly along the Atlantic coast, the tilling of the soil was merely a necessary supplement to the economic life of the people. It was not a source of wealth as were trading and shipping. Only in the notable case of "the Wadsworths of Geneseo" were large tracts acquired and held for leasing and development. Others sought to sell their lands as best they could—at a profit, if possible. Hence, the speculators, instead of drawing wealth from the land directly, aimed merely to extract wealth indirectly from their fellows' pockets.

Thus, the early land schemes, unlike many modern ventures of the same class, were not conducted on the principle of enhancing land values by making improvements and other applications of capital to bring out the natural resources and productive qualities of the soil. Their main idea was to obtain the advantages of the "unearned increment"—the added value which comes from growth of population and material wealth.

The national public land policy had much of the same motive. Both the individual states and the national government looked upon their public domains as assets to be cashed as quickly as possible and the proceeds to be applied to the extinguishing of their debts or for current use to meet government expenditures. This accounts for the important sales of large tracts of public land soon after the Revolution. The policy was changed in later years when land was disposed of in small quantities as encouragement towards settling rather than for immediate pecuniary gain.

Having acquired large acreages, the post-Revolutionary speculators were generally at their wits' ends to dispose of them. Three methods were generally followed. They would offer to resell in large tracts to wealthy men in Europe or America. Or they would set up "land offices" and offer parcels to individuals or small groups for settlements; or they might hold them as an investment for resale when lands were less abundant. The first method, as we shall see in the following chapter, met with success in very few instances. Wild lands in large tracts were too plentiful to invite purchases at enhanced prices by the wealthy seeking investment. Moreover, there were expenses attached to land ownership. This, the "land-poor" aristocracy of both Europe and America have sadly experienced. The land must be developed, roads must be built, and, worst of all, taxes must be paid. When the owners are wealthy non-residents, the local communities are likely to tax them unmercifully.

Robert Morris and his contemporaries failed to see all this in their manifold land deals—though they were made to realize it in the end. In the prospectus advertising the "North American Land Company," it was boldly stated:

The proprietor of back lands gives himself no other trouble about them than to pay taxes, which are inconsiderable. As nature left them, so they lie till circumstances give them value. The proprietor is then sought out by the settler who has chanced to pitch upon them, or who has made any improvement thereon, and receives from him a price which fully repays his original advance with interest.

How utterly misleading! First of all, the settler is slow in coming. Moreover, he is generally poor and must be given credit. He must also struggle against nature and savages, must build roads, clear rivers, construct schools and churches, pay taxes, and maintain his family against starvation and disease. History proves that the pioneer unlike the city immigrant cannot readily be made the object of exploitation.

Strenuous efforts were put forth by the early land jobbers to dispose of their holdings in Europe. A number of agents were sent abroad for this purpose, but they accomplished little. As already stated, Gouverneur Morris, in spite of his popularity and sociability, made relatively few sales of importance in France—though he did sell some land to Jacques Necker, Le Ray de Chaumont and a few other French *émigrés*. Joel Barlow, the Connecticut poet, whom William Duer sent to France during the revolutionary political upheavals there to dispose of his "Scioto lands" before he actually owned them, had hard sledding—and almost all of the French settlers he sent over to settle in Ohio returned to their native land, poorer and disgusted. William Constable was successful in selling a part of his Adirondack lands to Louis Chassanis and Le Ray de Chaumont, French noblemen, but this sale represented only a small part of Macomb's Great Purchase. Robert Morris' sales of Genesee lands to English and Dutch capitalists were made mainly in America through the agents of the purchasers.

As an aid to their efforts to dispose of lands in Europe, the speculators made use of edifying literature. Periodicals, pamphlets and treatises were published giving alluring descriptions of America, its resources and its advantages. Several of these were written on this side of the Atlantic. Thus, Tench Coxe, the prominent Philadelphia attorney, published in 1794 his *View of the United States of America*, for circulation in England. Robert

Goodloe Harper, a Congressman from South Carolina, and interested with Morris in land speculation, published a spirited defense of the North American Land Company (see illustration on next page). Similarly, Judge William Cooper, prominent as a land agent in New York State, wrote an alluring description, entitled *Guide to the Wilderness*, and Manasseh Cutler published in French and English his *Description of Ohio*. Brissot de Warville, about the same time, published in Paris and London his *New Travels in America*, which bristled with descriptions of investment opportunities in the new republic.

British writers were also employed. William Winterbottom published in 1795 an elaborate work of four volumes, entitled *An Historical, Geographical and Commercial View of the American United States*, in which he described several tracts of lands for sale and mentioned an American land agency office in Threadneedle Street, London. Gilbert Imlay, a former captain in the American army, and "commissioner in laying out lands in the back settlements" published in London, in 1797, his *Topographical Description of the Western Territory of North America*. This work went through several editions. The 1797 edition contained a description and plan of organization of the North American Land Company, promoted by Morris, Greenleaf and Nicholson, an account of which is reserved for later chapters.

A shorter and more direct appeal to the land-hungry English was made by one John Dewhurst in a pamphlet published in 1794, entitled *Observations on the Present Situation of American Landed Property*. Dewhurst was plainly a land agent. He begins with the bold statement that "there exists at the present crisis, the means of employing money to greater advantage and upon principles (when facts are known) more obviously secure than has occurred at any former period in any country in the world. *It is by the purchase of lands in America.*" He deplores the British prejudice against America and the fear of settling in distant places, and offers information on tracts of land principally situated in New York, Pennsylvania and New Jersey to all who will come to his office at 17 Norfolk Street, Strand.

The propaganda spread abroad by American land agents naturally invited opposition. Richard Parkinson, an Englishman, made

OBSERVATIONS

ON THE

North=American Land=Company,

LATELY INSTITUTED IN

PHILADELPHIA:

Containing an Illuftration of the Objeſt of the Company's Plan,
the Articles of Aſſociation, with a fuccinct Account of
the States wherein their Lands lie:

TO WHICH ARE ADDED,

Remarks on AMERICAN LANDS in general, more particularly the
Pine-Lands of the Southern and Weſtern States, in Two
Letters from *Robert G. Harper, Efquire*, Member
of Congreſs, for SOUTH CAROLINA, to
a Gentleman in Philadelphia.

LONDON:

PRINTED, BY H. L. GALABIN, INGRAM-COURT,
FOR C. BARRELL AND H. SERVANTE', AMERICAN AGENTS,
NO. 6, INGRAM-COURT, FENCHURCH-STREET:
SOLD ALSO BY J. DEBRETT, PICCADILLY; J. JOHNSON, NO. 72,
ST. PAUL'S CHURCH-YARD; AND W. RICHARDSON,
UNDER THE ROYAL EXCHANGE.

====

M.DCC.XCVI.

THE PROSPECTUS OF THE NORTH AMERICAN LAND COMPANY ISSUED IN LONDON.
MORRIS' EFFORT TO INTEREST BRITISH SPECULATORS
(Courtesy of the New York Public Library)

GOUVERNEUR MORRIS, STATESMAN, DIPLOMAT AND LAND AGENT

WILLIAM CONSTABLE, PRINCIPAL PROPRIETOR OF MACOMB'S PURCHAS

(From a portrait by Gilbert Stuart)

JEREMIAH WADSWORTH

a tour of America during 1798-1800, and published in 1805 a
book strongly condemning the purchase of American lands: "If
a man wishes to obtain property [in America] to any great extent," he remarked, "he cannot do it with comfort or satisfaction.
He may purchase a considerable portion for a small sum of money,
but he will derive little or no income from it. As he cannot let it
out to rent, he must cultivate it himself with a great number of
negroes, for white men are not only expensive, but ungovernable."
When speaking of the English "boosters" of America, among
whom he includes Tom Paine, William Cooper, Imlay, Priestley,
and others, Parkinson states:

> Those authors who have represented America as possessing pe-
> culiar advantages, are all men who have left this kingdom in anger,
> and described the plausible benefits likely to be obtained by adven-
> turous speculators before they knew any more of the country than
> those who have never seen it: they write with a determination to do
> all the harm they can to their mother country.[10]

Considerable opposition also developed from French sources.
The French minister in the United States, Joseph Fauchet, representing the new revolutionary government, in his official and
private letters uttered warnings to his countrymen against investments in American lands. The agents of *"les grands proprie-
taires,"* he wrote from Philadelphia, "are vile deceivers," and
their efforts to get Frenchmen to emigrate is furthered by such
émigrés as Talleyrand and the Duc de Noailles, who "thus hope
to cause a considerable part of the French population to desert
their country." Fauchet was particularly unfriendly to Robert
Morris, whom he called *le plus grand agioteur de ce pay-ci* (the
greatest of American speculators). In 1794, he published two
letters in France attacking Morris, especially respecting the character of the latter's Georgia lands, called the "Pine Barrens."
Fauchet claimed that he had evidence, that the title to these lands
was worthless and that Morris was "selling them to innocent
French investors." Morris in the same antagonistic vein replied
in a letter published in the *Philadelphia American Advertiser*,
denying that he invited the French to buy his lands. At this, the

[10] Richard Parkinson, *A Tour in America*, Vol. II, p. 642.

minister of the French Republic became further incensed and complained bitterly to his government of the "indecent diatribe" of Mr. Morris against him.[11]

Thwarted and hampered in efforts to attract large purchasers of their holdings at home and abroad, most of the speculators were either compelled to abandon their lands to their creditors or turn them back to the states for non-payment of taxes. As shall be shown later, only a few awaited the slow process of piecemeal disposal. For this purpose they employed land agents and opened up "land offices." Oliver Phelps who moved to Canandaigua is credited with opening there the first private land office in America. Traveling land agents, it appears, became a general nuisance. William Priest, an English musician, in his *Travels in the United States*, written in 1797, thus describes a harangue of a land agent:

When we made our stay at the tavern on the road [from New York to Boston] I observed one of my fellow travellers (who was very eloquent on this subject) take every opportunity of singing forth the praises of New Virginia (a rich tract of country west of the Alleghany mountains). . . . The northwest wind continuing . . . the morning was very cold; and we breakfasted with a number of strangers. Our orator does not lose this opportunity of holding forth on his favorite topic. I recollect the latter part of his harangue was to the following effect: "There," says he, (while the New Englanders were staring with their mouths open) "when I clear a fresh lot of land on any of my plantations, I am obliged to plant in six or seven years with hemp, or tobacco before it is sufficiently poor to bear wheat. My Indian corn grows twelve to thirteen feet high: I'll dig four feet deep on my best land, and it shall then be sufficiently rich to *manure* your barren hills; and as to the climate, there is no comparison; this cursed cold north-west wind loses all its severity before it reaches us: our winters are so mild that our cattle require no fodder, but range the woods all winter: and our summers are more moderate than on your side of the Alleghany."[12]

These "agents" in most cases did not sell parcels of land or give clear title and deed to property. They marketed merely the "shares," "scrip," or "warrants" of "companies" and "associa-

[11] See the Annual Report of the American Historical Association, 1903, Vol. II, p. 678 *et seq.*
[12] William Priest, *Travels in the United States of America*, p. 155.

tions" organized by the land jobbers. The "scrip" and "warrants" represented usually a claim to a definite acreage, but the "shares," though having a face value expressed in currency, were a claim to nothing in particular. Thus, Timothy Pickering, of Salem, who occupied various posts in Washington's cabinet, and who plunged deeply into land speculation, disposed of twenty-six tracts of land in Pennsylvania, aggregating about 19,000 acres to an "association" of thirty-four "subscribers," for $33,300. The "association" was divided into 333 shares of $100 each, eighty-three of which Pickering reserved for himself. Pickering was given power of attorney to take care of the lands and to dispose of them "according to his judgment."[18] The same method of land disposal, as we shall see later, was also used by Oliver Phelps, Robert Morris, John Nicholson, William Duer, John Cleves Symmes, Manasseh Cutler and others of the prominent land promoters of the period. Failure to sell the lands in a reasonable time generally made the "shares" worthless—since the usual outcome of the land deal was reversion to the state for non-payment of taxes.

The wild land speculation in America, which reached its zenith soon after the establishment of the new government under the Constitution, steadily and rapidly declined after 1795. At the beginning of the new century, public interest in land speculation had greatly subsided. The collapse of most of the large land companies, together with the adoption of a national policy to distribute the vast western public domain in small parcels at a nominal price, discouraged private land-jobbing schemes. The popular contempt for land speculators, however, persisted, so that statesmen and financers for many years thereafter refrained from openly associating themselves with wild schemes of land development. In the meantime, also, other fields of speculative endeavor such as commodities and securities had come into vogue. Land speculation, however, was again and again to play its part in the annals of pecuniary avarice and greed in the United States. We now pass on to the leading episodes in this drama of American cupidity.

[18] Pickering, *The Life of Timothy Pickering,* Vol. IV, p. 28.

CHAPTER III

PARCELING OUT THE EMPIRE STATE AT
WHOLESALE

WHEN the Revolutionary War was over, New York State was a mere skeleton of its present self. The white inhabitants were settled, for the most part, along the shores of the Hudson River, but pioneers had already moved westward along the Mohawk River as far as "the German Flats." Here, the sturdy Herkimer and his fellow Germans beat back Major St. Leger and his Indian and Tory allies, thus making possible the victory of Saratoga. Beyond these regions, to the west and north, was wilderness. The once powerful Six Nations had been decimated to a few scattered Indian villages. Though they still occupied the territory they could offer no resistance to the oncoming white man. The dangers of savage warfare which retarded the settling of the land were, therefore, removed.

But the ownership and control of the unsettled region west of the Mohawk Valley was still in dispute. Both Connecticut and Massachusetts claimed it. New York maintained that it was within its domain, and resisted the claims of the New England colonies to the region. The Indians, of course, had legal title to it—but that was no great obstacle. A few barrels of rum, and a supply of shawls, blankets and trinkets, could buy them off.

The Continental Congress, the only cementing force that held the young republic together, was anxious to promote harmony at home as well as abroad. It succeeded in having the sister states, Massachusetts and New York, negotiate a peaceful settlement of the controversy. On December 16, 1786, New York, in return for political authority over the territory, ceded to Massachusetts the preëmption right to "all that part of the state lying west of a line beginning at a point in the north line of Pennsylvania, eighty-two miles west of the northeast corner of the state, and running from thence due north through Seneca Lake to Lake Ontario." Within this vast domain, comprising more than six million acres, New York reserved for itself the ownership right of merely a strip of land one mile wide along the Niagara River.[1]

Massachusetts thus became the possessor—subject to the extinguishment of the Indian title—of a vast western empire, for which she had no earthly need, and which she would gladly dispose of at a price. Impoverished by the war, and with her treasury "scrip" passing current at about 30 per cent of its par value, Massachusetts in April, 1788, eagerly accepted an offer from Nathaniel Gorham and Oliver Phelps, two of her citizens, to purchase the entire tract for $1,000,000, payable in Massachusetts "consolidated scrip" in three annual instalments. The sale was made subject to the extinguishment of the Indian title, the cost of which was to be borne by the purchasers. In July, 1788, Phelps and Gorham, "by treaty" at Canandaigua, "purchased" from the Indians the easterly portion comprising about 2,600,000 acres, or slightly more than one-third of the total region. Payment for this section, which has since been known as the "Phelps and Gorham Purchase," was covered by the first of the three annual instalments, so that, on November 21, 1788, the title to the land was conveyed by Massachusetts to Phelps and Gorham. The other two-thirds still remained unpaid for. A sharp rise in the market value of Massachusetts "scrip," due to Alexander Hamilton's plan to have the federal government assume the states' indebtedness, was unfavorable to the two land jobbers. They were unable to meet the second instalment and so the unpaid-for portion reverted to Massachusetts.

The Phelps and Gorham acquisition did not pass without rivalry and opposition. Previous to the cession of the territory to Massa-

---

[1] Massachusetts also was granted 230,000 acres lying upon the Susquehanna River between the Owego and Chenango Rivers. This tract, known as the "Boston Ten Towns," was sold to Samuel Brown and associates of Stockbridge, Mass., in November, 1787. Several of the purchasers moved to the region and settled on the land.

chusetts, a group of prominent New Yorkers at Hudson, N. Y.,
formed the "New York Genesee Land Company." Among the
promoters and shareholders were John Livingston, Peter Schuyler, Dr. Caleb Benton, Robert Troup and other politicians. They
leased, or claimed to have leased, the Massachusetts lands from
the Indians for 999 years at an annual rental of $2,000 in Spanish
dollars. In February, 1788, just two months before the sale to
Phelps and Gorham, and before the extinguishment of the Indian
title, Benton and Livingston petitioned the New Lork Legislature to recognize the lease. The petition was peremptorily rejected, and Massachusetts also denied the validity of the lease.

The promoters, however, would not be downed. They employed
agents to go about the state, lavishing presents on the politicians
and the Indians to win their favor. They even suggested the
formation of a separate state. For this, one of the members was
jailed on a charge of treason. Livingston and his associates then
proposed a settlement by presenting a proposition to the New
York commission for holding treaties with the Indians to obtain
from the state a direct conveyance of all the Indian lands, the
Genesee Company to be remembered by a grant of 1,000,000
acres. Since Massachusetts had already been granted the preëmption right to the territory, this was likewise rejected. However,
in 1793, the New York Legislature passed an act for the relief
of the Genesee Company, by conveying to its members certain
lands in the northern part of the state known as the "Old Military
Tract," but there is no record that the land was ever claimed or
a deed granted.

Phelps and Gorham were not without the assistance of others
in their purchase from Massachusetts. Each originally associated
with himself a group of speculators, and these were contemplating rival bids for the domain. They soon came to an agreement
to present a joint bid in order to avoid competition. It is believed
that Robert Morris had a hand in the deal. He certainly knew
of what was going on, for when the purchasers were unable to
meet the second instalment of the agreed price, Morris stepped
in and made the purchase of the unpaid-for portion.

In the meantime, Phelps, acting as the agent of his associates,
was making efforts to dispose of the land they had acquired. He

immediately began surveys. To him may be ascribed credit for first employing the method of laying out the lands into rectangular townships of six miles square, though most authorities ascribe the inauguration of the system to Thomas Jefferson.[2] As soon as townships were surveyed, they were offered for sale in whole or in part. By 1790, about fifty townships had been sold to individuals and companies, about half of the area. The largest purchase was made by General Jeremiah Wadsworth, wealthy capitalist of Hartford and New York, with whom both Phelps and Morris had been closely associated during the Revolution in the Quartermaster's Department of the Army.

Wadsworth acquired a strip of land of about 30,000 acres, bordering on the Genesee River. Its chief settlement was a place called by the Indians "Big Tree," but later known as Geneseo, located not far from the present site of Rochester. Jeremiah Wadsworth conveyed some of the land to his young cousins, James and William Wadsworth, and appointed them his land agents. The tract comprised one of the choice sections of the Phelps and Gorham purchase, and was considered the most valuable. For this, Jeremiah Wadsworth paid one dollar per acre. Like other land purchasers of the time, he bought on credit, giving bond and mortgage as security for the debt.

James and William Wadsworth, accompanied by axmen, and provided with crude agricultural implements, moved to the tract in 1790, and took steps to settle it and to dispose of the neighboring lands. They imported cattle, and began the growing of staple crops. They also erected grist and lumber mills. Both fell ill with a fever—"the ague," for which this section was noted— and "became low-spirited," but not discouraged. It was soon found, however, that little could be accomplished at their place of settlement in Geneseo. Accordingly, James made repeated trips to Connecticut and New York City to effect sales both for himself and for other landowners. But he accomplished little. His next step was to draw up an elaborate prospectus of "the Genesee lands," and take it with him to England, in the hope of negotiating sales. Here he ran against the competition of the agents of Robert Morris and others who also were peddling American lands.

[2] See Payson Jackson Treat, *The National Land System*, p. 180.

The rivalry between them resulted in James Wadsworth's duel with two of the Kane brothers, whose sister was the wife of Robert Morris' son, Thomas Morris.[3]

James Wadsworth remained in England from February, 1796, to November, 1798. His prospectus, which made a strong point of a republican form of government as the only sure basis of prosperity, did not gain many friends for him among the English, and he returned somewhat embittered and prejudiced against all things British. He did, however, adopt, through necessity rather than choice, the British practice of settling lands through leaseholds rather than sales. Moreover, he and his brother used their "land" profits and commissions in extending their acreage, and thus became the largest individual owners of cultivated lands in New York State. The estate would have been considered a magnificent principality in Europe. The result of this policy was that the Wadsworths, almost alone among the early American landholders, retained their estates. Through generations of soldiers, statesmen and scholars, they have resided in the Genesee Valley as "Lords of Geneseo."

As already indicated, when Phelps and Gorham surrendered the unpreëmpted two-thirds of their purchase of the western part of the Empire State, Robert Morris became the purchaser. The sale was made to Samuel Ogden, March 8, 1791, by "deed poll, reciting that the purchase therein mentioned was made by him at the special insistence and request of Robert Morris." Previous to this deed, Morris, on November 18, 1790, had also acquired from Phelps and Gorham all their unsold lands, about 1,200,000 acres. Accordingly, Phelps and Gorham were "cleaned out," and Robert Morris became nominally the sole owner of about 5,000,000 acres of the soil of New York. Nathaniel Gorham died a bankrupt soon afterwards, but Oliver Phelps, as we shall see, continued in the land-grabbing business. In his deed to Morris, Phelps reserved a small tract for himself where the village of Canandaigua is located. Here he later took up his residence, erected the first "land office" in the state, and became prominent in local politics. He was joined in 1816 by his old friend and associate in land deals, Gideon Granger, who also

[3] See Henry Greenleaf Pearson, *James S. Wadsworth of Geneseo*, pp. 8-11.

emigrated from Connecticut to the wilds of western New York. Phelps died in 1809, a comparatively poor man. Granger lived until December 31, 1822.

Robert Morris, despite his reputed affluence, was not in a position to carry through his Genesee purchases alone. Like Phelps and Gorham, he had unnamed associates. These comprised the leading New York land jobbers of the period. Samuel Ogden, whose purchase of the state lands along the St. Lawrence will be described below, is reported to have had a share in the deal. He participated to the extent of 300,000 acres; Gouverneur Morris assumed responsibility for 250,000 acres; R. Loderston and William Constable took 100,000 and 50,000 acres, respectively. As the aggregate participation of these four associates amounted to but 700,000 acres of a total of about 4,000,000 acres, Morris, after all, bore the chief burden of the purchase. The price he paid to Massachusetts was £45,000 (in the state's currency), or approximately $200,000. In addition, Morris paid Phelps and Gorham £30,000 Massachusetts currency, for the 1,200,000 acres which he purchased from them directly.[4]

In those days these were large sums. Morris' resources were unequal to the burden so he made haste to dispose of his "Genesee lands." As the Indian title had not been extinguished on the tract acquired by him directly from Massachusetts, cash sales of this region were out of the question. Accordingly, his efforts were directed towards the sale of the Phelps and Gorham tract, which had already been "purchased" from the aborigines. This he accomplished apparently without much difficulty, for his London agent, William Temple Franklin, grandson of Benjamin Franklin, sold the whole section to an association, comprising Sir William Pulteney, John Hornby and Patrick Colquhoun for £75,000, or about twice as much as it cost Morris.

In later years, Morris regretted the bargain, claiming that he sold too cheaply. But he needed the cash to settle with Massachusetts for the western section of the Genesee lands, and to procure the Indian title. His shortage of ready money may be surmised from the fact that soon after his Genesee purchase he mortgaged

[4] See William Graham Sumner, *The Financier and Finances of the Revolution*, Vol. II, pp. 258, 259.

a portion of the acreage to W. S. Smith, as agent of Sir William Pulteney, for a loan of $100,000.

Having disposed of the "Phelps and Gorham Tract," Morris next proceeded to offer his remaining Genesee lands. He could not give a clear title to prospective purchasers because he himself had acquired only the "right of preëmption" from Massachusetts. It was necessary to get a bill of sale from the Indian owners. Before accomplishing this, however, Morris dispatched his son, Robert Morris, Jr., to offer the lands in England and Holland. He also continued to employ William Temple Franklin as a foreign sales agent.

While these were searching for purchasers, a group of Dutch bankers, some of whom had amassed fortunes from speculations in American government debts, sent to America a confidential agent to seek out money-making opportunities. This agent was Theophile Cazenove, a Swiss, who had taken up residence in Amsterdam, and who, through his brother's banking house in London, J. Henry Cazenove & Co., had influential British connections. He was "an expansive, jovial person, of infinite affability and bonhomie, and a man who knew the world and how to get on with it."[5]

Coming from the moneyed gentry of prosperous Holland, Cazenove was eagerly sought after and importuned by the numerous land jobbers of the time. That he was socially entertained by them, in both New York and Philadelphia, is without question. Before making any land purchases, however, he reported from time to time to his Dutch principals, furnishing them with details of money-making opportunities that were brought to his attention. He at first bought heavily of American government debts, but soon concluded that more money could be made in land purchases. Naturally, he was tempted to this conclusion when large tracts were offered him at less than a dollar an acre. In Holland land could be obtained only at prices a hundredfold higher.

Moreover, at this time, the numerous tribe of land jobbers, particularly those who were unable to meet maturing payments on their contracts, looked upon him as a godsend. James Wilson,

[5] Paul Demund Evans, *The Holland Land Company*, Buffalo Historical Society Publications, 1924, p. 5.

Alexander Macomb, William Duer, Andrew Craigie, and the whole Connecticut group of "wild land" grabbers, applied to him for loans. As Cazenove made his headquarters in Philadelphia, he was brought into close contact with Robert Morris, and soon came under his influence. Morris pointed out to him the great advantages of the "Genesee Country." He argued that, without the slightest difficulty, the purchase of a million acres would soon produce a profit of a million and a half dollars. The country offered remarkable resources in pot and pearl ashes, maple sugar and whiskey. Cazenove sent two Dutch engineers there to make a personal investigation. These convinced him that the territory was extremely favorable as to both climate and natural resources.

Accordingly, Cazenove, on December 13, 1792, contracted to purchase conditionally from Morris the two most westerly tracts of his Genesee lands, totaling 1,500,000 acres. For one tract of a million acres he agreed to pay £75,000 sterling cash. This amount was to be considered a three-year loan, secured by the land, if Cazenove's Dutch masters decided not to hold it. The remaining half million acres was to be paid at the same rate, i.e., £37,500 sterling, or about 1½ shillings an acre, provided the Dutchmen decided to take it. Morris agreed to make the necessary surveys and to extinguish the Indian title.[6]

When this deal had been completed and the papers signed, word was received that Robert Morris, Jr., had already sold in Holland 1,500,000 of the remaining acres of the Genesee lands directly to Cazenove's Dutch masters. This caused the elder Morris considerable consternation, since he had intended to retain a part of the Genesee lands for later sale at a higher price. However, he had already launched upon further wild land speculations and was greatly in need of cash. So he confirmed the sale. Thus, Dutch bankers had obtained an option to 3,000,000 acres of New York State soil, comprising a region one half as large as Holland and of greater prospective wealth and resources.

The Dutch evidently thought they had made a good bargain, for they immediately consolidated their purchases, formed a company (the "Hollandshe Land" company), divided the shares among themselves and set about to dispose of a part of their

[6] Evans, op. cit., p. 25.

holdings. They also, through the enthusiasm of their agent, Cazenove, acquired about one million acres additional lands in Pennsylvania. These came largely from Judge James Wilson, who, in his eagerness to corner the Pennsylvania land warrants, "bit off more than he could chew." One of the chief Dutch speculators, Peter Stadnitzki, published in Holland a prospectus entitled, *Information Concerning a Negotiation of Lands in America*.[7] This was for home consumption, as there is no record of an English or German translation, and it was never circulated on this side of the Atlantic. It may be assumed that it was read with great interest by Dutch speculators, since its author had, on previous occasions, pointed out to them the large profits gained from dealings in United States debt certificates. Similar profits, of course, could be made in speculations in American lands.

Robert Morris had thus disposed of all except about a half million acres of his Genesee lands. This unsold tract was, for a while, known as "Morris' Reserve." It was soon sold to W. & J. Willink, also Dutch bankers. As a result of Morris' efforts, all of New York State, lying west of Seneca Lake, with the exception of the mile strip along the Niagara River (that had been reserved to New York State in the compromise agreement with Massachusetts), was acquired by Dutch and English land speculators. This is all the more remarkable because when these foreign capitalists made their purchases, the New York laws prohibited alien ownership of lands. But in 1798, largely through Aaron Burr's influence, the statute was amended so as to give the Dutch and the English owners legal title to their Genesee purchases.

It took Morris some time to extinguish the Indian title. The delay was attributed to the Indian wars in Ohio. Finally, in 1797, Thomas Morris, Robert's oldest son, with the aid of the Wadsworths of Geneseo, gathered the Indians together at the Wadsworth homestead at Big Tree. Here also assembled representatives of the United States Government, of Massachusetts and of the Holland Land Company. Robert Morris personally could not be present, since at this time he was kept a prisoner by his creditors, in his country place on the Schuylkill, known as "The Hills." He could not satisfy "these cormorants," who eventually had him

[7] This pamphlet is very rare. A copy is in the Library of Congress.

marched off to jail. The father, however, had sent a speech to be read to the Indians. But the redskins insisted on dealing only with the "white man with the big belly." With whooping and yelling, they declared that the council fires were covered up. They were actually on the point of scattering, when young Thomas Morris, by the diligent use of his persuasive powers, helped along by a plentiful supply of whisky and of feminine trinkets—and with promises never fulfilled—again brought back both warriors and squaws. He finally induced them to sell their lands for $100,000.

Thus ended Robert Morris' first great land deal. It was the beginning of a number of similar gigantic speculations, which finally landed "the Financier" in a debtors' prison. In later years, Morris felt that he had been too hasty in selling this valuable territory. In 1800, when writing of his affairs while in the Prune Street Prison, he noted:

If I had contented myself with these Genesee purchases, and employed myself in disposing of the land to the best advantage, I believe that at this day I should have been the wealthiest citizen of the United States. That things may have gone otherwise, I lament more on account of others than on my own account.

The Dutch purchasers, after some legal entanglements in which Aaron Burr figured conspicuously, were put in possession of their New York lands. They almost immediately set up an organization for disposing of them in small tracts. Before following this part of the story, however, we will turn to other gigantic land transactions which came about through the early parceling out of the Empire State.

· · · · ·

When New York State became a free and independent commonwealth, it acquired title to the unpatented crown lands within its territory. It also took over the confiscated properties of the loyalists. These lands comprised vast domains lying north of the upper reaches of the Hudson River and westward to the section ceded to Massachusetts. Along with the other colonies who had struggled for seven years against the mother country, the state government had become impoverished. Cash funds were urgently needed. So when peace returned, the plan of raising money by sale of state lands was favorably received. The state legislature, on May 5, 1785, passed "An Act for the Speedy Sale of the Unappropriated Lands of the State." It empowered a land commission, comprising the principal state officials, to dispose of any unsold lands as it might deem proper.

As a preliminary step to offering lands, the commissioners ordered a survey made of two ranges of townships on the south side of the St. Lawrence River. It then offered these tracts at public auction. The proposed sale was advertised in the *Albany Gazette*, June 7, 1787; to take place at the "Merchants Coffee House" in New York City. An "upset price" of a shilling an acre was fixed by the commissioners. Another condition was that an actual settlement should be made on each forty acres within seven years after patents were granted to purchasers.

The auction commenced July 10, 1787. An endeavor was first made to sell in small tracts, but through agreement among the expectant purchasers, or possibly by collusion with the land commissioners, no bids were received. Moreover, it was agreed that successful bidders to any part of the tract would immediately convey their purchases to Alexander Macomb, who was the designated agent of the conspiring group of land jobbers contemplating the purchase of the entire section.

The deal was successfully carried out. Macomb's bids were accepted and his purchases forthwith conveyed, for a consideration of £3,200, to Samuel Ogden and associates "in trust" for himself. The transaction thus became known as the "Ogden Purchase." The principal participants in the deal, besides Alexander Macomb and Samuel Ogden, were General Henry Knox, Washington's Secretary of War, and Robert and Gouverneur Morris. The associates divided up the land among themselves, Ogden and Macomb taking 90,000 acres, Knox taking 44,114 acres, and Robert and Gouverneur Morris, 60,641 acres each. Macomb, because of insolvency, was later compelled to sell out his holdings to William Constable. Knox and Robert Morris also appear to have disposed of their commitments shortly after the sale.

As the territory comprised in the "Ogden Purchase" was still claimed by the British at the time of its sale by New York State, and a Canadian garrison still held Oswegatchie, on the present site of Ogdensburg, the purchasers could do practically nothing with their acquisition until after the signing of Jay's Treaty in 1795. In this compact, Great Britain definitely assigned the southern bank of the St. Lawrence to the United States.

In the meantime, the New York land commission was advertising for bids for other tracts in the northern Adirondack section, so that Ogden and his associates had opportunities to amplify their acquisitions. By 1792, the land commissioners had disposed of 5,542,173 acres for a sum slightly in excess of $1,500,000. Some small tracts brought three shillings an acre, some two and a half shillings, but the bulk of the lands went for less. Alexander Macomb, pioneer New York "plunger" and a friend of Governor George Clinton, one of the land commissioners, bid for a tract of 3,635,200 acres at eight pence per acre, payable in six annual instalments, and got it. His acquisition is still designated in deeds as "Macomb's Great Purchase." It now comprises most of St. Lawrence, Jefferson and Franklin counties, and constitutes today the heart of the wonderful Adirondack Reserve, the pride of every New Yorker.

Macomb made two applications for the land he wanted. The first, made in April, 1791, was rejected on the ground that it comprised too great an area. The second, made the next month, merely described more definitely the territory desired, but was about as large in area. It comprised almost all the unappropriated land between the St. Lawrence River and Lake Champlain, including the Thousand Islands. Its extent may be inferred from the map on page 70.

In his formal application, Macomb named his price and terms as follows:

I will give eight pence per acre, to be paid in the following manner, to wit: One sixth part of the purchase money at the end of one year from the day on which this proposal shall be accepted, and the residue in five equal annual instalments on the same day, in the five next succeeding years. The first payment to be secured by bond, to the satisfaction of your honorable Board, and if paid on the time limited and new bonds to the satisfaction of the Board executed for another sixth of the purchase money, then I shall be entitled to a patent for one sixth part of said tract, to be set off in a square, in one of the corners thereof, and the same rule to be observed as to the payments and securities and grants or patents, until the contract shall be fully completed. But if at any time I shall think fit to anticipate the payments, in whole or in part, in that case I am to have a deduction on the sum so paid, of an interest at the rate of six per cent, per annum, for the time I shall have paid any such sum before the time herein before stipulated.

Of course, Macomb in bidding for the vast acreage was acting in conjunction with other capitalists. His silent partners appear to have been William Constable and Daniel McCormick, wealthy New York merchants. Shortly after the purchase, when Macomb became bankrupt and was forced into a debtors' prison, he conveyed his interests to Constable and McCormick. In fact, there are letters of Constable which tend to show that the whole "Macomb Purchase" had been planned by him, and his name appears in connection with the earliest resales of the acquired properties.[8] Other land jobbers were also undoubtedly interested in the deal, among whom was Jonathan Dayton, speaker of the House of Representatives from 1797 to 1799, and a partner of John Cleves Symmes in an Ohio land purchase. Dayton has a "township" named after him in the "purchase." It is quite probable also that Gouverneur Morris may have had a hand in it, although he was abroad at the time. Macomb, we know, as early as April 16, 1791, appointed Morris as his attorney to sell the lands in France, but no sales appear to have been made. He also tried to sell his interest in the purchase to Cazenove, the Dutch emissary, but the latter was too shrewd to be enticed into the deal. He considered the location too remote, the climate too cold, and the soil of too poor quality.[9]

The sale of a big chunk of the Empire State at a price per acre of a loaf of bread did not pass without notice even in those early days. Cries of treason and fraud arose. One Dr. Josiah Pomeroy made oath that it was merely a scheme to annex New York to Canada. Handbills protesting against the grab were

[8] Alfred Lee Donaldson, *History of the Adirondacks*, Vol. I, p. 66.
[9] Evans, *The Holland Land Company*, p. 12.

THE MAP OF MACOMB'S PURCHASE WHICH JAMES CONSTABLE TOOK TO EUROPE.
THE ADJOINING TRACTS ARE MARKED AS "THICK SETTLED SECTIONS" WHEN
THEY WERE STILL WILDERNESS

(Reproduced from a copy in the National Library of Paris)

LE ROY DE CHAUMONT, PROPRIETOR OF NORTHERN NEW YORK LANDS

publicly distributed. Governor George Clinton, who was chairman of the state land commission, was bitterly attacked for approval of the sale, and was threatened with impeachment. Aaron Burr, who as the state's attorney-general was one of the land commissioners, also had to endure much political abuse.

Philip Schuyler, a Federalist opposed to the democratic administration of Clinton, wrote his son-in-law Alexander Hamilton, January 29, 1792:

> I have been pressed by several persons to draft a bill for the future conduct of the Commissioners of the Land Office, in the preamble of which they wish to convey a censure on the board for the conduct of the sale to Mr. Macomb. Considering a measure of this kind as a two-edge sword, I have advised that if even it were proper, it would not be prudent until matters more important to the state have been decided upon.

Thus, Schuyler feared he might involve his own party adherents in the scandal. Or he regarded the land as of so little value as not to be worth making its loss a political issue. Melancthon Smith, one of the wild land jobbers of the period who then had a seat in the legislature, strongly urged legislative approval of the deal and won out. In April, 1792, after an acrimonious debate, the New York Legislature "highly approved of the conduct of the Commissioners of the Land Office in the judicious sales by them." Consequently, when Constable and McCormick paid the required instalments of the purchase price, they received the state patents to the immense tracts.

On May 31, 1796, in New York City, in the presence of Constable and McCormick, "purchasers under Alexander Macomb," the Indian title to the property was extinguished. Under the purchase treaty, "the people of the State of New York agreed to pay the Indians, styling themselves, the Seven Nations of Canada, on the third Monday of August next the sum of one thousand two hundred and thirty-three pounds, six shillings and eight pence, and the further sum of two hundred and thirteen pounds, six shillings, and eight pence, lawful money of the state on the third Monday in August, yearly, thereafter"—if the five chiefs cared to come for it.

Macomb's purchase had hardly been officially confirmed when Constable sailed for Europe in the hope of disposing of the vast acreage to British and French speculators. At this time France was in the throes of revolution, and it appeared that the *ci-devant* aristocrats, robbed of their native estates, would be glad to exchange their valuables for American lands. America was pointed out to them as a haven of refuge. Constable, accordingly, through his friend Gouverneur Morris, advertised his lands among the hard-pressed aristocrats. His partial success in disposing of large parcels to several French notables is reserved for later consideration.

In addition to the Ogden and Macomb purchases, the State of New York, during the decade between 1790 and 1800, by various means, disposed of other sections of its unappropriated public domain. The political outcry against the land jobbers, however, put an end to the wholesale disposal of large tracts after the turn of the century. Subsequent sales were on a much smaller scale. Those who purchased tracts ranging from 1,000 to 100,000 acres comprised almost all the leading capitalists and politicians then in the state. The list of names of the "bidders" could have constituted the social register of the time. There were the Cuttings, the Lows, the Roosevelts, the Ludlows, the Fenimore Coopers, the Watkins and the Livingstons, names which survive not only in their living descendants but are still retained by the villages and townships comprised in their land purchases. Few of these held on to their acquisitions and large acreages were returned to the counties for non-payment of taxes. The bankruptcy of the chief land operators, together with the abundance of wild lands for actual settlements in the fertile western territory then being opened up by the federal government, discouraged speculation in eastern waste lands, with the result that after 1795 prominent New York capitalists returned to trading, banking and shipping as sources of wealth and income.

A contemporary opinion of the futility of land speculation, together with the reasons for its existence, is well stated in a letter written by William Henderson to William Constable, dated February 6, 1795. Henderson wrote:

The room for speedy profit on waste lands in general above a dollar an acre, I do not, for my part, think very great. Indeed, the sudden rise which they have taken may be considered in a great degree artificial! You will say perhaps, "Why then do you purchase?" I reply, "because they have been an article in which there is great speculation," and therefore may answer "to sell again."

Such has been the psychology of land speculation in America from that day to this. Land purchases were made with a view to resale while a speculation fever was on, and not for permanent investment. Purchasers did not care much where or what were the areas they bought. They traded in land deeds as if they were parcels of merchandise. They bought, sold, traded and mortgaged without surveys, and without adequate description of boundary limits. Deeds to purchases, in many cases, were never filed, and titles were frequently never claimed. When taxes became burdensome, the land reverted to the state for non-payment.

We cannot well pass over to the secondary phase of the parceling out of the Empire State without briefly telling the story of an interesting episode in the annals of early New York and Connecticut land speculation. A strip of land, 2½ miles wide and over 200 miles long, bordering the whole length of the Pennsylvania-New York boundary, and once known as "The Gore," had been claimed for many years prior to 1800 by Connecticut under her original charter grant. This claim was disputed by both Pennsylvania and New York. Notwithstanding Connecticut's doubtful title, a group of native speculators offered to purchase it from their state.

This was in 1795. Connecticut at that time, though much impoverished, desired to build an imposing statehouse at Hartford. Various means of raising funds for this purpose, such as public subscriptions, lotteries, and the like, were tried without success. An offer was made by two contractors, Andrew Ward and Jeremiah Halsey, to complete the construction of the statehouse in return for a conveyance of land "comprised within the original charter limits of this state, and extending on the north line of Pennsylvania from the northeast boundary to the northwest boundary." This offer was made notwithstanding that part of the land in question had already been sold by Massachusetts to Phelps and Gorham and the remainder to Robert Harper, James Watson, William Bingham, and others, by the New York commissioners of the Land Office.

The offer was accepted by the Connecticut Legislature, and the contractors immediately organized the "Gore Company" to claim possession of the slender strip of territory. Sundry new members were admitted as partners in the association. The whole deal was soon swept into the flames of the current Connecticut land gam-

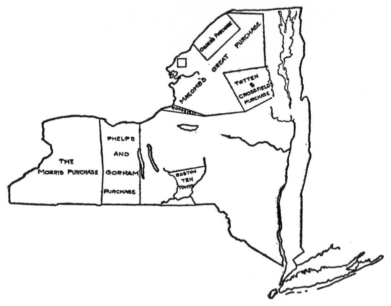

NEW YORK STATE PARCELED OUT AT WHOLESALE

bles. "If we are able to erect our public buildings, school our children and expound our Bible through wild lands with a dubious title, at a vast distance and covered with Indians, we are certainly a most favored people." Thus, wrote Samuel Hopkins to his friend, Oliver Wolcott. "The prospect pleases us," he added, "but the lapse of time only can show how much they are magnified by the fog of speculation."[10]

[10] See "The Connecticut Gore Land Company," in *Annual Report of the American Historical Association*, 1898, p. 162.

The Gore Company lost no time in offering the lands for sale. In this way the promoters expected to get funds to pay for the work on the statehouse. About twenty-five deeds for tracts in the "Gore" were passed within a few months after its organization. In the meantime, the land was advertised as having increased in value about tenfold. Five trustees were appointed to hold the land, and "scrip" and shares were issued to those who chose to buy them. Altogether 384 shares were distributed among Connecticut residents.

The "proprietors" soon had their troubles, however. The New York Legislature, hearing of the deal, passed an act directing the governor to remove all those who settled under the Gore Land Company claims, "and cause all the buildings of such persons to be destroyed." In accordance with this legislation, Governor John Jay issued a proclamation expressly charging and commanding all the magistrates and other citizens of New York "to oppose and prevent, by all legal means in their power, any such intrusion, entry, sale or purchase . . . and to give due notice of all such practices as may come to their knowledge; to the end that proper measures may thereupon be immediately taken to maintain the authority of the laws, and to bring the offenders to exemplary punishment."

In May, 1796, the "proprietors" memorialized the Connecticut Legislature to declare the state's right to the land as "they were unjustly impeded from making settlement." Connecticut then appointed James Sullivan, James Wadsworth and Alexander Wolcott to treat with New York regarding the title to "the Gore," but without avail. The offer to grant New York "the judicial right to the land on condition that a settlement be made with the "proprietors" of the Gore Land Company, was rejected. The dispute then was brought into the United States Courts. Alexander Hamilton appeared for New York and James Sullivan of Massachusetts for the Gore Land Company. The "proprietors" were assessed $12.50 per share for legal expenses; the case was dragged along without decision, and in 1799 an additional tax of $10.00 was levied on shareholders. Many declined to pay and their shares were resold at auction. A quietus was given to the whole gamble in 1800 when Connecticut renounced her claim to all lands west of her eastern boundary, except her "Western Reserve" in Ohio. In the meantime, the shares of the Gore Company had dropped from $1,000 to $70 per share and many innocent Connecticut speculators were ruined. After repeated appeals, in which it was stated that "many of the proprietors have been reduced from a state of affluence to penury and a state of bankruptcy," the Connecticut Legislature in May, 1805, finally awarded the company $40,000 payable in four installments, on condition that the state be given a complete release from the shareholders. Thus ended the Connecticut Gore Land Company. It was but one of the many wild schemes of wasteful speculation that infested the New England region in the early post-Revolutionary period.

CHAPTER IV

PARCELING OUT THE EMPIRE STATE AT
RETAIL

"I<small>F THE</small> whole Holland Purchase was brought to the condition of a garden, capable of yielding agricultural products to any given extent, it might be the means of affording a very comfortable support to the inhabitants, *but would never enable them to pay for their farms, until capital is invested in rearing towns and manufactures to purchase and consume the surplus products, and thus react upon the value of the land.*"

The foregoing statement was made by Benjamin Barton, in February, 1827, at a convention of delegates from the several counties comprising the Holland Purchase to consider "the relations subsisting between the Holland Company and the settlers on the said Purchase, and to propose some remedy by which the settlers may be alleviated." It illustrates correctly the difficulty in the way of filling up rapidly large areas of unoccupied waste lands with settlers whose single occupation is agricultural production. It points out, moreover, the desirability, if not the necessity, of the investment of large sums (in addition to the primary cost of the soil) by the owners of undeveloped sections, to foster and encourage the growth of the country.

The post-Revolutionary wild land speculators in New York and other states for the most part neglected this condition. As they were speculators or "land jobbers" and not *"land developers,"* they did not buy to hold and develop, and thereby gain a profit from the added values arising from making their properties more desirable as homesteads and settlements. Their aim was a "quick turnover" with as large a profit on as small an investment as possible.

When the wild land mania had subsided, however, and large tracts fell into the hands of those who purchased for actual real estate investment, the business side of the proposition took on a different aspect. It was now a matter of slow disposal—a complicated and continuous undertaking covering many decades. It is these experiences of the great New York State landholders in retailing and parceling out their properties after they were acquired from the original "speculators," which now concern us.

· · · · ·

As stated in the previous chapter, Robert Morris, soon after taking over from Phelps and Gorham the unsold portion of their patent from Massachusetts, resold it almost immediately to a syndicate of Britishers, comprising Sir William Pulteney, John Hornby and Patrick Colquhoun. These organized themselves into the Pulteney Association, and in 1792 sent over Captain Charles Williamson as their agent to dispose of the land. Naturally, Williamson, on his arrival in America, went to Morris in Philadelphia for advice and assistance. What Morris advised is not definitely known, but, as he stated in a letter to W. & J. Willink, Dutch bankers, March 16, 1795, "I chalked out his [Williamson's] plan and line of march. He has succeeded far beyond his expectations and I glory in it—notwithstanding I sold the property so cheap and knew at the time the sacrifice I was making."

Williamson, at the expense of his employers, soon began extensive schemes of development. He first built a road from Williamsport, Pa., on the Susquehanna River to Williamsburg on the Genesee River, so as to give a commercial outlet to his tract. He next planned the town of Bath, N. Y., "as a handsome progressive city." Here he constructed a theater, laid out a race track, and built a sumptuous hotel. He introduced the printing press to the town and published a weekly, *The Bath Gazette*. He also constructed a pretentious hotel at Geneva, N. Y., lying in the northeastern part of the Pulteney Purchase.

Thus the agent of the Pulteney Company seems to have been given a free hand with unlimited resources by the proprietors. Between 1792 and 1799, he had expended $1,374,470 but had received only $147,974 for lands sold.[1] Of course, he made efforts both at home and abroad to sell and colonize his lands. With this in view, he prepared and circulated anonymously a descriptive pamphlet entitled *Description of the Settlement of the Genesee Country, in a Series of Letters from a Gentleman to a Friend.* It was intended to entice the wealthy British as well as the immigrant settlers to take up parcels of land in his domain. "You will find the Genesee Country," he wrote, "abounding with situations both valuable to the farmer and amusing to the gentleman and man of leisure."

The place was a paradise for sportsmen. The newly created settlement at Sodus on Lake Ontario, he pointed out, stood unrivaled for "fishing, fowling, sailing or hunting, and perhaps no place in America can equal it." "Fish of various kinds, many of them from the ocean, can be had at pleasure, and a species of soft shell green turtle may be procured in plenty, little inferior to the green turtle brought from the West Indies." With such appetizing allurements, he hoped to create a British sporting center in the wilds of America.

In order to "hurry civilization," Williamson attempted "hothouse settlements" within the Pulteney Purchase. In "Coral Gables fashion," he furnished pastime and amusement to the inhabitants. One of his stunts was the holding of country fairs near the site of his "land office" in Bath. Here his lands were "boomed" between intervals of horse racing, dances and theatrical performances. To these affairs he invited the sporting gentry of the country, and entertained guests coming from as far south as Virginia. Those who attended these events came away with "terraphobia" (as land speculation was then derisively termed), just as "tourists" did in Florida more than a century later. A letter to the *Wilkesbarre Gazette*, in October, 1796, quoted by Isaac Weld, the English traveler, thus describes the allurements of Bath:

Gentlemen:

It is fearful to reflect that speculation has raged to such a degree of late, that honest industry and all the humble virtues that walk in

---

[1] O. Turner, *History of the Pioneer Settlement of the "Phelps and Gorham's Purchase,"* p. 274.

her train are discouraged, and rendered unfashionable. It is to be lamented, too, that dissipation is sooner introduced in new settlements than industry and economy.

I have been led to these reflections by conversing with my son, who has just returned from the Lakes of the Genesee. . . . He has been to Bath, the celebrated Bath, and has returned both a speculator and a gentleman, having spent his money, swapped away my horse, caught the fever and ague, and, what is infinitely worse, that horrid disorder which some call the "terraphobia."

We hear nothing from the poor creature now (in his ravings) but of the captain and Billy, of ranges, of townships, numbers, thousands, hundreds, acres, Bath, fairs, races, heats, bets, purses, silk stockings, fortunes, fevers, agues, etc., etc. My son has part of a township for sale, and it's diverting enough to hear him narrate its pedigree, qualities, and situation. In fine, it lies near Bath, and the captain himself once owned, and for a long time reserved, part of it. It cost my son but five dollars per acre; he was offered six in half a minute after his purchase; but he is positively determined to have eight, besides some precious reserves. One thing is very much in my boy's favor—he has six years' credit. Another thing is still more so —he is not worth a sou, and never will be, at this rate. . . . —A Farmer.[2]

It will be noted from the above that Captain Williamson, like other land agents of that day and this, sold land on liberal credit terms. All this brought in little cash to the proprietors. Consequently, they grew impatient. They became tired of constant capital outlays and small receipts from land sales. They protested to Williamson, and eventually refused to honor his drafts.

Finally, in 1801, the Pulteney Association was split up. Sir William Pulteney took over three-fourths of the unsold land, and the other partners the remainder. Captain Williamson was dismissed as the resident land agent, and returned to England. Robert Troup, a prominent New York politician, was appointed in his stead. He held the office for thirty years. Although the race track at Bath disappeared under a growth of scrub oak, and the theater was dismantled, the Pulteney lands rose steadily in value during Troup's administration, and sales were more frequent. An advertising campaign was carried on in New England

[2] Isaac Weld, *Travels in America*, (Fourth Edition), Vol. II, pp. 336, 337.

GENESEE LANDS.

THE Subscriber having received ample powers from the Family of the late Sir WILLIAM PULTENEY, of London, is now in a situation to fulfil all his past Contracts, and to continue his sales of the VALUABLE LANDS belonging to the Pulteney Estate, in the Genesee Country, on terms very advantageous to industrious settlers. ROBERT TROUP.

Albany, 19 May, 1806 4m58

LANDS FOR SALE.

Encouragement to Farmers.

UPWARD of 500,000 acres of Land, are offered for sale to settlers upon the following liberal terms, viz. the purchase money to be paid in four equal annual instalments, to commence at the end of three years from the date of the sale, with interest after the end of three years and not before.

The greater part of the above lands are of an excellent quality, well watered and the country remarkably healthy.

The rivers Cohocton and Chenesteo which are branches of the Susquehannah run through the lands, and are navigable in the spring of the year and some times in the fall for arks and boats that will carry from twelve to fifteen hundred bushels of wheat

The Susquehannah and Bath turnpike road, and the Lake Erie turnpike road (which latter is a continuation of the former) will pass upwards of thirty miles thro' these lands ; and there is every probability that these turnpike roads will be shortly made, and thus a safe and easy communication will be opened to Kingston on the Hudson river.

Roads are already opened and mills erected in different parts of these lands and in the adjacent country, so that the difficulties which first settlers in a new country always experience, are in a great measure removed. The above lands belong to the Pulteney estate. Their title is indisputable, and the subscriber is duly authorised to sell them. For further particulars apply to the subscriber at Bath, in the county of Steuben, in the state of New-York.

SAMUEL S. HAIGHT.

Bath, 25th Sept. 1806. 6m80

ADVERTISEMENT OF THE PULTENEY ESTATE IN THE *Hartford Courant,* JANUARY 14, 1807

and elsewhere to attract settlers. The War of 1812 brought new money into the region from the army supplies it furnished to the troops guarding Lake Ontario. Later, the building of the Erie Railroad through Steuben County, in which the estate was located, added materially to its importance and increased the sales to actual sellers.

However, when the affairs of the Pulteney Association were finally wound up about a century after its creation, it was estimated that if the sums represented by the original purchase price had been invested at the lowest prevailing interest rates, it would have been a more profitable investment of the proprietors.[3]

. . . . .

Theophile Cazenove, to whom was assigned the task of disposing of the vast domain of the Holland Land Company, was not permitted by his Dutch masters to follow a policy of land booming such as was attempted by the agent of the English purchasers of a part of the Genesee Country. Instead of entering upon schemes of development, he quietly and unostentatiously set about to offer small tracts here and there to settlers.

Moreover, the Dutch, in spite of their vast acreage, acquired from Morris, did not appear to be in a hurry to get rid of their enormous commitment. They even sought and obtained more land. In 1791, through Cazenove, they purchased a thousand out of a total of 2,500 shares of the Pennsylvania Population Company, an association which had been organized by John Nicholson, to take over about 450,000 acres of Pennsylvania lands lying just south of the Holland purchase. As stated in the previous chapter, they also acquired about a half million additional acres in the same region from Judge James Wilson, who had preëmpted tracts through speculation in Pennsylvania land warrants, but who was unable to make payments thereon when due.

The tract of the Pennsylvania Population Company was incorporated with those of the Holland Land Company, and for a time the two concerns were generally regarded as one. However, disputes regarding the titles and other difficulties in Pennsylvania led to the dissolution of the Population Company in 1813. Its

[3] See "The Pulteney Purchase," by Paul D. Evans, in the *Quarterly Journal of the New York State Historical Association*, Vol. III, p. 102.

lands were sold to Judge William Griffith, of New Jersey, and J. B. Wallace, a Philadelphia attorney, for $180,000. Griffith later sold his interest to Wurtz Brothers, merchants of Philadelphia, for $150,000, payable in English goods. These Wurtz Brothers were interested in buying up lands containing coal, and a decade later were instrumental in organizing the Delaware & Hudson Canal Company. When their anthracite speculations proved a success, they withdrew from partnership with Wallace, receiving $310,000 for their interest, two-thirds of which, however, was in debts due from settlers.

Difficulties beset Cazenove and his Dutch masters in trying to profit from their land deals. Since the owners were aliens, they were not legally permitted to hold lands in New York State. Williamson had avoided this handicap for his English employers, by becoming an American citizen soon after his arrival at Philadelphia, and by receiving in his own name title to the Pulteney Purchase directly from Morris. The Dutch, however, tried to get around the law by placing their holdings in the name of "trustees," but this was a clumsy expedient. Accordingly, measures were taken to obtain exemption from the New York law against alien ownership of landed property. As already stated, it was accomplished on April 2, 1798, largely through the political influence of Aaron Burr.

In his early political career, Burr endeavored to get rich along with the other land jobbers of the time by buying large tracts on credit. He was a shareholder in the Pennsylvania Population Company, owning one hundred shares, which, however, he forfeited for non-payment. He also had contracted under a bond with Cazenove to purchase 100,000 acres in the northern part of the Holland Purchase, but he soon found payments beyond his financial means. He was, therefore, threatened with suit against his sureties. In the hopes of bettering a bad situation, he had united with other hard-pressed land speculators, in commissioning James Wadsworth, who was then in England trying to sell Genesee lands, to find English purchasers for their insecure holdings. To make the task easier, Burr, who was a member of the New York Assembly, put through a bill granting aliens the conditional right to hold land in New York.

The correspondence of Cazenove with his Dutch masters confirms the belief that Burr obtained the passage of the law through bribes furnished by the Dutch owners. They paid altogether $10,500, of which $3,000 went to Josiah Ogden Hoffman, the attorney-general, and $5,500 went to Burr himself, albeit as a two-year loan. Burr never repaid the loan, but his contract for

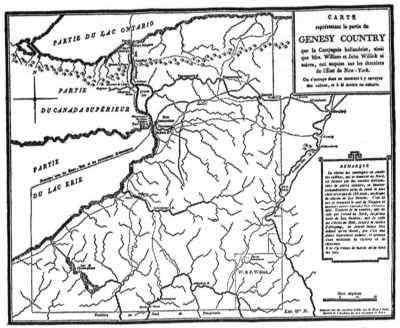

AN EARLY MAP OF HOLLAND PURCHASE, PUBLISHED IN FRANCE IN 1803 IN JEAN PHILLIPPE LOUIS BRIDEL'S *Le pour et le contre, ou avis à ceus qui se proposent de passer dans les Etats-Unis d'Amerique*

the purchase of land from the Holland Land Company was canceled. So he escaped from a bad financial situation.[4]

Although the New York law permitted the Dutch proprietors to take title to the land, it did not give them the right to reënter lands once the title had passed from their hands. This prohibition was a serious handicap to the alien owners. They dared not sell land on credit by taking a mortgage for the unpaid portion of the sale price, since, as aliens, they could not bid in the land

[4] Evans, *The Holland Land Company*, p. 209; also Wandell and Minnigerode, *Aaron Burr*, Vol. I, p. 178.

under foreclosure. This led to sales conditioned on the final payment being made. Hence, no deeds were granted to purchasers until they had paid in full. Settlers on the lands were for the most part poor, and few could keep up their interest payments, to say nothing of the required instalments of the principal. The result was a permanent condition of vassalage on the part of the purchasers. These could not sell their farms and reap the benefits of the improvements made thereon, because they possessed no deeds confirming title. As late as 1802, in all Genesee County, there were only thirty freeholders—in fact, "not enough to make up a jury."

The State of New York in 1817, however, had begun the construction of the Erie Canal. The Holland Land Company was asked to donate the necessary right of way through its property. When this was promised, a law was passed on March 5, 1819, repealing the restriction of reëntry of aliens on property sold by them. Even with the prohibition removed, the Holland Company continued its old practice of making contract sales, and deeds were offered at time of purchase only in special cases.

When the "boom" in the wild land mania collapsed after the Morris-Greenleaf-Nicholson failure in 1795, Cazenove realized that it was impossible to dispose of large tracts of the enormous territory under his control. He accordingly built up an organization for retail disposal. Land agents and subagents were employed in eastern towns and seaports as well as abroad. Land offices were opened in various settlements within the purchase. The principal office was set up in the newly created town of Batavia, N. Y. (located at about the central point of the domain), and Joseph Ellicott was placed in charge.

Ellicott was a renowned, though an eccentric surveyor. He was a brother to Andrew Ellicott, the engineer, who completed the plan of Washington, the "Federal City." He held the office as resident land agent of the Holland Land Company for twenty-one years. In this capacity he laid out the city of New Amsterdam, now Buffalo, gave its streets the jaw-breaking names of the Dutch proprietors and made it a flourishing town. He was careful enough to take the choice lots for himself. Through a series of roads built through different parts of "the Purchase," he made the lands accessible to new settlers.

Through these means settlers came in steadily, though slowly. Every encouragement was given them when no expense was involved. Little cash payment was required of land purchasers and if instalments of interest and principal were not paid when due, the defaults were added to the capital of the debt, and the interest computed on the total amount. In some cases when cash could not be paid, cattle and produce were accepted. As the Dutch owners had paid cash for their lands, they did not press remittances from their debtors and appear to have been satisfied to allow balances due them to accumulate at 7 per cent interest, when the prevailing rate in Holland was 3 per cent. With this liberality to new settlers the wild lands were gradually converted into farms.

Theodore Dwight, President of Yale College, who passed through the Genesee country in 1810, wrote enthusiastically of its rapid settlement: "It is questionable," he says, "whether mankind has ever seen so large a tract changed so suddenly from a wilderness into a well-inhabited and well-cultivated country."[5] He estimated the white inhabitants then at between two and three hundred thousands "all planted within 26 years." And Captain Williamson also wrote in 1799, ten years earlier:

A wilderness changed, in so few years, to the comfortable residence of a numerous body of industrious people, who enjoy the comforts and conveniences of life in a degree superior to most parts of the United States, affords matter of curiosity to the intelligent traveler, and many respectable characters undertake the journey for no other motives.

Though the liberality of the Holland Land Company toward its creditors is generally admitted, this very liberality in time became a cause of great discontent. The purchasers, unable to pay in full for their lands, practically became tenants-at-will of the company. Complaints of this condition poured in. The proprietors themselves grew tired of the situation, and in 1820 offered to resell to the state all of their lands in the Genesee

[5] Theodore Dwight, *Travels,* Vol. III, p. 510.

country. Gideon Granger, as their attorney, submitted the proposion to Governor DeWitt Clinton, who passed it on to the legislature, with the remark: "This measure from a financial point of view may be rendered beneficial. It will relieve a considerable portion of our population from evils which are actually experienced, and from influence which may be injuriously exercised. It will enable the State to extend encouragement to the meritorious settlements which have already taken place."[6]

Granger argued that "eighty to one hundred thousand people were subject to the will of the Hollanders for their prosperity," and inasmuch as the unsold lands could be acquired at about one dollar per acre, and the bonds, mortgages, contracts, etc., at a considerable reduction from face value, the state would be making a good bargain by accepting the proposition. It was estimated that about 1,750,000 acres (about one-half of the original acreage) still remined unsold, "much of it considerably valuable."

The legislature did not take kindly to the proposition, so that conditions remained unchanged. Wearied of steadily growing defaults and of inadequate cash receipts, the proprietors appointed, in 1821, a new agent, Jacob S. Otto, to replace Joseph Ellicott. Otto abandoned the former policy of leniency. Many of the settlers were served with threats of dispossession. During the next ten years, these dissatisfied debtors held public meetings, distributed pamphlets and had "almost weekly conventions." All this engendered political opposition to the Holland Company. It resulted in the repeal of the company's exemption from state taxation on its unsold land, and to legislative threats to tax debts due on land sales contracts for land belonging to non-residents.

Charles Butler, who at this time lived in Geneva, N. Y., and who in later life became a wealthy New York capitalist through speculation in western lands, sought a remedy for the situation. In March, 1830, the New York Life Insurance and Trust Company was incorporated and empowered to lend on mortgages, up to one-half of the value of the land. Butler went to New York and made application to it for loans on behalf of the debtors of the Holland Land Company. He then became the Holland Company's land agent. In this way mortgages were substituted for

* See *New York Assembly Journal*, 43rd Session (1820), p. 581.

unpaid balances on sales contracts. Other New York trust companies also granted loans, so that many of the farmers in the section, instead of being tenants-at-will, became freeholders.

But the political animosity against the Holland Land Company continued. Moreover, the law requiring the payment of taxes on its unsold lands made its business unprofitable. Efforts were then made to wind up its affairs. The lands and sales contracts were offered to local capitalists. In the meantime, real estate and farm lands were booming throughout the country, and the Dutch proprietors were thus given the long sought for opportunity to dispose of their holdings. A syndicate headed by Trumbull Cary and George Say of Batavia, N. Y., acquired early in 1835 the unsold lands and purchase contracts of the Holland Land Company in Chautauqua County for about $1,000,000. The transfer of ownership, however, did not allay the dissatisfaction of the debt burdened settlers. In fact, the efforts of the new proprietors to force payment from them, led to actual riots. A mob set fire to the company's land office at Maysville in Chautauqua County and another threatened to destroy the main office at Batavia. For a while the latter place was surrounded with block houses and a constant guard kept on hand.

In order to mend matters, Cary and Say called upon William H. Seward, prominent politician and later Lincoln's Secretary of State to treat with their discontented tenants. Seward resided in Auburn, just east of the Holland Purchase. He knew the calibre of the up-state farmer, and when the agency of the proprietors in Chautauqua County was offered him, in 1836, he accepted. He immediately began to follow the plan of Charles Butler in converting the outstanding sales contracts into mortgages.

When Seward was running for Governor of New York in 1838, his political opponents accused him of selling the debts owed by the settlers "to Wall Street," and of using Nicholas Biddle to raise money in England at 5 per cent, whereas the settlers were made to pay 7 per cent. This accusation was answered in a brilliant address to the citizens of Chautauqua County. In this, Seward made a vigorous defense of his policy as agent of the Cary land syndicate. "In less than eighteen months," he said, "four thousand persons whom I found occupying lands, chiefly

TO THE SETTLERS

ON THE

Holland Land Company's Lands,

IN THE COUNTIES OF GENESEE, NIAGARA, CHATAUQUE, CATTARAUGUS AND ALLEGANY.

The Agent general of the Holland Land Company having relinquished the plan of effecting a sale in gross of their property in the state of New York, feels it his duty to give this public notice of his determination to continue the administration of the concerns committed to his care, on the same general principles which have hitherto governed him, with such modifications as will be hereinafter noticed. Various considerations induced him to attempt a whole sale of the Holland Land Company's property. He was led to believe by the tenor of the memorials presented to the Legislature, by several of the inhabitants residing within the limits of the Holland Land Company's territory that the measure would have been agreeable to and consequently have met with the support of the major part of the purchasers under the company. Such appears not to have been the case, and so far as the opposition of the settlers to the contemplated transfer may have been founded on their aversion to a change of creditors, the preference thereby manifested towards the Holland Land Company is a source of high gratification to the Agent General.

It will always be his aim and pleasure to justify the expectations which an honourable confidence in the justice and liberality of the Company may have inspired in the minds of the settlers.

The unhappy times upon which the generality of nations have fallen are shared by the American people; the low prices of produce and the consequent scarcity of money are evils felt by the cultivators of the soil, to which no effectual remedy can be afforded by the Agent General. All he can essay to do, is to offer an alleviation of the evils so universally complained of, and this he will do with a readiness, the liberality of which he trusts will be ascribed to its proper motive. He has no object in view but the promotion of the true interest of the company and the general welfare and prosperity of the purchasers. He is well aware that these objects are inseparably united—they go hand in hand—He recognises no superiority of claims in the settlers, save those founded on moral character, and he solemnly disclaims all knowledge of or partiality for political parties. The feelings and sentiments of the settlers in political as in religious matters, ought to be and must be sacred in the eyes of the Company and of their General and sub-agents. With these they have neither the right nor the wish to interfere, satisfied with the exercise of their own privileges, the only legitimate question in deciding on the application of a purchaser is, is he honest, is he industrious?

The instructions by which the sub-agents at the several offices opened in the territory are to govern themselves, (until revoked or modified) contain the following injunctions.

All the unsold being surveyed into lots, a valuation of them is to be carefully made, and posted up in a conspicuous place in the offices.

The purchaser of a single lot containing about one hundred and twenty acres, is to be admitted into contract at the fixed price.

To the purchaser of two adjoining lots a reduction will be granted of 4 per cent. on the fixed price.

To the purchaser of three do. do. of 6 per cent. on do.
To the purchaser of four do. do. of 8 per cent. on do.
To the purchaser of five and upwards of 12 per cent. on do.

The benefit of these deductions however, is limited to those contractors, who, on the execution of the contract, shall pay in specie or good current Bank notes at least one-twentieth part of the consideration money. The credit not to exceed ten years, the legal interest of 7 per cent, on the purchase money, to commence on the expiration of the third year from the date of the contract, and the principal to be made payable in six yearly instalments.

To meet the views of persons inclined to purchase for Cash a deduction of $5 per cent. will be made on the credit valuation prices of a single lot, and a further abatement in price, agreeably to the foregoing scale will be granted to cash purchaser of two or more lots.

Settlers whose contracts have expired, and which consequently are subject to forfeiture may have them renewed, by adding the amount of the simple legal interest due on the old contract, to the principal, the whole payable in ten equal yearly instalments with seven per cent interest payable annually. If all arrears of interest be paid on renewing the contract an allowance of twenty per cent on the amount so paid will be made, so that every $100 will be received as $120.

The same allowance will be made to those who having paid up all arrears of interest shall on renewing their contracts make a payment on account of the principal.

The Agent General avails himself of this opportunity seriously to call on all the debtors of the Holland Land Company for payment. There is a point beyond which indulgence and forbearance cannot safely be carried. It is equally the interest of both debtor and creditor that debts should not be suffered to accumulate. An impartial discrimination will be made between the settler, who is entitled to a continuance of indulgence and he who has abused it, Against the latter class coercive measures will be used, unless they come forward and by making partial payments prevent the disagreeable necessity of having recourse to them.

To those settlers who within one year shall pay 4-4th of the present arrears of interest an allowance of fifteen per cent will be made on the sum paid, so that every $100 will be received as $115—and the same allowance will be made on all payments of such arrears to the amount of 4-4th within either of the three following years.

To those settlers who have punctually paid up their arrears of interest and who shall pay, within one year 4-4th of the arrears of the purchase money an allowance of ten per cent will be made on the sum paid, so that every $100 will be received as $110—and the same allowance will be made on all payments of such arrears to the amount of 4-4th within either of the three following years.

To avoid the inconvenience to the Company, and frequent injurious effects to the Settlers, arising from the facility of transferring and assigning the contracts, the Agent General has authorised the sub-agents to execute deeds to those settlers who have paid one fourth part of the purchase money and all arrears of interest; and for the balance due to accept a Bond and Mortgage. This mode the Agent General feels assured will in most cases be preferred by the settlers.

Aware of the difficulties (doubtless much increased by the hardness of the times) under which the tillers of the ground labor, of finding a ready market for their surplus produce, the Agent General has resolved in his mind the means of procuring for the settlers the opportunity of discharging in kind at least this interest of their debts. Sensible of the many inconveniences which the settlers suffer in this respect, he has conceived that it would greatly tend to their relief if places of deposit were opened at the sub agencies where the produce of the farmer would be received in payment. The introduction and organization of this system requires much consideration and preliminary preparation. The Agent General is engaged in procuring the requisite information on the subject, which, when digested, will, he trusts, enable him to obviate the difficulties which seem to oppose the general introduction of this measure, for the present he must confine himself to a few articles and that to a limited amount. He has instructed the sub-agent to commence this system of facilitating the mode and means of payment and to accept, on account of arrears of interest, Cattle, suitable for the New York, Philadelphia, and Montreal markets, Wool, Bees-wax, Hemp, Flax and Flax Seed, the price of the above articles to be agreed upon between the settlers and the sub-agent at the time of delivery, or the company becoming accountable to the settler for the proceeds of the produce, after deducting the charges actually paid for their transportation to market.

In addressing to the settlers on the Holland Land Company's lands the foregoing proposals and rules of government, the Agent General entertains the fond hope of having afforded them a convincing proof of the unaltered disposition of the Holland Land Company to act with liberality and kindness towards their settlers and of their strict adherence to those principles of equity, impartiality and moderation which they have always professed and from which their Agent General has never knowingly permitted a departure. He flatters himself that his principles and motives will be properly appreciated, and serve to encourage and promote, among the yeomanry of Genesee, those habits of industry and economy, unanimity and cordiality, by which only the Cultivators of the Soil can expect to prosper and acquire independence, and which will insure to them all the domestic comforts which they can desire and procure them the honorable title of being useful citizens of a free, independant, and powerful state.

PAUL BUSTI.

Philadelphia, April 24th, 1821.

J. Harding Printer, back of No. 76, South Second street.

BROADSIDE OF HOLLAND LAND COMPANY, APRIL 24, 1821, ANNOUNCING THE FAILURE TO PLAN TO SELL OUT TO THE STATE, AND OFFERING NEW TERMS TO SETTLERS under expired and legally enforceable contracts of sale, and excited and embarrassed alike by the oppression and uncertainty of ever obtaining titles, became freeholders." Seward was elected governor in 1838, and again in 1840, so that his land dealings proved in the end no detriment to his political ascendancy.

While Seward was endeavoring to adjust the delicate situation of the new proprietors in Chautauqua County, Jacob Le Roy and Herman Redfield, in behalf of the Farmers Loan and Trust Company of New York, were negotiating for the purchase of the Holland Company's lands and securities in other counties. An agreement was finally reached in December 31, 1835, whereby about 90,000 acres of unsold wild lands, and a mass of mortgages, unexpired sales contracts and other indebtedness, were sold for $2,282,382, payable one-half in cash and the remainder within two years.[7]

This left but a few remaining properties of the company in two other counties. These were likewise sold to New York capitalists, who raised the necessary funds through loans from the Farmers Loan and Trust Company of New York City. Thus, by 1836, the Holland Land Company faded entirely from the picture. Only its old stone "land office," still standing at Batavia as a local "landmark," and a few boundary posts, now kept in local museums, are a reminder that a group of Dutch capitalists once owned about a seventh of the total area of the Empire State.

And little profit came from their speculation! According to Paul Evans, the historian of the Holland Land Company, the original investment of the company "was retrieved with interest of five to six per cent," but he gives this estimate "merely for what it is worth."[8]

· · · · ·

The story of the disposal of the northern New York lands comprised in the Ogden and Macomb purchases is further proof of the futility of waste land speculations. In this section, the lands were sold and resold in large tracts, usually in townships or parts of townships. The original purchasers, as a rule, attempted to be relieved of their acquisitions at a profit as soon as

[7] Evans, *The Holland Land Company*, p. 393.
[8] Evans, *op. cit.*, p. 435.

possible, and in many cases, when profits were not forthcoming, they either turned their titles over to their creditors or permitted their holdings to revert to the state for unpaid taxes.

William Constable and Gouverneur Morris had the largest hand in the disposal of these properties. Morris, as stated in the previous chapter, became a "general land agent" both at home and abroad. When he returned from France in 1798, he continued to occupy himself with numerous land deals and remained in this business to the end of his long career as lawyer, author, statesman, diplomat, and financier. He died in 1816.

When Constable arrived in France in 1792, to offer his vast empire of waste woods and mountains to distressed *émigrés*, he naturally sought the aid of the astute American minister, who could bring him into contact with prospective purchasers. It was undoubtedly through Morris' assistance that Constable sold a tract of "Macomb's Great Purchase," comprising 630,000 acres, to Pierre Chassanis, just a few days before Louis XVI was guillotined. Chassanis was a brother-in-law of James Donatien Le Ray de Chaumont, who in turn was the son of Donatien Le Ray de Chaumont, the host in France of Benjamin Franklin. These French noble gentlemen formed a company, called the "Compagnie de New York," and issued a prospectus, the title page of which is shown herewith. According to this document, "The subscribers agreed to emigrate to America and establish a settlement on the north side of the Black River, near Lake Ontario." The territory was to be known as *"Castorland,"* which was translated into English as "Beaverland." A seal bearing a cut of a beaver was adopted as the concern's insignia.

The six hundred thousand acres mentioned in the prospectus were reduced to 200,000 acres in 1793, and were represented by two thousand shares, all of which were sold at the original offer of 800 livres per share. The price received by Constable for this tract was £25,000 in English currency.

The prospectus of "Castorland" gave an alluring description of the country, describing trees, plants, roots, birds and fish. There were very favorable conditions for producing maple sugar and potash, two important and necessary articles of commerce at the time. The success of similar colonies recently established was

DESCRIPTION

TOPOGRAPHIQUE

DE SIX CENTS MILLE ACRES DE TERRES

DANS L'AMÉRIQUE SEPTENTRIONALE,

Mises en vente par Actions, suivant le Plan d'Association ci-joint.

PROSPECTUS.

Le Bureau de la Compagnie eft à Paris, rue de la Juffienne, n°. 20

1792

pointed out, particularly Judge Cooper's venture on Lake Otsego. Each "share" of the company was to be an "integral part and fraction of the purchase" and no money was to be paid to Constable, the vendor, "until after the title was received from America, clothed with all the formalities required by the usages of the country."

The proprietors of Castorland lost no time in sending two agents to America. These men, after many delays and hardships of travel, reached the location of the purchase. As at this time real estate in New York could not be legally held by non-resident aliens, the agents returned to New York City and sought the aid, first, of Alexander Hamilton, and subsequently of Aaron Burr, to get the legislature to remove this obstacle. This accomplished, the two agents again visited Castorland with a corps of surveyors, but sickness and hardships severely hampered their activities. In the meantime, the guillotine in Paris had ended the careers of several of the original shareholders. One of the agents, Pharoux, was drowned in the Black River in 1795, and the other, through sale of a part of the company's property, received sufficient cash to pay his bills, and so returned to France. The colony was not long afterward abandoned, and the lands passed to other proprietors—chiefly to Gouverneur Morris, in payment of commissions, and to Le Ray de Chaumont, who had become an American citizen and had taken up his residence in this back country.

When Chassanis and his associates could only obtain subscriptions to about a third of the 600,000 acres that they had agreed to buy from Constable, the latter in April, 1793, resold the returned portion, about 400,000 acres, to Charles J. Michael de Wolf, of Antwerp, for 300,000 florins ($125,356). De Wolf then transferred the land for 680,000 florins to a group of Belgian capitalists who called themselves the "Antwerp Company." They, however, did not propose a colonization scheme similar to that attempted by Chassanis. In 1800, they appointed Le Ray de Chaumont and Gouverneur Morris their joint agents to hold and dispose of the land, "in trust." Their agents could accomplish little in making sales, and most of the land was later acquired by Le Ray de Chaumont.

Thus, James Le Ray, as he was known in the United States, was the residual legatee of large tracts in the original Macomb purchase. He was an enterprising *émigré*, who came to America in 1789, to collect the debts owing to his father by the Revolutionary Government. The land mania took a strong hold on him. He acquired tract after tract in northern New York. Much of it he resold, but his generosity, combined with his inability to make large profits in land deals, as well as other difficulties, kept him "land poor." Like his father in France before him, he became a bankrupt, and was compelled in 1824 to surrender his estates to his son for the benefit of his creditors. His landed property at the time of making the assignment consisted of:

30,759 acres in Franklin County	appraised at	$22,500
73,947 acres in St. Lawrence County	appraised at	106,000
143,500 acres in Jefferson County	appraised at	574,000
100,000 acres in Lewis County	appraised at	133,000
348,206 acres	appraised at	$835,500

Strange to relate, the affairs of Le Ray's estate were so well managed by his son that all American claims were satisfied in full. While his property was being liquidated, Le Ray abandoned his land office at LeRaysville, and retired to France.

Le Ray was a noteworthy French-American citizen. His activities in settling the northern area of New York State are far surpassed by his contributions to the economic and social welfare of the inhabitants of the region. He was very much interested in scientific agriculture, and in other progressive developments, and endeavored to introduce new crops and new industries in the land of his adoption. He was instrumental in bringing to his lands the finest breed of merino sheep, taking these from the celebrated sheepfold of Rambouillet. He built roads, established schools, endowed churches. He was fond of his children, and has perpetuated their Christian names in such places as "Alexandria Bay" (named after his daughter) and "Cape St. Vincent" (after his son), both on the St. Lawrence River, where he was for a time a dominating spirit. He died in Paris in 1840, at the age of eighty-one.

Le Ray was associated in land deals with Gouverneur Morris, and it is undoubtedly through his influence that Morris succeeded in selling several tracts to Jacques Necker. Necker bought this land ostensibly for his daughter and her children. Like Morris, he feared that "all kinds of property in Europe are uncertain and wavering" and wished to transfer part of his wealth to peaceful America. Madame de Staël, his daughter, later added purchases made on her own account. One purchase comprised 23,000 acres in the town of Clare, St. Lawrence County. The total acreage owned at her death was estimated at 30,000 acres.

The Duke of Rochefoucauld, who had witnessed the many tragedies of land speculation in America, cautioned Madame de Staël against her speculations, but Le Ray assured her that they would prove profitable undertakings. Morris also aided in allaying her fears. As Madame de Staël, who was hard pressed by Napoleon, and chased all over Europe, had expressed a wish to settle with her family in America, Morris encouraged her by pointing out that "with us [in America] it is within the reach of every one to attain the objects of his desire, and he who is successful, enjoys the consciousness of possessing an influence over the course of affairs." Though he admitted that building castles in the United States was a folly as ruinous as building castles in the air, the setting up of "a little summer establishment in a new country, which is rapidly advancing, and to pass there from three to five months of the fine season; to remain four months more either in Philadelphia or New York, and to spend the remainder of the year traveling, is a mode of life by no means repugnant of common sense." But despite the allurement held out by Morris and Le Ray, and an expenditure of $20,000 in building roads and other improvements on her property, Madame did not come to America. Her wilderness estate passed to her children at her death in 1817. These ordered it sold, and the land reverted to American ownership.

Madame de Staël was not the only French celebrity whom Le Ray induced to risk a fortune in an American land venture. It was he who was responsible for the purchase, in 1816, of a large tract of the northern wilds of New York by Joseph Bonaparte, elder brother of the emperor. How it was brought about is thus related by Vincent Le Ray:

Mr. Le Ray de Chaumont was at his estate in Touraine in 1815, when he heard of Joseph Bonaparte's arrival at Blois. He had known this prince before his great elevation, and was his guest at Mortefontaine when the treaty of September 30, 1800, between the United States and France was signed there, but he had ceased meeting him afterwards. Seeing, however, that misfortune had assailed the prince, he remembered the man and hastened to Blois. The prince, having invited Mr. Chaumont to dinner, said suddenly to him: "Well, I remember you spoke to me formerly of your great possessions in the United States. If you have them still, I should like very much to have some in exchange for a part of that silver I have there in those wagons, and which may be pillaged any moment. Take four or five hundred thousand francs and give the equivalent in land." Mr. Le Ray objected that it was impossible to make a bargain where one party alone knew what he was about. "Oh," said the prince, "I know you well, and I rely more on your word than on my own judgment." Still Mr. Le Ray would not be satisfied by his flattering assurances, and a long discussion followed, which was terminated by the following propositions, immediately assented to by the prince: Mr. Le Ray Chaumont would receive four hundred thousand francs, and would give the prince a letter for Mr. Le Ray's son, then on the lands, instructing him to convey a certain designated tract if, after having visited the country, (whither he was then going) the prince confirmed the transaction; otherwise, the money to be refunded."[9]

Joseph Bonaparte, in time, came to America, visited the tract, and accepted it. This, however, may have been from necessity rather than choice, as Le Ray was unable to repay the loan. The former King of Spain could not take title to the estate, since he was an alien, so the deed was made out to Peter Duponceau, the learned Philadelphia lawyer of French extraction.

The original Bonaparte purchase was estimated at 150,000 acres, but it later was reduced to 26,840 acres, valued at $40,260. As "Count Survilliers," Joseph Bonaparte took up his residence in America at Bordentown, N. J. But he occasionally visited his vast woodland estate in the Adirondacks. He recognized the qualities

[9] See Franklin B. Hough, *History of Lewis County, N. Y.,* p. 71.

of the lands as a hunting preserve, but complained that he could not find 200 acres of level ground to build a lodge on. In honor of his favorite deity, the goddess of the hunt, he named his township "Diana." A beautiful lake in his domain still retains the name of Bonaparte. He petitioned the New York Legislature for the privilege of acquiring title to the land, and the Act of March 31, 1835, which conferred upon him this right, is evidence that he meant to retain it. He did not hold it long thereafter, however, but sold the whole property for $80,000 to John La Farge, a merchant of Havre and New Orleans. La Farge took up his residence for awhile at Penets Square near the tract, but about 1838 he moved to New York where he engaged extensively in real estate and other business transactions and amassed considerable wealth. He was the confidential agent of Louis Philippe who, as King of the French, realized the instability of his job and invested heavily in America.

Although Joseph Bonaparte made but few and infrequent visits to his Adirondack estate, a local poet of the region, Caleb Lyon, memorialized the occasions in pleasing verse, thus:

Here he forgot La Granja's glades,
Escurial's dark and gloomy dome,
And sweet Sorrento's deathless shades
In his far off secluded home.

The hunter loved his pleasant smile
The backwoodsman his quiet speech
And the fisher's cares would he beguile
With ever kindly deeds for each.

He lived for others not in vain
His well kept memory still is dear.
Once King of Naples and of Spain
The friend of Bernardin St. Pierre.[10]

Gouverneur Morris, to whom may be ascribed the interest of Le Ray de Chaumont, Jacques Necker and Madame de Staël in the northern wilderness of New York, is also responsible for the

[10] Abstracted from Franklin B. Hough's *History of Lewis County, N. Y.,* p. 79.

large land venture of another prominent European capitalist. It was he who persuaded David Parish, scion of a prominent Scotch family, "The Lairds of Rossie," (who for several generations successfully conducted international banking at various European centers), to buy a large estate in northern New York.

Morris, while in Europe, became intimate with John Parish of Antwerp, whose son, David, came to America in 1804 on a financial mission. When Morris returned to America in 1798, and continued his occupation as leading American land hawker, he urged John Parish, through correspondence, to place a part of his fortune in American estates. "Your oldest son," he wrote November 12, 1806, "should own a large tract. This is the way to become a real baron without a name."

Accordingly, David Parish, after taking up his residence in America, became a land baron. Through Morris' advice he purchased the whole township of Ogdensburg, comprised in the original Ogden purchase, together with many hundreds of acres in the vicinity. For this he paid about $2 per acre. After the tract was bought David Parish did not know what use to make of it. Morris and Le Ray suggested that the land might. be used for raising merino sheep. The soil, they said, was an exact repetition of the Spanish district where sheep produce the most wool.

Parish, therefore, commenced operations by importing about 3,000 merino sheep from Spain at heavy cost. Merino sheep were then selling at fabulously high prices. He also built a "baronial mansion" at Ogdensburg, "the Red Villa" designed by the French architect, Renée, whom Parish brought over with him in 1811. This villa he equipped in European style, and visited it occasionally.

The wool raising idea, for awhile, took a strong hold on him. Vincent Nolte, who in 1853 wrote an entertaining account of his American experiences,[11] relates that while traveling with Parish from Philadelphia to Baltimore, he noted some merino sheep in a field. "Look," Parish exclaimed, "how they jump about. They yield splendid wool." But success does not seem to have attended

[11] *Fifty Years in Both Hemispheres, or Reminiscences of the Life of a Former Merchant.*

Parish's wool-raising scheme. Aside from building a fine residence and a church at Ogdensburg and laying out the towns of Parishville and Rossie (where he attempted to establish iron works), he allowed the estate to retain its primeval condition. Yet, Nolte estimates that he invested more than $350,000 in the proposition. He brought over his nephew, George Parish, to take charge of it, and returned to his banking business in Europe. George occupied the "baronial mansion" for a number of years, bringing there his mistress, Madame Vespucci, a Tuscan beauty, who had gained social prominence from her claim of descent from Americus Vespucci. After George was recalled to Germany as "Baron von Softenburg," in 1834, Madame Vespucci retained possession of the mansion for a few years. But she also wearied of the monotony of northern life, and returned to Europe. The "old red villa" at Ogdensburg was allowed to become a ruin. Its grounds were later cut up and the whole Parish estate was offered for sale, and gradually parceled out.

Thus, David Parish failed to realize his ambition to become an American baron. Though hardly a trace of his ownership of a vast northern New York barony remains, his sojourn in America was not without substantial benefit to his adopted land. It was he who suggested, in 1813, to Stephen Girard and John Jacob Astor that they, in coöperation with him, purchase the entire issue of $16,000,000 United States bonds, and thereby enabled the nation to carry on successfully the "Second War for American Independence."

Not all the prominent purchasers of the northern New York wild lands were of foreign nationality. Both William Constable and Gouverneur Morris, following their attempts to dispose of large tracts of the Macomb Purchase in Europe, made offerings of large and small parcels to native capitalists. Constable, who seems to have been a persuasive real estate salesman, as well as a great shipper and trader, succeeded in selling, for £100,000, in June, 1792, about 1,280,000 acres, or almost one-third of the total purchase, to Samuel Ward, a prominent private banker in New York. This tract was located in the westerly portion of the Macomb Purchase and is designated in the maps as the Boylston

Tract. Aaron Burr is reported to have been a silent partner in the purchase transaction, but upon ascertaining that there was no prospect of quick profit, he withdrew; so Ward completed the purchase alone. Ward, however, did not want to hold the land, and soon returned a large part of it to Constable. He tried to make out of it a quick "turnover" of his money. The portion he retained (668,000 acres) he soon resold in parcels to others.

James Greenleaf made a beginning of his vast land-jobbing business, by buying 210,000 acres from Samuel Ward for £24,000, in New York currency. Greenleaf mortgaged his entire tract to Philip Livingston for $38,000, to effect the required payment. He then proceeded to seek a purchaser. He was fortunate in finding one in John Francis, the son-in-law and partner of John Brown, a wealthy Providence shipper and manufacturer. Francis had come to New York City, where Greenleaf then resided, to dispose of a cargo of goods which was expected to arrive at the port. While awaiting the arrival of the vessel, he was entertained in "high society" by Greenleaf and Livingston, who were constantly talking of their land speculations. Whether they purposely got the young merchant under the influence of liquor or not is, of course, not recorded—but there is pretty good evidence that Francis, without consulting his rich father-in-law, turned over to Greenleaf $210,000, or some such sum, of the proceeds of the cargo money, for an imperfect claim to the same number of acres of the northern wilderness of New York.

It is reported by an eyewitness that when John Brown, the richest man in Providence, learned of the foolish transaction put over on his son-in-law, "he dropped his head into his hands and wept bitter tears of mortification and disappointment."[12] The son-in-law died about four years thereafter, probably also from mortification, so John Brown was left to struggle along with his wilderness estate. In 1798, he obtained clear title to the property, at an aggregate cost of about $250,000. He was required to buy off Livingston's first mortgage, and made other outlays to perfect his title. The estate became locally known as "John Brown's Tract," and covers the most delightful section of the Adirondacks, as it comprises the Fulton Chain of Lakes.

[12] Alfred Lee Donaldson, *History of the Adirondacks*, Vol. I, p. 101.

Brown retained the tract until his death in 1803. And he sought to exploit it. He built a road into the region and endeavored to encourage settlements therein, but with little success. At Old Forge, a saw mill, a grist mill, a few houses, and a frontier tavern and schoolhouse were built. The whole estate was divided into eight townships. To each of these townships, Brown, in the hope that they would inspire good New England morals in the wilderness, gave such names as "Industry," "Perseverance," "Frugality," "Sobriety," "Economy," and the like. When he died, he willed one or more townships to each of his heirs. Some of these soon gave up the land rather than pay the taxes due thereon.

After John Brown's death, his son-in-law, Charles Frederick Herreschoff, the progenitor of the famous yacht builders of Bristol, took over the management of the Adirondack estate. He offered strong inducements to settlers to come to the tract, and allotted them farms, on condition that they clear and cultivate the land. By this means, he hoped to sell neighboring parcels to later comers.

Of course, he didn't succeed. The country was fine for hunting, fishing and camping, but farming on it was out of the question. Accordingly, about 1815, Herreschoff, like David Parish, indulged in the sheep-raising mania. A herd of fine merinos were driven over the Berkshires all the way from Rhode Island to take up a domicile in the northern wilderness. But no profit came from this venture. Herreschoff next tried iron mining. The name of "Old Forge," where his smelting operations were carried on, is all that remains of this venture. Finally, in 1818, when financially ruined, and utterly discouraged in trying to exploit the John Brown Tract, Herreschoff blew out his brains. This is but one of the many tragedies growing out of the wild land mania which infested the Empire State in the decades following the Revolutionary War.[18]

Thus, the great wild land purchases in northern New York, as a whole, brought little satisfaction to those who originally or subsequently acquired them. The area bordering along the St. Law-

---

[18] Donaldson, *op. cit.*, pp. 89-110.

rence River, due to its water power facilities, it is true, has become an industrial and commercial region of moderate importance, but its progress has been slow. Much of the region elsewhere is still barren waste land. Some of it has been cut over for lumber, and much of it denuded for pulp. Some of it is still held as private game preserves and woodland estates of the very rich, but the greater part has again been taken over, albeit at heavy expense, by the people of the State of New York, as their public domain—a playground and forest reserve for all time.

CHAPTER V

THE OHIO LAND LURE

"I HAVE learnt from experience," wrote Lord Dunmore, Colonial Governor of Virginia, to his chief, Lord Dartmouth, on December 24, 1774, "that the established authority of any government in America, and the policy at home, are both insufficient to restrain the Americans, and they do and will remove as their avidity and restlessness incite them . . . They acquire no attachment to a place, but wandering about seems engrafted in their nature, and it is a weakness incident to it that they should forever imagine that the lands further off are still better than those upon which they are already settled."

Thus, the lure of the wooded hills and fertile plains west of the Alleghanies, as we have already seen, dates back to colonial times. This vast, inland empire stretching as far west as the Mississippi, threatened to disrupt the incipient union of the thirteen states, but the spirit of compromise prevailed. The conflicting and overlapping claims to territory were gradually surrendered to the national government. The question arose: "What is to be done with it?" "Give it to the soldiers," demanded some. "Use it to pay off the national debt," said others. "Keep it for future use," still others counseled, and there were those who held that any who desired should have the right to settle on it.

Before deciding on a policy of disposal of its western domain, Congress adopted a plan of government for it, and a system of administrative control. It passed the Ordinances of 1784, 1785 and 1787. It created the Northwest Territory. It prohibited slavery and guaranteed religious liberty in it, and provided that the primary disposal of the soil should be left to the federal government without interference or hindrance by local, state or territorial authorities.

As early as 1784, Congress took up the question of disposing of western lands. It was provided that no areas were to be sold until after they had been surveyed. All surveys were to make

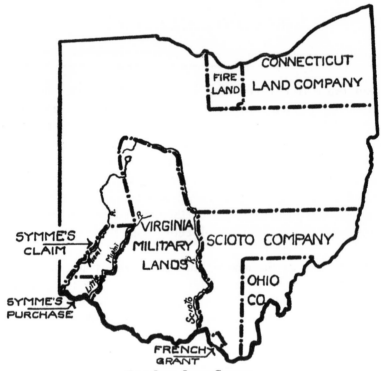

THE OHIO LAND GRANTS

provisions for "ranges," "townships," and "sections." As soon as a sufficient number of ranges were surveyed and the maps prepared, one-seventh of the land therein was to be reserved for the soldiers, and the remainder could be sold or otherwise disposed of by acts of Congress.

Little time was lost in waiting for bids for land. In 1785, Nathaniel Sackett, in behalf of himself and his associates, petitioned the Congress for a grant of land, the boundaries of which would now cover most of the present State of Ohio. Sackett offered no consideration "except an ear of Indian corn annually as rental, if demanded." He did, however, make it a condition of the proposed grant that the land be settled and cultivated by those who obtained it. To effectually prevent land jobbing, none of the settlers were to be permitted to sell their land for a space of years.

But the Continental Congress was too heavily in debt to give away the land freely. No heed, therefore, was given to Sackett's petition. In the meantime, a reverend gentleman from Massachusetts, Dr. Manasseh Cutler, had been pondering over a colonization scheme in the Ohio country. He was desirous of providing the hard-pressed New England yeomen with better and cheaper lands, and incidentally, he may have had ideas of pecuniary gain. He was born at Killingly, Conn., May 28, 1742, and graduated from Yale College in 1765. He then studied law and began the practice of his profession at Martha's Vineyard, but soon gave this up for theology. Becoming a Congregational minister, he served as chaplain in the American army during the Revolution. It is quite probable that he became interested in the Ohio country through his friend, Rufus Putnam, a hardy Revolutionary soldier, who had made a trip beyond the Alleghanies, and returned an enthusiast. Anyway, in 1786, Cutler, together with Putnam, formed a colonization association, which he called the "Ohio Company of Associates."

Of course, they offered shares in this enterprise "for a consideration." The capital was to be a million dollars in Continental certificates. It required a full year before one-fourth of this capital was subscribed, but it was thought the remainder could be readily obtained if Congress would give the "associates" an option on a compact body of land on reasonable terms. This required a modification of the land ordinance of 1785. Accordingly, the Reverend Manasseh Cutler journeyed to New York to treat with Congress. Here, it is said, he was largely instrumental in shaping the Ordinance of 1787, which established the government of the Northwest Territory.

If the Reverend Dr. Cutler had no dreams of pecuniary gain or "land grabbing" deals when he came to New York to present his petition to Congress, he probably caught the fever then, or at least was subjected to a severe risk of contagion. For at that time, Colonel William Duer was secretary of the Board of the Treasury. This "Board," composed of three members, managed the depleted finances of the new republic. Duer, therefore, would have a hand in arranging terms with Cutler regarding the purchase of western lands. He dined and wined Cutler on his arrival, and promised him assistance. In fact Duer put a business slant on Cutler's undertaking, and proposed a partnership.

Cutler's negotiations with Congress were discouraging, however. Cash was demanded, and the poor New England clergyman did not have this in sufficient amount. A minimum price of one dollar an acre had been placed on the public lands, payable within three months after purchase. As the "Ohio Associates" petitioned for 1,000,000 acres, Cutler knew that his shareholders could not raise the required sum in so short a period. Duer then advised that, as a bait to the impoverished government, Cutler should increase his application to 4,000,000 acres, and that 3,000,000 acres be assigned to a "company," composed "of a number of the principal characters of the City" of which he, Duer, would, "in profound secret," be the head. With so large a sum in prospect, Congress would be willing to grant liberal credit terms. As a further inducement, Duer proposed to give Cutler a large personal share in his land concern which was to take over the excess acreage. This excess acreage, as shown on the accompanying map, comprised the territory east of the Scioto River and west of the actual grant to the "Ohio Associates."

Cutler acceded to the proposition, and a bargain was struck with Duer, July 20, 1787, following "an elegant oyster dinner" in Brooklyn. In accordance with its terms, William Duer, together with Samuel Osgood and Walter Livingston, close friends and associates on the Board of the Treasury, used their influence (as Cutler noted in his diary), "to bring over my opposers in Congress." The outcome was the approval by Congress of a purchase by Cutler and associates of a tract in Ohio, covering five or six million acres, at one dollar per acre payable in specie, or in "loan office certificates reduced to specie value, or certificates of liquidated debts of the United States." Payments were to be $500,000 on the execution of the contract, another half million dollars

MADAME DE STAËL, WHO SPECULATED IN NORTHERN
NEW YORK LANDS

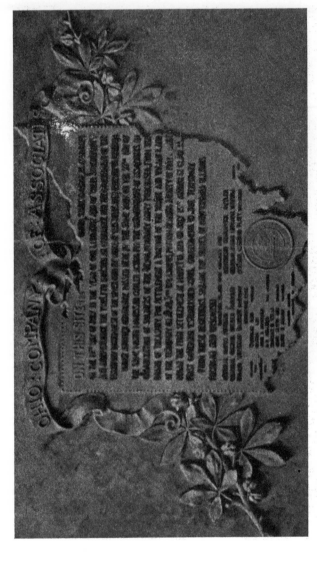

Bronze Tablet Commemorating the Grant to Ohio Company of Associates, on the Portal of the Sub-Treasury Building, New York City

when the tract was surveyed, and the balance in six equal semi-annual instalments with interest. Whenever the aggregate sum of $1,000,000 was paid, a patent for a million acres was to be given. The title to the remainder was to pass upon such conditions as the Board of the Treasury might agree with the purchasers.[1]

Thus, the Ohio Company and William Duer's so-called "Scioto Project" were launched as a joint proposition. The former may have been primarily a colonizing scheme, without the stigma of speculation, but the Scioto Project was an out-and-out land gamble. In order to put the proposition through, Duer had promised to advance $100,000 to Cutler to enable him to effect the first payment of a half million dollars. He also was to obtain assistance, if necessary, for the Ohio Company to complete the payments required of it in order to obtain full title to the quantity of land the "associates" actually desired. The payment for the remaining three to four million acres was to be made by the "Scioto Associates," and if these payments were not made, the Ohio Company would still have full title to its lands, and would not be injured by such failure. In fact, the Ohio Company shareholders were kept in blissful ignorance of the real connection of the Scioto speculation with their own enterprise.

Cutler returned to Boston in August, 1787, and reported his success to his associates. He had, he said, "arranged the greatest contract ever made in America." Some of the "shareholders," however, objected to the option on the additional 3,000,000 acres included in the contract with Congress, and "declared that they would withdraw from the company if anything beyond the original purchase was undertaken."[2] No action on the proposition was necessary, however, and the matter was allowed to stand. The principal efforts of the "Directors and Agents" of the Ohio Company were to complete the list of shareholders and obtain the first half million dollars (in depreciated government debt certificates) required for the initial payment. For this purpose handbills were circulated, traveling agents employed, and newspaper articles were published throughout New England.

An appeal was made to both investors and "settlers" with such

[1] See Joseph Stencliffe Davis, *Essays in the Earlier History of American Corporations*, Vol. I, pp. 132-136.
[2] See Cutler, *Manasseh Cutler*, Vol. I, p. 496.

good effect that despite the extreme scarcity of money at the time, a large part of the sum was acquired. Duer and associates, in accordance with the private arrangement with Cutler, made up the deficit, amounting to $143,279. Duer personally subscribed for $30,000 of the "shares" of the Ohio Company. On October 27, 1787, Cutler paid over to the Board of the Treasury a half million dollars in debt certificates of the United States then worth anywhere from $60,000 to $130,000.

From this time on, the affairs of the Ohio Company were severed from those of the Scioto Project. Its history has been recorded in glowing eulogies as the earliest phase of the westward movement. A commemoration tablet in bronze to this effect has been placed on the old Sub-Treasury building in Wall Street, New York. It notes that under an ordinance "passed here," Manasseh Cutler, acting for "The Ohio Company of Associates, an organization of soldiers of the Revolutionary Army, purchased from the Board of the Treasury for settlement, a portion of the waste and vacant lands of the (Northwest) territory." On April 7, 1788, it continues, "Rufus Putnam, heading a party of fifty-eight, began the first settlement at Marietta, and on July 15th, Arthur St. Clair, as first Governor, established civil government in the territory. From these beginnings sprang the States of Ohio, Indiana, Illinois and Wisconsin."

So runs the legend. The project was free from the stigma of speculation. "No land Company in America," enthusiastically writes Archer B. Hulbert, an American historian, "was ever formed with an eye more single in the welfare of the poorest investor; no land company in our history surpassed the Ohio Company in its manifold efforts to better the causes of the common people."[3]

Such acclamations, to be swallowed whole, must be taken with a grain of salt. Undoubtedly, the Ohio Company was more of a colonization scheme than a land speculation. But a plain appeal to human cupidity was made in the original prospectus. Among the "shareholders," moreover, were many who had not the least intention of emigrating west and who had not the slightest per-

[3] Archer B. Hulbert, *The Records and Proceedings of the Ohio Company,* Vol. I, p. lxxvi.

sonal interest in fostering land settlement for the downtrodden and impoverished Revolutionary soldiery. Thus, Alexander Macomb, the great land plunger of New York, held five shares in 1796. Alexander Hamilton was down for five and a half shares. William Duer put in $30,000 (in debt certificates) as "an investment." The Scioto "trustees" originally held one hundred and forty-three shares, representing about 200,000 acres, which shares, however, were forfeited for non-payment. Many other of the "investors" also had their holdings forfeited because of failure to meet payments when called for. They were not interested in acquiring western wild lands. They wanted merely to profit from the rising market value of their "shares."

Measured by the financial outcome, the Ohio Company was not much of a success. In March, 1792, the company petitioned Congress for relief. It had made one payment of $500,000 in debt certificates, which, computed at the then market value, was equal to less than 33 1/3 cents per acre; but before the second payment was due, the rise in the value of federal securities, due to Hamilton's funding scheme, together with the Indian war in the Ohio country, and the proposals of Congress to reduce the price of western lands to settlers, threatened the company with ruin. If the second payment could not be made, the title to the lands would not pass, and the settlers could be evicted. Congress yielded to the petition by reducing the average price of the lands to 50 cents per acre. The Ohio Company, therefore, received about 1,000,000 acres of land for $500,000 in government debts, worth during the time of purchase from 12½ to 50 cents on the dollar. For about 215,000 acres it presented soldiers' warrants.

Despite the Ohio Company's strenuous colonization efforts, when the directors of the company endeavored to make final assignments of the lands to settlers and shareholders in July, 1793, there were but 230 males of 18 years and upwards on the purchase. Indian warfare and frontier hardships had discouraged emigrants. Yet, the venture was of inestimable value to American progress. "It extinguished a half million of the public debt at a time when the treasury was all but bankrupt; it was a concrete example of the wealth of the western lands; it seemed to pave the way for other remunerative sales, and better than all this, it placed on the frontier a most desirable body of settlers, many of them veterans of the Revolution."[4]

. . . . .

Though the Ohio Company's success, from a financial viewpoint, was disappointing, that of the Scioto Project, its illegitimate half-sister, was a complete fiasco. Two days after the purchase contract was signed with the Board of the Treasury on behalf of the "Ohio Company of Associates," Colonel William Duer, on behalf of himself and a small "inside" group of speculators, entered into an agreement with Manasseh Cutler and his assistant, Major Winthrop Sargent, by the terms of which the Ohio Company's option on the Ohio lands, exclusive of the 1,000-000 acres to be taken up directly by the settlers, was divided into thirty equal shares, "thirteen to belong to Duer and his assignees, thirteen similarly to Cutler and Sargent, and the remaining four to be disposed of abroad for joint account." The two groups were to share equally in profits which might accrue in attempting to negotiate the sale or mortgage of the same, "either in Europe or America . . . and in paying the purchase money due to the United States."[5]

This contract formed the sole basis of the Scioto Project. The concern was never chartered. It was not even a recognized "association." When Duer was hard pressed by his French investors for an explanation of the real character and composition of his "company," he is reported to have made the following statement:

The company known under the name of the Company of the Scioto, was originally composed of thirty (30) shares belonging to as many owners. The persons who held these shares were for the most part those who had much influence in the formation of the Company of the Ohio at Marietta, or in the Legislative or Executive branches of the Government. The original shares have since been much sub-divided, but the general management of the Company's affairs, as well in America as abroad, has been entirely trusted to myself alone, and I have for aid and counsel, two agents, who are Messrs. Royal Flint and Andrew Craigie.[6]

[4] Payson Jackson Treat, *The National Land System*, pp. 57, 58.
[5] J. S. Davis, *Essays in the Earlier History of American Corporations*, Vol. I, p. 139.
[6] *Ibid.*, p. 231.

Thus it was William Duer's "bubble." He seems to have interested, both financially and otherwise, a group of prominent capitalists and land jobbers in New York and Boston. Besides Royal Flint and Andrew Craigie, there were Christopher Gore, of Boston, Nalbro Frazier, a Philadelphia merchant; James Jarvis, John Holker, William Constable, Melancthon Smith and Seth Johnson of New York. Several others were probably concerned in it, but the real "proprietors" may never be known, as the whole affair was conducted in an underhanded manner without responsible officers or offices, and without minutes or records of proceedings. No attempt was made to interest the public in the venture, and no efforts were employed to attract home settlers to the lands, though there was an abortive plan of French colonization.

William Duer, like Robert Morris, Alexander Macomb, William Constable and other land jobbers of the epoch, believed that American waste lands could be readily sold in Europe. And he attempted to follow the practice the speculators then called "dodging," i.e., selling the land in Europe before paying for it here.[7] The "Scioto Associates" certainly acted on this principle. All they had was a contract to take over a portion of the option of the Ohio Company, an option not originally desired by Manasseh Cutler and his associates, but forced upon them through the need of Duer's political influence in obtaining a land grant from Congress. On the basis of this option they despatched to France the young Hartford editor and poet, Joel Barlow, to offer the lands. They thus expected to attract the hard-pressed and persecuted aristocracy as purchasers.

Barlow's task was not easy, and his expense to the "Scioto Associates" was heavy. Despairing, after many efforts, of selling large tracts to individuals, he decided to form a French subsidiary company, called the "Compagnie du Scioto." This company agreed to purchase from the "Scioto Associates" 3,000,000 acres at about $1.00 per acre, payable in instalments. It was given the privilege of reselling in large or small tracts, and could send out settlers to take possession of the land. Barlow acted as its agent and manager. Because he gave "shareholders" and land

[7] See Chapter II, p. 36.

purchasers the right of immediate settlement, he expected "to raise the reputation of the lands to such a degree that they will sell them all off in the course of one year at a great profit."

With this object in view the "Compagnie du Scioto" issued in Paris a glowing prospectus for "an Establishment on the Ohio and Scioto Rivers in America." It contained much the same material used by Manasseh Cutler in his advertisement of the Ohio Company's project. The rough maps exhibited were seriously misleading, and the statements and plans of the enterprise highly overdrawn. Barlow, however, was "furnished with testimonies of so flattering a nature, and with credentials of the first authority to the most respectable houses in Paris" that he aroused the cupidity of the intelligent Frenchmen and created a flood of public enthusiasm for the speculation. His land office in Paris became so popular that he wrote his principals that they might reckon their profits at "above a million," and he even suggested a proposal that the French Government exchange its American securities for shares in the "Compagnie du Scioto." "The present circumstances are so favorable," he added, "and the object so popular, many portions are already sold, and the people are preparing to embark in January."

This news was not entirely pleasing to the "Scioto Associates." They had no intention of establishing colonies and had made no provision for receiving foreign settlers. They had hoped that some opulent French capitalists would take their property off their hands "en bloc" at a great pecuniary profit to themselves. In fact, they never intended that Barlow should divide up the tract into "shares," and they certainly could not back up Barlow's warranty clause in his sales to Frenchmen, guaranteeing purchasers against every kind of eviction and attack.

However, they were overjoyed at the prospect of a handsome profit, and made some preparation to receive the *émigrés*. Barlow was fearful, however, that he had gone too far in making outright sale of lands that his principals did not possess. On January 15, 1790, he wrote Duer:

Don't for God's sake fail to raise money enough to put the people in possession. . . . Make every sacrifice rather than fail in this essential object. If it fails, we are ruined. All our fortunes, and my character will be buried in the ruins.[8]

The first shipload of the French settlers arrived in Alexandria, Va., in March, 1790. Duer had sent an agent, Colonel David Franks, one of the proprietors of the old Illinois Company, to remove them as quietly and as secretly as possible, to a site selected for their settlement. They and their wares were placed in wagons and carted off to the Ohio country, but not without difficulties. Franks notified Duer they complained bitterly against the cheap claret furnished them, and demanded French wines. Near Winchester, Va., they entered into a fistic encounter with the native farmers. Moreover, Franks was not furnished by Duer with sufficient funds to pay the cost of cartage, and the wagoners threatened to have him jailed for debt.

The discontent was increased by the heterogeneous character of the human consignment. Among the Frenchmen who arrived were several *ci-devant* notables who had purchased large tracts. They had organized themselves into an association called the "Society of Twenty-four." These included the Marquis de Lezay-Marnésia, Count de Barth, Viscount de Malartic, and Madame de Leval. They brought with them renters and sub-purchasers, and "indentured servants of the worst class—even taken from the prisons." When they arrived at the place of settlement, euphoniously called "Gallipolis," they were painfully disappointed, and sent home letters denouncing the promoters of the speculation. They were unfitted for and could not endure the hardships of pioneer life. Many soon deserted.

Some of the "notables" went to New York and presented their bitter protests to Duer. They were appeased for a while by assurance of protection from prominent government officials to whom Duer had introduced them. Duer also entertained them well and placed them into the best society. He succeeded partly in interesting them in his Maine lands. But the poorer immigrants were not so easily stalled. They experienced hunger and other privations as well as Indian attacks. The few that remained suffered miserably. In the meantime, Duer, together with Alexander Macomb and Andrew Craigie, and others of the "Associates" had

[8] Davis, *op. cit.*, p. 221.

become involved in a disastrous speculation in government bonds and bank shares. Several, including Duer, took up their residence in the debtors' prison. *And they never paid for the Scioto lands.*

But Joel Barlow, poet and diplomat, who was really responsible for the colonization scheme that brought scandal into the Scioto deal, speculated successfully in France following its collapse, became rich, and returned to America. Here, he purchased an estate near the national capital; endeavored to establish a national university, and ended his career in Cracow, Poland, in 1812, while United States Minister to France.

Congress, merely as a charitable act, later made provision for the few Frenchmen who remained in the Gallipolis colony. A law was passed giving them patents to small allotments of land in the Scioto Valley. Thomas Ashe, an Englishman, who visited the Ohio country, in 1806, describes the wretched French colony, and concludes that "never was a place chosen, or rather approved of with less judgment." Of an estimated number of 500 families, not more than sixteen families were left in 1800.[9] Thus ended the Scioto fiasco. It was conceived in the iniquity of avarice, nurtured in secret and underhanded dealings, and was closed out as a national disgrace. John Bach McMaster, the eminent American historian, who, despite his exaggeration and inaccuracy in his short account of the project, aptly described it as "the most shameful piece of land jobbery that ever disgraced our country."[10]

. . . . .

Aside from Cutler's purchase on behalf of the "Ohio Company of Associates," in which the Scioto Project was involved—Congress made only one other sale of a large tract of public land for colonization purposes. This is known as the Symmes' "Miami Purchase." In its outward aspects, it is an Ohio land venture very similar to that of Manasseh Cutler and his associates.

John Cleves Symmes, in his application for a western land grant, pictured himself, as Cutler had done before him, a friend of the Revolutionary soldier and a promoter of western settlement. He was born in 1742, at Southold, L. I., of old American pioneer stock. He was the fifth generation of the Symmes, and

[9] Thomas Ashe, *Travels in America, Performed in 1806,* Vol. II, p. 86.
[10] John Bach McMaster, *History of the American People,* Vol. II, p. 146.

JOEL BARLOW
(From a portrait by R. Fulton)

WILLIAM DUER
(From an etching by Max Rosenthal)

JOHN CLEVES SYMMES

(Reproduced from Bond's *The Correspondence of John Cleves Symmes*)

the fourth generation of the Cleves family in America. As a young man he took up the work of a surveyor, which may account partly for his later interest in lands. It is not known definitely whether he read law, but his letters indicate that he possessed considerable learning, and as an associate justice of the Supreme Court of New Jersey and a pioneer federal judge in the Northwest Territory, he acquitted himself well.

In 1770, Symmes moved to Sussex County, then on the western frontier of New Jersey. He joined the patriotic cause at the outbreak of the Revolution, and served in the New Jersey militia. His military record commended him as a tried and able leader. His record in the civil service of his adopted state was also honorable. Removing to Morristown, N. J., in 1780, he was elected to the Continental Congress in 1785. Here he acquired the political influence and the personal contacts which were of valuable assistance to him in putting over his scheme of western colonization.

Jonathan Dayton, who became Symmes' partner in the Ohio land deal, was also a Revolutionary veteran and a member of Congress from New Jersey. Dayton remained in Congress after the adoption of the Constitution, and was Speaker of the House during the years 1793-1797. The strength of his political influence, together with his superior business acumen, helped Symmes in his negotiations with Congress. Although at times the two partners were somewhat at loggerheads in their business relations, they never suffered a complete rupture of their friendship.

Such is not the case of Symmes' relationship with Elias Boudinot, his third partner in the Ohio land purchase. Boudinot also was a Jerseyite, and of greater political prominence than either Symmes or Dayton. He was at one time President of the Continental Congress, and was a member of Congress under the new Constitution, from 1785 to 1795. Like Symmes, he became very much interested in western lands. It was his powerful political influence which was largely instrumental in putting through Symmes' "Miami Purchase." He also acquired a half interest in the tract which Symmes reserved for himself as a speculation, and, in addition, became the owner of large sections in other parts of the purchase. Toward the end, Boudinot and Symmes had a dispute regarding the division of the "reserve lands" and the former took legal action to compel Symmes to furnish him with deeds for his portion.

Although Boudinot and Dayton, as members of Congress, pushed through the Miami Purchase, and became active participants in the deal, the origination of the idea and the execution of the plan must be credited to John Cleves Symmes alone. It is said that the "western urge" was communicated to Symmes by his neighbor, Benjamin Stites, who went on a trading trip down the Ohio River in 1786. Stites became an enthusiast regarding the prospects of the Ohio country, and selected the region between the two Miami rivers as offering the best locations for settlement. In the spring and summer of 1787, Symmes himself visited the region and was likewise impressed with its resources and prospects.

At first he planned a colony on the Wabash River above Vincennes, in the region formerly claimed by the United Illinois and Wabash Land Companies, and went as far as to issue a "prospectus" addressed to the people of Kentucky. This is described "as a masterpiece of its kind in the inducement it offered to settlers." In this document, Symmes announced that he hoped to "induce Congress to lend a favorable ear" to his petition, since he meant "not to solicit a grant merely for himself, but on behalf of all those who will signify to him their wishes to become adventurers, and will subject themselves to a proper system for safe settlement and the government which it is expected will be established by Congress."[11]

Notwithstanding his proposal of adherence to the government "which is expected to be established by Congress," the fact that Symmes addressed his appeal to the "People of Kentucky"— then strongly dissatisfied with the federal administration—and invited settlement, "with artillery and military stores" before he ever had title to the land, led General Josiah Harmar, who was the military governor of the district, to send a copy of the prospectus to the Secretary of War for the information of Congress. Congress did nothing about the matter, however, and on his return to the East, Symmes gave up the idea of the Wabash set-

---

[11] Beverley W. Bond, Jr., *The Correspondence of John Cleves Symmes,* pp. 278-281.

tlement, and turned his attention to obtaining a grant in the Miami section.

Doubtless, he was influenced in this choice by the Congressional grant that had just been made to the Ohio Company in the Muskingum Valley. The lands bordering on the west of this grant, comprising the district between the Scioto and Miami rivers, had been reserved by Congress for the holders of Virginia military land warrants, so the section nearest to the Ohio Company's land available for private purchase was the region lying on the Ohio River between the Miami and the Little Miami rivers. It was an ideal location for a settlement, since the rivers afforded navigation for commerce with the southwest. Symmes impetuously petitioned Congress for the whole of this region, comprising about 2,000,000 acres. He later reduced his demand to 1,000,000 acres, but was particular to designate the most favorable boundaries. He insisted upon, and he received, the same terms as Manasseh Cutler and Winthrop Sargent had been granted, when acting for the Ohio Associates. The contract was signed October 15, 1788, and the first payment of $82,198 in debt certificates and soldiers' warrants was made.

In the meantime, Symmes, in a determined effort to secure settlers, and in order to make the required initial payment, had been issuing prospectuses, pamphlets and advertisements. He invited Revolutionary veterans with land warrants, and owners of federal debt certificates, to enter the deal. One of his advertisements which appeared in the *Brunswick Gazette*, January 7, 1788, reads, in part, as follows:

The subscriber having succeeded with Congress in obtaining that most excellent tract of land on the northwest bank of the Ohio, between the great and little Miami rivers, begs leave to state some particulars to those gentlemen who may not meet with a small pamphlet already published on the subject.

In the first place it ought to be observed, that no dispute respecting titles in the first instance, can possibly arise, these will be clear and certain, as the whole purchase will be surveyed into sections of one mile square, and every line well marked, and the sections numbered, and every number which may be sold shall be recorded to the first person applying to the subscriber therefor. The land is allowed (all circumstances considered) to be the best tract in the federal country: It lies in north latitude thirty-eight degrees, and the same with Virginia. Horses, cattle and hogs can live well in the woods, where there is abundance of food through the winters, which are very moderate: Every kind of grain and vegetable raised in the middle states grows here, with the addition of cotton and indigo, which may be raised in sufficient quantities for family use. The land is generally free from stone and a rich, easy soil for tillage. There are no mountains and few hills, so that the country for the most part is level: It is extremely well watered throughout, and surrounded on three sides by rivers navigable in the boating seasons; vessels may be built here of two hundred tons burden, and being fully freighted may be navigated with safety to New York, or any other sea-port. The finest timber of every kind known in the middle states, with many other sorts of more southerly production, grow in plenty here, but there is very little underwood or brush. Millstones and grindstones are found in some of the hills. Wild game and fish may be taken in abundance. Salt is now made to any quantity, in Kentucke, opposite this tract on the south-east side of the Ohio, where seven counties are already considerably settled and where any number of neat-cattle may be had very cheap.

As payment was to be made in "debt certificates," Symmes exchanged land warrants for this currency. He also made actual sales of land prior to the grant, something which was destined to cause him considerable trouble. But the important transaction which concerns us, as a land speculation, was his reservation of the most valuable section of the grant for himself. This reserved section, consisting of over 40,000 acres, bordering on the Ohio River, and covering the present city of Cincinnati, he divided up into twenty-four shares. He made Elias Boudinot an equal partner in this territory and then offered and sold to speculators a considerable part of these shares on their joint account, even before he started west with his settlers. All this was done in advance of the signing of the definite purchase contract. Symmes was so anxious to launch his undertaking that he actually set out for Ohio in July, 1788, three months before he obtained the right to the land, leaving to Boudinot and Dayton the task of completing the legal formalities.

MIAMI LAND-WARRANT.

No. 231   MIAMI LAND-WARRANT.

THIS entitles mr Joseph Lamb, his Heirs or Assigns, to locate one quarter of a Section, in which the Fee of 160 Acres shall pass, subject to the Terms of settlement.

Dated the 3d Day of April A.D. 178 3

Signed by John Cleves Symmes.

Counterfigned by. Benjamin Stites

A MIAMI LAND-WARRANT

(Collection of the Historical and Philosophical Society of Ohio)

JONATHAN DAYTON

It is generally believed that Symmes' object was patriotic and idealistic, and that it was free from the stigma of land speculation. That this is an erroneous view is proven by his correspondence and his activities subsequent to making the purchase. The fact that, from the very inception of his enterprise, he made a reservation of the best section for the benefit of himself and partners is an indication that his humanitarianism was diluted with personal avarice. In his Trenton circular, addressed, "To the Respectable Public," issued November 26, 1787, he openly stated:

The subscriber hopes that the respectable public will not think it unreasonable for him, when he informs them that the only privilege which he reserves for his trouble in the business, is the exclusive right of electing or locating that entire and exclusive township which will be the lowest point in the point of land formed by the Ohio and Miami Rivers, and those three branching parts of townships which may be northwest and south of such entire township.

When this reservation, together with his hasty departure west before the contract was signed, became known, it aroused considerable political opposition to his grant. Both Dayton and Boudinot had much difficulty in overriding the opposition. Competitive land companies insidiously attacked the idea of a "proprietor's reserve" by advertising that their own projects permitted all to come in on equal terms. Judge Symmes met their attacks in a public statement, published in the *New Jersey Journal*, March 19, 1788, in which he denied that the proprietors' lands along the Ohio and Miami Rivers were the most desirable. The suspicion persisted, however, and an unsigned squib, in the same newspaper, ironically described Symmes' emigrants as "going west to the emolument of certain gentlemen who have a particular genius for land jobbing." In a letter to Dayton, dated August 21, 1788, Symmes boldly stated:

My appropriation of a township at the confluence of the two Rivers, and the mode adopted by me in disposing of the same, I still conceive, to have been my province alone, and of which no one with propriety can complain.[12]

[12] Bond, *op. cit.*, p. 38.

The proprietors' "reserve" selected by Symmes, despite his public statement to the contrary, covered the most accessible and fertile lands in the Miami Purchase. It includes today within its limits the City of Cincinnati, that Queen City of the West, in which Symmes originated the "town-jobbing" business, which became a mania in the Northwest Territory for many years thereafter. Each owner of the twenty-four shares representing the "proprietors' reserve" was required to pay £200 per share into a joint account of the original proprietors, i.e., Symmes and Boudinot. For this payment, each share was to receive "a square" in the proposed city (i.e., Cincinnati) and a proportionate part of the remaining reserved section. In later years, some dispute arose among the shareholders over the divisions of the lands, and, as already noted, Boudinot was impelled to enter suit against Symmes to obtain his allotment.

Symmes lost no time in pushing land sales. For this purpose, he engaged a number of agents in New Jersey as well as in the new settlement. Sales continued for some time on a moderate scale in all parts of his purchase. When final surveys of the tract were made, however, they revealed that it contained only slightly more than one-half of the expected million acres. The proprietors soon discovered that they had "oversold."

This, at first, did not seriously disturb Symmes. He persisted continuously to make demands on Congress for the full million acres designated in the contract. One of his handbills, dated January 20, 1797, almost ten years after the date of his purchase, reads as follows:

TO THE PUBLIC

It being a matter, no longer doubtful, that Congress will establish their Contract with the Subscriber, in the fullest extent of One Million of Acres of Miami Lands, It is hoped that all who wish to become purchasers, will not longer suffer themselves to be amused with the idle reports against the Contract, but purchase immediately from some Persons who have a right to sell. And those Gentlemen who have already contracts for Miami Lands, are desired to make payment as soon as possible to Wm. H. Harrison at Fort Washington, as the Secretary of War has agreed to receive Twenty

Thousand Dollars at Fort Washington from the Subscriber, if the money be paid immediately for the use of the Army.

JOHN CLEVES SYMMES

Jan. 20, 1797.

Thus Symmes was confident that he would get his million acres. He accordingly continued to sell lands lying outside his grant. This caused him considerable annoyance later, and ultimately led to his financial ruin. Numerous suits were filed against him by purchasers whose titles were rejected by the government. The judgments obtained by them brought him into a condition of bankruptcy. His large land holdings were seized and sold piecemeal under the hammer.

Moreover, after 1790, Congress adopted Hamilton's plan of disposing of the public domain in small plots on easy terms to individual purchasers, and steadfastly refused to accede to Symmes' petitions for the unpatented sections of his million acres. He had contracted to pay for his grant at the rate of only 66 2/3 cents per acre, payable in depreciated debt certificates. As Congress had placed a minimum price of $2.00 per acre on public lands, Symmes saw a remarkable opportunity for profit in his land deal with Congress. But Congress was obdurate. The agitation against land grabbing was too strong to be politically ignored. The petition of two designing land grabbers—Royal Flint and Joseph Parker—for an Ohio grant was rejected. A similar petition for a tract on the Mississippi River just south of Ohio, made by Colonel George Morgan, one of the proprietors of the old Indiana Company, was also given little heed. Henceforth, public land was not to be sold at wholesale to speculators.

The total acreage that Symmes had patented to him amounted to but 311,862 acres. The actual cost in specie was probably less than $50,000, but, of course, Symmes and his associates incurred other expenses in acquiring and improving the tract. Naturally, he was much embittered by his inability to receive all the acreage he contracted for. This is reflected in his last Will and Testament, in which he complains of having been treated "with the blackest ingratitude" by the United States. "Many of those," he stated, "who now laugh at my calamity, . . . would this day be toiling in poverty had not my enterprise to this country, my benevolence on the property that they have plundered from me, have made them rich."

Symmes undoubtedly served the country well in settling the Miami lands on the Ohio. He took up his residence on his grant and was active in the administration of its welfare. His difficulties were many. Indian attacks, settlers' complaints, shortage of provisions, riots and disease were prevalent. He bore all with indomitable courage. He is described by Thomas Ashe in 1806 as living in a noble stone mansion, surrounded by improved farms, villages, and country seats. "The banks of the River," noted Ashe, "are settling with unparalleled success, and the title to all the adjacent lands is bought up by individuals and speculators who propose selling again at an advance price. Most of the prairie ground are now as high as from twenty to fifty dollars per acre, and the woodland adjoining the river at from five to sixteen dollars per acre."[13] Symmes had paid Congress for the same land less than twenty years previous but a few cents an acre.

As is customary in human experience, the pioneer and promoter did not profit. Symmes died February 26, 1814, in almost hopeless poverty. Though his venture was a great financial disappointment to him, due, as he claimed to "the unjust claims against him founded upon the deepest conspiracy that had ever destroyed the earnings of an industrious, frugal and adventurous life," be brought to completion his dream of a western colony which gave a fresh impetus to American territorial growth and expansion at the beginning of the nineteenth century. His claims to fame rest not alone on his enterprise in western settlement, but because of his emigration to the frontier. Through his western venture he became the father-in-law of the warrior President, William Henry Harrison, and a great-grandfather of Benjamin Harrison, also a President of the United States.

Symmes had associated with him a number of prominent land jobbers, whose cupidity and zeal were attracted by the speculation. In addition to Jonathan Dayton and Elias Boudinot, there was James Wilkinson, soldier of the Revolution, who had settled in Lexington, Ky., where, in addition to carrying on an extensive

[13] Thomas Ashe, *Travels in America, Performed in 1806,* First Edition, Vol. II, p. 248.

trade with Louisiana, he speculated heavily in western.lands. Re-entering the army in 1791, he continued his land deals, and later was suspected of treasonable intrigues with the Spanish, and of complicity in Burr's Conspiracy. Even after his removal from the army in 1815, he kept up his interest in land speculation. He died in Mexico City in 1825, when on a mission to obtain a Texas land grant.

Israel Ludlow, prominent land surveyor in the Ohio country, who laid out the Symmes patent, also became mildly infected with the land mania. Still another was General Arthur St. Clair, first governor of the Northwest Territory.

Jonathan Dayton, together with St. Clair, Ludlow and Wilkinson, jointly purchased from Symmes the tract between the Miami and the Mad rivers. On this, Ludlow laid out the town of Dayton in 1795. The proprietors offered in Cincinnati the "in-lots" at ten dollars a lot, and the "out-lots" at still lower prices. The town jobbing proposition gave fair promise of success, until the site was declared to lie outside the area of Symmes' original grant. At this time, Jonathan Dayton was speaker of the House of Representatives, occupying, as Symmes expressed it, "honor's easy chair" at $12 a day. His great political influence and his "wire-pulling," however, were not powerful enough to lead Congress to yield to the petition to have the town bearing his name placed within the Symmes Purchase. The "lot purchasers," therefore, had to pay the "government price" to the national land office, if they desired a clear title. Some of them did this, but many of the purchasers of the "out-lots" abandoned their properties.

. . . . .

Symmes' Miami Purchase was the last sale of government land at wholesale. But it was not the last of the wholesale Ohio land gambles. The State of Connecticut had persistently claimed title under its charter grant to territory beyond its eastern boundary. After much haggling and bickering with the federal government, a compromise plan was adopted whereby Connecticut in 1786 ceded to the nation all lands beyond the Alleghanies, but reserving a strip of territory, comprising about 3,500,000 acres, bordering on Lake Erie. This became known as the "Connecticut Western Reserve." A part, covering about one-half million acres, was set aside by the state and allotted to the residents of New London and other Connecticut towns that had suffered from British depredations. These were known as the "Fire Lands." But the greater portion was left undisturbed.

The state authorities did not press its disposal. Its citizens, however, already intoxicated by their profits from speculation in government debt certificates, and seeking for further opportunities for gain, were eager to get possession of this fertile and accessible western domain. In order to obtain the support of the dominant Congregational Church, a bill was introduced in the Connecticut Legislature in 1791, proposing the sale of the land and using the proceeds for the support of the ministry, thus dispensing with a portion of the state tax which was then levied for their maintenance. Two years later, the bill was again introduced in amplified form, allotting the proceeds to the support of all ecclesiastics in the state. Though it passed, it created such strong opposition that in May, 1795, an amendment to the measure was passed, applying the proceeds to the establishment of a general school fund.

A committee was then appointed to effect the sale of the Western Reserve. Rival bids were received. One group of bidders was headed by John Livingston, of New York City, and another by Oliver Phelps, both previously concerned in the western New York speculation. Phelps succeeded in buying off Livingston by proposing to turn over to the latter's syndicate all the land in the Western Reserve in excess of 3,000,000 acres. The "Excess Company" was organized to receive this surplus. This bubble concern was later sold for $50,000 to General William Hull, the surrenderer of Detroit to the British. When the final survey proved there was no excess acreage, Hull was threatened with the total loss of his investment at one fell swoop. In order to avoid trouble with him, the successful bidders for the Western Reserve gave him a share in their purchase.

Having eliminated competitive bidders, a syndicate, headed by Oliver Phelps, struck a bargain with the Connecticut commission appointed to dispose of the Western Reserve. For an aggregate sum of $1,200,000, the entire unappropriated Ohio lands of Connecticut were sold to a group of thirty-five individuals, each of whom gave a separate bond to secure his portion of the purchase. Payment in cash was to be made September 2, 1800, with interest at 6 per cent computed from September, 1797. Thus, the purchasers had ample time to raise the required funds before their payments fell due. Oliver Phelps, however, because of the magnitude of his individual participation, agreed to pay on demand. It is quite evident that Phelps, who had safely crawled out of his gigantic New York land venture, was the chief promoter as well as the chief participant of the deal. Of the total sum of $1,200,000, he subscribed for $168,185 on his own account, and jointly with Gideon Granger, Jr., he assumed $80,000 additional. The remaining thirty-three subscribers took up various amounts ranging from $85,000 downward. All were New Englanders, and the chief participants were stockholders and "managers" of the recently organized Bank of Hartford.

The purchasers immediately organized themselves into an association called the "Connecticut Land Company." The shares numbered 400 and were distributed in accordance with the portion of the purchase price paid by each subscriber. Each share, therefore, represented $3,000 of the purchase money, but it was convertible into an indefinite quantity of land based upon the results of a survey. It was the apparent intention of the shareholders to take over this land and dispose of it at a profit. As a survey had not been made at the time of the purchase, the separate proprietors deeded their respective claims to the land in trust to John Caldwell, Jonathan Brace and John Morgan. Moreover, it was required of the purchasers that they extinguish the Indian title, and also stand the cost of the surveys. Accordingly, each share was assessed $10 to cover these costs. In order to prevent the largest shareholders from dominating the affairs of the association, a limitation was placed on the voting power, but in the partition of the territory, every share was entitled to its proportionate quantity of land. Isaac Cleaveland, a Connecticut surveyor, and also one of the proprietors, was appointed the general agent of the company. He went west to make the surveys, and, incidentally, he laid out the city of Cleveland.

When surveys of the purchase were completed, it revealed a total of 2,841,471 acres. Although some townships were sold in units to speculators, a large part of the lands were drawn by lot by the individual proprietors, the last drawing taking place in 1809. The resolution originally adopted by the proprietors to resell only to actual settlers was not generally carried out.

It is quite evident that both the Connecticut state authorities and the purchasers tried to avoid the appearance of "speculation" or "land jobbing" in the deal. The sale was made to the "subscribers" individually, though no definite "plots" could be assigned to each. Each bought a "pig in a poke." But this was not uncommon in those days of "wild land" sales. Moreover, the question of the title and jurisdiction of the purchase was not settled. Connecticut's claim to western territory was never fully acknowledged by the other states. Neither did the federal government consent to the political suzerainty of Connecticut in the Western Reserve. When the agents of the Connecticut Company began to survey the region, General Arthur St. Clair, Governor of the Northwest Territory, claimed authority over it. A dispute arose. This seriously handicapped the resale in Connecticut of the proprietors' preëmption rights. They grew impatient, and demanded that the status of their purchases be fixed. Finally, in 1800, in return for a surrender by Connecticut of all claim to territory west of her eastern boundary, Congress acknowledged her ownership right of the Western Reserve, and accepted the political jurisdiction over it.

Then began the Connecticut trek to the west! It threatened to depopulate the state. A rage for moving seized rich and poor alike. The Connecticut Company's lands were eagerly sought after and sold at favorable prices for the proprietors. In 1809, they divided up the little that remained unsold and disbanded. A small group of the shareholders pooled their plots, and under the cognomen of the "Erie Company," continued to dispose of lands to settlers until 1812.

So popular was the western lure to the Connecticut gentry that legislation was urged to countermand it. "Young people in their plays at social gatherings marched to rude melodies which taught them to dream that toward the setting sun lay an earthly paradise with gates open to welcome them. From hill and valley the processions hurried away. Today, many of our rural towns are scarred and paralyzed by an outflow which has built up the continent to no small degree at their expense."[14]

Washington Irving's description, in his charming *Legend of Sleepy Hollow*, of Ichabod Crane's desire to marry the fair Katrinka Van Tassel, and, with her dowry, purchase supplies, oxen and a covered wagon and move westward, is a contemporary delineation of the Connecticut Yankee's urge:

As the enraptured Ichabod rolled his great green eyes over the fat meadow-lands, the rich fields of wheat, of rye, of buckwheat, and Indian corn, and the orchard burdened with ruddy fruit, which surrounded the warm tenement of Van Tassel, his heart yearned after the damsel who was to inherit these domains, and his imagination expanded with the idea how they might be readily turned into cash and the money invested in immense tracts of wild land, and shingle palaces in the wilderness. Nay, his busy fancy realized his hopes, and presented to him the blooming Katrina, with the whole family of children, mounted on top of a wagon, loaded with household trumpery, with pots and kettles dangling beneath; and he beheld himself bestriding a pacing mare, with a colt at her heels, setting out for Kentucky, Tennessee, or the Lord knows where.

But it was not Kentucky or Tennessee that Ichabod Crane's Connecticut brethren sought as a place of prosperous abode in the early part of the nineteenth century. Many cleared wild tracts in the Holland Purchase in western New York, but a large number passed by way of the "Pittsburgh Pike," or the Buffalo gateway, to the fertile plains of the Western Reserve. Here they laid out farms, built roads, planned canals and started the city of Cleveland and other flourishing communities. Here came the ancestors of the Shermans, the Bancrofts, the Hayes, the Garfields, and the Cookes. Here in a space of ten years were settled 150,000 white inhabitants, sturdy and steady, zealous to undertake great things; and, when the land further west offered profitable gain or a promise of a larger supply of material goods, they, like their ancestors, took up the westward march and went.

[14] P. H. Woodward, *One Hundred Years of the Hartford Bank*, p. 74. See also R. J. Purcell, *Connecticut in Transition*, p. 154.

CHAPTER VI

THE GEORGIA "YAZOO" LAND FRAUDS

Now we come to the most notorious and widespread of the early American land gambles.

The State of Georgia, at the southern end of the colonial confederacy, had performed its share in bringing about political independence, and following the Revolution, like its sister states, laid claim to the immense territory lying immediately to the west. South Carolina, however, contended that a part of this land was comprised within her original charter limits, while the federal authorities maintained that it was national domain, because it had been obtained directly from the British crown. The Spanish king also asserted political authority over much of the region as a part of Louisiana ceded to him by the French.

While all these competing and conflicting claims were being debated, the Chickasaws, Choctaws, Cherokees and Creeks roved over the region at will. It was in their possession, and few white settlers dared to invade their ancient hunting grounds. Over these tribes, the United States had established a protectorate, and forbade Georgia or any other state to deal with them directly or to take any action to dispossess them. In view of these difficulties and uncertainty of title, the impoverished State of Georgia was quite ready to accept any financial consideration for her doubtful claim, and sought to dispose of the lands at the earliest and most favorable opportunity.

Nor were purchasers lacking! Despite its primeval condition, and the fierce savage tribes, the territory had distinct commercial advantages. It bordered on the Mississippi River, that Father of

Waters which afforded the chief means of commercial intercourse between the interior settlements and the Gulf of Mexico. It contained numerous well-watered streams emptying into the Mississippi, and therefore gave accessibility to trade and barter, a prime factor in creating land values. One of these tributary streams was the Yazoo River. For some reason or other, the name "Yazoo" originally was applied to the whole territory, which now comprises the entire areas of Alabama and Mississippi.

In 1785, some enterprising citizens of South Carolina and Georgia, with an eye to business, planned to get possession of a favorable section of the Yazoo country. As customary, an effort was made to buy off the Indians. John Wood, one of the promoters, succeeded in "purchasing" from the Choctaws a tract of two or three million acres lying near the mouth of the Yazoo River. The exact quantity was of little concern. Application was then made to Georgia for a grant of the lands. But the state did not yet feel ready to dispose of the territory, when its title was so strongly doubted. However, the legislature of Georgia organized the territory into a county, and gave it the then popular French name of "Bourbon." Settlers were invited to move there. To these settlers, lands were to be granted at not more than 25 cents an acre. Few settlers came, however. They preferred not to run the danger of Indian tomahawks and Spanish bullets. One John Holder, a captain in the Revolution, however, in 1789, proposed to conduct four hundred Kentucky settlers to the present site of Vicksburg, but failed utterly.

The Georgia land speculators were not discouraged. Through the influence of an unprincipled character, styling himself Thomas Washington, but whose real name was Walsh (and who eventually was hanged at Charleston for counterfeiting South Carolina debt certificates), a "land association" was formed to acquire the region. It was called the "South Carolina Yazoo Company." The original promoters, in addition to Thomas Washington, were Alexander Moultrie, William Clay Snipes and Isaac Huger of South Carolina. Among those who joined later was Alexander McGillivray, a famous chief of the Creek tribe. The "association," on November 20, 1789, presented an elaborate petition to the Georgia Legislature urging the confirmation of a grant of land.

They announced that they had already begun settlements in the region "as well from a motive of general good to mankind and of happiness and prosperity to Georgia and the union; as their own." This, they thought, would please the authorities of Georgia, who wished settlers as a buffer against the unfriendly Indian tribes. They also appealed on the ground of commercial development. They had, they claimed "established Connections in Europe, America and in this State; whereby an affrican trade and European Commerce" would "take place at the Yazoo to an immense and vast amount."[1]

In view of the wild land mania of the period, it would be expected that others would also seek "grants." Three other companies presented petitions. These were "the Virginia Yazoo Company," in which Patrick Henry is reputed to have been the moving spirit; the "Tennessee Yazoo Company" and the "Georgia Yazoo Company." Each of these offered compensation for the lands, the Georgia Company bidding the highest price. But the Georgia Company's bid was ignored despite efforts to make it the favored applicant, and little heed was given to a motion to demand a higher price than was offered for the region. Thus far, the promoters or "jobbers" were exclusively Southerners, though it is possible that northern capitalists had a hand in the business.

Georgia was evidently desirous of getting rid of the territory regardless of the price that might be obtained for it. Perhaps it was because the legislators were influenced by personal pecuniary awards. At least, it is recorded that without much opposition or debate, an act was passed by the Georgia Legislature, with the sanction of the governor, on December 21, 1789, granting the South Carolina Yazoo Company a western tract "bounded by the Mississippi River, the thirty-third parallel, the Tombigbee River and a line drawn from a point just above Natchez." This grant contained over 10,000,000 acres, covering the southern section of Mississippi and Alabama. The Virginia Yazoo Company received a grant, north of that given to the South Carolina Company, estimated to contain 11,400,000 acres. The Tennessee Company's grant bordered on the southern boundary of Tennessee, and contained 4,000,000 acres. Thus, more than twenty-five mil-

[1] Charles Homer Haskins, *The Yazoo Land Companies,* pp. 6, 7.

lion acres were disposed of. The total compensation to be received by Georgia was slightly more than $200,000, or less than one cent per acre, payable in the state's depreciated debt certificates. Moreover, immediate payment was not demanded, but a period of two years was allowed the purchasers in which to tender compensation. But, in the purchase contracts, the state relieved itself of the expense of keeping peace between the grantees and the Indians while extinguishing the Indian titles.[2]

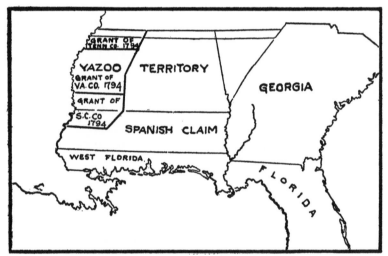

FIRST PARTITION OF THE YAZOO TERRITORY

What a bargain for these southern land grabbers! After the sale was made, the three "companies" set to work to secure their grants. The South Carolina Company, which was the most active in pushing its purchase, appointed Dr. James O'Fallon, a Revolutionary soldier, its agent, to proceed to New Orleans and secure the favor of the Spanish Government. On his way, O'Fallon visited Tennessee and Kentucky. He secured the coöperation of John Sevier, Governor of Tennessee, whose land grabbing was largely responsible for the settlement of that state,[3] and of Gen-

---

[2] Haskins, *op. cit.*, p. 8.

[3] "All the settlers [in Tennessee], who had any ambition to rise in the world were absorbed in land speculations. . . . They were continually in correspondence with one another about the purchase of land warrants and about laying them out in the best localities."—Theodore Roosevelt, *The Winning of the West* (New Knickerbocker Edition), Vol. II, p. 360.

eral James Wilkinson, then in Kentucky, who was carrying on intrigues with the Spanish Governor of Louisiana regarding the separation of Kentucky from the Union. Both these adventurers were won over with promises of shares in the company's purchase. Colonization plans were laid, and a "battalion" of militia was organized, "these troops being intended to insure the great security of the Company's rights."

It was expected that Wilkinson and Sevier would each lead hundreds of families to take up lands in the purchase. George Rogers Clark, the western Revolutionary hero and conqueror of the Northwest Territory, also was probably concerned in this venture, as it was rumored that he would be chief in command of the "battalion."[4]

The act of Georgia in disposing of territory, the claim to which was not recognized, and the prospect of consequent Indian warfare disturbed the peace of mind of the First President of the United States. On Friday, April 30, 1790, he entered in his diary:

Conversed with the Secretary of the Treasury, on the Report of the Secretary at War's propositions, respecting the Conduct of the State of Georgia, in selling to certain companies large tracts of their Western territory and a proclamation which he conceived expedient to issue in consequence of it. But as he had doubts of the clearness of the ground in which it was proposed to build this proclamation, and do other acts which were also submitted in the report I placed it in the hands of the Secretary of State to consider and give me an opinion thereon.[5]

Jefferson, the Secretary of State, who was outspoken in his denunciation of land grabbing, and who, besides, disliked Patrick Henry, was firm in his opinion that the grants were illegal.[6] The President accordingly, issued his proclamation on August 25, 1790. It warned the purchasers of the Georgia lands from interfering at all with the treaty rights of the Indians, or in any way disturbing the ownership of their lands.

But the intrepid O'Fallon persisted with his plans to estab-

---

[4] See Claiborne's *"Mississippi,"* etc. Vol. I, p. 157, note.
[5] *The Diaries of George Washington*, Vol. IV, pp. 124, 125.
[6] See Jefferson's *Works*, edited by H. A. Washington, Vol. VII, pp. 467-469.

lish the South Carolina Yazoo Company on its lands. He even wrote to Estéban Mero, Spanish Governor of Louisiana, that he "had insensibly prevailed" upon the members of the South Carolina Yazoo Company "to get their consent to be the slaves of Spain, under the appearance of a free and independent colony, forming a rampart for the adjoining Spanish territories and establishing with them an eternal, reciprocal alliance, offensive and defensive."[7]

O'Fallon's persistence brought another proclamation from the President, and the United States District Attorney was directed to arrest him, if necessary. At this, O'Fallon's courage failed, and he gave up the enterprise. Wilkinson had deserted him, and his associates declined to share responsibility for his actions. So he returned to Kentucky, where he married a sister of George Rogers Clark, and settled down. Moreover, the shares of the South Carolina Yazoo Company did not attract purchasers. There was difficulty in raising the required funds. Although the agent of the company offered to settle with Georgia in "debt certificates," the state treasurer refused to accept them, as the legislature had passed a resolution requiring that debts due the state be received in specie only.

The Virginia Yazoo Company, likewise, died abortively. There is considerable historical evidence that Patrick Henry, who we have already shown had been active in grabbing western lands in the pre-Revolutionary period, was deeply concerned in this speculation. His name appears among the shareholders, and it was even thought that he intended to desert Virginia and depart to the wild Yazoo territory.

Before entering upon the deal, Henry endeavored to assure himself that Georgia had title to the lands. When convinced of this, he, together with David Ross, Abraham B. Venable, Francis Watkins and other prominent Virginians, formed the "Virginia Yazoo Company." Before presenting their petition for a grant, they made overtures for a consolidation with the South Carolina Company. When this move failed, they purchased direct from the State of Georgia. Unlike the directors of the South Carolina Company, however, the Virginians made no colonization plans.

[7] Haskins, *op. cit.*, p. 11.

They preferred "to complete their payments to the State for the lands purch'd; next to quiet the Indian claims agreeable to Law, and to have the permission and approbation of the General Govern't for settlement and that the first Emigrants shall be accompanied with Civil and Militia officers Legally appointed."[8]

Patrick Henry, however, was for settlement, even though federal approbation was lacking. Thus, Washington, on April 8, 1791, entered in his diary:

> Was informed by Jno. Lewis, who had, not long since been in Richmond, that Mr. Patrick Henry had avowed his interest in the Yazoo Company; and made him a tender of admission to it, which he declined; but asking him if the Company did not expect the Settlement of the lands would be disagreeable to the Indians, was answered by Mr. Henry that the Co. intended to apply to Congress for protection, which, if not granted, they would have recourse to their own means to protect the settlement.[9]

It never became necessary for the Virginia Company to take this action, for their offer of payment to Georgia in depreciated debt certificates was not accepted. Patrick Henry had bought up a large amount of this paper at about 10 per cent of the face value in preparation for the payment. He profited greatly by this, because Hamilton's funding scheme, whereby the federal government assumed the state's obligations, soon raised the value of the debt certificates. Thus, Hamilton became the political idol of Henry, much to the disgust of Thomas Jefferson.

The promoters of the Virginia Company attempted again to secure the same grant in 1794, when Robert Morris, Wade Hampton, a wealthy South Carolina planter, and other capitalists already immersed in other land speculations agreed to furnish the funds. This move was also unsuccessful, and the threat to sue the State of Georgia was never carried out. When the Virginia Yazoo Company's claim came before Congress in later years, it was thrown out on the ground that its perpetrators were concerned in the fraudulent Georgia sales of 1795. Thus, the

[8] Letter of David Ross to Governor Randolph, April 10, 1791, quoted in Haskins, *op. cit.*, p. 19.
[9] *The Diaries of George Washington*, Vol. IV, p. 157.

James Wilson, Associate Justice of the U. S. Supreme Court

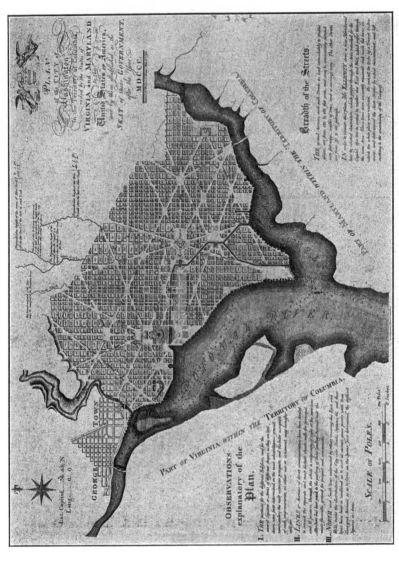

THE FIRST PLAN OF THE CITY OF WASHINGTON, ENGRAVED IN 1792 AND USED IN SELLING THE "LOTS"

Virginians received nothing for their trouble, and the money advanced by them in preparation for the speculation was lost though they probably profited by the advance in the market price of the Georgia debt certificates.

The outcome of the Tennessee Yazoo Company's purchase did not differ much from that of the other two companies. Zachariah Cox, one of the boldest adventurers and entrepreneurs of the old Southwest, was the leading spirit of this concern. He had an eye for business and saw clearly the advantages of commercial settlements in promoting trade between the upper Mississippi River region and the Gulf. After the Tennessee Company received its grant, he, in coöperation with John Sevier, attempted to form a settlement at Muscle Shoals. Cox was warned off by both the Indians and the federal government. In 1795, he and his associates again renewed their efforts to settle the territory. He was arrested by federal troops at Natchez for opening a land office, escaped, and was recaptured at Nashville, but was soon released. He next planned the construction of a canal to connect the Mississippi with the Mobile River, and thus open up commerce between the interior and the Gulf of Mexico, without molestation by the Spanish authorities. In this enterprise he was also unsuccessful. He finally ended his restless life in New Orleans.

Thus, the first attempts of southern land jobbers to profit by Georgia's disposal of her disputed western domain ended in a complete fiasco. George Washington, during a tour South in 1791, remarked in his diary that the "people in South Carolina and Georgia appear to have abundant means to live on grounds where they are settled," and that they "appear to be happy, contented and satisfied with the general government under which they are placed." He noted, however, that:

In Georgia, the dissatisfied part of them at the late treaty with the Ck. Indians were evidently Land Jobbers, who maugre every principle of Justice to the Indians, and policy to their Country, would, for their own immediate emolument, strip the Indns. of all their territory if they could obtain the least countenance to the measure; but it is to be hoped the good sense of the State will set its face agains such diabolical attempts. And it is also to be wished—

and by many it was said it might be expected—that the sales by the State to what are called the Yazoo Companies will fall through.[10]

The President's wish and expectation were not realized. The fever of wild land speculation was prevalent. At this time, Robert Morris and his associates, as noted below, were carrying on their Georgia "Pine Barrens" speculation, with reputed enormous profits. The fertile Yazoo lands were, therefore, a tempting morsel. The Georgia legislators were again importuned to sell the state's western domain. Nay, more! They were bribed to do so. This time the jobbers were not merely small groups of southern gentlemen arranged by states. They comprised the leading northern capitalists and statesmen, too numerous to list. They hailed from Boston, Hartford, New York and Philadelphia, as well as from lesser known sections in both the North and the South. Their participation involved the common folk of every commercial center in their speculations.

The first proposal for a resale of the Georgia lands was made November 12, 1794, by John Wereat, agent of a triumvirate, consisting of Albert Gallatin, Alexander J. Dallas and Jared Ingersoll, all prominent Pennsylvanians. They offered to purchase the former grant of the South Carolina Yazoo Company, at the original price. This price was insignificant, however, when compared with rival bids. Gallatin's agent then raised his bids, but they were again rejected. The Pennsylvania speculators then apparently withdrew, and disclaimed further connection with their agent's proposals.

Next, four separate companies made an offer of $500,000 payable in specie for a region comprising the bulk of Georgia's western lands. The legislature considered this proposal and a committee brought in a favorable report. The bill was passed without much opposition, but the governor vetoed it. He doubted whether it was a proper time for disposing of the domain. The price, moreover, was too low, and the sale to large "companies" smacked of land jobbing and monopoly. He insisted also that in any sale, proper provision should be made to give Georgia citizens preference in settling in the territory.

In the meantime, John Wereat, probably acting on his own

[10] *The Diaries of George Washington*, Vol. IV, p. 196.

account and in the expectation of being "bought off" by other bidders, continued to raise his bids, but, as he had not reached the pockets of the legislators, they paid no attention to his offers. They gave the excuse that he did not furnish sufficient security. A new bill of purchase, embodying some of the governor's suggestions, was then introduced and hurriedly passed. The governor yielded. The act was signed on January 7, 1795. *By its terms, approximately 30,000,000 acres of American soil, comprising the bulk of the States of Alabama and Mississippi, were sold for $500,000 or about a cent and a half an acre.*

The purchasers were four separate companies, to each of which was allotted a definite stretch of territory. To the "Upper Mississippi Company" was assigned the northwest section, comprising about 3,000,000 acres for $35,000. The "Tennessee Company" obtained for $60,000 practically the same territory as that granted the former concern of the same name, containing 4,000,000 acres. The southwestern section comprised approximately 7,000,000 acres, and was sold to the "Georgia Mississippi Company" for $155,000. The "Georgia Company" received the largest grant of all, about 17,000,000 acres, for $250,000. One-fifth of the purchase price, in each case, was deposited with the state treasurer. Undoubtedly, additional but unknown sums went to individual legislators before the passage of the act.

The unpaid balance of the purchase price in each case was required before November 1, 1795, and was secured by a mortgage on the land. There was reserved in the purchase 2,000,000 acres for the citizens of Georgia, who were entitled to membership in any one of the companies, and whose subscriptions counted as part of the purchase price. Georgia did not guarantee title against other claimants, and disclaimed responsibility for the acts or the claims of the Indians. The Indian title was to be extinguished in each instance by the purchasers, with the approbation of the federal government. Within five years after such title was secured, each company was required to begin colonization within its respective purchase.

They were not small fry or common land jobbers who consented to these provisions. Among those chiefly concerned in the deal was a noted United States Senator, General James Gunn, of

Georgia. He was the leading member of the Georgia Company. General Wade Hampton, richest of southern planters, and grandfather of the Congressman and Confederate general of the same name, was a large shareholder in two of the companies.

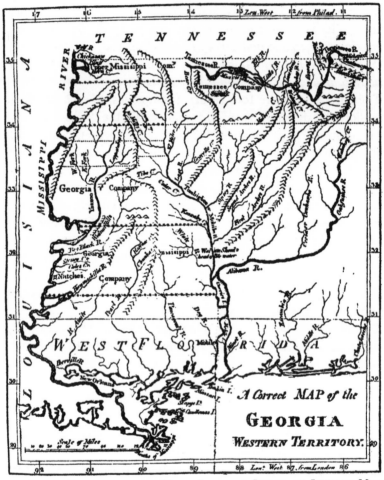

THE SECOND PARTITION OF THE YAZOO LANDS AS SHOWN BY JEDIDIAH MORSE IN HIS *American Gazetteer*, PUBLISHED IN 1797

Robert Morris and James Greenleaf were also heavily concerned. Greenleaf is reported to have participated financially in the deal more than any other one individual. He was soon forced to assign his proprietorship to others, however, because of approaching bankruptcy. Among his assignees were Nathaniel Prime, the New York banker, James Wilson and Andrew Craigie. Oliver Phelps, whose land-jobbing activities have already been described, also was a participant in the Yazoo deals. Congressman Robert Goodloe Harper, who was associated with Morris, Greenleaf and Nicholson in the North American Land Company, and who prepared the prospectus of this company, was also a participant. So was Congressman Thomas P. Carnes, another heavy "investor." The Honorable James Wilson, Judge of the United States Supreme Court, though at this time heavily involved in Pennsylvania land "scrip" speculations was a large subscriber. He held ten shares, representing 750,000 acres in the Georgia Company alone. He also obtained about 2,000,000 additional acres through assignment from Greenleaf. Zachariah Cox, despite his disappointment at the outcome of his first Tennessee Company, was again a prominent member of the second purchase. He held, on his own account, 450 shares in the new Tennessee Company, and was the agent of a number of other shareholders. He had as fellow shareholders his former land jobbing associates, John Sevier and William Blount, both pioneer Tennessee politicians and land grabbers.

Arrangements were quickly made, by the speculators, to divide the shares of each company into subshares for resale, and to subdivide the tracts for wholesale distribution. As Theodore Dwight, a contemporary observer, noted: "The territory was split up into endless divisions and sold in almost every part of the Union. On the ocean of speculation great multitudes of sober and industrious people launched the earnings of their whole lives, and multitudes became indebted for large sums which they never possessed."[11]

Almost immediately after the law authorizing the sale was passed, a part of the Georgia Mississippi Company's grant was resold for $1,138,000 (a great advance in price over the original cost of $155,000) to the "New England Mississippi Land Company," for consumption among the land-hungry Yankee gentry. James Greenleaf engineered the deal, and it was to him that the deed was first conveyed. It was in this subdivision that Gideon

[11] Theodore Dwight, *Travels*, Vol. I, p. 188.

Granger, Jr., the Postmaster-General, who was active in Ohio land deals, and Perez Morton, prominent Massachusetts statesman, were concerned. For this connection, Granger had to bear the gibes and jokes of his political enemies, particularly John Randolph, of Roanoke, the bitter foe of the Yazoo gamblers.

The "Mississippi scrip," as the shares of the New England Mississippi Company were commonly called, were scattered throughout this section. Its land office in Boston for a while resembled John Law's "Mississippi Company's" home in the Rue de Quincampoix, Paris. Speculators vied with each other to get first in line to enter subscriptions for their shares. The "company" had bought its tract on credit, and sold on equally liberal terms. The "scrip" passed from hand to hand. The holders, in blissful ignorance for a time of what was going on in Georgia, indulged in fanciful dreams of fabulous wealth.

But their hopes were soon to be dispelled. When the Georgia folk began to realize the rotten deal put over by their legislators, a howl of protest arose. There was indignation from the mountains to the sea. The grand juries of every county but two presented the act authorizing the Yazoo sale as a public grievance. The state constitutional convention which assembled in May "had its table heaped with petitions, memorials and remonstrances. Hardly a freeman in the state but put his name to some such document. Every member of the Legislature of 1796 came solemnly pledged to repeal the Act."[12]

Vengeance was sought on the speculators, and Georgia became a perilous residence for all concerned in the deal. James Gunn, the United States Senator from the state, and leader of the "Georgia Company," was repeatedly burned in effigy. Other legislators, who were accused of bribery in connection with the deal, were threatened with violence, and subjected to the most scurrilous newspaper attacks.

The new legislature that met in January, 1796, immediately proceeded to the question of repeal. In three weeks' time, a bill was reported, denying the validity of the grants, and recommending their repudiation. Accordingly, on February 13, 1797, the Georgia Legislature unanimously announced the sale unconstitu-

[12] McMaster, *History of the People of the United States,* Vol. II, p. 480.

tional and void. "The two Houses then formed in procession, marched to the front of the State House, and drew up before a bonfire in the road. The Committee handed the paper, on which the hated act was printed, to the President of the Senate. The President passed it to the Speaker of the House. The Speaker gave it to the Clerk. The Clerk delivered it to the doorkeeper, and he flung it into the flames."[13]

The hopes of the Yazoo speculators were not so easily extinguished. They looked for protection to the clause in the United States Constitution reciting that "no State shall pass any law impairing the obligation of a contract." But the embittered Georgia freemen did not "give a rap" for the Constitution. They ordered the bartered territory surveyed and cut up into small plots, and decreed its distribution among Georgia citizens by means of a lottery. This was slow work, and before it was completed Georgia had agreed to cede its Yazoo territory to the United States for the sum of $1,250,000. A reservation was made, however, that 5,000,000 acres should be set aside by the federal government to satisfy the claims of the former purchasers.

Although subsequent to the repudiation, Georgia officials offered to refund the payments that had been made to land purchasers, few took advantage of the offer. Instead, they made haste to sell their lands. Prospectuses were distributed throughout New England, and the Middle States. The lands of the Upper Mississippi Company were sold mostly in South Carolina. The Georgia and Mississippi companies disposed of many of their shares and "scrip" even before the newspapers announced the repeal of the grants. Speculators in these shares lost heavily. Boston alone is said to have sunk over two million dollars in Georgia "scrip." La Rochefoucauld, in his *Travels*, thus describes the mania: "Every class of men, even watch makers, hairdressers, and mechanics of all descriptions, eagerly ran after this deception."

Imagine the disappointment of the "scrip" holders when the newspapers announced the repudiation of the grants. "The shock throughout the Union cannot be described," remarked Theodore Dwight, who was then President of Yale College and a witness of the spectacle. Men gathered on street corners to discuss it. News-

[13] *Ibid.* Vol. II, p. 480.

GEORGIA

SPECULATION

UNVEILED;

IN TWO NUMBERS.

———————————

By ABRAHAM BISHOP.

———————————

HARTFORD:

Printed by Elisha Babcock,

[*COPY-RIGHT SECURED.*]

1797
One of the "Yazoo Frauds" Pamphlets

papers and pamphleteers arrayed themselves for and against the speculators, and a remarkable stream of controversial literature resulted. In one of these pamphlets the author gives some sound advice to the "scrip" holders. He recommended that these refuse to honor the notes they gave for payment. "By your success," he says, "millions of dollars now pledged on this speculation, will be restored to the channels of industry," and he ended by calling the speculation "a system of fraud and swindling, more complicated in its machinery and varied in its operations than any which has disgraced the character of man in this or any age."[14]

It is quite evident, from the pamphlets issued by the defenders of the land companies, that their chief reliance for protection was upon the United States courts. Several suits were entered against the State of Georgia, and in one Patrick Henry was employed as attorney. Congress was soon embroiled in the muddle. When word of the second sale reached President Washington, he immediately announced it to Congress with the admonition that unless something was done about it, Indian troubles might be expected.

Congress was slow in acting, but on the advice of the Attorney General regarding Georgia's doubtful title to western lands, a law was passed, authorizing a commission to settle the disputed ownership. The hopes of the "scrip" holders were revived. Now they could deal with Congress. Surely, a just and democratic body of national representatives, an organization that was always known to uphold property rights, would not deny them indemnification!

The "scrip" and "shares" of the various companies again became an object of speculation. They began to flow into the coffers of rich capitalists. These had in mind the government "debt certificates" and "indents" issued during the previous decade, which were paid off at par. The Yazoo claims may likewise some day be paid off at face value! What a great chance for speculative profit for those who could afford to tie up their money for a while!

These wealthy "scrip" holders, while garnering the floating supply from the impoverished owners, began to "pull wires" to have their claims recognized by the federal government. Among the "humble" petitioners who repeatedly importuned "the Honorable

[14] Abraham Bishop, *Georgia Speculation Unveiled*, Hartford, 1797.

Congress" for a consideration of their Yazoo claims were such well-known capitalists as Nathaniel Prime, who organized the first American private banking house; Leonard Bleecker, a founder of the New York Stock Exchange; James Perkins and Leonard Jarvis, New York capitalists; James Sullivan, eminent attorney of Boston; James Strawbridge, of Philadelphia, and a host of others, who, though not participating in the original purchase, had acquired thousands of dollars in claims from others.

But their speculations did not result in "easy money." There was at this time no Alexander Hamilton to put through a funding plan, and settle their claims in full. Instead, there developed the most determined opposition, both in and out of Congress. These "Yazoo claims" became a bugbear to the national legislature. They popped up at each session of Congress from 1800 to 1814. At first a proposition was made to compensate the "scrip" holders at 25 cents per acre, but Congress would not stand for this "profiteering." When compromises were proposed, the fiery and bombastic Virginian, John Randolph, of Roanoke, resisted them at every point. Throughout the rest of his political career, he was "Anti-Yazoo" to the core. Because James Madison and the northern Democrats favored settling the claims, they won Randolph's bitter enmity, and brought about the first split in the Democratic Party. In one of his "fire and brimstone" orations, delivered in 1804, Randolph soundly berated his fellow Democrats who were supporting the Yazoo claims as abettors of the Federalist cause:

What is the spirit against which we now struggle and which we have vainly endeavored to stifle? A monster, generated by fraud, nursed in corruption, that in grim silence awaits its prey. It is the spirit of Federalism! That spirit which considers the many made only for the few. . . . When I behold a certain party supporting and clinging to such a measure almost to a man, I see only men faithful to their own principles. . . . But when I see associated with them, in firm compact, others who once rallied under the standard of opposite principles, I am filled with apprehension and concern. . . . If Congress shall determine to sanction this fraud upon the public, I trust in God we shall hear no more of the crimes and follies of the former administration. For one, I promise that my lips upon this subject shall be closed in eternal silence. I should disdain to prate about petty larcenies of our predecessors after having given my sanction to this atrocious public robbery.[15]

Congress dilly-dallied with the "Yazoo Claims" until after March 16, 1810, when Chief Justice John Marshall rendered his opinion in the case of *Fletcher* vs. *Peck*. There could be no doubt, Marshall claimed, that the Georgia legislation rescinding the sale of the Yazoo lands was an act impairing the obligation of a contract and was therefore contrary to the Constitution. That the act secured its passage through corruption and bribery was immaterial to the Chief Justice, and, even if a court had examined the title and set it aside because of fraud, it could not cause innocent third parties to suffer. Thus, it was manifestly the duty of Congress to indemnify the Yazoo claimants.

After a delay of four years, Congress finally agreed to a settlement, and thus the curtain was rung down on the final act of the Yazoo Frauds. In 1815, the Secretary of the Treasury reported a total payment by the United States to the Yazoo claimants, of $4,282,151.12, in a new but reliable kind of "Mississippi scrip," bearing the seal of the national government. The amount was divided in accordance with the payments made by the original "scrip" and "share" holders. All who voluntarily surrendered the evidences of their claims, or who had received back any of the purchase money, were, to this extent, barred from participation in the award. However, as it is quite evident that most of those who presented their claims were not the original purchasers, but had acquired them cheaply from distressed and disgusted holders, the benefits of the settlement, therefore, accrued to wealthy speculators and not to those who first sought a profit from an ownership of the wild Georgia back lands.

.   .   .   .   .

The western territory of Georgia was not the only section of that state that figured prominently in the early wild land manias. Georgia, like most of the other colonies at the outbreak of the Revolution, became possessed of immense tracts of waste lands without inhabitants. These had been the property of the colonial proprietor, General Oglethorpe, who, unlike the Penns and the

[15] Haskins, *op. cit.*, p. 36.

Calverts, did not take up his residence on his boundless domains. Before the Revolutionary War was over, the state government endeavored to dispossess itself of its proprietary heritage. It was land poor, and needed taxable resources. As early as 1777, when its first state constitution was adopted, an act was passed, granting 200 acres to every white head of a family, and 50 acres for each member and for each slave, but limiting the maximum "head right" to 500 acres. Of course, ownership was not recognized unless the land was settled. This right to free land was, in 1780, extended to non-residents.

The "head right" system, however, did not accomplish the desired result of populating the state, so in 1789 the law was amended, by giving authority to justices of the peace to issue warrants for unappropriated land. All that was required of claimants was a survey of the land at their expense. This liberality resulted in a raid on Georgia lands, located principally in the present counties of Franklin, Washington and Montgomery. Warrants for small plots were easily obtained and resold, and most of them got into the hands of land jobbers.

Large tracts were also freely disposed of by Georgia. Count d'Estaing, the French admiral who assisted the colonies, was granted a substantial acreage for his Revolutionary services. D'Estaing sold his land to the Count de Colbert, who resold it in England to Robert Morris, through the agency of William Constable and Gouverneur Morris.[16] Robert Morris then proceeded to add to his Georgia possessions. In association with John Nicholson, he soon become the leading proprietor of Georgia waste lands. How these large holdings were obtained has never been satisfactorily explained. It is the "unsolved riddle of Georgia's land history."[17]

Yet, it is known that four early governors of the state granted lands in large quantities to single persons without the slightest authority under the law, and contrary to all laws on the subject of "head right" grants. It is quite possible that Morris and Nicholson purchased from the grantees, who had received their titles in this way. It is also possible that they may have received

[16] Ellis Paxton Oberholtzer, *Life of Robert Morris*, pp. 307, 308.
[17] S. G. McLendon, *History of the Public Domain of Georgia*, Chap. IX.

patents direct from the state authorities. There are early records which show that Morris and Nicholson paid state taxes on the land for a few years. It was the taxes that the Georgia government desired.

To most of these "free" Georgia lands the name of "Pine Barrens" was given. Their sandy soil was covered with a luxuriant growth of pine trees, for which Georgia, for over a century, was famous, and which in later years not only afforded a lucrative article of export, but was the basis for its naval stores' industry. But "barren" they certainly were in the post-Revolutionary days when they were sold to Robert Morris and other land jobbers. As mentioned in a previous chapter, "whatever land was offered for sale, they appeared ready to buy; and actually bought quantities which outran every sober thought."[18]

The Pine Barrens, though of so little value that neither Indians nor white settlers could be attracted to them, became an important part of the lands of the North American Land Company, which was organized in 1795, when Morris, Greenleaf and Nicholson pooled their holdings. The inventory of the company showed that out of a total of 6,000,000 acres, Georgia lands comprised 2,314,796 acres.

Morris, as previously noted, endeavored to get French purchasers for these Georgia lands. There was already considerable French influence in South Carolina and Georgia, and these lands were advertised as most suitable for the *émigrés*. But he was brought face to face with the outspoken opposition of Joseph Fauchet, French Minister to the United States. Though the Pine Barrens were hawked about even before the second Yazoo grants were made, and it was reported that they were a profitable speculation, they lacked buyers. There was, of course, considerable doubt as to the validity of Morris' title to them—and this point was strongly emphasized by Fauchet. Most of the grants had not been surveyed in accordance with the legal requirements. In 1798, the Georgia Legislature, with the Yazoo fiasco fresh in mind, passed a law requiring all landowners to survey and identify their holdings every ten years, beginning in 1799. The purpose was to compel holders under fraudulent grants to prove

[18] Theodore Dwight, *Travels*, Vol. I, p. 188.

their titles. The heritors of the North American Land Company, after Morris and Nicholson's failure, could not do this. Moreover, it was not worth the expense. As taxes were not paid, the lands went back to the state. In fact, the State Comptroller of Georgia reported in 1839 that "not more than half the land in the region was worth owning or paying taxes for."[19]

Yet, large tracts of it, in after years, were offered privately for sale or colonization. In 1801, George Sibbald issued a pamphlet in Augusta, Ga., entitled *Notes and Observations on the Pine Lands of Georgia*, showing the advantages they possessed. It was specifically addressed to persons emigrating. Sibbald stated that he owned large bodies of pine land in Washington, Montgomery and Bullock counties, beginning about 30 miles south of Savannah. "The surveys I hold," he said, "are well known in this State to be the first land surveyed in large tracts." Although he names some of the original grantees, he does not divulge how he obtained title to them, but it may be assumed that he bought them in at tax sales. He petitioned for, and received, an exemption from taxes on the land until 1805 "on condition that he leave the State and seek emigrants." The land was offered to settlers and immigrants at 50 cents per acre.

It is not known to the author whether Sibbald's lands constituted part of the Pine Barrens of Morris and Nicholson. But a later proffer of lands in the region shows conclusively what became of the Pine Barrens speculation. In a pamphlet printed in Kingston, N. Y., in 1865, entitled, *An Account of the Lands belonging to Robt. L. Pell, in the State of Georgia*, it is stated specifically that among the original grantees were John Nicholson, Robert Morris, Jr., James Greenleaf, James Wilson, R. L. Pell, James Cooper and John Shorter, and trustees of the North American Land Company. Pell published the pamphlet in order to sell the lands. He claimed ownership to four million acres of "valuable land for timbering." His holdings, therefore, included other tracts besides those acquired by the North American Land Company. The district in which the property was located underwent rapid exploitation by timber magnates after the Civil War. Among those who invested heavily here in timbering projects was Wil-

[19] Absalom H. Chappell, *Miscellanies of Georgia*, Part II, p. 49.

liam E. Dodge, one of the founders of Phelps, Dodge & Company, renowned in the annals of the American copper industry. Dodge County in Georgia was created as a testimonial of his large interest in the Georgia "Pine Barrens."

It is a sad commentary on Robert Morris' business judgment that lands which he eagerly acquired as a speculation and actively sought to sell were still in as wild and primeval condition almost a century after his death. But he seems never to have inquired regarding the quality or locations of properties, as long as he could obtain them cheaply and on credit. Either he had the utmost confidence in the rapid filling up of unoccupied regions in the country, or he became madly intoxicated by the prevailing wild land mania. He, Nicholson and Greenleaf purchased indiscriminately in the South, West and East—from the sluggish Savannah to the shores of Lake Erie. The modern searcher of land titles in any district east of the Alleghanies and south of New England is apt to find the name of Robert Morris or that of his partners in the early deeds. As stated by Allen C. Clark, "When a tract in the Carolinas or the Virginias is subject to negotiation, the lawyer from the metropolis must need travel through primeval forest whose solemn stillness is unbroken save by the cawing of the inhabitants of the air and the reverberating music of the axe, to the little remote brick courthouse, there to ascertain if the title is a continuous chain from the original owner—Robert Morris."[20]

.   .   .   .   .

To the story of the "Yazoo" and "Pine Barrens" speculations could be added others of a similar nature, also concerned with distant and unsettled regions along the moving frontiers of American territory. As noted by Lord Dunmore, the last Virginia colonial governor, an "engrafted trait" of Americans is "to forever imagine that the lands further off are still better than those upon which they are already settled." This trait undoubtedly has been a potent force promoting rapid national expansion, and, despite its tragedies of feverish speculation, it has been an important factor in America's economic progress.

But historians with their minds concentrated on politics have

[20] *Greenleaf and Law in the Federal City*, p. 26.

belittled or ignored this force. Thus, Theodore Roosevelt, in his early work, *The Winning of the West,* when commenting on the activities of the land companies in the old Southwest, remarked: "These land companies possessed on paper a weight which they did not have in actual history. They occasionally enriched and more often impoverished the individual speculators; but in the actual peopling of the waste lands they counted for little in comparison with the steady stream of pioneer farmers who poured in, each to hold and till the ground he in fact occupied."

And yet, the chief exponent of the "strenuous life" admits that the land companies "did possess considerable importance at certain times in the settlement of the west, both because they in places stimulated that settlement and because in other places they kept out the actual settlers."[21] But, as the following chapters will show, the stimulation to settlements was a permanent force, while the retardation was but temporary and sporadic. Speculation is essential to human progress. Adventure and Cupidity, hand-in-hand, have spread civilization.

[21] *The Winning of the West* (New Knickerbocker Edition), Vol. II, p. 411.

CHAPTER VII

WASHINGTON—AMERICA'S FIRST "BOOM TOWN"

"IN AMERICA," wrote the Duke de La Rochefoucauld in 1797, "where more than in any other country in the world, a desire for wealth is the prevailing passion, there are few schemes which are not made the means of extensive speculations; and that of erecting the Federal City presented irresistible temptations, which were not in fact neglected."[1]

Thus, observed the philosophical French *émigré* after he had visited the embryonic national capital located on the "banks of the Potowmack." The framers of the Constitution, wishing to have a seat for the federal government, independent of the territory or jurisdiction of any state, provided that Congress shall "exercise exclusive legislation in all cases whatsoever, over such District (not exceeding ten miles square) as may, by Cession of Particular States, and the Acceptance of Congress, become the Seat of the Government of the United States."

The question of a national capital had been suggested even during the dark days of the Revolution, and in the critical period following the peace with England, but no action accomplishing this end had been taken. In the meantime, however, speculation was rife as to a most suitable site. On January 29, 1783, before the news of the peace treaty had arrived, the trustees of the corporation of Kingston, N. Y., sent a memorial to the New York Legislature, praying that "their estate be erected into a separate

[1] See *Travels Through the United States of North America in the Years 1795, 1796 and 1797*, by the Duke de La Rochefoucauld-Liancourt. Translated by H. Neuman, London, 1799, Vol. III, p. 622.

district for the Honorable Congress of the United States," and they offered for this purpose "a sufficient quantity of land." The application was formally presented to Congress by Alexander Hamilton and William Floyd, the New York delegates. The corporation of Annapolis, Md., made a similar offer and tendered for the purpose 300 acres in the town. Its citizens argued that Annapolis "is more central than any other city or town in the federal states." Both tenders were referred by Congress to the executives of the various states with a notice that the matter would be brought up for consideration the following October.

New Jerseyites also were desirous of having the seat of the Congress within the borders of their state. On June 19, 1783, their legislature expressed a willingness to invest Congress "with such jurisdiction, authority and power over a district of twenty miles square as may be required by Congress, as necessary for the honor, dignity, convenience and safety of that august body." In addition, they proposed to grant £30,000 in specie, "for the purpose of procuring lands and erecting buildings thereon for the suitable accommodation of Congress."

Virginia also sent in an offer, suggesting the town of Williamsburg. In addition to 300 acres of land adjoining the said city, it would "present the palace, the capitol and all the public buildings, together with a sum of money not exceeding £100,000 this state's currency, to be expended in erecting thirteen hotels for the use of the delegates in Congress." As an alternative, Virginia offered to cede a district at any place on the Potomac, and to appropriate a sum of £100,000 in Virginia currency for hotels, as well as 100 acres of land to be used as sites for public buildings. If Maryland also desired to cede territory for the same purpose, Virginia would coöperate and bear a share of the expense.

Thus, the hint of a location on the Potomac was given. Before Congress proceeded to the consideration of these rival offers, a mutiny of the Pennsylvania troops in Philadelphia in June, 1783, made it plain that, if this "august assembly" of the thirteen federated states was to function freely and untrammeled, it must have a seat of government independent of any other authority. No formal action was taken, however, until more than a year later, though in the meantime Congress moved to Princeton, then to Annapolis, then to Trenton, and next to New York. It seemed as if the members were "trying out" the various locations.

Speculation continued, however, as to the place of permanent abode. The passion for gain and the belief that wherever the selected "district" would be located there would take place a pronounced increment in land values, caused the deliberations of Congress to be closely watched. While convened at Trenton in December, 1784, Congress passed a resolution appointing commissioners to lay out a district on the banks of the Delaware, near the Falls, of not less than two nor more than three miles square, and to erect buildings thereon, "in an elegant manner," for the use of Congress. Although the commissioners were empowered to expend $100,000 for this purpose, no attempt was actually made to carry the plan into effect. The next month, Congress moved to New York, where it remained until after the adoption of the Constitution.

Shortly after the passage of the resolution of Congress, authorizing a site on the Falls of the Delaware River, Robert Morris, who was one of the three commissioners appointed to execute the plan, bought a tract of 2,500 acres in the neighborhood. This site he called "Morrisville." It was one of Morris' first important land speculations and its purchase created the suspicion that his motive was to gain a profit at the expense of the nation. Morris' biographers deny this, however, and point out that he never urged his site upon Congress as a location for a "federal district," and that he continued to hold and develop the land until it was sold by the sheriff subsequent to his bankruptcy in 1798.

Moreover, it does not appear from the Morris correspondence that he was disappointed, when the Trenton site proposed by Congress in 1784 was later abandoned. William Maclay, Morris' fellow Senator from Pennsylvania, who bore him considerable ill-will, noted in his journal on August 25, 1789, that Morris had refused his request "to bring forward all the places which had been mentioned for a permanent residence of Congress at one time." Instead, Morris answered "rather roughly," *"Let those that are fond of them bring them forward; I will bring forward the Falls of the Delaware."* And this he did, "although the Presi-

dent was every moment looked for to attend the Senate session."[2]
In fact, Maclay later remarked that he (Morris) "has had no
other object in view than the Falls of the Delaware, since he has
been Senator; at least, this has been his governing object."

Maclay came from Harrisburg, Pa., and of course was deeply
interested in having the federal site fixed on the Susquehanna
River. Morris' residence was in Philadelphia, and he therefore
favored a site close to this metropolis in eastern Pennsylvania.
His personal interests may have influenced his attitude, but it does
not appear as Maclay declares that he was unwilling to "consent
to it [the federal seat] being anywhere else, unless it be on his
own grounds at the Falls of the Delaware." In fact, Morris, a
few days after Maclay penned the above, made a motion in favor
of Germantown, near Philadelphia, and appears to have abandoned his support of the Falls of the Delaware.

Whatever may have been Morris' purpose with reference to his
purchase of 2,500 acres near Trenton Falls (it is possible he saw
its advantages as an industrial site), he did not hesitate to enter
upon a gigantic speculation in the new Federal City, after Congress, on July 16, 1790, definitely voted to locate the seat of
government on the river Potomac "at some place between the
mouths of the Eastern Branch and the Connogochaegue."[3] The
site was selected in January, 1791.

It was some time before the commissioners, appointed to execute the plan of the Federal City, could start things going. First
of all, they had to buy off the former property owners. Each of
these wanted special privileges for his site, with reference to the
location of buildings and the planning of the district. One, "the
obstinate Mr. Burnes," was obdurate and would not meet
the terms of the commissioners. It required a patriotic address by
the "Father of his Country," to get the landholders to agree to
sell out. He met them at Georgetown, the village located in the
selected area, and in the course of his remarks, "represented that
the contention in which they seemed engaged did not . . . com-
port either with the public interest or that of their own; that
while each party was aiming to obtain the public buildings, they

[2] *The Journal of William Maclay* (1927 Edition), p. 131.
[3] Wilhelmus Bogart Bryan, *A History of the National Capital,* pp. 38, 39.

might, by placing the matter on a contracted scale, defeat the
measure altogether; not only by procrastination but for want of
the means necessary to effect the work" . . . and that "instead
of contending," they had better, "by combining more offers make
a common cause of it."[4]

Washington's advice was heeded. As the President noted in his
diary, on March 30, 1791:

> The parties to whom I addressed myself yesterday evening . . .
> saw the propriety of my observations: and that whilst they were
> contending for the shadow, they might lose the substance; and there-
> fore mutually agreed and entered into articles of surrender for
> public purposes one half of the land they severally possessed within
> bounds which were designated as necessary for the City to stand with
> some other stipulations, which were inserted in the instrument which
> they respectively subscribed.[5]

The "instrument" which they subscribed stated that "in consideration of the great benefit we expect to derive from having
the federal city laid off upon our lands," the subscribers agreed
to convey in trust the whole of their lands upon condition that
"the President shall have the sole power of directing the federal
city to be laid off in what manner he pleases."[6] The lots, it was
agreed, were to be divided equally between the public and the
former owners, and those taken by the public were to be paid for
at the rate of £25 per acre, with a deduction for streets. Thus,
one-half of the area of the proposed city was acquired by the
District Commissioners, representing the public, to be disposed
of as they saw fit. The other half could be retained by the original
owners. As the commissioners needed money for laying out the
City and constructing public buildings, they soon had "lots for
sale." So did the former landowners. These were also desirous
of realizing the profit that would come from the selection of the
site of the Federal City on their properties.

The first public sale of lots "in the Federal City" was scheduled
to begin October 17, 1791. It was expected that Major Charles
L'Enfant, the City's designer, would have his map prepared,

[4] *The Diaries of George Washington,* Vol. IV, p. 154.
[5] *Ibid.*
[6] Bryan, *op. cit.,* p. 134.

showing the complete layout and the location of lots, but this distinguished "French gentleman" procrastinated and blustered, and finally was dismissed in disgust. When the sale began, not only was a general plan of the City lacking, but the bad weather prevented prospective buyers from meeting on the ground which was to be "auctioned off." Yet the occasion was marked by the presence of George Washington, the incumbent President, and Thomas Jefferson and James Madison, two future Presidents of the United States.

The results were extremely disappointing. After three days of auctioning, only thirty-five lots were sold for an aggregate sum of $8,756. The actual cash received was but slightly more than $2,000, since, in accordance with common usage from that day to this, liberal credit terms were granted. Only a quarter of the purchase price was required in cash. The balance was payable in three annual installments.

The price of lots ranged from $160 to $534. Whoever bought or held the lots was required to build thereon. The promoters of the Federal City, moreover, would permit no cheap or temporary structures. Buildings must be of at least two stories, and of brick or stone. No building was to be higher than forty feet and, on the avenues, not lower than thirty-five feet, thus assuring an harmonious sky line. The idea was sanctioned, therefore, that the Federal District was to be a *magnificent city*—an artistic city; in other words, a modern real estate development, and not merely a "scene of speculative land operations or of the erection of buildings for the use of the Government."[7]

Modern, up-to-date real estate sales methods also were used in "booming" the new city. As there was much political opposition to the selected site, and much unfavorable gossip regarding the likelihood that Congress would ever move to "the residence city," some sort of "boostering" was deemed essential. Newspapers were used then as now. On September 30, 1791, about two weeks before the first sale was scheduled, there appeared in the *Maryland Journal* the following alluring account of the proposed city:

The plan [of the city] was designed and drawn by the celebrated Major L'Enfant, and it is an inconceivable improvement upon other

7 Bryan, *op. cit.*, p. 162.

cities of the world, combining not only convenience, regularity, elegance of prospect and a free circulation of air, but everything grand and beautiful that can possibly be introduced into the City. It will not only produce amazement in Europe but meet the admiration of all future ages.

Such it was proposed to be—and such a city it has become—but when George Washington, President of the United States, Thomas Jefferson, his Secretary of State, and a few other curious or interested spectators gathered at Suter's Tavern in Georgetown on October 17, 1791, to sell unsurveyed city lots covered with woods and cornfields, the grandeur and beauty of the future national capital might have been conceived, but not seen. Certainly it taxed the imagination of even the most hopeful, for at the end of the third day, in spite of free "wine and wood" furnished the prospective lot purchasers, "the business seemed to flag," as Washington stated, and the auction was called off.

But with all this, the First President, who was undoubtedly the most interested party in the proposed plan of developing the magnificent city that bears his name, was not discouraged. He informed Congress the following week, in the course of his regular message: "There is prospect, favored by the rate of actual sales which have already taken place, of ample funds for carrying on the necessary public buildings. There is every expectation of their due progress."[8]

The actual prospect, nevertheless, was a poor one. In the spring of 1792 there occurred in New York and Philadelphia the first of the many financial panics with which our country has since been cursed. The speculations of William Duer, Alexander Macomb and other capitalists in New York; the reign of terror in France; and the suspension of specie payments by the Bank of England, "produced general stagnation of money contracts." So Jefferson wrote to the District Commissioners. These officials were hard pressed for funds and desired additional lot auctions to obtain current cash. It was not until a year later, however, when the cornerstone of the "President's palace" had been already set, that the second public sale of lots was attempted. As on the pre-

[8] *The Writings of George Washington,* edited by Ford, Vol. 12, p. 81.

vious occasion, the sale continued for three days, but with scarcely greater success than the first offering.

The heaviest and most interested lot purchaser on this occasion was Samuel Blodget, Jr., one of the many enterprising and ingenious seekers after wealth of his generation. He was born in Woburn, Mass., in 1755, and served on the staff of General Washington in the Revolution. Subsequently, he engaged in the East Indian trade, and made visits to Europe in 1784 and 1790. In March, 1792, he founded the Tontine Association in Boston, and this proving fairly successful, he came to Philadelphia and promoted the "Universal Tontine." As he failed to get the necessary subscribers, he suggested that the funds already in hand be applied to the establishment of a general insurance company. As a result of this suggestion, there was organized in November, 1792, the Insurance Company of North America, in Philadelphia, the oldest concern of its kind in the Western Hemisphere. Blodget took a minor part in its organization, though he and his father were among the first stockholders.

At this time, his chief activities were centered in the Federal City, whither he, in all probability, went to attend the first sale of lots in 1791. His interest in the city's promotion, he stated years afterwards in his pamphlet,[9] was stimulated by the persuasion of "his former commandant, Washington, to purchase property to the amount of above $100,000 in and adjoining the city, one day to become the noblest of the universe."

Blodget soon became the right-hand man of the commissioners of the Federal City, and for a time was the chief manager of the enterprise. Washington consented to his appointment as "Superintendent," though he acknowledged that he "knew very little of him, . . . and after what has happened shall be cautious about recommending."[10] The public sale of lots proving unsatisfactory as a means of obtaining funds to further the construction of public building, Blodget was despatched to Boston to negotiate a loan based on the unsold city lots as security. Nothing came of this endeavor. Blodget next suggested that agents be employed "to pass through the several states to dispose of lots," but Wash-

[9] *Economica, a Statistical Manual for the United States,* published in 1813.
[10] Washington's *Writings,* Vol. 12, p. 212.

ington seemed to object to this, because it appeared "to be hawking the lots about."[11]

Still undaunted, Blodget's gambling propensities were again manifested in his next suggestion to the commissioners. He proposed a lottery as a means of raising funds. The principal prize was to be "a grand hotel," to be erected in the City at a cost of $50,000. Whether the commissioners officially sanctioned the idea or not is in dispute, but the lottery was duly advertised January 19, 1793, as "by the commissioners appointed to prepare the public building, etc., within the City of Washington," and signed "Samuel Blodget, agent for the affairs of the city." The drawing of prizes was scheduled to take place in the fall of 1793, about the date of the next sale of lots. Before the date arrived, however, some mix-up occurred, and the commissioners, fearing the city's funds might be put in jeopardy, repudiated the lottery transaction and placed the entire responsibility for it on Blodget and his associates.[12]

This led to Blodget's financial ruin. He was required to convey by deed to trustees all his property in the Federal District, as well as his stock of 7,160 shares (par value $10) in the Insurance Company of North America, to secure payment of the lottery prizes, and to protect the commissioners from damage suits in consequence of the lottery.

Unabashed by this outcome, he proposed still another lottery known as "Federal Lottery No. 2," to which he also endeavored to give an official character, but which was likewise repudiated. His "former commandant," General Washington, was seriously irritated by the audacity of the "City Agent," as Blodget styled himself, in trying to put over a second lottery scheme after the failure of the first. "I was at a loss," he wrote Thomas Johnson, on January 23, 1794, "how to account for a conduct so distant from any of the ideas I had entertained of the duties of a Superintendent, but it appears evidently enough now, that speculation has been his primary object from the beginning."[13]

But Blodget persisted, and announced that the drawings of the lottery would commence December 22, 1794. The principal prize

[11] *Ibid.*, p. 214.
[12] Bryan, *op. cit.*, pp. 205-208.
[13] Washington's *Writings*, Vol. 12, p. 407.

was to be a house to cost $30,000. The total amount to be raised was $400,000. If a surplus resulted after paying all prizes, it was to constitute a fund to be used for the proposed national university in the city, which was one of the promoter's pet ideas.

Blodget pledged all his Washington lots to secure the prizes. As neither the hotel—the prize of the first lottery—nor the buildings constituting the principal prize of the second were ever completed, the successful ticket holders obtained judgments against him, and he was "cleaned out" entirely of his Federal City property. He was also dismissed as "Superintendent." He continued to reside in Washington, however, where he wrote the first book that was printed there,[14] and, as already noted, also prepared in later years a statistical and economic treatise on the United States. He was imprisoned for debt in 1802, but on being given "the liberty to walk out of prison (within the bounds of the District), for the preservation of his health" under a bond of $10,000, he failed to return, though he soon reappeared in Washington and busied himself in promoting a "national university." He died in comparative poverty on April 11, 1814, at Philadelphia, "and no stone marks the grave of the founder of Washington City."[15]

The failure and repudiation of Blodget's schemes, and the inability to sell "lots" at retail as a means of raising funds to erect public buildings, brought into the Federal City the greatest landgrabbing triumvirate that ever operated in America. James Greenleaf, then a young man of but twenty-seven, had just returned from Holland, where, with the coöperation of Dutch bankers, he had engineered some profitable deals in American debts. He accounted himself wealthy and was looking about for new and speculative ventures. In some unknown manner, he was attracted to the Federal City as a field of operations. It is quite probable that Washington, the President, suggested it to him. Or perhaps, he, hearing of the financial straits of the District Commissioners, had offered to negotiate for them a loan from Dutch bankers.

[14] The title of the work is *Thoughts on the Increasing Wealth and National Economy of the United States of America.*

[15] *A History of the Insurance Company of North America,* p. 109. Blodget's heirs sued to recover his Washington real estate, and the "descendants of the third generation" are reported to have been successful.

Whatever may have been the real reason, he came to the District Commissioners in August, 1793, armed with a letter of introduction from the President. In this letter, Washington wrote: "This gentleman has it in contemplation to make certain proposals to you for building a number of houses in the Federal City, provided he can have lots upon such terms and conditions as may correspond with his interest in the undertaking, while it tends, at the same time, to promote the object of the City . . ."

As to Greenleaf's financial ability to execute his plans, the President would give no advice. "He has been represented to me as a gentleman of large property and having the command of much money in this country and in Europe. But I can say nothing on this head from my own knowledge." Yet, he added, "I have reason to believe that if you can find it consistent with your duty to the public to attract Mr. Greenleaf to the Federal City, he will be a valuable acquisition."[16]

The immediate result of Greenleaf's visit was an offer by him to purchase three thousand lots at $66.50 per lot, to be paid for in seven annual installments. On these lots, during the period of the installments, he was to erect an average of ten houses annually, according to the required specifications. He agreed to make no sales prior to January 1, 1796, unless on every third lot sold a house should be erected within four years. But what was more important to the commissioners, he offered further to make them a loan of $2,200 each month at 6 per cent, until the public buildings were completed.

The President was undoubtedly pleased with Greenleaf's bargain with the District Commissioners. "You will learn from Mr. Greenleaf," he wrote Tobias Lear, his secretary, "that he has dipped deeply in the concerns of the Federal City—I think he has done so on very advantageous terms for himself, and I am pleased with it notwithstanding on public ground; as it may give facility to the operation at that place, at the same time that it is embarking him and his friends in a measure which although [it] could not well fail under any circumstances that are likely to happen, may considerably be promoted by men of Spirit with large Capitals."[17]

[16] Bryan, *A History of the National Capital*, Vol. I, p. 215.
[17] Washington's *Writings*, Vol. 12, p. 329.

Greenleaf undoubtedly had Robert Morris' backing in this project. He, in fact, had already become an associate of Morris and Nicholson in their land speculations, and he was regarded as a valuable acquisition, since he led these two land jobbers to believe that his banking relations in Amsterdam, where he had been recently appointed American consul, would serve them as a means of obtaining loans or disposing of their properties. Morris and Nicholson, accordingly, became partners in Greenleaf's wholesale purchase of Washington lots, each taking a one-third interest. But neither assumed responsibility for Greenleaf's proffered loan to the District Commissioners.

Greenleaf's first proposition was soon altered by a revised agreement. The number of lots purchased was six thousand instead of three thousand. The average price was raised from $66.50 to $80.00. In the second contract, Greenleaf openly associated with himself, as principals, both Morris and Nicholson. There was naturally no objection to this, as these two men were then reputed to be the richest capitalists and "high financiers" in the country.

The terms accepted by the speculating syndicate were rather stiff. They were required to expend large sums for building within a seven-year period. This handicapped them in reselling because the same obligation to build was imposed on those who purchased from them. Morris, who was for "land jobbing" rather than "land holding," did not, at the time, take the conditions seriously. "Nobody can suppose," he wrote the President on September 25, 1795, "that Mr. Nicholson or myself entered into these engagements with an expectation of holding the property. It was from the beginning and it is now our intention to sell them when it can be done to our satisfaction and I believe the interest of the City will be more certainly promoted by interesting a number of individuals, than by any one or two men continuing to hold a large number of lots."[18]

Selling, however, was not easy, and meeting installment payments or providing building costs was still more difficult. Yet, the three capitalists went ahead with their purchases. They bought also additional lots from the private owners. From Daniel Carroll and Notley Young, two of the former landowners in the District,

[18] Allen C. Clark, *Greenleaf and Law in the Federal City,* p. 114.

they purchased nearly seven hundred additional lots. Washington and the commissioners were highly pleased with all this since considering "the uncertainty of settled times and embarrassed commerce," they were happy to have the assistance of "Mr. Morris' capital, influence and activity."

Altogether, the syndicate purchased 7,235 lots in the Federal District. In view of their heavy commitments in land purchases elsewhere, and the prevailing disturbed financial condition of both Europe and America, they had bitten off more than they could chew. They sought in vain for financial aid in Europe. Greenleaf attempted to get a loan in Holland, offering to pledge the city lots as security. A negotiation through Messrs. Daniel Crommelin & Sons, Amsterdam bankers, was engineered by Sylvanus Bourne, then American vice-consul at Amsterdam, but the subscriptions fell considerably below the required amounts. The fact that Greenleaf and his associates lacked a clear title to the pledged property (since title was not to pass until payment was made in full) was ignored by him, but he put up as additional collateral such amount of 6 or 3 per cent United States bonds, "as with the interest to accrue thereon will be sufficient to pay the annual interest of this loan until the final discharge of the same." This collateral made the proposition apparently sound.[19]

Before the Dutch loan negotiations were assured, however, Morris and Nicholson, in their dire need of funds, began issuing and circulating drafts on Dutch bankers. The volume and amount of their bills increased enormously. "Had their success been uncurbed, they would have appreciably drained the money supply of the Dutch. The mere acceptance by the Dutch bankers of the management of a popular loan in the lots was made by the syndicate a sufficient warrant to draw."[20] These Dutch transactions not only got Morris into difficulties a few years later, but gave the District Commissioners considerable trouble in straightening out their deals with the syndicate.

No attempt appears to have been made by Morris, Nicholson and Greenleaf to unload their Federal City "lots" in England,

[19] Clark, *op. cit.*, p. 86.
[20] *Ibid.*, p. 89.

though, as we have already seen, they tried at this time to sell there the wild lands which they had transferred to the North American Land Company.[21] George Washington, however, may have had in view possible British purchasers of the Federal City lots, for his private secretary, Tobias Lear, undoubtedly with the President's encouragement, published in New York, in 1793, and in London, in 1794, the first book ever written regarding the City of Washington. It was entitled *Observations on the River Potomac, the Country Adjacent, and the City of Washington,* and its pages furnished pleasing prospects and alluring commercial industrial possibilities of the proposed seat of government and its surrounding territory. As the originator of the "Potomac Company," which was to make the Potomac River the principal highway of commerce between the western back country and the seaboard, Washington had a double interest in promoting the progress of the Federal City.

Others also had the notion that the seat of the federal government would be the nation's chief commercial and industrial center. Writing of the proposed plan to open a passage "from the Ohio to the Potomac," Isaac Weld, the Englishman, who visited the new Federal City, in 1795, wrote:

Considering the vastness of the territory, which is thus opened to the federal city, by means of a water communication; considering also that it is capable from the fertility of its soil, of maintaining three times the number of inhabitants that are to be found at present in all the United States; . . . there is good foundation for thinking that the federal city, as soon as navigation is perfected, will increase most rapidly in population, and that at a future day . . . it will become the grand emporium of the West, and rival in magnitude and splendor the cities of the old world.[22]

Though this may have sounded fanciful to jealous and incredulous Englishmen of the time, there was at least one British capitalist who was attracted by its allurements. He was Thomas Law, wealthy and aristocratic East Indian trader, who, in 1794, decided to take up residence in America. While sojourning at Philadelphia, he learned, in a conversation with the President,

[21] See Chapter II, p. 50.
[22] *Travels Through the States of North America, Etc.,* by Isaac Weld, Jr.

of the speculative prospects of the new national capital. Greenleaf then met him. The result was that Law bought a number of lots from Greenleaf's syndicate, and with his two sons moved to the nascent city on the Potomac.

The remarkable feature of Law's purchase is that he paid Greenleaf an average of $266 per lot for five hundred lots, which Greenleaf had, but a little over a year previous, bought for $80 per lot. Law selected his lots south and east of the site of the Capitol, and along the banks of the river, called the Eastern Branch. It was then believed that this section would become the city's chief commercial center. It turned out otherwise, however. The sections in which Law's properties were located developed more slowly than those in the neighborhood of the President's "residence." In fact, until about three decades ago, the lots south of the Capitol were covered largely by negro shacks and decaying and dilapidated warehouses.

Thomas Law's real estate transactions in the new national capital were second only in magnitude to those of Morris, Greenleaf and Nicholson. Unlike these men, he continued solvent in spite of his financial disappointments, and he kept up his faith in the future value of his real estate. Writing to Greenleaf, on January 8, 1795, he stated enthusiastically, "You may say that I had rather sell my horses or books or anything rather than part with a foot at present of Washington City."[23] He succeeded in escaping from the effects of the subsequent failure of Morris, Greenleaf and Nicholson, to meet their instalment payments to the District Commissioners, by having received, at his own insistence, a clear title to the real estate that he purchased. For a number of years he lived as a prominent, respected and public spirited citizen of Washington City, though his real estate ventures caused him serious loss of his fortune. In 1796, he married Elizabeth Parke Curtis, granddaughter of Mrs. George Washington. This brought him into close association with General Washington, while the latter was in retirement at Mount Vernon. But the marriage was not a happy one. A separation ensued in 1802.

Aside from the resale of lots to Thomas Law and a few others,

[23] Clark, *op. cit.*, p. 101.

Greenleaf's syndicate, which had agreed to furnish funds to the District Commissioners through instalment payments, soon found it impossible to sell their holdings and thereby raise the necessary funds. Nevertheless, they started in with considerable zest to erect the required buildings, and in 1796 constructed a whole city block, which was called the "Twenty Buildings." This row of brick buildings, which was dedicated with much ceremony by the personal presence of Robert Morris, was never actually inhabited, and as late as 1824 was described as "a fallen and dilapidated ruin."

When their funds were exhausted, the speculating triumvirate petitioned for relief from their contracts. As they could not sell lots because they had not the deeds, the commissioners decided to offset their cash payments by conveyances. In this way, they received title to about 1,000 lots, or about one-seventh of their total purchases. In the meantime, rival interests among the real estate operators in the city were causing a serious situation. Instead of concentrating building and improvements in one section, each erected structures wherever it suited his own interest. "Each began in his own quarter, with the hope of drawing thither the new-comers," remarked La Rochefoucauld, in the diary of his travels. "Each vaunted of the advantages of that side of the city where his property lay and depreciated others. The public papers were no longer filled with the excellences of the Federal City, but with those of one or other of its quarters." The effect was a few scattered buildings, "most of them built for speculation and remained empty," in a territory of seventy square miles.

La Rochefoucauld lays part of the blame for this haphazard planning to the District Commissioners. "The commissioners were not altogether clear of this venal contest," he remarked. "Two of them possessed lots near George-Town; and if that had not been the case, their habits and prejudices relative to the city would have determined their opinion as to the advantage of beginning to build in one quarter or another, and would not have permitted them to remain indifferent spectators of the emulation of the several proprietors . . . Each proprietor supported with arguments the interests of the quarter where the mass of his

AN EARLY VIEW OF WASHINGTON

(Reproduced from an old engraving in the Library of Congress)

THOMAS LAW, AN ENGLISHMAN WHO BOUGHT REAL ESTATE IN THE
FEDERAL CITY

(Reproduced from Clark's *Greenleaf and Law in the Federal City*)

property lay, but he built with great caution, and with constant fear of some of the opposite interests prevailing."

"Were the houses that have been built," notes Isaac Weld, another contemporary commentator, "situated in one place all together, they would make a very respectable appearance, but scattered about as they are, a spectator can scarcely perceive anything like a town." He states further:

Excepting the streets and avenues, and a small part of the ground adjoining the public buildings, the whole place is covered with trees. To be under the necessity of going through a deep wood for one or two miles, perhaps, in order to see a next door neighbor, and in the same city, is a curious, and, I believe, a novel circumstance.[24]

Tom Moore, the Irish poet, who visited Washington in 1804, about eight years after Weld, expressed the same sentiment in verse:

> This embryo capitol, where fancy sees
> Squares in morasses, obelisks in trees
> Which second-sighted seers, ev'n now, adorn
> With shrines unbuilt and heroes yet unborn,
> Though naught but woods and Jefferson they see
> Where streets should run and sages ought to be.

More than thirty-five years later, Charles Dickens, another critical and skeptical Englishman, whose proneness to exaggeration should be duly discounted in all he has written about America, gave a similar description of Washington:

It is sometimes called the City of Magnificent Distances, but it might with greater propriety be termed the City of Magnificent Intentions; for it is only on taking a birds-eye view of it from the top of the Capitol that one can at all comprehend the vast designs of its projector, an aspiring Frenchman. Spacious avenues, that begin in nothing, and lead nowhere; streets, mile-long, that only want houses, roads and inhabitants; and ornaments of great thoroughfares, which only lack great thoroughfares to ornament—are its leading features. One might fancy the season over, and most of the houses gone out of town for ever with their masters. To the admirers of cities, it is a Barmecide Feast; a pleasant field for the imagination

[24] Weld, *Travels, etc.,* Fourth Edition, p. 286.

to rove in; a monument to a deceased project with not even a legible inscription to record its departed greatness. . . . Such as it is, it is likely to remain.[25]

Dickens was undoubtedly a popular novelist and a pleasing satirist in his day—but judging from the above remark, he was a poor prophet.

Notwithstanding the disappointment of the projectors, the progress of the building of the Federal City in its early days was being heralded at home and abroad. La Rochefoucauld ascribes this to the speculators: "The building of a house for the President, and a place for the sittings of Congress," he wrote, "excited, in the purchasers of lots, the hope of a new influx of speculations. The public papers were filled with exaggerated praises of the new city; in a word, with all the artifices which trading people in every part of the world are accustomed to employ in the disposal of their wares, and which are perfectly known, and amply practiced in this new world."

George Washington was seriously concerned about the progress of the city of his name. From the day of its inception until near to the day of his death, he had its progress at heart, and it appears to have given him more worry than most other of the troublesome affairs of the state. He also had faith in it as a field of pecuniary speculation, and is known to have advised others to invest their fortunes in it. He, himself, bought some lots. A printed deed, signed by the three District Commissioners, shows that he purchased on April 23, 1794, "lot No. 4 in square 21 of the City of Washington, for £200 Maryland currency," and that the fee was conveyed on October 3, 1798. Other lots owned by him were in square 632 (on the west side of North Capitol Street between B and C streets). On these lots, Washington constructed residences, which remained standing until 1908, when they were torn down to increase the area of the Capitol grounds.

The final outcome of Morris, Greenleaf and Nicholson's speculations in Washington real estate and other land deals was, as already stated, disastrous to them. Their failure also almost wrecked the plans for a national capital—since their defaults put

[25] *American Notes.*

the District Commissioners into a serious financial muddle. These officials were confronted with the necessity of suspending building operations. On May 15, 1795, about a year and a half after Greenleaf made his first wholesale purchase from them, the commissioners notified him that unless the payments due them were made, they would take legal steps to enforce the obligations. But Greenleaf's position was then almost hopeless. He was at odds with his partners. These blamed him for their unfortunate town-lots venture. He had contracted, Morris stated to Washington, "with his hand and seal to provide us with money, to carry through the operations which, at his instance, we were tempted to undertake, but the French invasion at Holland put it out of his power to fulfill his engagements."[26]

Greenleaf's retort was an offer to sell out to his partners. A bargain was struck between them. Morris and Nicholson paid Greenleaf for his share in their joint properties with their personal notes. Their bankruptcy soon followed, so the notes were uncollected. Thus, the controversy did not end. Greenleaf also soon became a bankrupt. He continued years thereafter to claim an interest in the Washington lots of Morris and Nicholson, as well as in the assets of the North American Land Company.

A controversy of rancorous bitterness was carried on in newspapers between John Nicholson on one hand and James Greenleaf on the other. Robert Morris took no direct part in it. In fact, he did not like this method of airing their differences, and wished for a "settlement with Mr. Greenleaf in the Counting House and not in the Public Prints." But he was bitter toward Greenleaf to the end. When endeavoring within prison walls to straighten out his affairs, he penned his memorandum on Greenleaf, thus:

James Greenleaf. This is an unsettled account; and I suppose, ever will be. Here commenced that ruin which has killed poor Nicholson, and brought me to the necessity of giving an account of my affairs. But I will forbear to say more, lest I shall not know where or when to stop.

All three of the partners were fellow prisoners in the Prune Street Prison. Morris' sojourn there was the longest. He was not released until August 26, 1801.

[26] Bryan, *op. cit.*, p. 257.

The struggle of Robert Morris and John Nicholson to keep out of a debtors' prison marks one of the most tragic scenes in American financial annals. Kept within their homes for over a year by their creditors, whom they called "the cormorants" and who, armed with writs of attachment, camped in their gardens and on their doorsteps, and watched their every move, the partners maintained a communication with one another through the secret exchange of notes. Humor and pathos, rancor and regret, hope and despair, were commingled in them. "We must work like men to clear away these accursed encumbrances to satisfy the cormorants," Morris wrote encouragingly from "The Hills," his country place on the Schuylkill, on October 25, 1797. And again, in a despairing spirit, he informs Nicholson, "two hundred thousand acres of my land in North Carolina, which cost me $27,000 are sold for a year's taxes. By heaven, there is no bearing of these things. I believe I shall go mad . . . God help us, for men will not. We are abandoned by all but those who want to get from us all we yet hold."

Finally, in January, 1798, when Morris was preparing for his somber march to Prune Street Prison—that "hotel with the grated doors"—he informed Nicholson mournfully that "Confidence has furled her banners, which no longer wave over the heads of M. and N."

Morris went to prison, February 16, 1798. Nicholson, despite the fact that Morris taunted him for being "a great and sometimes a good lawyer," soon joined him. Nicholson, as already pointed out, died within a year.[27] Morris remained slightly more than three and a half years. Sixty-eight years old, and broken in spirit, he made no attempt to recoup his fortunes. Gouverneur Morris obtained from the Holland Company an annuity of $1,500 annually for Mrs. Morris for release of her dower rights in the Genesee lands, and this constituted his chief support in his last years. Gouverneur noted in his diary in 1803 that his old-time friend, Robert, visited him at Morrisania, his New York estate, "lean, low-spirited and as poor as a commission of bankruptcy can make a man." "But," he also notes, referring to the annuity, "I sent him home fat, sleek and in good spirits and possessed of

[27] See Chapter II, p. 37.

the means of living comfortably for the rest of his days." Within three years thereafter, he died.

When Greenleaf, Morris and Nicholson failed to meet their obligations on their Washington real estate, the commissioners of the Federal District decided to resell "as many of the lots sold to the syndicate as may be necessary" to make good the unpaid installment, especially "when they reflect that 95,000 pounds have been raised and actually received from sales of city lots by them [i.e., the syndicate] while they profess to be unable to pay their annual installment of only $68,500." The commissioners did not force sales of the lots, however, and they even succeeded in receiving a portion of the installment due from the syndicate. Yet it was only after December, 1796, when the State of Maryland lent the commissioners $100,000 "in United States 6% stock" that they were able to proceed with the building plans, and put the district into shape for the "residence" of the national government in 1800.

James Greenleaf, though adjudged a bankrupt after the collapse of his Washington speculations, continued for a while to maintain a residence in the city, and became the "trustee" of the syndicate's creditors. From this occupation he managed to get a small income for many years. He resided a few years in Allentown, Pa., the home of his second wife, Ann Penn Allen, though he credited himself to Philadelphia. While in Allentown, he took an active part in its affairs, but made frequent visits to his old battleground in the District of Columbia, where he defended vigorously the rights of creditors of the syndicate to their property claims in the Federal City. At some time before 1831, he again took up his permanent residence in Washington, then a thriving political center, and spent the remainder of his days as a retired gentleman of taste, though of very limited means. He died September 20, 1843, obscure and alone.

The failure of James Greenleaf, Robert Morris, John Nicholson, Samuel Blodget, Jr., and Thomas Law—the most conspicuous figures in the "Federal City" speculation—to be profitably rewarded for their ventures, was not due to fantastic visions of stupendous growth in land values, or even to lack of foresight. They merely ignored the inherent and difficult problems of town building. As pointed out by the Duke de La Rochefoucauld, one of the keenest of observers of early American society: "He . . . who is engaged in the establishment of a new city, can rarely confine to himself the conduct of the enterprise. If he is not counteracted in the whole of his views, he is sure to be so in the greater part of them. The proper inhabitants that he receives on his estate are of no advantage to him. They are even burthensome, as they occupy the space he wishes to fill with others, whose wealth may advance his fortune. Benevolence is banished from his system, by the necessary calculations of his interest. If those calculations induce him to expend sums for buildings, it is to erect taverns, shops, to open billiard tables, and to create lotteries; in a word, to furnish the means of dissipation and pleasure. . . . It is such objects as these that draw crowds of inhabitants to cities; and without them, cities will never be extensive."[28]

And thus it was with the Federal City, America's first "boom town."

[28] *Travels Through the United States of North America in the Years 1795, 1796 and 1797*, Vol. III, p. 648.

CHAPTER VIII

FILLING UP THE "OLD NORTHWEST"

WHEN the year 1800 ushered in the new century, land speculation in America was at low ebb. The wild land mania had subsided, and those who participated in it, if not already bankrupt, were compelled to hold their acquisitions or proceed slowly to dispose of their tracts at retail. The tendency was toward speculations on a more moderate scale.

This move was fostered by the national land policy. Congress, after the disappointments of the Ohio grants, provided for the sales of western public lands in small allotments, instead of in large tracts. Through the suggestion of William Henry Harrison, son-in-law of John Cleves Symmes, Congress in 1800 passed a law reducing the minimum area of tracts allotted to single purchases from 640 acres to 320 acres.[1] Harrison was the Congressional delegate from Ohio, and his residence in that unsettled region brought home to him the difficulties of the pioneers in endeavoring to pay for large tracts. He urged the sale of the public lands in alternate half and quarter sections on an instalment payment basis.

The adoption of this policy gave a new impetus to western migration. It discouraged the engrossment of large areas by fixing the price of public land at $2.00 per acre regardless of the quantity purchased. Payments could be made in instalments covering a period of four years.

To facilitate sales to all comers, land offices were established

[1] Payson Jackson Treat, *The National Land System*, p. 94. In 1804 the minimum acreage that could be purchased was reduced to 160 acres, i.e., a quarter section.

at accessible places in districts where surveys had been made and the unappropriated lands made available for settlement. Accordingly, land offices were established at Cincinnati, Chillicothe, Marietta and Steubenville, to serve the Ohio country. Whenever a new tract was surveyed and opened up for settlement, a public auction of sections and half sections was held for a period of three weeks. Thereafter the unsold portions could be obtained at the minimum government price.

The lure of fertile sections in the new "ranges" drew actual settlers to the West. Of course, the private land companies and individual speculators continued to offer their lands, but to meet the competition of the government land offices, and still make a profit on their sales, they had to offer more liberal terms of credit or some other special inducement to attract purchasers. The prospect of fancy profits in private land deals was thus considerably reduced. It was only through town-site building and the construction of internal improvements that the interest in land speculation could be maintained.

Yet, the old "land grabbers," who still held large areas of unsold wild lands, endeavored to keep up a speculative interest both at home and abroad. Gouverneur Morris, that prince of land agents, was kept on the job. In 1806 he published a small pamphlet, in the form of a series of letters entitled *Notes on the United States of America*,[2] which was manifestly for the purpose of attracting land purchasers from abroad. "Judicious speculations in land," he wrote, "have yielded more in the last ten years than in the twenty preceding on the antecedent forty." And, he added, "It is reasonable to believe that they will continue to be advantageous."

In answering the question whether the best speculation is in acquiring large rather than small tracts, he states emphatically that "experience favors the purchase of large tracts at a moderate price."

Of course, Morris was biased in his opinion. He was still selling the northern New York lands and other large areas acquired by wealthy speculators during the wild land mania. "He who purchases a small tract of choice land, must pay a large price,

[2] Philadelphia, 1806, 48 pp.

but, [he admits] he has the moral certainty of a speedy sale. He who purchases a large tract unexplored, pays less, but much of it may be bad, and the sales will not speedily be completed." In large tracts, however, "there is much less to be apprehended from the mistakes or misrepresentations of surveyors, and frequently the proportion of good land is so great that if made to bear the whole price, it will be as cheap as a small tract leaving the inferior quality a clear profit. Moreover, when the best lands are sold and in cultivation, those which adjoin them find as good, and sometimes, a better market."[3]

Gouverneur Morris, as a wealthy New York landlord and as a "wild land" speculator, was qualified to give advice. We have already shown how he put over sales to Madame de Staël, David Parish, Le Ray de Chaumont, and other distinguished foreigners. To these, and to other purchasers, he advised the disposition of their lands at retail to settlers, though the wholesale method was the easiest, if not the most profitable mode of disposal.

He also discussed the advantages and risks of making improvements on lands to attract settlers. "The landholder," he said, "who gives a salary to his agent, is certain of nothing but the expense. He will generally be pestered with costly projects of roads, mills, and villages which seldom answer any good purpose." He advocated, therefore, a commission basis of payment to agents. But he also suggested that purchasers of large tracts may profit by "settling in the center of their domain," and developing it for the purpose of gradual disposal. Judge William Cooper at Cooperstown, N. Y., and the Wadsworths in the Genesee country had done this with success.

Undoubtedly, Gouverneur Morris was a man of eminent shrewdness and foresight, and his writings indicate him to have been one of the keenest minds that the United States has ever produced. It was he who first proposed the construction of the Erie Canal, and it was he who was largely responsible for the land development activities which assisted in the rapid settlement of the unoccupied areas of northern New York.

But he was, nevertheless, visionary, and somewhat mistaken in holding that speculators would be attracted to the more set-

[3] *Ibid.,* p. 37.

tled eastern sections of the United States in preference to the undeveloped West. The tide of emigration surged over the Alleghanies, and though settlers gradually filled in the vacant lands in the western portions of New York and Pennsylvania, the chief attraction was the Ohio and the upper Mississippi valleys. This section has since become known as "the Old Northwest."

This westward movement, in the early nineteenth century, was in large part induced by land speculation, though the opportunities of buying large tracts for speedy resale at a profit had almost vanished. Speculation, therefore, had to take a different course.

What was commonly called "town jobbing" in these early days became the new form of land grabbing. Choice sites for communities became the land speculator's dream. Whenever a government land office opened up a new district for settlement, business men, surveyors, lawyers, politicians, territorial officers and others scrutinized the maps in the hope of discovering the possibilities of a favorable town site. When individuals decided that a certain section or half section was a desirable location for a "town," they sought to preëmpt it. If they learned that others were after the same site and would offer competitive bids, they would endeavor to buy them off. Bribery and corruption became rife. "Town jobbing" became a common practice.

The important beginnings of town jobbing west of the Alleghanies can be traced to the large Ohio grants. All three of the principal "companies," i.e., the Ohio Associates, the Symmes Purchase, and the Connecticut Land Company, laid out towns. The Ohio Associates founded Marietta; Symmes selected the site for the city of Cincinnati; the Connecticut speculators laid out the "village" of Cleveland. All these towns were divided into squares and lots. The central part of the town plot was composed of the "in-lots" and the surrounding sections were designated "out-lots." Both classes of lots were generally offered for sale simultaneously.

From such beginnings originated the "townsite mania." It has continued with little interruption ever since. When Symmes thought he had done a good job with Cincinnati, he encouraged Jonathan Dayton, Governor Arthur St. Clair, and General James Wilkinson, in 1796, to select a site (which he believed was within the bounds of his grant) for the town of Dayton. "The in-lots of the new town called Dayton," Symmes wrote, on January 20, 1796, to Jonathan Dayton, "are selling in Cincinnati at ten dollars per lot." Then, referring to Dayton's election to the speakership of the House of Representatives, he added, "I hope you will find 'honor's easy chair' both agreeable and profitable, for $12 a day is very pretty." Thus a lot in a new town was worth almost as much as the Speaker's daily pay, and since in the same year a favorably located lot in Cincinnati (which was then but partly built) sold for $150, the new "in-lots" in the proposed town appeared cheap. "Out-lots" naturally sold for less, but as the town boomers generally owned the neighboring land, the success of the town project meant also an enhancement of the agricultural lands for sale by the same owners.

It would be tiresome to relate the tales of the numerous cities, towns, ports, and emporiums which were planned and fostered in the unsettled western country. Many were started, continued for a brief space of time, and then disappeared. Others thrived, and became great centers of population. But the number of those that survived and progressed, compared with the total number projected, is very small.

Some towns were the outgrowth of colonizing efforts. In a number of instances whole groups moved from a New England community to a new location in the Ohio country. The Licking Land Company, formed in 1804 by citizens of Granville, Mass., was but one of the many ventures of this kind. They bought a part of a tract in Ohio which was reserved for holders of military warrants. They acquired these warrants from the original holders. They then moved as a single caravan across Pennsylvania into the Ohio Valley and took possession of their purchase in 1805. Two years later they formed Granville township, and laid out in the middle the town of Granville, "with 100 acre farms around it."[4]

Other towns as in the case of Cleveland, Chillicothe and Cincinnati, were the result of careful and deliberate site selection and town planning. Most frequently, however, the aim was town-lot

[4] Hubert Howe Bancroft, *Retrospection*, p. 77. See also *The Old Northwest Genealogical Quarterly*, Vol. 8, p. 241.

selling, and nothing else. "Gain! Gain! Gain!" exclaimed Morris Birkbeck, the Illinois pioneer, while journeying through the Northwest in 1817. "Gain is the beginning, the middle, and the end, the *alpha* and *omega* of the founders of American towns, who, after all, are bad calculators, when they omit the important element of salubrity in their choice of situations."[5] He noted that wherever there was a small cluster of houses, a town was laid out by some one who named it after himself, and who sold lots at auction:

> On any spot where a few settlers cluster together . . . some enterprising proprietor finds in his selection what he deems a good site for a town: he has it surveyed and laid out in lots, which he sells, or offers for sale by auction. . . . The new town then assumes the name of its founder:—a store-keeper builds a little framed store, and sends for a few cases of goods; and then a tavern starts up . . . as the boarding-house of the weary traveller; soon follows a blacksmith; a schoolmaster, who is also a minister of religion becomes an important accession to this rising community. Thus the town proceeds, if it becomes the metropolis of the neighborhood. Hundreds of these speculations may have failed but hundreds prosper; and thus trade begins and thrives around these lucky spots.[6]

The founding of Toledo, Ohio,. on Lake Erie, may be taken as a typical example of early Ohio town jobbing. Located at the mouth of a sluggish stream, the Maumee River, it was originally purchased from the government in February, 1817, by two groups of speculators from Cincinnati, each of which began laying off lots on different sides of the river. One group, because of some unknown association, named their side "Toledo" the other "town" was called "Port Lawrence." These two rivals began selling lots at about the same time. In order to avoid competition, they soon combined as the "Port Lawrence Company." They attracted few purchasers, however, and failing to make the final payment to the government, the land was forfeited. In 1821, however, the surviving promoters succeeded in making an arrangement with the land office, whereby they received back a part of their original

[5] Morris Birkbeck, *Notes of A Journey in America,* (Dublin Edition, 1818), p. 71.
[6] *Ibid.,* p. 105.

purchase (i.e., the "Toledo" side). They again advertised their "town lots." This time the venture was more successful, and Toledo remained on the map. It did not begin to thrive, however, until the boom days prior to the Panic of 1837. The town of "Port Lawrence" on the opposite side of the river, was also revived—and the lots, which had been neglected for almost twenty years, were again put up for sale.[7]

An English traveler, by the name of Joseph Biggs, whose diary was discovered a few years ago, thus describes the process of town jobbing in the Old Northwest:

A speculator makes out a plan of a city with its streets, square and avenues, quays and wharves, public buildings and monuments. The streets are lotted, the houses numbered, and the squares called after Franklin or Washington. The city itself has some fine name, perhaps Troy or Antioch. This is engraved and forthwith advertised and hung up in as many steamboats and hotels as the speculator's interest may command. All this time the city is a mere vision. Its very site is on the fork of some river in the far West, 500 miles beyond civilization, probably under water or surrounded by dense forests and impassable swamps. Emigrants have been repeatedly defrauded out of their money by transactions so extremely gross as hardly to be credited.

It must not be thought, because of the prevalence of town jobbing in this period, that agricultural or wild land speculation was totally absent. There was plenty of it. It did not, however, have the "wholesale" character of the post-Revolutionary land deals; nor did it involve as many persons of social and political prominence. At this period, certain large tracts of western land were set aside as soldiers' bounties. By buying up the military land warrants, individual speculators could acquire large areas, and some capitalists took advantage of this land-grabbing opportunity.

An outstanding figure in early Ohio land speculation was General Duncan McArthur, an early governor of the state. McArthur was born in Dutchess County, N. Y., in 1772, but when still a boy moved to western Pennsylvania. He later became an Indian

[7] See Clark Waggoner, *History of Toledo, Ohio,* pp. 370-372.

fighter and surveyor in Ohio, and assisted General Nathaniel Massie, in 1796, in laying out the town of Chillicothe—one of the most successful town-jobbing ventures in early Ohio. While still occupying a log cabin in Chillicothe, he commenced surveying and locating lands in the Virginia Military Reserve. He soon acquired a reputation for land jobbing superior to any in this business. Through accumulation of Virginia military warrants, he began to reap the advantage of personal knowledge of the most accessible and fertile sections. Fortune favored his land speculations. Though he was confronted with numerous lawsuits regarding his titles, he in time became by far the largest land holder in the Scioto Valley.

Politics and war also appealed to him. He volunteered in the War of 1812 and joined General Hull in his defense of Detroit. He learned of Hull's surrender of the post on his return from a reconnoitering expedition, and before becoming a prisoner of war, "tore off his epaulets, and broke his sword" in indignation. He was paroled and returned to Ohio. He later became a major-general of the militia and the successor of General William Henry Harrison to the command of the American forces in the Northwest Territory.

McArthur continued his land acquisitions after the war with all the adroitness and dexterity with which he could take advantage of the defects in the locations and surveys of other land speculators. In these successful land deals he took as much pride as an ambitious general in outmaneuvering his adversary on the field of battle. His land manipulations were evidently emulated by others in his home town. "My landlord at Chillicothe," noted William Faux, an English traveler in Ohio in 1818, "states he recently bought seventy-five acres of good land in Ohio, at the small price of 75 cents per acre. It was at a forced sale, and the land has been privately resold at three dollars an acre." "The General," he added in speaking of McArthur, "looks dirty and butcher-like—very unlike a soldier in appearance, seemingly half-savage, and dressed as a backwoodsman." Perhaps this appearance was due to the contempt in which land jobbers in Ohio were then held. "Land here gives a man no importance," Faux remarks. "Storekeepers and clerks rank much above farmers, who are never seen in genteel parties."[8]

General McArthur's lands were largely in the section of the Virginia Military Reserve, in which there had been a mix-up in the surveys. Two surveys of this area had been made, each of which fixed different boundary lines, leaving a vacant area between. In this vacant section, McArthur bought about 14,000 acres from settlers who had originally located there under Virginia warrants. His titles to these lands were contested, but the United States Supreme Court, in 1829, gave him a favorable decision.

These "shady" land deals gained for the general a host of political enemies. Yet he succeeded in 1824 in getting into Congress and was elected Governor of Ohio in 1830. McArthur's own brother-in-law and biographer notes in referring to the general's land speculations, "his conduct is not worthy of imitation and though he acquired great wealth, it brought to him more vexations and enemies than all other acts of his life." It may have been by way of Divine retribution, that the roof of a building fell on him, causing his death in 1839. He died rich in land, but detested and scorned, for "notwithstanding that he was liberal in feeding the hungry and clothing the naked, he was admitted to be a close and severe dealer."[9]

Chillicothe, McArthur's home town, together with Cincinnati, and Lexington, Ky., were the chief centers of land speculation in the Old Northwest during the first three decades after 1800. In this section, the unoccupied public lands were rapidly filling up. The New Englanders were settling along the borders of Lake Erie; Virginians and Pennsylvanians were taking up the southern areas; and foreign immigrants were preëmpting half sections or buying from speculators throughout the whole region.

As in former years, both speculators and settlers conducted their operations on a credit basis. Farms and town lots were sold "on liberal terms," and "wild cat" banks were organized to afford loans. The Second Bank of the United States, which was char-

[8] William Faux, *Memorial Days in America*, pp. 183-193.
[9] John McDonald, *Biographical Sketches of General Nathaniel Massie, General Duncan McArthur, etc.* This book was written in 1838, one year before McArthur's death.

tered in 1816, did a large business in granting loans secured by mortgages on land. At one time it had under pledge almost all the area of Cincinnati. In 1823, defaulted real estate loans in that city alone exceeded two million and a half dollars. When interest was regularly paid, the debtors were not disturbed. When the arrears accumulated, the mortgage was foreclosed and the property sold, only to be repurchased by the bank.

All this brought on bitter political opposition to Nicholas Biddle's "money monopoly" and finally defeated the request for a renewal of the bank's charter. Voicing the western sentiment against the bank, "Old Bullion" Thomas Hart Benton, in the United States Senate, exclaimed: "I know towns, yea, cities . . . where this bank already appears as an engrossing proprietor . . . All the flourishing cities of the West are mortgaged to this money power. They may be devoured by it at any moment. They are in the jaws of the monster! A lump of butter in the mouth of a dog! One gulp, one swallow, and all is gone."[10]

Individual capitalists, as well as the banks, prospered by the pecuniary needs of real estate debtors. Foremost among those who became rich by buying up the holdings of distressed speculators was Nicholas Longworth, grandfather of the late Speaker of the House of Representatives. Coming from Newark, N. J., to Cincinnati in the wake of Symmes' settlers, Longworth took up the practice of law. From the beginning of his business career, he displayed confidence in the future of his adopted city. He bought up every piece of land and every town lot that his cash permitted. He even accepted land in payment of legal fees.

On one occasion (so the story runs) he defended a man accused of horse stealing. His client had no cash, but offered, in payment for legal services, two second-hand copper stills which were in the possession of a friend. Longworth learned that the friend had a lot of several acres near the city, and proposed that this be given him in lieu of the copper kettles. The substitution was gladly made. On this transaction alone, Longworth is reported to have made a fortune, for in 1856 the "kettle land" was estimated to be worth two million dollars.

Longworth's other property in and near Cincinnati and in the

10 Ralph C. H. Catterall, *The Second Bank of the United States*, p. 67.

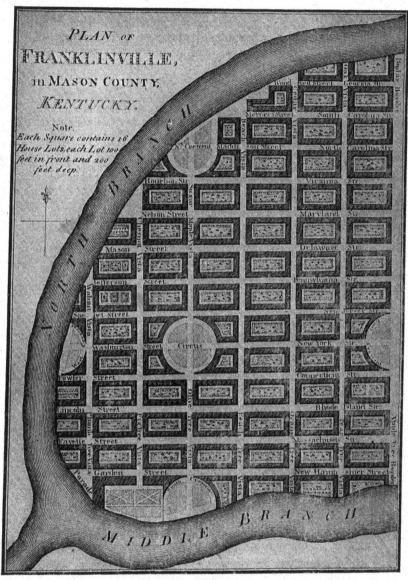

AN ILLUSTRATION OF EARLY WESTERN TOWN JOBBING, TAKEN FROM WILLIAM WINTERBOTTOM'S, *An Historical and Geographical and Philosophical View of the United States of America*, LONDON, 1795. THE PLACE DOES NOT EXIST TODAY

NICHOLAS LONGWORTH

A Contemporary Portrait of Nicholas Longworth Embellished with
His Favorite Fruit and Beverage

The Banks of the Ohio. Mr. Longworth's Vineyards

region extending from Hamilton to Sandusky was worth still more. When he died in 1863, he was reputed to be the richest real estate owner in the United States, with the possible exception of William B. Astor, of New York City.

The original Nicholas Longworth had two hobbies: land grabbing and vine growing. He devoted much of his time to grape and strawberry culture. His vineyard on the Ohio River was a showplace for travelers. He worked zealously to encourage the manufacture of wine in the Ohio Valley, and in this he then had government encouragement. Bounties of public land were offered to those who would cultivate the vine and the olive. Persons skilled in the manufacture of Rhenish and Moselle wines were imported from Europe and given responsible positions in Longworth's wineries. His addresses and papers on grape growing and horticulture were widely read and much appreciated. To him may be ascribed the inspiration of the hymn in praise of "American Catawba":

> Ohio's green hill-tops
>   Glow bright in the sun,
> And yield us more treasure
>   Than Rhine or Garonne.
> They give us Catawba,
>   The pure and the true,
> As radiant as sunlight,
>   As soft as the dew.

In the course of a few decades following the first settlements, the Ohio and Kentucky waste lands were rapidly converted into farms. So land jobbing moved westward into the Indiana and Illinois country. Here was a different type of soil and topography: the prairie. Strange to relate in these times, "grass lands" were not looked upon favorably by the early American cultivators. Any ground which could not grow trees was regarded as of little value, and was passed over even by those who selected home sites east of the Alleghanies.

This prejudice had to be overcome. It was a handicap to western land jobbing. However, when it was proven that bountiful corn and wheat crops could be raised on the Illinois lands without the difficult preliminary work of clearing and grubbing; and when sleek cattle thrived by feeding on the native grasses, the ancient prejudice departed. New settlers began to move into the fertile western plains beyond the Mississippi and Illinois rivers.

It will be recalled by the reader that just prior to the Revolution, the Indiana and Illinois lands were "preëmpted" by a group of politicians and Indian traders through spectacular purchases from the supposed Indian owners. Largely to offset opposing claims to the territory, Virginia, during the Revolutionary War, sought possession of the region and sent George Rogers Clark to drive out both the Indians and the English. In 1780, the Virginia authorities established a court at Vincennes (then a well-established French settlement) which assumed the right of granting lands freely to every applicant whom they approved.

The members of the court naturally were kind to themselves. "An arrangement was made," notes William Henry Harrison, Governor of Indiana Territory in 1802, "by which the whole country, to which the Indian title was supposed to be extinguished, was divided between the members of the court." Most of them, however, abandoned the land in a few years, because they could find no purchasers. When settlement in the territory began, however, after 1800, the claims of these "grantees" were bought up by speculators who infested the western country. These resold to others in different parts of the United States. "The price at which the land is sold," wrote Governor Harrison to James Madison, "enables anybody to become a purchaser; one thousand acres being frequently given for an indifferent horse or a rifle gun."

Many ignorant persons were induced to buy these fraudulent titles, and a number began to settle upon the land. "I should not be surprised," wrote Harrison, "to see five hundred families settling under these titles the ensuing Spring." He feared that upon learning of their invalid titles, the settlers would petition Congress to confirm their ownership. "The extent of these speculations was unknown to me until lately," the governor stated. "I am now informed that a number of persons are in the habit of repairing to this place [Vincennes] where they purchase two or three thousand acres of this claim, for which they get a deed properly authenticated and recorded, and then disperse themselves over the United States to cheat the ignorant and credulous. To check this practice, I have forbidden the recorder and prothonotary of this county from recording or authenticating any of these papers."[11]

.   .   .   .   .

Though William Henry Harrison, hero of Tippecanoe, railed against the unprincipled land jobbers that "infested" his Indiana territory, he, himself, participated in one of the questionable and corrupt speculations in the Old Northwest. When George Rogers Clark, and his Virginians, took possession of the Illinois country and drove out the British, he found French colonies established along the Kaskaskia River. These simple-minded French pioneers feared the Americans because of both their pillaging and their Protestantism. Some fled the country and settled in Louisiana. Others who remained were sought to be appeased by grants of land. Thus, in Vincennes, each head of a family was given 400 acres, drawn by lot. After the Ordinance of 1787, many again became frightened, as they were told they would be required to change their religion—and left their settlements.

As might be expected, they sold their land titles for almost anything. Their claims were eagerly bought up by both resident and non-resident land grabbers. Among those who bought these titles were William Henry Harrison, the first secretary, and General Arthur St. Clair, the first governor of the Northwest Territory. Neither, however, went into this business of land grabbing on a large scale.

But Harrison's name appears several times, in the lists of those who presented claims to the Frenchmen's lands in Kaskaskia.[12] St. Clair personally presented no claims, but it is clearly evident that his son, John Murray St. Clair, was closely associated with one John Edgar, merchant of Illinois, who garnered more land claims in this region than any other individual. St. Clair, as governor of the territory, passed upon the validity of these claims, and he seems to have approved a vast number held by John Edgar and, jointly, by Edgar and his son.

John Edgar settled in Kaskaskia in 1784. He was a native of

[11] *American State Papers,* "Public Lands," Vol. I, p. 123.
[12] *Ibid.,* Vol. II, p. 125 *et seq.*

Ireland, and brought with him to the Illinois country a stock of merchandise, useful to the pioneer inhabitants. He soon built up an extensive trade, established a flour mill, and entered local politics. He was also appointed a "Major General of Militia" as well as a "judge" in the Northwest Territory. He became very friendly with Governor Arthur St. Clair, whom he occasionally entertained in his sumptuous backwoods palace.

In the *St. Clair Papers*, published in 1883, there is a letter written by Edgar to Governor St. Clair, which indicates their close association. On April 11, 1801, after congratulating the governor on his reappointment "in spite of the opposition of your enemies," he wrote, "I must now take the liberty of refreshing your memory concerning the deeds for the three surveys which I sent you last Spring, for which I now begin to feel myself anxious." And, in a more familiar vein, he added: "Present if you please, Mrs. Edgar's and my compliments to Mrs. Dill, Mrs. Vance and the rest of the family."[13]

St. Clair brought upon himself severe criticism because, among other things, of his approval of several Kaskaskia claims. He was rebuked by Washington for his actions, and finally was removed by Jefferson in November, 1802. His confirmation of a grant of 30,000 acres to John Edgar and his son was subsequently annulled on the ground that it was made after St. Clair had authority to act as a land commissioner. St. Clair's son, however, remained in Illinois, but the general returned to western Pennsylvania after his dismissal, where he died in 1818, a poor and broken-down old man. He acquired no wealth because of his political position in the Old Northwest; though, when surrounded by ravenous land jobbers in this back country, he undoubtedly was under great temptation to join in their schemes. But he seems to have passed up the opportunity.

Next to Edgar, to whom were confirmed 49,200 acres, the largest jobbers in the Kaskaskia claims were William Morrison and Nicholas Jarrot. Jarrot was a jobber of no political importance, but Morrison, like Edgar, was prominent in early Illinois politics. He was a native of Pennsylvania, who emigrated to Kaskaskia in 1790. He also was a leading merchant in the Illinois country,

---

[13] William Henry Smith, *The St. Clair Papers*, Vol. II, p. 533.

and operated stores in several of the settlements, and became a large land holder. Like Edgar, he advocated the establishment of slavery in Illinois, probably in the belief that this institution would enhance the value of his lands. He died in 1837.

The determination of the Kaskaskia claims gave Congress and the government land officials an almost endless amount of trouble. The matter was under consideration for many years. It was brought out in the proceedings that several of the leading land grabbers had employed false and corrupt witnesses in support of their claims. Thus, John Edgar was accused of forging deeds and of buying forged deeds. François Vigo, William and Robert Morrison, Nicholas Jarrot, and Robert Reynolds also presented claims which were considered fraudulent and invalid. Vigo was a lieutenant of George Rogers Clark's in the winning of the Northwest, and for many years he and his heirs prosecuted a claim before Congress for compensation for military supplies and loss of his property in the French settlements.

A goodly number of the claims presented by the Kaskaskia jobbers was rejected. However, out of a total of 2,294 claims presented, 1,171 or about one-half were confirmed. But it was not until about 1820 that the clearing up of old land titles in the Kaskaskia district ceased to take up the time of Congress and the land officials.

. . . . .

The rapid growth of the Old Northwest and the consequent rise in real estate values there did not fail to attract British speculators. Of course, during the Napoleonic Wars, the Britishers could spare very little capital to send abroad. They found better use for it as subsidies to their allies in the conflict with the Continental conqueror.

Conditions were different after 1815. The London banking house of Baring kept up close business relations with American firms. The Barings, however, appear to have avoided commitments in American lands. But they acted as agents and advisers of Englishmen, who desired profit and riches from rising American land values.

How much capital was invested in this period by British speculators in our soil may never be known. No one has even tried to estimate it, but there is much evidence indicating that British speculative interest in American growth and prosperity was greatly aroused in this period and that agents were employed by British capitalists to acquire both agricultural lands and urban real estate in the United States.

The interest of the British was stimulated by the letters and publications of Morris Birkbeck, a distinguished British immigrant, who proposed the establishment of English farm colonies in America. Despairing of improvement in the condition of English tenant farmers, Birkbeck came to America with his son in 1817. Before sailing, he issued a prospectus or "proposals for the establishment of a colony of English," in which he stated that he intended to acquire one or more entire townships of government land. These lands he proposed "to offer on terms proportionately favorable to a number of our countrymen."

Arriving at Norfolk, in May, 1817, Birkbeck almost immediately began a journey westward via Washington and Richmond. He was unable to buy a tract in the Ohio country, because of the prevailing high land prices, and because, as he noted, "the best locations were already taken up." Good Ohio lands were then selling at $20 to $30 per acre, representing a tenfold increase in twenty years.

Birkbeck proceeded into Indiana and Illinois. He described this region in his *Notes on a Journey in America*, published in both London and Dublin in 1818. This was followed shortly by his *Letters from Illinois*, issued in London and in Philadelphia. These publications attracted considerable attention both in Great Britain and in the United States.

In these publications Birkbeck described the methods of purchase and settlement of western public lands and the prevalent speculation in town sites. "Land Jobbers traverse this fine country," he wrote back home, "like a pestilent blight. Whenever they see the promise of a thriving settlement from a cluster of entries being made in any neighborhood, they purchase large tracts of the best land and lock it up in real mortmain, for it is death to all improvement."

"One of the greatest calamities," he exclaims, "to which a young colony is liable, is this investment of the property of non-residents, who speculate on their prosperity, whilst they are doing all they can to impede it. . . . This holding back from cultivation of millions of acres, tends to scatter the population of these new countries; increasing the difficulties of the settlers manifold. . . . The western States are suffering greatly from this evil."[14]

Birkbeck had, as a partner and companion, George Flower, a wealthy and well-known English writer on rural economics. Flower arrived in America a year in advance of Birkbeck, and was advised by Thomas Jefferson to settle in Virginia. He went west, however, with Birkbeck, and each took up 1,500 acres of government lands at "Big Prairie" in Edwards County, Ill., just south of Vincennes. They paid more than they intended to, and blamed the high price on "the invasion of speculators" into the region. Flower, in his *History of the English Settlement in America*, thus described their attitude toward the speculator:

Having expended all the money we could then command, by securing but little more than half the land we intended for our own families, we were fearful, as the point of our settlement was designated, that speculators might buy the lands immediately around those we purchased, and thus defeat our object in preserving lands at the Government price to those we hoped to induce to come from Great Britain.

Immediately following the selection of the site for their colony, the two partners sent alluring letters home, advertising the virtues of the soil, the topography and the climate. These letters were given wide publicity in the British press, and threatened to cause a rush of English farmers to the Illinois country. "No man, since Columbus," remarked William Faux in 1819, "has done so much toward peopling America as Mr. Birkbeck, whose publications, and the authority of whose name had effects truly prodigious; and if all could have settled in Illinois whom he had tempted to cross the Atlantic . . . it had now been the most populous state in the Union."[15]

And here are some of the allurements pointed out by Birk-

[14] *Letters from Illinois*, by Morris Birkbeck (Philadelphia, 1818), pp. 81, 82.
[15] William Faux, *Memorial Days in America*, p. 298.

beck in his *Letters from Illinois,* which "tempted" so many British to cross the Atlantic:

I am so well satisfied with the election [of the site] we have made, that I have not for a moment felt a disposition to recede; and much as I should lament that our English friends should stop short of us, some amends even for that would be made by the higher order of settlers, whom similar motives bring constantly into our very tract. Society we shall not want, I believe; and with the fear of that want every other fear has vanished. The comforts and luxuries of life we shall obtain with ease and in abundance; pomp and state will follow quickly.

A few months later, he wrote:

As to the comforts and accommodations of life, we have our books, our music, our agreeable and kind neighbors, good food and clothing, and before two years are ended we expect to have as good and well furnished a house as we left. It is astonishing how small are the privations we are subject to. . . .
I *own* here a far better estate than I *rented* in England, and am already more attached to the *soil.* Here, every citizen, whether by birthright or adoption, is part of the government, indentified with it, not *virtually,* but in fact. . . . I love this government. . . . I am becoming a patriot in my old age; thus a new virtue will spring up in my bosom.

He was enthusiastic about America as a field of investment. "The power of capital here," he wrote, "is great almost beyond calculation; the difficulty seems to be in the choice of objects out of the various ways of doubling and redoubling it, which present themselves to the enterprising. . . . We have no rent, tithes, or poor rates and scarcely any taxes. . . . For about half the capital that is required for the mere cultivation of our worn-out soils in England, a man may establish himself as a proprietor here, with every comfort belonging to a plain and reasonable mode of living." And finally, in an appeal to the British gourmandizing impulse, he wrote: "We are now feasting on wild turkeys. We have not sat down to dinner for the last month, I believe, without a fine roast turkey. They weigh about twelve pounds, and are sold five for a dollar."

William Cobbett, the radical British politician, who resided in the United States in 1818, and made a short visit to Birkbeck's colony, issued a public statement that Birkbeck's account of the fertility and salubrity of Illinois was overdrawn.[16] Birkbeck made a scathing reply, showing up Cobbett's ignorance. He accused Cobbett of "lending his active aid to eastern land speculators, who wish to see Illinois in ruin and utterly discarded."

These controversies whetted the curiosity of the English. Several investigators left for America to verify the situation. Among these were William Faux, "an English farmer," Adlard Welby and Henry Bradshaw Fearon, all of whom published accounts of Birkbeck's settlement.[17]

Faux admits that his account was written "to show men and things as they are . . . and to discourage British emigration." To quote from his preface:

When I saw thousands of my countrymen hurrying thither, as though they fled for life, and from the city of destruction, I became very anxious to know the real nature of their prospects. . . . I may truly say, that throughout the whole of this enterprise, I have been in a high degree influenced by a sense of patriotic duty. The same sentiment impels me to the completion of my task, in the hope that the truth, so long perverted and concealed, may contribute to destroy the illusions of transatlantic speculation.

While on his way to Illinois, Faux gathered here and there discouraging accounts of Birkbeck's venture from persons who professed to have been there. One informer even accused Mr. Birkbeck and his family of eating "the rattlesnake, the flesh of which is fine, sweet and white as an eel." That Faux was credulous of these wild stories is indicated in his note: "By the papers, today, I see that Miss Courtney, the daughter of an emigrant in Mr. Birkbeck's settlement, was killed in a few hours by the bite

[16] See "Letters to Morris Birkbeck, Esq.," in Cobbett's *A Year's Residence in the United States of America*, Third Edition, 1822.

[17] William Faux, *Memorial Days in America; and Tour of the United States to ascertain the condition and probable prospect of British Emigrants*, 1820; Adlard Welby, *Visit to North America and the English Settlements in Illinois, with a Winter Residence in Philadelphia*, London, 1821; Henry Bradshaw Fearon, *Sketches of America, etc., with remarks on Mr. Birkbeck's Notes and Letters*, London, 1818.

of a huge spider.''[18] But when he finally arrived at Birkbeck's settlement, he did not find conditions as bad as had been painted to him, and he speaks highly of some of its aspects. His descriptions, however, did not encourage British emigration to Illinois.

Both Birkbeck and Flower were pestered by letters from land speculators in England and in eastern United States. "As early as 1817," wrote Flower in his memoirs, "I was solicited to purchase land from persons living in Eastern cities—I was reluctant to do so, though regretting to disappoint some friends."

MORRIS BIRKBECK

Neither of the two Illinois colonizers prospered. Because of rivalry in a love affair, which resulted in Flower marrying a young lady who had accompanied them to the West, the partners separated. Birkbeck's colony became known as "Albion." At first it had fair prospect of success under his guidance. He became interested in politics, took up the fight against introducing slavery into Illinois, and in 1822 became Secretary of Illinois. He had endeavored to acquire the preëmption right to 40,000 additional

[18] *Op. cit.*, p. 138.

acres, and petitioned Congress for a grant, but the Illinois representative in Congress politely informed him that it would be refused because of "the fear of speculation." His colony in the end was not successful, and after his death in 1825 it began to disintegrate. Even his sons deserted the place and settled elsewhere.

George Flower likewise met with financial reverses in his colonization schemes. His settlement called "Wanborough" has disappeared altogether. Flower, having wasted his resources in the experiment, took refuge in Robert Owen's colony at New Harmony, in 1849, whither he removed "with household furniture, some plate, and $250 in cash to begin life anew." He died January 15, 1862.[19]

. . . . . .

While in the opening years of the nineteenth century, land grabbers and town-site jobbers were operating in the western country, the eastern capitalists were not idle in reaping the benefits of rising land values in cities and towns. It was in this period that John Jacob Astor, Nicholas Emmerich, Henry Brevoort, Stephen Whitney, Peter Goelet and a host of other "old merchants of New York" were accumulating fortunes in urban real estate. Their example was followed by Jacob Ridgeway and Stephen Girard in Philadelphia. These men were merchants, shippers and bankers. They did not make a business of their real estate transactions. It was merely a means of placing their surplus funds acquired in the course of trade. They bought largely for cash, and they rarely mortgaged their properties. They left their estates free and clear to their descendants, and these, through long term leases, which freed them from taxes, obtained incomes affording lives of luxury.

John Jacob Astor, it is true, entered upon one or two speculative schemes. He bought up the claims to the confiscated lands of departed Loyalists. Chief among these were the claims of Roger and Mary Morris, whose ancestors owned an estate comprising 51,100 acres, or nearly one-third of the area of Putnam County, N. Y. Astor is said to have paid the heirs $100,000 for

[19] *History of the English Settlement in Edwards County,* by George Flower, *Chicago Historical Society Collections,* Vol. I.

their rights. The confiscated land had been divided into more than seven hundred farms, on which 3,500 people were settled. Astor threatened suit to oust them. This created consternation among the settlers. Most of them had obtained their titles from the state. It was the state's duty to defend them.

The New York Legislature appointed a commission to treat with Astor. They had to acknowledge the legality of his claim, and asked for a redemption price. Astor at first named $667,000, one-half of the estimated market value. This was considered extortionate and no settlement of the dispute was made.

Astor did not press the case, but the owners of the land were kept in a state of suspense and clamored for a settlement. Their titles were questionable. They could not mortgage or sell their lands. They hesitated to make improvements thereon. Finally, after ten years of bickering, the legislature passed a law providing for a settlement. Astor was to bring five separate suits, and if the United States Supreme Court decided three in his favor, he was to be paid $450,000, subject to a deduction of $200,000, should the court hold that the value of buildings and other improvements placed upon the land by title holders under the state could not be claimed by the contestant.

Astor accepted the offer. The state employed Daniel Webster and Martin Van Buren to plead its cause. Astor's attorneys were Emmet & Ogden, the leading law firm then in New York, though it is suspected that Aaron Burr acted secretly as his counsel. Astor won the necessary three cases, and in 1830 there was issued to him, in lieu of cash, $500,000 in New York State bonds. As more than twenty years elapsed between Astor's payment of $100,000 and his award, his actual profit, allowing for interest accumulations at 6 per cent, and attorneys' fees, was probably less than 100%—in fact, less than the profit on his urban real estate during the same period.

But Astor did not buy real estate for a profit on "turnover." He bought to hold indefinitely, for income, and his descendants still live from the rentals of scores of lots and plots, obtained at bargain prices by their ingenious and farseeing progenitor. Land-poor individuals, institutions and estates found him a willing purchaser of vacant and non-income producing properties, provided he thought they were cheap. He bought numerous lots from the Trinity Corporation—the largest landowner in early New York. He bought from distressed traders and merchants, and from defaulting mortgagors, and when the crash of 1837 came he still had cash to buy at ridiculously low prices.

Nor did he care to sell, until he obtained a price with which he could make a better investment. And he did not spend money on building and improving property, unless he could reap the immediate reward of such expenditure. Occasionally he asked for and received grants of city land, and though political corruption or graft may have been at the bottom of some of these transactions, he generally rewarded the community by undergoing the expense of cutting streets, draining or filling in the donated plots or the surrounding areas.

America, in the first two decades of the nineteenth century, recovered from the collapse of the visionary schemes of wholesale land grabbing, which marked the post-Revolutionary period. It was in these decades that the European immigration and the western movement, which the earlier speculators had prematurely expected, began to take place. This "filling-in" process was mainly fostered by native speculative enterprise, rather than the leadership of wealthy and politically prominent promoters. A keen observer of American institutions in this period, Michael Chevalier, a Frenchman who visited the United States in 1834, aptly remarked that "inasmuch as speculation in the United States created utilities, it was beneficial." "Here," he says, "one lives a hundred fold more than elsewhere. All is circulation, motion, and boiling agitation. Experiment follows experiment, enterprise succeeds to enterprise. Riches and poverty follow on each other's traces, and each in turn occupies the place of the other."

CHAPTER IX

LOUISIANA "SPANISH GRANTS" AND THEIR "ANTEDATERS"

ON JANUARY 29, 1804, less than a year after France ceded Louis-iana to the United States, Thomas Jefferson wrote to Dr. Joseph Priestley:

"I very early saw that Louisiana was indeed a speck in our horizon, which was to burst in a tornado."

Jefferson undoubtedly did not mean a tornado of land claimants, land jobbers and land-grant thieves, but he could, with truth, have as well made this remark. The vast, boundless region—which scarce a half century before had engendered dreams of fabulous wealth creation on the part of John Law and the other promoters of the Mississippi Bubble—had hardly been taken over by the new American republic, when hosts of schemers and "get-rich-quick" adventurers began to present their "claims" to a large part, if not practically all of the territory.

Under the terms of the treaty of cession, the United States agreed to incorporate the ceded territory into the Union as soon as possible and to accord to the inhabitants "all the rights, ad-vantages and immunities of citizens,—and in the meantime, they shall be maintained and protected in the free enjoyment of their liberty, property and the religion they profess."

This clause meant that all land titles, land grants and other rights given by the Spanish and French administrators must re-ceive recognition in so far as they did not conflict with the princi-ples of the Federal Constitution.

Just as soon as the Louisiana Purchase became known, land speculators in the region began to get exceedingly busy. They sought out and bought up all sorts of questionable titles, grants and conveyances, and when they could not find enough of them, they manufactured them. "No sooner was it known that the province of Louisiana was sold to the United States," wrote Moses Austin, a resident of Upper Louisiana, to Albert Gallatin, "a general and fraudulent sale of lands took place. . . . Concessions for any quantity of land were duly granted, bearing date of 1799 or further back, if the claimants demanded.—The number of acres granted was governed by the sum paid. It is not necessary to say to what extent the speculation was carried on."[1]

And Rufus Easton, a Connecticut Yankee, who was one of the many Easterners who settled in St. Louis within a year after Louisiana was acquired, wrote to Jefferson in a similar vein: "About the latter end of June 1803, information arrived in this country of its cession to the United States when instructions were given to the various agents of the governor . . . that grants and concessions be dated back to the year 1799, which was the general antedate . . . and that surveys thereof would be made of any tract from fifty to fifty thousand acres to any person upon payment of one hundred dollars for five hundred acres, and so great was the thirst for speculation, when money could not be obtained, horses and other property were received for payment."[2]

Because the Spanish governors had been desirous of attracting settlers to the Upper Louisiana territory, the local officials had granted free land under liberal "head rights" and "colonizing contracts." This policy was not continued under the brief régime of the French, with the result that the dates of the fraudulent grants were set back to the Spanish period, i.e., before 1800. So freely were the Spanish grants given that some local officials were in the habit of attaching their signatures to the certificates before the amount and location of the land was noted thereon. Naturally, these sheets got abroad and began to command a price among the so-called "antedaters." These "antedaters" were mostly Americans some of whom had emigrated into Missouri and

[1] *The Austin Papers,* Part I, p. 117.
[2] Quoted in Louis Houck, *History of Missouri,* Vol. III, p. 36.

"squatted" on land without receiving an actual grant or conveyance from Spanish officials.

The frequency of these land grants bearing date of the closing year of the Spanish régime in Louisiana was soon recognized as strong evidence of corruption and fraud. As early as February 29, 1804, President Jefferson informed Congress that "Attempts are now making to defraud the United States." He estimated that two hundred thousand acres of land, "including all the best [lead] mines, have been surveyed to various individuals in the course of a few weeks past . . . All the official papers, relative to these lands, bear the signature of M. . . . ., the predecessor of the present Lieutenant Governor." "To understand the nature of this fraudulent transaction," the President added, "it will be necessary to state the mode of acquiring titles. The settler applies to the commandant by way of petition, and prays a grant of certain lands described by him. At the bottom, on the back of the same petition, the commandant accedes to the prayer, and directs the surveyor to run out the lands prayed for. This petition and order entitle actual settlers to grants on application to the proper officer at New Orleans . . . Under these circumstances, they seem to have an equitable claim to their lands and really expect a confirmation of them by the United States."

The "M. . . . . ." mentioned in Jefferson's report undoubtedly refers to Lieutenant-Governor Zenon Trudeau, who was Spanish Commandant of Upper Louisiana in 1799, and who was living at New Orleans at the time of the Louisiana Purchase. He was induced, through bribes of speculators, to sign numerous blank sheets of paper. On these sheets the petitions for lands and the orders for surveys were later inserted by the speculators. In this way, the best lead and iron mines in Missouri are said to have been "granted" during the period when the Louisiana territory was being transferred to the United States.

Old land cessions were also resurrected and the deeds altered by erasing names. Moreover, Carlos Delassus, the last of the "commandants" of Upper Louisiana is reported to have made large grants to members of his family and to his friends. These grantees thus became the largest land holders in the region now constituting Missouri.

JOHN JACOB ASTOR
(From a painting by Chappel)

AARON BURR

(Reproduced from an engraving in the Smithsonian Institution)

Congress in 1805, upon learning of the frauds, appointed commissioners to determine the validity of Louisiana land titles. And what a difficult job they had! They required every holder of real estate obtained under Spanish and French dominion, ranging from village lots to princely domains, to prove ownership of their properties. The work extended over a period of thirty years. Corruption and fraud, threats and violence, suits and countersuits, characterized the proceedings throughout. At times, the land commissioners suffered bodily attacks, and the lawless spirit and greed for land made it necessary for them to carry arms for their personal protection.

The land grant controversies entered prominently into local politics in Missouri. The fiery Thomas H. Benton, grandson of Thomas Hart, notorious Yazoo and Tennessee land grabber, was appointed United States Senator from Missouri in 1820 largely because he favored liberal grants to claimants. Other politicians took the opposite view. Among these was John B. C. Lucas, Benton's opponent, appointed by Jefferson a member of the Louisiana Land Claims Commission. Lucas' attitude of persistent opposition to the speculators fastened upon him the hatred and ill will of many of the influential politicians; but he persisted in his policy, notwithstanding it led to his defeat by Benton in the senatorial contest in 1820.

While the government commissioners were hearing and deciding land claims, the "Spanish grants" were being hawked about among speculators. Eastern capitalists, as well as speculators on the spot, bought them up. Familiar names appear among the lists of those whose claims were denied or granted. Daniel Boone, who moved from Kentucky into Louisiana territory in 1798, and became a commandant of a district under the Spanish, claimed and was granted 1,000 arpents (about 850 acres) by Congress in 1813, though he had not cultivated or improved the land as required in the original concession. Moses Austin, who settled in Upper Louisiana in 1797, and began mining lead at Mine-a-Burton, near St. Genevieve, Mo., was finally refused title to his "square league" of land on the ground that the grant was not made and completed prior to October 1, 1800. Rufus Easton, a judge and politician, who had early informed Jefferson of the "antedaters," also had a number of claims, which were denied confirmation. Easton's ire, on one occasion, was so aroused by the opposition to him of one of the land commissioners, that he made a personal attack on him "with a bludgeon," for which he was sentenced to fourteen days in jail. William Russell, a large jobber in the Spanish grants, submitted as many as 309 claims in the space of a few years, but of these only 23 were approved. John Smith T., a notorious land thief, also presented a number of claims to both small and large plots, most of which were rejected. And so the cases ran, the decisions creating both political and financial animosities, in the old Upper Louisiana country.

General James Wilkinson's name, curiously, is not conspicuous among the Spanish land grant claimants. Wilkinson, we have already seen, had been concerned in western land deals. His integrity has been a mooted question among historians—and the fact that he was in command of American troops in Louisiana, and, together with Governor Wm. C. C. Claiborne, received the surrender of the province from the French Government, would have given him the opportunity of engrossing lands. Yet, as pointed out by his great-grandson, "one of the strongest proofs of the integrity of Wilkinson is the fact that the eight volumes of American State Papers, which contain all the Spanish land grants, and include hundreds of American settlers, do not show one grant in Wilkinson's favor . . . Wilkinson never got enough land from the Spaniards to serve him as a grave."[3]

Yet, as admitted by the ardent defender of his ancestor, one entry among the Spanish land grant claims in Louisiana shows that General James Wilkinson bought on May 12, 1816, from Moreau, the original grantee, Dauphin Island at the mouth of Mobile Bay. The American commissioners, on the application of Wilkinson's heirs, refused to confirm the grant because he "was not allowed to hold land under Spain, not being a Spanish subject."

The ousting of squatters was a most difficult task for the national government. Many Americans, prior to the Louisiana cession, had emigrated into the Spanish domains and had taken up lands merely on the verbal permission of the Spanish officials.

[3] *Louisiana Historical Quarterly*, Vol. I, No. 2, pp. 104, 105.

These settlers, because of willingness to live under Spanish laws, were called "Hidalgos" by the Ohio people. They could furnish no evidence of title, and when ordered to remove, frequently caused disturbances. The cry of "squatter sovereignty" arose. Politicians sought offices by favoring this principle. Thus, John Scott, who in 1816 presented himself as a candidate for Congressional Delegate from Missouri,—and got the job,—boldly stated in his platform: "Neither justice or policy requires that the people of this territory should be removed from land which they have ameliorated by their labour, and defended by their bravery, before any opportunity of buying was afforded them; and indeed, before they have received the pay which the government owes them for defending even the country itself against our savage enemies."[4]

Some of the Spanish grant cases were fought through the courts for many years. The litigation of Antoine Soulard for land granted him in Missouri covered a period of almost half a century. Soulard was a former officer in the French navy, who settled in Upper Louisiana and became a surveyor. He was recommended by the last French Governor, Carlos Delassus, to the American authorities, as one who could furnish the most reliable information regarding titles to Spanish grants, including those in New Madrid, the last post in Louisiana where free grants were made. Soulard and his two sons were granted more than 5,000 arpents (4,200 acres) in various parts of Upper Louisiana, by Delassus. In addition, he received a grant of 59 arpents in and near the city of St. Louis. This latter grant became extremely valuable after the American occupation. It was assigned to E. H. McCabe, who prosecuted the claim. Though in the opinion of the land commissioners the claim was valid, the United States Court finally rejected it in 1830. In the meantime the land had been sold by the United States, but in 1856 the heirs of McCabe petitioned Congress for other lands to offset their claim—and Congress finally reported favorably upon the petition.

Another and more extended claim was that known as the "Clarmorgan Grant." Jacques Clarmorgan, a native of Guadalupe, was a merchant, fur trader, explorer, and land speculator in the Upper Louisiana territory during the Spanish régime. As a reward for

[4] *Austin Papers,* Part I, p. 258.

"exploration services as far as the Pacific Ocean," he petitioned, on March 1, 1797, for a tract of land "on the west side of the Mississippi River, at a distance of a few leagues above the mouth of the Missouri River and bounded by Charmette (Dardenne) Creek and the Copper River, with suitable water frontage, and extending toward the west until the 'inland hills' are reached." The total acreage was estimated at 500,000 arpents (425,000 acres) and today would comprise a large part of Arkansas, just below New Madrid. The petition, it was claimed, was granted July 3, 1797, by Baron de Carondelet, Governor-General of Louisiana. In addition, Clarmorgan acquired other immense tracts in the same region along the Missouri and Mississippi rivers. The total acreage of his lands was estimated at about one million arpents. Land speculation, however, was not his only business. He was the promoter of the Missouri Fur Company in St. Louis, which traded extensively with the Indians. After the American occupation, he became a judge in the Louisiana territory. But his fur company proving unsuccessful, he left St. Louis after a few years and settled in Mexico. His land claims were then assigned to others "as his legal representatives."

For many years, these "legal representatives," "trustees" and "assigns," as they variously called themselves, sought confirmation of Clarmorgan's grants, stressing particularly the claim for the 500,000 arpents near the mouth of the Missouri River. Congress appears to have paid little heed to the repeated petitions for recognition of the claim, though the settlement of the region was retarded for a time because of its existence. The land was finally surveyed and opened to public entry and, because of its desirability, was soon taken up by settlers.

The federal commissioners again and again considered the question of the validity of the Clarmorgan grants. In their final report made August 25, 1835, they stated that "the great importance of this claim has induced the commissioners to make a consideration of every fact connected with it." And they concluded that this grant to Clarmorgan was never validated by the officers of the Spanish Government, and was abandoned by the claimant himself soon after it was obtained. Moreover, when the Surveyor-General of the United States made his surveys in the territory, he was not notified of the claim. "These circumstances induced the board to believe that the claimant abandoned his claim with the knowledge of the officers, to seek remuneration otherwise; or has been guilty of the neglect of his privileges under the grant. . . . The board, therefore, could not recommend this claim for confirmation." Despite this rejection, speculation in the claim continued.

A peculiar interest is attached to the proceedings with reference to the Clarmorgan Claim, because of the participation of Daniel Webster. In spite of the repeated refusals of Congress to confirm the grant and the final adverse decision of the Board of Land Commissioners, there was formed in 1837 the "Clarmorgan Land Association" to take over the title. Like other land-grabbing concerns, the association was not incorporated, but it had a president and board of directors composed of prominent individuals. William A. Bradley was president, the "Hon." D. Webster, Senator, and the "Hon." S. L. Southard, formerly governor of New Jersey, were directors. The "association" took over title to the claim from John Glenn and Charles M. Thurston, Baltimore capitalists, who purchased it from Pierre Chouteau. It issued 536 "shares," each share representing 1,000 arpents (850 acres).

The "Hon." D. Webster gave the "association" a favorable legal opinion of the validity of the Clarmorgan grant. Moreover, the deed of trust under which the title was held by the "association" was acknowledged before Chief Justice Taney of the United States Supreme Court. All this was published in two pamphlets entitled *Papers relating to the Clarmorgan Grant* and *The Clarmorgan Grant.*

The shares of the "association" were not conspicuously offered for sale at a fixed price. In small type on the bottom of the title page of each pamphlet, there is the bare statement:

The interest in this tract is divided into 536 parts, each part, therefore, will represent the interest of 1000 arpents and a fraction,

and further;

For opinion of the present and prospective value, see paper "A" and "B," the first by Dr. Linn, Senator from Missouri, and the other by Mr. Harrison, Representative.

In this modest way, shares in land companies were then advertised. To have boldly solicited purchasers would have condemned the proposition as a speculative land-jobbing scheme.

Success seems not to have attended the efforts of the Clarmorgan Land Association. Congress, however, continued to receive petitions to compensate the "heirs" and "assignees." Thus, in 1848, Henry Clarmorgan, "one of the legal representatives of James E. Clarmorgan" petitioned Congress. As late as 1851 another petition was received, and a Senate Committee upheld the right to compensation and "reported a bill."[5] But there is no record that a bill was passed for a settlement of the claim, nor was the matter ever carried into the courts.

Another "Spanish grant" which was destined for many years to fill the annals of Congress, was known as the "De Bastrop Claim." It is of considerable historical interest not only because of the persistency of its prosecution through several decades, but because it furnished the pretext of Aaron Burr's "western expedition," and also because it finally came into the possession of Stephen Girard, who philanthropically willed the land jointly to the cities of New Orleans and Philadelphia.

Philip Henry Neri, Baron de Bastrop, was one of the most picturesque and commanding figures associated with the early history of the Louisiana territory, and with Texas as well. He was a man of kindly, winning and magnetic personality, an adventurer who sought to undertake great things, but who met with misfortunes throughout his career. Although a native of Holland, he entered the service of Frederick the Great, becoming a member of his famous body-guard of giants. Frederick ennobled him with the title, "Baron de Bastrop," but Napoleon confiscated his property in 1795 and compelled him to flee to America. For a time he resided in Virginia, where he carried on trading with Europe, and where he claimed to have acquired a large landed estate at Harrison, W. Va. For some reason, possibly because of failure to pay his debts or because of passing out worthless bills of exchange, he took refuge in Louisiana. Here he became

[5] Senate Report #354, 32nd Congress, 1st Session.

friendly with the Spanish governor, Carondelet, with whom he made a contract in June, 1797, for a grant of about 850,000 acres, on the Wichita River.

Bastrop agreed to settle five hundred families on his grant. Before the families were settled, however, or before Bastrop had time to carry out his plans, the execution of the contract was suspended by the Spanish Government. He, therefore, never received a patent, though he had succeeded in mortgaging a part of the property to Abraham Morehouse, of Kentucky, whose financial assistance he had solicited in the deal.

Bastrop moved into Texas soon after the United States took possession of Louisiana. In consideration of a debt of $350,000 he deeded to Morehouse, on January 25, 1804, two-thirds of his pretended grant. The remaining third is reported to have been foreclosed in 1801, under a mortgage given in New Orleans. Or, perhaps, it was all mortgaged in New Orleans, and then sold by de Bastrop to Morehouse. The baron's reputation for honesty in business dealings was not of the best. Haden Edwards, of Nashville, Tenn., whose Texas deals in 1827 were opposed by Bastrop, accused the baron of having borrowed $400,000 of American merchants by giving fraudulent bills of exchange on Dutch bankers, and then fleeing to New Orleans. He may have been such a scoundrel, but he has two American towns still bearing his name—one located in Louisiana and one in Texas.

Just how Aaron Burr at one time obtained a part—reported as 400,000 acres—of de Bastrop's grant, is not entirely clear. It is fairly certain, however, that it came, either directly or indirectly, from Abraham Morehouse, since the latter, through his assignees or representatives, remained in "full and complete possession until 1846, and had even paid taxes thereon." Colonel Charles Lynch, of Lexington, who sold the property to Burr, either obtained it from Morehouse or was acting as Morehouse's agent.

"I have bought of Col. Lynch 400 M. acres of the tract called Bastrop's, lying on the Washita," Burr wrote a Mr. Latrobe in October 26, 1806. "The excellence of the soil and climate are established to my satisfaction by the report of impartial persons. I shall send on forty or fifty men this autumn to clear and build cabins. These men are to be paid in land, and to be found for one year in provisions. It is my intention to go there with several of my friends next winter. If you should incline to partake, and to join us, I will give you 10,000 acres. I want your society; I want your advice in the establishment about to be made. In short, you have become necessary to my settlement. As the winter is your leisure, I reason, if you should incline to go and view the country, you may do it at my expense."[6]

It is quite evident from this letter that Burr had at least intended making a settlement on the land, even though it may have been a mere pretext, or as a base for military operations against Mexico, or in order to separate Louisiana from the Union. Burr was certainly well acquainted with land jobbing and land development schemes. We have already seen that he was concerned in one way or another in several of the great New York land purchases. He was a close friend and political associate of Jonathan Dayton, through whose instrumentality it is quite likely that he obtained knowledge of the de Bastrop tract. Dayton and General Wilkinson, we have already noted, were partners in western land deals.

Though some fifty or sixty of Burr's men started to the Wichita River from Kentucky, nothing ever came of his purchase. It is quite probable that he made only the first payment of $5,000, and that, because of defaults in subsequent payments, the land reverted to the seller. Burr was interested enough, however, to draw a map of his "tract," which is now one of the prized possessions of the New York Public Library.

The connection of Bastrop's grant with Burr's conspiracy became generally known. As illustrative of the humor of the time, a political handbill issued during Burr's treason trial stated that "his quid Majesty [meaning Burr] was charged with the trifling crime of wishing to divide the Union and farm Baron Bastrop's grant." But the public was to hear more and more of the Bastrop grant long after the excitement of Burr's treasonable designs subsided. The Louisiana land commissioners refused to confirm the claim, and the petitions to Congress were equally unavailing.

[6] Wandell and Minnigerode, *Aaron Burr*, Vol. II, pp. 87, 88.

Finally, the case came to the United States Supreme Court for decision, and there received a "knock-out" blow.

It came before the highest tribunal in this way: Stephen Girard was requested by the French bankers, Laffitte & Co., to collect a debt owing to them by one Carrère of New Orleans. Carrère offered 12,500 arpents of land on the Wichita, in settlement. This Girard accepted and credited Laffitte & Co. with the amount of the debt. He was glad to do this as he, in partnership with Robert E. Griffith and James Lyle, had already secretly bought, in 1822, other tracts in the Bastrop grant from the trustees of the heirs

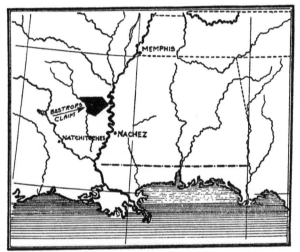

LOCATION OF THE DE BASTROP CLAIM, BASED UPON MAP IN THE
U. S. LAND OFFICE

of Abraham Morehouse. They bought four-tenths of the whole tract for $21,000. The purchasers divided it into 21 shares of $1,000 each, Girard taking 10 shares. Girard, however, later increased his participation, paying 15 to 21 cents per acre, until he had in all 200,370 acres. The estate he placed under care of Judge Henry Bye, of Monroe, La., under whose direction Girard spent $42,690 improving 30,000 acres.

Girard thought he was making a safe investment. He wrote Laffitte & Co., on June 7, 1829, "Congress has not done anything in it [i.e., the grant] nor do I expect they will do it for some time to come in consequence of the large tracts which they own themselves in that neighborhood, and are anxious to sell. I own myself upwards of 180,000 arpents of the aforesaid tract, and have commenced a settlement thereon, where I have upwards of 30 slaves, besides overseers, and feel perfectly tranquil as it respects the nature of the title."[7] But all Girard ever received from his investment of upwards of $100,000 was a few thousand dollars from cotton and produce grown on the land. At his death he willed one-third of the tract to New Orleans, and two-thirds to Philadelphia. The city of Philadelphia brought suit for a confirmation of the grant. The Supreme Court held that Bastrop had not perfected his title, and denied the validity of the grant. The city appealed to Congress in 1859, to override the decision of the court, but no action of this kind was ever taken.

Thus ended the famous de Bastrop Grant. The Maison-Rouge Claim which was of a similar character and was also comprised in the "Washita" lands likewise never received recognition.

Another interesting and long-drawn-out claim for lands obtained originally under Spanish grants also attracted public attention for a long period of years. This was known as the Myra Clark Gaines Case. It involved, among other property, valuable real estate within and adjacent to New Orleans.

Daniel Clark was an Irishman who settled in New Orleans in 1784, when a youth of seventeen. Here he became a Spanish subject, and waxed wealthy in trade and commerce. He was politically and socially prominent, and, of course, was rewarded with liberal grants of land. He also bought up the grants of others, including the worthless Maison Rouge Claim. Among his acquisitions was a tract now in the parish and city of New Orleans which had been originally granted to Elisha Winter in 1791. The right to this land was approved by the Board of Land Commissioners in 1812. The patent was engrossed and made ready for the President's signature, but, because of some objection, the Secretary of the Interior arrested the patent. Clark died soon after the grant was confirmed, but before its ratification by Congress. Before his death, he conveyed this New Orleans property together with all his other real estate to Joseph Belle-Chaise,

[7] John B. McMaster, *The Life and Times of Stephen Girard,* Vol. II, p. 409.

with the confidential understanding that they were to remain under his control for the use and benefit of Myra Davis.

But Myra Davis was Clark's own daughter—the fruit of a secret marriage with Madame Zubime De Granges. At least, the United States Supreme Court so decided in several suits brought before it. Her paternity was not discovered until Myra was a woman. Daniel Webster, her attorney, gave the court convincing arguments of his client's rights to the vast estate of the crafty New Orleans politician, Congressman, and personal friend of Aaron Burr. In 1867, when Myra Clark Gaines was already an elderly woman, the Supreme Court also confirmed her legal title to the immense acreage of real estate that had belonged to her father. Some of this was recovered through suits of ejectment, but much of the wealth thus obtained by the persistent litigant was swallowed up in court costs and legal fees.

As already noted, a valuable part of the estate consisted of 700 acres adjacent to New Orleans. This had been considered as national domain and was comprised in the grant of 200,000 acres awarded to General Lafayette by Congress in 1824. Lafayette needed money, and sold the land. Thus, innocent purchasers came into possession, and when the legal ownership was decided by the court, the property was worth many millions. It was thus up to Congress and the city of New Orleans to compensate Myra. This was finally done after Myra Clark Gaines ended her litigious career in 1885.

The Myra Clark Gaines case is remarkable for the extended period of the litigation. It began in 1834 and was not settled until almost a half century thereafter. In delivering an opinion in the case in 1860, United States Supreme Court Justice Wayne remarked, "When, hereafter some distinguished American lawyer shall retire from his practice, to write the history of this Country's jurisprudence, this case, will be registered by him as the most remarkable in the records of its courts."

Still another case involving valuable New Orleans property attracted nation-wide interest. This was the claim to the New Orleans beach front area by Edward Livingston, Andrew Jackson's friend and Secretary of State. Livingston was a member of the Scotch colonial clan of that name, which for several generations held, under manorial rights, most of the present Columbia County in New York. The family had a reputation for land grabbing, though Edward Livingston had become an attorney and was mayor of New York from 1801 to 1803. Thomas Jefferson then appointed him United States Attorney for the New York District. While acting in this capacity, he confessed to a shortage of public funds entrusted to him, due, as he claimed, to the dishonesty of subordinates during his illness. This led him to take refuge in New Orleans in February, 1804. The place then had a reputation as a resort for all those whose integrity had been questioned. In New Orleans, Livingston became a lawyer, politician and land jobber. Like Daniel Clark, he was friendly to Burr and became innocently involved in the latter's conspiracy. In this way he won the animosity of General James Wilkinson, then military commander of Louisiana territory,—and, naturally, Jefferson also became prejudiced against him.

Livingston had accepted, as a fee for legal services, some water front land in New Orleans. Much of it was the result of tidal action piling up the river silt. In 1808, the United States Government laid claim to this alluviation and ousted Livingston. To get the case before the country, Livingston sued Jefferson as a citizen for trespass. Jefferson then personally took part in the controversy. In 1812 he published his pamphlet of 103 pages entitled, *The Proceedings of the Government of the United States in maintaining the Public Right to the Beach of the Mississippi, etc.* In this tract Jefferson took the opportunity to deny the charge that he was induced to seize the land because of malice toward Livingston.

The next year Livingston answered Jefferson in an equally vigorous manner. Livingston's reply was a pamphlet of three hundred printed pages. Both documents attracted nation-wide interest among the legal fraternity and were reprinted in the current law journals. Livingston accused Jefferson of endeavoring to deprive him of his property, from the sale of which he expected to discharge his shortage to the government. The controversy went from Congress to the courts, and then back to Congress. It was not settled until after Livingston's death in 1836, when his widow received a large indemnity for the appropriated lands. In the meantime Jefferson and Livingston became reconciled. On April 4, 1824, just about one year before his death, Jefferson wrote Livingston a friendly letter congratulating him because the good people of New Orleans had restored him again to the "councils of our country," and expressing the sentiment that his election to Congress would bring aid "to the remains of our old school in Congress, in which your early labors had been so useful."[8]

.   .   .   .   .

Not all land speculations in the old Orleans country were founded on disputed Spanish and French grants. In this region, after the American occupation, town jobbing and land engrossment was as rampant as in the Northwest Territory. Towns were laid out along the rivers or at crossroads, and lot auctions were advertised widely by handbills, newspaper announcements and other means. Speculators also gambled on the probable or possible locations of state or territorial capitals or on county seats.

Thus, Stephen F. Austin, destined in after years to become the "Founder of Texas," took up some land at Little Rock, Ark., in the expectation that the capitol of the new territory would be located there. Others interested in lands elsewhere in the territory used their political influence to oppose Austin's selection. "Were it not for this man, Russell," Austin wrote his brother-in-law, in speaking of one of his opponents, "our unfortunate family might yet be enabled to secure small, but decent competence, for if his opposition were removed, there would be no difficulty in getting the seat of the Government moved to Little Rock."[9] Austin's speculation in Arkansas failed, but he was soon to take up another and more elaborate venture in Texas.

Stephen F. Austin and his family, through whom three generations of land speculators can be traced from Connecticut to Texas, also took part in the short but exciting "run-up" of what were commonly known as the "New Madrid Claims." In December, 1811, the populous settlement of New Madrid, Mo., was visited by a severe earthquake. It tore up the land and demolished

---

[8] Jefferson's *Works*, edited by H. A. Washington, Vol. VII, p. 342.
[9] *The Austin Papers*, Part I, p. 359.

buildings. The inhabitants fled from the region, and took refuge in the outlying sections. Though not required to do so by the Constitution or the statutes, Congress in 1815 passed a measure affording relief to the sufferers. The landowners were permitted to give up their holdings in the affected region and, in return, were granted certificates entitling them to locate an equal area on government land of their own choosing.

Thus, the door for wild speculation was opened. Before the earthquake sufferers actually knew that a law for their relief was passed, a host of speculators came down from St. Louis and started to buy up their "certificates." As the certificates gave a choice of location to the holders, they were eagerly sought after by town jobbers. The result of the rush was that of a total of 516 certificates finally issued, only 20 remained in the hands of the earthquake sufferers.

The private papers of the Austin family, then residing at Herculaneum, Mo., near St. Louis, furnish some interesting side lights on this speculation. The Austin family at the time were in financial difficulties. Their bank in St. Louis crashed and their Spanish "grant" to "Mine-a-Burton" had been rejected by the Board of Land Commissioners. Stephen Austin was, therefore, on the lookout to repair the family fortune. In his journal he noted, "I have this day given a power of attorney to W. M. O'Hara to purchase any amount of Madrid Claims and locate them for our joint account, and I have received a power from him to lay out towns and sell lots on the claims we hold jointly."[10]

Austin and his partner bought the claims at the rate of from $10 to $12 per acre, payable during five years. He was so confident of a profit from his purchases that he once wrote his brother-in-law he was determined to sell all his flour "and buy Madrid claims with the money, which I will locate on my improvement in the Long Prairie." "I advise you," he wrote again, "to return [from Alexandria, La.] as quick as possible with all the money you can and buy Madrid claims."

Imagine the disappointment to the speculators when William Wirt, United States Attorney-General, gave an opinion, in 1820,

[10] *The Austin Papers*, Part I, p. 337.

that the persons to whom the New Madrid warrants were issued had no right to transfer them, and that patents to the land claimed "must issue to the person who was the owner at the date of the Relief Act or his heirs." "The Act," he stated, "attaches no assignable quality to the charity, which it disposes. . . . It was not the intention of Congress to make these charities a subject of speculation. The law was passed to help the poor who have been rendered indigent by the visitation of God, not to enrich the speculator."[11]

This thunderbolt created consternation among the land jobbers of Missouri. They made political fodder of it. As late as 1825, the General Assembly of Missouri, on behalf of the New Madrid speculators, petitioned the "Honorable Senate and House of Representatives of Congress to take the case of the claimants— [meaning, of course, the speculators]—under consideration and grant unto them such relief as justice, expediency and good policy may dictate." Concerning the speculation in the certificates, the legislative petition frankly stated:

These certificates [for public land] have been sold and transferred for a valuable consideration from one person to another, until they have passed through the hands of many individuals of the most worthy and respectable class of our citizens, from the time that they were first issued. They were purchased with great eagerness (and when lands were high) by the new settlers coming into this state . . . who have located on them. Should the patents to the land be withheld, it would be the means of breaking up many families, and cause the ruin of many of our most worthy and respectable citizens.[12]

Congress, in its public land policy, has frequently shown sympathy for actual settlers, but that august body has never had a high regard for or given much consideration to petitions of land speculators. In the case of the New Madrid Claims, there was little reason to be sympathetic. An agent of the General Land Office, writing to his chief from St. Louis, November 22, 1823, expressed the view that the law for the relief of the earthquake sufferers "has given rise to more fraud and more downright

---

[11] *American State Papers*, "Public Lands," Vol. III, p. 494.
[12] *Ibid.*, Vol. IV, p. 155.

villany than any law ever passed by the Congress of the United States, and if the claims are not immediately decided upon will involve the citizens of Missouri in endless litigation and trouble."[13]

It does not appear that many great fortunes were founded on land speculation in the Middle West during the first decades of the acquisition of the Louisiana territory. The amount of un-occupied land was too vast. Congressman Adam Seybert, in his statistical survey of the United States, published in 1816, esti-mated that the government's acreage was then in excess of 400,-000,000 acres. Surveys were continuously being made by the General Land Office and settlement was being opened to lands further and further west of the Mississippi River.

In New Orleans and St. Louis and other parts of Louisiana and Missouri, it is true, there were a number of large land-owners, some of whom began their acquisitions during the old French and Spanish régimes. Others acquired their estates after the American occupation. Notable among these was John McDonogh, who at the time of his death in 1850 was the largest landowner in Louisiana. McDonogh was of Scotch-Irish stock. He was born in Baltimore, December 29, 1779, and upon coming of age he took up his residence in New Orleans. Here he be-came a merchant and shipper, but soon his chief occupation was buying up land. He bought a number of Spanish grants in West Florida, some of which were rejected on the ground of invalidity while others were allowed. His real estate in New Orleans alone was valued in 1850 at over $2,000,000 and in addition he owned a large part of both the cultivated and the unimproved area of the State of Louisiana.

McDonogh was a queer personality. He was self-centered, in-dustrious, patriotic, and, though somewhat miserly, liberal in his views. He was peculiarly shy of women and, therefore, never married. His three objects in life appear to have been: first, the ownership of real estate; second, the liberation of the slaves, and last, a system of free public education.

He accomplished the first with great success. He secretly

[13] *Ibid.*, p. 47.

MOSES AUSTIN
(From a portrait in the Jefferson Memorial Library, St. Louis, Missouri)

STEPHEN F. AUSTIN IN 1836
(From a portrait in the Capitol at Austin, Texas)

STEPHEN F. AUSTIN IN HUNTING COSTUME
(Reproduced from Eugene C. Barker's, *The Life of Stephen F. Austin*)

fostered slave emancipation (though he himself was a slave owner) and supported the work of the American Colonization Society; and he left almost all his fortune for the support of public schools in Baltimore and New Orleans. The McDonogh School, at McDonogh, Md., near Baltimore, is supported through his bequest; and New Orleans, for almost a century, has used the McDonogh fortune in aid of public education.

McDonogh never really speculated in land. Like John Jacob Astor, he bought to hold, and it is said of him, that he rarely offered property for sale. Yet he did little to improve his real estate holdings. He seems to have invested his money upon the principle that time and the increase of population in Louisiana would vastly augment the value of his property. Accordingly, at his death the buildings on his New Orleans property were exceedingly dilapidated. There was, moreover, in the neighborhood of New Orleans at that time a quantity of land belonging to his estate that was still covered by the original forest, though it could have been cut up into building sites and farms and sold at a handsome profit to him. Vincent Nolte, a German trader, who was conspicuous in New Orleans business affairs, thus describes McDonogh in his reminiscences: "McDonogh talked very little, and seldom mixed in general conversation, especially with ladies, whose society he avoided as much as possible. When he did open his lips, all that fell from them was the praise of certain lands he had just purchased, and this theme was inexhaustible. It was not in Louisiana alone that he carried out his system, but in the neighboring states, and he continued it for more than forty years."[14]

Congress gave Napoleon $15,000,000 for the Louisiana territory. It was a lot of money in those days. And there were many who doubted that the region was worth the price. Aside from the districts of New Orleans and St. Louis, and a few other scattered settlements along the Mississippi River, the whole domain was then a boundless wilderness infested by savage Indian tribes.

All this was changed within a few years after the American

[14] Vincent Nolte, *Fifty Years in Both Hemispheres*, p. 86.

flag was raised in New Orleans. The onslaught of speculators, lawyers, politicians, pioneers and adventurers converted much of the barren empire into thriving and progressive farms and communities. Hardly a decade after the United States came into its possession, the combined wealth of a few individual new-comers exceeded the whole purchase price paid by the national government. Much of this was acquired through prudent urban real estate speculation and town jobbing. Immigrants from the East, such as John McDonogh, Edward Livingston and John B. C. Lucas, waxed wealthy in their real estate deals. Lucas alone, notwithstanding his hatred of the "antedaters" and land thieves, acquired a large portion of the present city of St. Louis. A tract of land here which he originally purchased for about $700 was in a few decades worth several millions. Like Astor, Longworth and McDonogh, he did not sell but left his estate intact for his heirs. These founded the private banking house of Lucas & Co. for many years one of the leading concerns of its kind in the Middle West.

CHAPTER X

THE TEXAS FEVER

IT WAS mentioned in the previous chapter that the Austin family, which had resided for several decades in Missouri, became impoverished. Their mining property at Mine-a-Burton was taken away; their investment in bank shares was unfortunate, and their land speculations, including the New Madrid fiasco, were failures. Things became so bad that the father, Moses Austin, wrote his son-in-law on April 21, 1821, that he was "without a dollar to get his shirt washed."

In this situation, the old pioneer, who had trekked from Connecticut to western Virginia, and then into Spanish Upper Louisiana, again sought a new field to repair his fortunes. He was disgusted with the American régime. It had taken away his grant and otherwise treated him unfairly. "As I am ruined in this country" [i.e., United States], he wrote his son, "I found nothing I could do would bring back my property again, and to remain in a country, where I had enjoyed wealth, in a state of poverty, I could not submit to."

Off to a new country again! Hearing that the old Spanish system of granting land to colonizers or *empresarios* was still in vogue in Texas, where Spain continued to rule, he set out in October, 1820, for the southwest wilderness "with a gray horse, a mule, a slave boy, and fifty dollars in cash." On December 23, 1820, he arrived in Bexar, then the capital of the Mexican province of Texas and there presented his petition for a land grant. He received little encouragement, however, and was about to return dejected, when he happened to meet an old Louisiana acquaintance, none other than Baron de Bastrop, who, to escape his American creditors, had fled to the Spanish domains. De Bastrop, though poor, was politically powerful in the province, and he intervened in Austin's behalf. The petition was then received and approved, but it was necessary to await its confirmation by the Spanish governor. In the meantime, Austin set out on his return journey, and after much suffering and privation, reached home on March 23, 1821. He died shortly thereafter.

Stephen F. Austin, his eldest son, was then in New Orleans, looking for a means of livelihood. When he heard of the death of his father, and learned that the grant had been confirmed by the Spanish authorities, he decided to carry out the colonization scheme. The grant was for a tract of two hundred thousand acres on the Colorado River, about two hundred miles from Natchitoches, the American western border town. Three hundred families were to be settled on the grant, after which the unappropriated land was to go to the *empresario* as a premium. It was this premium land, together with the "commissions" charged settlers, that was the bait Austin sought.

But he was without funds. He needed financial backing. It came in the form of a partnership with Joseph H. Hawkins, who had befriended him in New Orleans. With money furnished by Hawkins for a half-interest in the venture, Austin bought and fitted out a small vessel and engaged a number of emigrants to sail to Texas.

In the meantime, he was advertising his proposed colony. Notices of it appeared in the newspapers of the Mississippi Valley, and aroused great interest. The news of the venture spread south, east and north. Applications from emigrants began to pour in. These came from Maryland, Virginia, Tennessee and more distant places. A large number came from the neighborhood of the Austin's old home. Stephen Austin and his brother-in-law advertised the project in the neighborhood, and as times were then hard in the lead mining districts of Missouri, many residents were eager to join. His old mother wrote him encouragingly that "the Texas fever was raging," and expressed a desire to join him "in Texas."

Before leaving to take up residence among his colonists, Austin issued an open letter describing the plan and purpose of the project. The colonists were to be given land in accordance with the size of their families and the number of their slaves, if any. They must settle on the land and make improvements thereon within a year. Colonists were also expected to provide themselves with arms, materials and stores. Each was to pay $12.50 per hundred acres, payable in instalments, in return for which his land was to be surveyed and his colonization papers drawn up.

It was this "commission fee" which brought criticism upon the project as a land-jobbing scheme. The public did not know then about the "premium lands," but there was considerable suspicion that there was a lure of this character to induce the promoters to carry out the venture. Moreover, it was generally known that one of the reasons why the Mexicans desired settlers in the wilds of Texas was to keep off the Comanches and other savage tribes which threatened the country. The Comanches were the arch enemies of the Spaniards, but were favorably inclined towards Americans. Yet, the settlers had to be continually prepared against Indian attacks, and occasionally were in Indian fights. Probably some of them liked this excitement.

Austin, from time to time, during the early period of colonization, issued public statements denying the speculation motive. In a public address to his colonists issued June 5, 1824, he vigorously defended himself against profiteering:

It has been objected . . . that I am making an immense fortune . . . a great Speculation out of the Settlers. Let us examine carefully this subject by the application of Arithmetical calculation to it, and see what appears to be the result. The Surveying Averaging One League with Another, and taking the bends of the Rivers and Oblong Leagues, will cost about $70 per League, which for 300 would be $21,000.—The Taxes, due to the Government . . . is $165.4 cash on each league, which for 300 (is) $49,600.4 making together $70,660.4 to which I made myself personally responsible . . . To raise this sum, I should have had claims on the settlers for $555 per League, which for 300 would have made $166,500 payable in property at a distant period and in small instalments, and that property received for double or treble what it would actually bring in Cash.[1]

[1] *The Austin Papers,* Part I, p. 820.

In another publication issued from San Felipe de Austin, the seat of his colony, in 1829, he again refuted the accusation of profiteering. "It is very evident," he wrote, "that mere speculation was not the object, as some have stated, for little would be left, at best, after paying the expense of surveying, the office fees, the commissioner's fees, the stamp paper, and defraying the necessary expense. . . . The object, therefore, must have been the general good of all, and not the private speculation of one individual."[2] Regarding the fee of $12.50 per hundred acres, he "considered that he was justly entitled to a remuneration for his labor and expense," and he ran the risk of "not saving something for himself, out of said funds." His father also had spent much time and money in the enterprise, "besides privations."

However, as Austin noted incidentally, the contracts of the colonists to pay the fee for their lands were rarely carried out, so he had to depend on the "premium lands," under the general colonization law of Mexico, to cover his costs.

Yet, in spite of these protestations, there is evidence that Austin originally undertook his colonization project as a speculative land venture. It was the "premium lands" allowed the *empresario* under the Mexican colonization law that he looked for as a profitable reward. In giving instructions to his surveyor in 1823, when the required 300 families had not yet arrived, Austin asked the favor that he "select some good places for me, say about six or eight league tracts. . . . It will be a real service to me if you can do this, and mark them, and let it be known that they are reserved . . . also to find the best place for a town . . . it will be valuable at some future day . . . also, I want a good situation on some creek where there is a body of good land suitable for a stock farm . . . also some good mill seats, if it can be had." And then, by way of justification for these preëmptions, he adds, "It is no more than just that I should have a pick as well as others. . . . I have too much public business to attend to, to do anything for myself and must call on friends to aid me."[3]

Austin's partner, Joseph H. Hawkins, who financed the first colony, certainly had a profit-making view of the venture. Because

[2] See *Laws, Orders and Contract on Colonization 1821-1829*, p. 7.
[3] *The Austin Papers*, Part I, p. 690.

of financial troubles coming a short time after he had advanced funds to Austin (estimated by his heirs at about $30,000), he was eager to cash in. On February 22, 1822, he wrote Austin, "After your 300 families are introduced, would it not be well to raise the price of your land? Perhaps my own necessities have led to this view. I am bent down almost to the ground. Of the $7,000 advanced for the *Providence* [a vessel], I have not one cent return. . . . If I could obtain through your efforts the means to pay my debts, I would join you immediately and spend my life plowing the soil." And by way of encouragement to Austin, he added: "You and your colony excite more interest than the assembled sages of the Nations."[4]

Austin's many difficulties at colonizing prevented him from raising cash to meet the needs of his impoverished patron and partner. The latter died in 1824, and his widow, and children, moved to Kentucky to "accept charity of her sister." Moreover, before Austin could settle his colony, Mexico threw off the Spanish yoke and he had to go to Mexico City, at Hawkins' expense, to get a new confirmation of his grant. He remained there many months, and made or renewed the acquaintance of General James Wilkinson who, like himself, was in Mexico City for the purpose of obtaining a domain in Texas. A number of other American and foreign land jobbers, under the guise of promoting colonization schemes, also were present or had agents in the Mexican capital. One of these was General Arthur G. Wavell, an Englishman who had been a general in the Chilean War of Independence, and who became an officer of the same rank in the Mexican forces. At this time, however, he was seeking land. He became very friendly with the young *empresario*, Stephen F. Austin, and entered into an agreement with him to share equally all lands granted to either, with the exception of the grant which Austin already held jointly with Hawkins.

Thus, Austin had in view more Texas lands. Wavell set out for England to form a company to obtain the necessary capital. While at sea, his vessel was waylaid by pirates. This delayed matters somewhat, but on his arrival in London he took up the proposition with several capitalists without success. He could do

4 *Ibid.,* p. 476.

nothing because Austin had no fee title to lands, so the effort to get British financial assistance failed.

When Austin returned to his colony from Mexico City in 1823, he became somewhat discouraged regarding the profitable outcome of his venture. His colony was a success. Indeed, a howling success, one might say, because the noise of it echoed far and wide and attracted land jobbers to Texas. He even took up a second grant on much the same terms as the first. But he was becoming disgusted because of the intrigues and manipulations of other scheming *empresarios* and gave more attention to Texas politics than to profit. On December 17, 1824, he wrote his sister in Missouri: "My lot is cast in the wilderness, but I am content. . . . I am fast losing the desire I once had to make a fortune."[5]

In another letter, written about six months later, he expressed the same sentiments: "My labors, although arduous, and in every way perplexing, will not yield me anything for some years, and then not the fortune which some have supposed. . . . I shall benefit others much more than myself in the proposition . . . but, thank heaven, I am not avaricious." And still later (December 12, 1825), he wrote prophetically: "The enterprise I undertook is better calculated to enrich those who come after me than to benefit myself."

Stephen F. Austin's younger brother, James Brown Austin, who was his associate, was even more eager for fortune. In 1827, when there were rumors that Mexico would sell Texas to the United States, he wrote his sister, enthusiastically: "Should this take place (which, in my opinion, will sooner or later) we would not take less than a half million dollars for our interest in this country."

Yet neither realized much in the way of pecuniary gain from the bothersome colonizing labors in founding the State of Texas. Though Stephen lived to see the wilderness, which he inhabited and did so much to populate, develop into an independent republic, he died in 1836 (at the age of 43), a disappointed and almost heartbroken hero. He was never able to pay his indebtedness to the heirs of his friend and patron, Joseph H. Hawkins, though he made strenuous efforts to do so—and offered them a full one-

⁵ *The Austin Papers*, Part I, p. 992.

half division of his "premium lands." In this he was fulfilling
the terms of his contract inasmuch as Hawkins was a joint partner in his first colonization enterprise. His own estate was never
of great value. On October 6, 1834, he wrote his brother-in-law
from a Mexican prison, where he had been incarcerated on a
charge of sedition: "It has been hinted to me more than once
that a sum of money, say $50,000, would stop my enemies and
set me at liberty. All I have on earth would not bring me that
sum, nor the half of it in cash, but it is reported here that I have
many millions in the banks of the United States."[6]

In his distress, he ordered the sale of all his land, and the
settlement of all his business. "Do what you can to save my
property," he wrote. "Every honest and good man in Texas will
assist you in so doing."

In his last years, when land grabbing became a pestilence in
Texas, Austin was greatly embittered against the speculators. His
own secretary, Samuel M. Williams, he thought, betrayed him
by entering into gigantic land deals. His defeat as the first president of Texas by Sam Houston is ascribed to the suspicion that
"Williams would use him to protect the speculators." Yet Austin
himself was chiefly responsible for "booming" Texas. He lighted
up the flames, and the conflagration spread beyond his powers to
control it. It was he who was responsible for "the Texas fever,"
which his mother informed him was raging in his old neighborhood in Missouri and which spread gradually through almost
every section of the United States.

From 1820 to 1840, the Texas wilderness was the lure of land-
hungry, adventurous Americans. From the swamps of Florida
and Louisiana to the hills of Kentucky and Ohio, the sign
"G.T.T." (gone to Texas) could be found on many cabin doors.
Some went to find new homes. But many went to get land grants,
and to form Texas land companies. English translations of the
Mexican colonization laws were published and freely distributed
throughout the United States in order to awaken public interest.
Pamphlets descriptive of Austin's colony and the favorable features of Texas lands were published in Baltimore, Philadelphia,

* *Mississippi Valley Historical Review,* Vol. XI, p. 123.

New York and elsewhere. "Shares" in Texas land associations, and "Texas land scrip," were offered to speculators in all parts of the country.

One of the earliest Texas land "companies" was organized in Nashville, Tenn., about 1821. This became known as the "Texas Association." Among its original stockholders were Sam Houston, Ira Ingram, John M. Robinson, Sterling C. Robertson and

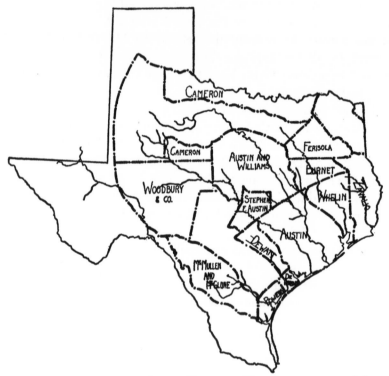

THE PRINCIPAL TEXAS GRANTS BASED ON MAP PUBLISHED IN 1836

a host of other Nashville business and professional men, some of whom later became prominent as Texans. On March 2, 1822, the Texas Association addressed to the new national government of Mexico a petition for a grant of land to settle a colony in Texas. It is quite probable that the news of Austin's venture led them into the speculation. Two of their members—Robert Leftwich and Andrew Erwin—were sent to Mexico to plead the cause of the "association" for a grant. They arrived about the time that

Austin was in the Mexican capital seeking a confirmation of his colonization contract. Erwin soon returned to take his seat in the Tennessee Legislature, but Leftwich continued to urge his grant before the Mexican officials. He received the aid and encouragement of Austin because the region selected by Leftwich was just west of his own colony, and therefore offered a buffer to the fierce Tahucano, Waco and Comanche tribes of Indians. Austin himself may have selected the site. The Leftwich grant and three others were confirmed by the Mexican authorities.

The members of the Texas Association were overjoyed. The seventy-four shareholders forthwith divided each share into eight parts, making 592 shares in all and distributed them among their particular friends in certificates, intending that each certificate should entitle a man to a league square of land. These certificates shortly rose in value "about 100 pr. ct. advance."[7]

A Dr. Felix Robertson, one of Nashville's "most worthy citizens," was engaged "to go out as agent and take with him a large connexion and many respectable friends." Robertson explored the grant, but returned the next year to Tennessee without accomplishing anything. Another agent, Benjamin F. Foster, was then sent "with three or four other young men" to begin a settlement, but they also returned.

By this time the Texas Association had spent $22,000 in the process of obtaining and endeavoring to settle their grant, and the shareholders were becoming much disheartened. Their "Texas scrip" fell to almost nothing in value. A new agent, Hosea H. League, who had been associated with Austin's colony, was then appointed. As the Texas Association's grant had been made directly to Leftwich, it was necessary for League to get a confirmation from the Mexican authorities for its reassignment. Austin agreed to take up this task. In addition to getting a reaffirmation, he had the grant enlarged to a point north of the present city of Waco. But still settlers did not come to the colony. As the time for settlement was limited, the whole affair was in danger of lapsing. League wrote anxiously to his "directors" to send on emigrants, but one of them replied that "the Texas fever seems to have died." "I have circulated your letters and endeav-

[7] *The Austin Papers,* Part II, p. 1186.

ored to procure a meeting," he wrote, "but could not succeed. Notwithstanding the apparent apathy, they [the directors] value highly their stock, and yet hope to realize fortunes from it, they know not how."

League became discouraged, joined Austin's colony, and turned over his agency of the Texas Association to Sterling C. Robertson. In the meantime, the Mexican authorities, becoming alarmed at the disaffection of the growing hordes of Anglo-Saxon colonists, issued an order prohibiting entrance into Texas without a passport, and forbidding new settlers, except those coming to colonies already established. This put a damper on the Texas Association's grant. Settlers that they had sent out from Nashville had to be placed in Austin's colony.

Austin was then accused of enticing settlers away from the Texas Association's lands. The outcome of the controversy was that Austin, in partnership with his secretary and associate, Samuel M. Williams, took over the rival association's rights. This was done, not by an assignment to Austin, but by a new contract with the Texas authorities by which Austin and his associates agreed to bring in colonists, and to receive "premium lands" as a reward. It is quite evident that the members of the Texas Association of Nashville had no intention of settling the land, either with their own families or with others, and consequently did nothing towards colonizing, but instead sold out their shares to speculators.

A companion colony to Austin's, and one with which he coöperated in harmony, was that of Green De Witt, like himself a Missourian. De Witt received his grant in 1825 for the purpose of settling four hundred families on the Guadalupe River, about seventy miles from Austin's location. It was, according to Austin, "a fine country, well watered, and very healthful."

Austin frequently gave advice and encouragement to De Witt and assisted him in getting settlers. He was very desirous of having other colonies around him, both as means of greater protection against the Indians and as a basis for creating higher land values. Moreover, the more Americans in Texas, the less mystery there would be regarding the situation of his own project. "I have seen some distressing tales told about us in some of the newspapers in the U. S.," he wrote his sister, October 28, 1825, "particularly in the *Arkansas Gazette*. That paper has always evinced most deadly hatred towards the settlement of this colony and its barking editor catches from every dirty buckskin scoundrel that has been driven from this country for his villainous acts . . . something to insert in his invaluable repository of truth and information to prevent any one from emigrating to this colony."

While Austin, De Witt and other honest *empresarios* were gradually filling eastern Texas with actual settlers, a gigantic Texas land speculation was set on foot in the United States. This took the name of the "Galveston Bay and Texas Land Company." It was organized in New York on October 16, 1830, to exploit the so-called "contracts" of Lorenzo de Zavala, Joseph Vehlein and David G. Burnett to settle colonists on land in southern Texas.

The region comprised the Galveston Bay district—a most desirable site—which Stephen F. Austin had endeavored in vain to obtain from the Mexican Government as early as 1824. The three grants were contiguous, but were made separately in 1824, 1828 and 1829. The contractors pooled their interests, and with the aid of some large New York and Boston capitalists, formed an association to take over their rights. Three members of the company, Anthony Day and George Curtis, of New York, and William H. Sumner, of Boston, were appointed trustees of the shareholders, to promote the fulfillment of the contracts and to obtain the approval of the Mexican Government.

The Board of Directors of the "company" comprised some of the leading figures of the period in New York's financial circles. Chief among these was Lynde Catlin, president of the Merchants Bank. Catlin, at this time, was thick with the Joseph brothers, brokers, who were reputed to be representatives of the Rothschilds. The Josephs, as we shall see in the following chapter, became involved in Samuel Swartwout's speculations. Swartwout was a favorite of President Jackson, who appointed him Collector of the Port of New York. He thus had plenty of money at his command —and in the end never accounted for over a million of government funds. It was probably through Swartwout that the Josephs assisted in financing Texas land deals along with many local New York real estate developments.

Though Samuel Swartwout's name does not appear among the directors of the Galveston Bay and Texas Land Company, he was undoubtedly interested in it in some way. His family had started trading in Texas, and carried on a shipping business between New York and Texas ports, and are reported to have "established a cotton plantation there."[8] His interest in Texas affairs continued until the financial crash of 1837, and he was one of the subscribers, along with J. L. and S. Josephs & Co., to the Texas Republic loan floated in New York in 1836. The loan was not a success, so Swartwout wrote Austin: "*Nothing but lands will satisfy the lenders,* and that at a low rate. I will not advise your government but I will repeat to you what I said to you and Wharton here . . . let your lands pay the expenses of the war, if you sell them only at five cents an acre."[9]

Another politician, who at this time became interested in Texas land gambles and who was identified with the Galveston Bay and Texas Land Company, was General John T. Mason of Michigan. Mason, a prominent attorney, became an agent as well as a large "scrip holder" of the association. He was sent to Mexico City as a lobbyist to obtain the consent of the government to the transfer of the grants from the original "contractors." The petition he presented made some rash promises. The "company" agreed to settle twelve hundred families before January 1, 1838. They had already made expenditures of $125,000 in the enterprise, and would do more, but they must have encouragement. The Mexican Government must allow settlers to come, and the settlers should be given title to lands.

All this fell flat. Nothing was then done by the company to take possession of the grants beyond sending out fifty-seven "emigrants," to prepare temporary quarters and to raise food for the European settlers they expected to bring over. Even these were not allowed to make a landing.

But, in the meantime, the promoters issued stock to themselves, and sold "Texas scrip" broadcast. In a pamphlet of more than

[8] Dyer, *Early History of Galveston*, p. 14.
[9] *Austin Papers*, Vol. III, p. 342.

seventy pages that they issued, it was subtly hinted that there was some uncertainty as to whether the "contractors" had the right to assign their grants, and that there was a Mexican law forbidding the admittance of American settlers.[10] These handicaps, however, were only temporary. They expected shortly to get a complete affirmation of the enterprise. But what of the hindrances! "Facilities of emigration to Texas, from the Atlantic States and Europe, deserve consideration. . . . The emigrant takes a passage at a trifling expense in some vessel bound for Texas. He is landed at Galveston. By means of navigable rivers, he can ascend with his family and effects in a keel or small boat to the very spot he has selected for his future residence." And as to excellence of climate and soil, why, Texas is incomparable!

Another pamphlet, issued about a year later, stated:

It is now the last of December, and our country is buried in ice and snow. A deep gloom is settled on the countenance of the poor, as well as on the face of Nature. General distress pervades our city . . . It is a consoling reflection that we are not bound to endure the rigors of a northern winter: that God, in mercy, has created more genial climates where there is neither snow or ice, where Nature, clad in her gayest livery always looks cheerful, and where the earth produces gratuitously for herds and flocks, and everything that can draw substance from its bosom. *Such a country is Texas.*[11]

With these perorations, they offered "Texas scrip" to speculators and settlers. Its price ranged from 5 to 10 cents an acre. It carried a "claim" to land, but gave no title to ownership. It was not even a preëmption right, except that in the event that applications from emigrants exceeded the number desired, the "contractors" then would select settlers from those among the scrip holders who desired to emigrate. But the scrip purchasers never had any idea of emigrating to Texas and becoming Mexican citizens. Nor did they wish to become backwoodsmen. They bought merely because of the raging Texas fever, and hoped to resell at a profit. As a writer in the *North American Review*, July, 1836, remarked: "Such is the cupidity and blindness, that any-

[10] *Address to the Reader of the Documents relating to the Galveston Bay and Texas Land Company, etc.*, New York, January, 1831, pp. 4-7.
[11] *Constitutions, etc., of the Galveston Bay and Texas Land Company*, p. 45.

thing that looks fair on paper, passes without scrutiny, for a land title in Texas."

Stephen Austin's cousins in New York kept him informed of the great Texas land gamble. On December 16, 1830, John P. Austin wrote him: "You will see from the enclosed that a company has been formed here to colonize the grant of Zavala, Vehlein and Burnett. . . . From what I can learn, it is the most extensive land company that was ever known in this or any other country, probably extending its interests throughout the United States; and its Board of Directors is composed of the most respectable and influential men among us, with the President of one of our banks at its head."[12]

And again, on March 15, 1831, Henry Austin wrote him: "The Galveston Bay Land Company is running wild in their operations. Selling land by hundreds of thousands of acres at five cents an acre. Sending out steam machinery for mills, boats, etc. I fear they will do much harm by calling attention of the Government too much to that quarter."[13]

The promoters of the Galveston Bay project endeavored to get Austin's coöperation, but he kept his hands clear of it. He would not use his influence with the Mexican Government to permit a settlement. Without his help, however, they continued to enlist the support of powerful agencies in Mexico. Mason resigned as lobbyist of the company in 1834, when he received on his own account, "an eleven league grant." Another was appointed in his place. Finally, in 1834, when the Mexican Government was in a turmoil, the company sent out a local agent, Jacob de Cordova, to Galveston, who began the sale of "scrip" on the spot, and who located the emigrants. These emigrants, however, were certainly not the eager "scrip" holders who rushed to buy Texas lands at 5 cents per acre. When the Panic of 1837 burst over the Galveston Bay and Texas Land Company, Lynde Catlin its president, was dead, the Josephs bankrupt, and Samuel Swartwout had absconded.

Though Stephen F. Austin did not openly oppose the deals of

[12] *The Austin Papers*, Part III, p. 556.
[13] *Ibid.*, p. 615.

the Galveston Bay and Texas Land Company, he expressed the opinion that such land speculations were injurious to Texas. In a statement to the Texan Senate, December 5, 1836, he remarked: "It is well known that nothing but injury to this country has resulted from the companies who have had colonization contracts in Texas. They have uniformly made it a matter of illegal speculation by selling 'land scrip' and deceiving the ignorant and credulous in foreign countries. The credit of Texas and all faith in any of our land titles has been destroyed in the United States by such proceedings, and immigration has been retarded rather than promoted by them."[14]

The grant of the Galveston Bay and Texas Land Company did not take in Galveston Island, on which the present city and port are located. A place of rattlesnakes, and a resort of pirates in the old days, the island remained vacant until 1836, when the Texas Legislature sold the eastern part of it to Colonel Michel B. Menard, an Indian trader residing at Nacogdoches, Texas, for $50,000. Menard then bought the remaining section from Juan M. Seguin, who had received it as a "grant" in 1832. The whole was then sold to the "Galveston City Company," an unincorporated association, of which Menard and associates took a two-thirds interest, and Robert Triplet the remaining third. The stock, comprising 1,000 shares, was then offered to the public at $1,500 per share, 10 per cent down and the residue in six, twelve and eighteen months in equal instalments.

The first public sale of town lots was made in 1838, although a few lots had been previously disposed of. Lots continued to be offered, and holders of shares of the association could surrender their certificates for lots at face value. The company was incorporated in 1841, and continued to have lots for sale until the end of the last century. As a town-jobbing scheme it was orderly and fair—coming, as it did, immediately after the boom period preceding the crisis of 1837.

The rapid colonization by American and foreign emigrants of Texas under the *empresario* or contract system, whereby, in re-

[14] Eugene C. Barker, *The Life of Stephen F. Austin*, p. 373.

turn for settling an area, the contractor was given a part of the land as a "commission," was destined to bring about the loss of the province to Mexico. Like the Virginian colonists of old, the American-Texans became dissatisfied with "Mexican tyranny," when this tyranny attempted to change the system of land settlement. As already noted, the Mexican Government, in 1830, wishing to put a curb on the heavy influx of undesirable non-Catholic immigrants, issued an order forbidding entrance of settlers into Texas, except when destined for colonies whose loyalty had been tested. This was treated by many as a "scrap of paper," much like the British proclamation of 1763 against western settlement.

Austin used his political influence to have the restriction law repealed. Following the repeal, the Texas authorities were more liberal than ever in distributing lands, and a whole host of land grabbers entered the province. The old *empresario* system was abandoned, and direct sale to speculators substituted. Thus, in 1830, James Bowie (whose name is immortalized by a weapon) went to Saltillo, the capital of the province, and returned with fifteen or sixteen "eleven league grants" which he purchased from Mexican citizens. General John T. Mason, Bowie's associate after he resigned as lobbyist for the Galveston Bay and Texas Land Company, proposed a "foreign" millionaire company to purchase twenty million acres on the eastern frontier for a mere pittance. He failed in this large proposition, but he did receive a grant of one hundred leagues—a principality in itself. Samuel M. Williams, Stephen F. Austin's confidential secretary, despite the disapproval of his chief, came in for splendid donations of land, receiving, in association with others, as much as four hundred leagues. Other similar grants were made to both Mexicans and Americans. The object of the sale of vast areas by the Texas authorities—then largely Anglo-Saxon—was for the purpose of replenishing the impoverished treasury of the province.

Naturally, this reckless policy in disposing of the soil aroused local indignation. The American settlers revolted. Austin was with them, for he became the bitter enemy of land grabbing. He broke with Samuel W. Williams, because the latter became actively concerned in land grabbing. "Speculation and honesty cannot contend in Texas," he wrote Williams, when reprimanding the latter for his gigantic land steals.

"General" Sam Houston was brought in from across the border to lead the revolting Texans to victory. Houston, who, as already noted, was one of the original members of the Texas Association, had deserted Nashville soon after the formation of the company and had taken up life among the Indians along the Texas border. He knew the frontier man's desire for free land, so when he was invited to Texas as military leader of the revolution, he promised all recruits liberal land grants. But he, like Austin, also detested the land jobbers, and among his first official acts after the liberation of Texas was the annulment of a number of the large grants or so-called purchases of Texas lands that had aroused the ire of the hardy Texas backwoodsmen.[15]

But the Texas fever continued even after independence. The financial interest of the American people in the soil of Texas, whether real or fictitious, was widely diffused, extending from Boston to New Orleans. It could not fail to create a sympathy and a bias for the new republic. Land grabbers continued to rush to Texas. Though many of the fraudulent grants were annulled after Texan independence was achieved, and land speculators were generally detested, the need of state funds and the desire for settlers caused a liberal sale of its large domain by the public authorities. Samuel Swartwout, so states Philip Hone in his diary, "had taken government money and engaged in wild speculations in Texas lands." As already noted, Swartwout had advised Stephen Austin that if a Texas loan was to succeed in New York, it must have Texas land "at a very low rate per acre as a reward to lenders." Texas, indeed, had then millions and millions of acres of unsettled lands, but in the dark days following the Panic of 1837, speculation was dormant, and the vast acres remained untouched. Mr. Louis Sterne, of Philadelphia, who, as a youth went to live in Texas in 1853, noted the cheapness of land at that time. "A large portion of the money which I earned," he writes, "I invested in land in Texas. I bought 40,000 acres, which cost me ten cents an acre. When the title was made out, the parties

[15] See *Texas Historical Association Quarterly Magazine*, Vol. X, pp. 76-95.

from whom I bought the land, on discovering that I was still a minor, declined to complete the title or refund the money." And he adds, mournfully, "The city of Fort Worth is now located on the site."[16]

The Government of Texas, subsequent to the separation from Mexico, continued to offer "premium lands" to colonizers, though on a more restricted scale than formerly. One of the grants made in 1844, under a contract of colonization, was a tract of 6,098 square miles, or 3,902,720 acres, on the Upper Trinity River, in the present Navarro County. This became known as the "Mercer Colony," the contract having been undertaken by General Charles Fenton Mercer, of Virginia. The contract was signed by "President" Sam Houston, just one day before he vetoed the bill passed by the Texas Congress repealing the colonization law under which the grant was made.

Mercer incorporated "the Texas Association" to take over the grant. This concern spent considerable money in surveys and in advertising. The contract with Texas required him to settle 500 families during the years 1845 to 1850 inclusive. Each family was to receive 640 acres, and for each family Mercer's association was to receive "ten premium sections." General Mercer made some attempt at European colonization. He organized the "German Emigration Company" for this purpose, but did not succeed in settling the grant within the required time. He subsequently sold out his interest to George Hancock, of Kentucky.

Hancock died in 1875, and his executors sued Texas for the "premium lands," claiming that more than the required number of settlers had been brought in. It was stated that 1256 families were settled under the terms of Mercer's contract and that the land commissioner of the state of Texas had issued patents for lands to these emigrants. The plea was denied by the United States courts and, incidentally, a judge remarked: "General Mercer, I know to be above suspicion, but he was a *speculator*, and unfortunately, for the interest of humanity, gentlemen of his order and class think it all laudable and right to make all they can out of governments."

[16] L. Sterne, *Seventy Years of an Active Life.*

Another large Texas land grant put over by "President" Sam Houston during the interval of Texas independence was made to W. S. Peters and associates in 1842. Peters, who had the support and assistance of General Mercer, likewise organized a land company—the Texas Emigration and Land Company—but with even less success in carrying out the terms of his contract. In fact, Peters' grant was rescinded by the Texas legislature in 1844, though Sam Houston tried to block the measure by his veto. The avenger of the Alamo was not altogether free from land grabbing influence.

After the "Texas fever" subsided, many other immense and valuable tracts could be bought there almost for a song. Today, individuals and corporations own vast domains. As cattle ranges or as goat farms, as cotton fields or oil pools, these lands have gained or lost value, creating at times millionaires and at times paupers. But none who ever entered Texas for fame and fortune has done so much for the Lone Star State, and has been rewarded so meagerly as the *empresario*, Stephen F. Austin, the Founder of Texas.

CHAPTER XI

GENERATING THE PANIC OF 1837

IN *Niles Register*, that renowned weekly compendium of American political and economic information during the first half of the nineteenth century, there appeared in the issue of May 9, 1835, the following headlines:

SPECULATION! SPECULATION!!
SPECULATION!!!

We offer a selection of articles as to what is going on in the way of speculation. Verily, the people are mad.

Then follows this excerpt from the *Baltimore Advocate*:

All the world is going mad after timber land, Canton stock, South Cove Company, and like speculations, which are taking the place of the lottery mania that used to possess the community. One gentleman, the other day, pocketed his $20,000 by selling out Canton [land] Company shares, and this, with the stories of sudden riches made by speculations in the timber lands of Maine, is making industrious people neglect their steady business.

Another excerpt deals with stock speculation in New York. It "became so extravagant that the Board of Brokers' room was not large enough for their accommodations. Some one suggested that there were excellent accommodations in the lunatic asylum."

Whether in land or in securities, the mania was having a tremendous sweep. It carried away all classes—workers, farmers, bankers and statesmen. Michael Chevalier, the French economist who visited America in 1834, was amazed by it. He compared it to Law's Mississippi Bubble. "Everybody is speculating," he wrote, "and everything has become an object of speculation. The most daring enterprises find encouragement; all projects find subscribers. From Maine to the Red River, the whole country is an immense *rue Quincampoix*. Thus far, every one has made money, as is always the case when speculation is in the ascendant. . . . The American, essentially practical in his views, will never speculate in tulips, even in New York, although the inhabitants have Dutch blood in their veins. The principal objects of speculation are those subjects which chiefly occupy the calculating minds of the Americans, that is to say, cotton, land, city and town lots, banks and railroads."[1]

Lands, city and town lots, indeed, took up a large share of the speculative ventures. It comprised the public domain, timber lands, suburban developments, city real estate and town-site jobbing.

. . . . .

As already noted, the national government had instituted a land policy which discouraged the sale of large tracts to speculators. Lands were sold through local land offices in small plots at public auction, or privately to settlers. The price was fixed, first at $2.00 per acre and later at $1.25 per acre. This system, combined with the steady offering of immense quantities of the public domain, checked for a time the purchase of public lands for resale at a profit. It was only when new "ranges" were surveyed and opened for settlement that speculators were offered opportunity of gainful purchases of favorable sites. But all sections in new ranges must first be offered at public auction, so that competitive bidding sometimes drove up the price of choice sites to a high level.

It was this competitive system of disposing of the national domain, during the first three decades after 1800 that placed a damper on speculation in public lands. In fact, "jobbing" in uncultivated lands was not a lucrative business. Many purchasers found it advantageous or necessary to forfeit their first payments and return their acquisitions to the government.

Moreover, the national land business became a national burden. As Andrew Jackson pointed out to Congress in December, 1833:

[1] Michael Chevalier, *Society, Manners and Politics in the United States* (1839), p. 305.

"From the origin of the land system down to the 30th September, 1832, the amount expended [on the public lands] . . . has been about $49,701,280, and the amount received from sales, deducting payment on accounts of roads, etc., about $38,386,624. The revenue arising from the public lands, therefore, has not been sufficient to meet the general charges on the Treasury, which have grown out of them, by about $11,314,656."[2]

But when, in the early thirties, the speculative fever raged throughout the country, and government lands, as well as other property, could be purchased with "rag money," created by "wildcat banks," then "the land office business" began in earnest. The auctions were attended by veritable mobs. They were scenes of great excitement. Premiums were paid for choice places near the auctioneers, and bribery and corruption in the process of receiving and registering bids were common.

The irregularities in bidding at public land auctions were numerous, and space does not permit details. A common form of fraud was a secret agreement among the bidders to withhold offers for a selected section. Another was to bid up choice sites to abnormally high figures to scare away competitors. The effect of this, wrote an official investigator, in 1834, "would be to enable one man to monopolize the entire sales, and bid off the lands at whatever price he might put down competition; of course, the people attending the sales will have dispersed in a few days after the sales have been closed. They have no idea but that all things in regard to the transaction are fair. A short time after the sales, the person thus purchasing by agreement, forfeits the land; the whole affair is cancelled; the receipts destroyed, and the land becomes subject to entry in the usual manner, and this being known only to a few privileged individuals, of course they can then enter the land at the minimum price."[3]

Another kind of public land fraud and corruption was in relation to preëmption claims. Certificates entitling certain individuals, such as soldiers, settlers and Indians, to the preëmption or selection of lands in a location were commonly called "floats," because anyone claiming land under a preëmption right was said to have

[2] *Messages and Papers of the Presidents*, Vol. III, p. 63.
[3] *American State Papers*, Public Lands, Vol. VII, p. 524.

a "floating" claim to it. Such claimants, of course, were required to be bona fide cultivators and occupiers under the Preëmption Act of 1834. Many individuals taking up land with "floats," however, were merely "fake" settlers, and soon sold out to speculators. Whole towns were planned or built up on these "floats." In 1836, Benjamin F. Linton, the United States District Attorney of Western Louisiana, reported that there was in his district one "notorious speculator in floats" whom, however, he does not name. But we may surmise that it might have been John McDonogh, whose land acquisitions in this section have already been referred to.

Because of the great excitement attending the national land office sales during the speculation fever just prior to the 1837 financial panic, "doing a land office business" became a common expression for great commercial activity and merchandising success. The tremendous increase in the public land sales indicates the extent of the virulent speculation fever. In 1825, receipts from public land sales amounted to but $1,216,090. They rose to $2,329,356 in 1830, then continued as follows:

YEARS	ACRES SOLD	RECEIPTS
1831	2,777,857	$3,557,024
1832	2,462,342	3,115,376
1833	3,856,227	4,972,285
1834	4,658,219	6,099,981
1835	12,564,479	15,999,804
1836	20,074,871	25,167,833
1837	5,601,103	7,007,523

Thus, the big bulge occurred in 1835 and 1836. President Jackson noted it anxiously. He appeared not pleased with the heavy receipts from land sales, for he and his cabinet soon realized that the land was paid for in "rag money," i.e., in bank notes that were in many cases irredeemable and worthless. Accordingly, he issued on July 11, 1836, his celebrated "Specie Circular." It simply ordered that the land offices should accept only gold or silver or "land scrip" (i.e., soldiers' warrants) in payment for public lands.

What a foolish idea, protested the land grabbers! Pay with

specie? Who has specie? Not even the banks kept it in their tills. Surely, those who wished to speculate in government lands could not pay in specie, when there was none circulating in the country.

Thus, the excitement of speculation in public lands abated. The land sales fell off. The land offices were deserted. When the crash came in the ensuing year, the Treasury found that instead of "cash" for lands already sold, the "old cat" was returned to its doorstep. Millions of acres reverted to the government because of default in required payments. Congress, by a large majority, passed a bill annulling the "Specie Circular," but Jackson was firm in his "hard cash" policy. He permitted Congress to adjourn without signing the bill.

Daniel Webster took a keen interest in public land speculation both for political and for personal reasons. As a true statesman, he traced its cause and effect. The government itself was partly responsible, he said, because it did not raise the price of its lands when everything else was going up in price. But, in his estimation, land speculation is not necessarily an evil. With characteristic oratory, he told the Senate, May 31, 1836:

> In everything else, prices have run up; but here [i.e., public land], price is chained down by statute. Goods, products of all kinds, and indeed all other lands may rise, and many of them have risen, some twenty-five and some forty and fifty per cent; but government lands remain at $1.25 per acre; and vast portions of this land are equal, in natural fertility, to any part of the globe . . . The government land, therefore, at the present prices, and at the present moment, is the cheapest safe object of investment. The sagacity of capital has found this out, and it grasps the opportunity. Purchase, it is true, has gone ahead of emigration; but emigration follows it, in near pursuit, and spreads its thousands and its tens of thousands close on the heels of the surveyor and the land-hunter . . . Nor are we to overlook, in this survey of the causes of the increase in the sales of public lands, the effects, almost magically, of the great and beneficent agent of prosperity, wealth and power, *internal improvement*.[4]

The optimism of the Senator from Massachusetts was not without personal bias. That he was concerned in western land

---

[4] *The Works of Daniel Webster*, Vol. IV, p. 262.

deals is not so well known as his other personal affairs, for his biographers have passed over it, possibly as a "shady," if not a purely private matter. He was accused by Senator Hayne of South Carolina, and other southern statesmen of seeking to hinder the westward movement for the sake of maintaining eastern political influence, and his "Reply" to this brought forth the greatest bit of oratory and the soundest exposition of the Federal Union that ever echoed through the halls of the Capitol. Webster did not oppose the rapid development of the West, even though it brought land speculation and fraud in its wake. He saw in it a fertile field for Yankee investment, and pointed out that with railroads, canals and other public improvements, they, in the East, "could almost see the smoke of the settlers' cabins."

Webster's western land purchases were in Illinois and Wisconsin. In partnership with Caleb Cushing, a Massachusetts attorney and politician, who furnished the funds, he acquired from John S. Haight, a tract of 600 acres near Rock Island, Ill., "on the branches of the Rock River, which (he thought) was the choice spot in that country." Haight had bought it at a government land auction, but was unable to pay for it in cash, following the announcement of the "Specie Circular." It was valued at five dollars an acre, which Webster informed Cushing was "probably not too high." "I have not the least doubt that the investment will prove an advantageous one," he wrote enthusiastically. Yet, after holding it until 1850, he could not sell at a profit, and offered it to Cushing in settlement of a debt. Cushing did not accept at once, and in the meantime, the land was sold to cover a tax bill of $300. The purchaser then offered the right to redeem it for $400, but Cushing, after investigation, found that it was not worth the price. Such were the fleeting and changeable land values in those days.

Webster's investment in public lands is reported to have been as much as $60,000, but this is doubtful. Webster probably never had that much money. He certainly did not have the $3,000 cash to meet the bill of exchange which Haight drew on him for the purchase price, and requested that Cushing advance the amount. However, had the land been held, its value would more than cover this sum, as the property is now a part of the town site of Rock Island.[5]

Henry Clay, like Webster, feared no evil from land grabbing. In defending the national land policy in the Senate in 1832, he pointed out that "To supply the constantly increasing demand [for land], the policy has been highly liberal. . . . Large tracts, far surpassing the demands of purchasers, in every climate and situation, are brought into the market at moderate prices. . . . For $50 any poor man may purchase forty acres of first rate land."[6]

"Yet," he exclaimed, in referring to the land speculators, "a friend of mine . . . bought in Illinois last fall about two thousand acres of refuse land at the minimum price, for which he has lately refused $6.00 per acre. An officer of this body [the Senate] now in my eye purchased a small tract of 160 acres at second or third hand, entered a few years ago, and which is now estimated at $1,950. *It is a business—a very profitable business,* at which fortunes are made in the new States, to purchase these refuse lands, and, without improving them, to sell at large advances."[7]

Aside from the speculation in public lands, which was killed by the "Specie Circular" (much to the satisfaction of Andrew Jackson, who wanted, as Webster remarked to Cushing, "to keep money out of the Treasury"), there was a rampant rage for all sorts of landed property in all parts of the country. Perhaps there is no better description of the mania of the time than that given by Michael Chevalier:

The amateurs in the land at the north dispute with each other the acquisition of the valuable timberlands of that region; at the southern extremity, the Mississippi swamps and the Alabama and the Red River cotton lands are the subject of competition, and in the West, the corn fields and pastures of Illinois and Michigan. The unparalleled growth of some new towns has turned the heads of the nation, and there is a general rush upon all points advantageously situated; as if, before ten years, three or four Londons, as many

[5] See Claude F. Feuss, *Caleb Cushing,* Vol. I, pp. 230-232, and Vol. II, pp. 85-88.
[6] Colton, *et al., The Works of Henry Clay,* Vol. V, p. 429.
[7] *Ibid.,* p. 503. Italics are mine.—A. M. S.

Parises, and a dozen Liverpools were about to display their streets and edifices . . . In New York, building lots have been sold sufficient for a population of two million souls, and at New Orleans, for at least a million. Pestilential marshes and naked precipices of rock have been bought and sold for this purpose. In Louisiana, the quagmires, the bottomless haunts of alligators, the lakes and cypress-swamps, with ten feet of water or slime, and in the North, the bed of the Hudson, with 20, 30 or 50 feet of water, have found numerous purchasers.[8]

Though there may be some exaggeration in all this, there can be no doubt that in the five years just prior to the 1837 panic, the fever of land speculation was the most virulent the United States has ever experienced. As Chevalier noted, it was not confined to any class of real estate. Wild lands, swamp lands, improved agricultural lands, town lots and city real estate were all included.

. . . . .

One of the conspicuous fields of speculation at this time was in Maine timber lands. Reference has already been made to the post-Revolutionary gamble in Maine lands.[9] Massachusetts owned this territory, and because of its impoverishment during the War for Independence, was desirous of realizing cash for it. Accordingly, the Maine lands were put on the market, in competition with the western New York domain and the Ohio lands. "Eastern Lands for Sale," was placarded throughout the state. Notwithstanding the sales efforts, however, less than 5,000,000 of the 17,000,000 acres of unoccupied lands in the "Maine District" were disposed of up to 1821. Considerable portions, moreover, were donated for charitable and educational purposes. Altogether, Massachusetts received only about $800,000 net for its sales.

When Maine was incorporated into the Union as a separate state in 1819, an arrangement was made with Massachusetts whereby the unappropriated areas were to be gradually sold, and the net proceeds divided on a "fifty-fifty" basis between the two commonwealths. But the property was regarded as of such doubtful value that Massachusetts made a proposal to sell her share

[8] Chevalier, *op. cit.,* pp. 305, 306.
[9] See Chapter II, p. 39.

for $150,000, payable in 40 years at 5 per cent. Maine accepted, but the Upper House of the Old Colony failed to ratify the agreement.

It will be recalled that one of the large speculative purchases in the Maine district was made jointly by General Henry Knox and William Duer.[10] Knox, who had become President Washington's first Secretary of War, wished to conceal his land-jobbing activities, and he feared the exposure that would result because of his inability to make the required payments. He therefore gladly dumped the tract on William Bingham of Philadelphia, and it thus became known as "Bingham's Million Acres."

Bingham died in 1806, and his estate was divided among his five sons-in-law. These desired hard cash rather than wild acres burdened with annual tax assessments, so they appointed agents to settle the lands. Actual settlements were required before patents could be granted. The agents were selected from both political parties, in order to get "extensions" of the period in which settlers were to be placed on the land, as well as other favors from the State of Massachusetts. One of these agents was the well-known statesman, General Harrison Gray Otis. With all his skill and political influence, General Otis could not settle enough land to pay the taxes. Otis' successor, General William King, experienced so much worry from the estate that he was driven to insanity and was placed under a guardian. After spending the cash of the "heirs" in building roads and making other improvements, the agents, one after another, gave up their jobs.[11]

By using methods bordering on bribery the heirs of Bingham finally obtained a patent for the land from Massachusetts. They then proceeded to offer both the timber and the lands for sale. In September, 1828, whole "townships" were offered at auction, at a minimum price of 75 cents an acre. This move started the wild speculation in Maine timber lands. Some townships were bought at the minimum price one day, and resold at an advance of 25 per cent the next. Purchasers flocked from Boston and elsewhere to bid for townships. Rumors were spread that there would be a shortage of timber. Maine woodlands, with their fine growth of merchantable timber, would, therefore, become extremely valuable.

"The wildest speculation that ever prevailed in any part of the United States," says Hugh McCulloch, a native son of Maine, "was in the timber lands of Maine. In 1832, or about that time, it became known to the people of Massachusetts that a good deal of money was being made by a few investors in Maine timber lands. . . . These lands were offered for sale . . . at very low prices, and those who bought early and judiciously did make what were considered large fortunes. . . . The desire became so strong, and the excitement so great, that a courier line was established between Boston and Bangor, by which orders to buy, and subsequently to sell, were rapidly transmitted, and for months little was talked about but Maine lands. Brokers offices were opened in Bangor, which were crowded from morning till night, and frequently far into the night, by buyers and sellers. Not one in fifty knew anything about the lands he was buying, nor did he care to know so long as he could sell at a profit. . . . The same lands were sold over and over again until lands which had been bought for a few cents were sold for half as many dollars. As is always the case when speculation is rampant, and inexperienced men become speculators, dishonesty was in the ascendant. . . . It happened, strangely enough, that the largest losers in the Maine land speculation were prudent men, who kept aloof from it until it had reached its highest point, and the tide was ready to turn."[12]

The tide did turn, and thousands of speculators were defrauded or ruined. The craze spread beyond the limits of New England. An issue of the *Baltimore Advocate*, in May, 1835, stated that "The timber lands are all the go in this market, and even the worthy Catholic Bishop, it is understood, is dipping in, having purchased a whole township which he is selling to the Irish to make a Catholic State somewhere in the woods of Maine."[13]

Fraud and corruption accompanied the excitement. Tracts were sold that did not exist. "In the interest of large holders, maps were prepared, on which lands were represented as lying upon water courses which were scores of miles away from them." Notes

[12] Hugh McCulloch, *Men and Measures of Half a Century*, pp. 214-216.
[13] *Niles Register*, May 9, 1835, p. 168.

were given and endorsed without the least expectation of making payment. In one of the lawsuits arising out of these Maine land transactions, the defendants denied the validity of a debt on the ground that "eastern land speculation in general was so tainted with fraud, deception, cheating, lying and swindling, that the very term had become proverbial for these vices." And on this ground the jury failed to return a verdict.[14]

One of the Boston capitalists caught in the trap of the Maine speculation was Josiah Perham, the original promoter of the Northern Pacific Railroad. Perham thought he had amassed a fortune in the speculation, but he held on to his purchases until the crash came. Then he lost all. With characteristic optimism, that later developed his ideas for promoting transcontinental transportation through free land grants, he set about to regain wealth and pay off his creditors. This he did in time, through his profits as a Boston wool merchant. And in this way he acquired the confidence and support of those who joined in his railroad enterprises.[15]

.   .   .   .   .

While New Englanders were running wildly after Maine timber lands, they were equally concerned in the western land fever. As in previous boom periods, a vast number of land companies were organized to foster speculation. One of the boldest enterprises of this nature was the "American Land Company." This was organized in 1835 by prominent New York capitalists, though it included in its management several Bostonians. Among its chief promoters was Charles Butler, of Geneva, N. Y. It will be recalled that Butler originated the plan whereby the western New York farmers who purchased from the Holland Land Company on credit could obtain deeds to their properties by mortgaging them, and applying the proceeds to pay up their debts due the land company. He thus became involved in the land business, and casting his eyes westward to the boundless unoccupied acres, was lured into the current land gambles.

Butler's optimism regarding western land opportunities was intensified by a journey to this region in 1833, "attended with great

---

[14] *Hunt's Merchants Magazine,* Vol. 2, p. 496.
[15] See Chapter XIV, p. 295.

DANIEL WEBSTER, WHOSE INTEREST IN WESTERN LANDS WAS BOTH PRIVATE
AND PUBLIC

(From a portrait by J. Ames)

CHICAGO IN 1831
(From an old print)

privations, fatigue, exposure, and difficulty." He returned to New York thoroughly infected with the "Michigan fever." His interest in the West was to continue long after the American Land Company faded into nothingness, for in the years following the Panic of 1837 he, in conjunction with his brother-in-law, William B. Ogden, was active as a promoter of western railroads and other large enterprises.

Butler had associated with him other prominent eastern capitalists. This is indicated in the list of trustees and directors of the American Land Company. They included Erastus Corning, wealthy merchant of Albany and one of the promoters of the Mohawk and Hudson Railroad (the first to furnish a journey on rails in America), Campbell Bushnell, a prominent attorney, and John B. Jones and John W. Sullivan of Boston. The largest shareholders, in addition to the trustees, were William B. Ogden, Herman Le Roy, wealthy New York banker, J. L. & S. Josephs & Co., the brokers already referred to as interested in Texas land gambles, and J. D. Beers and Co., another prominent New York brokerage house. The first annual report of the company lists over 150 shareholders, among whom was the celebrated American historian, William H. Prescott. He was down for twenty shares.

The authorized capital of the American Land Company was $1,000,000—quite a large sum in those days. The shares were $100 par value. About 80 per cent of this capital was subscribed in less than a year, though the company received only about $500,000, the unpaid subscriptions being represented by "accepted drafts from agents for purchase of lands." The purpose of organization is stated thus:

The specific object of this Association is the investment and employment of its capital in the purchase of land situated in the United States, particularly in the western states and territories.

It seems, however, that the main purpose was the "purchase of cotton lands in the southwestern states, at or near the Government price," and that this "was the leading motive of a large number of subscribers." Anyhow, about 70 per cent of the company's capital was applied to this purpose in the first year. Local agents were appointed to make purchases, and William B. Ogden (descendant of the "Jersey Ogdens"), destined to become Chicago's leading citizen and capitalist, was appointed "general agent to look after local agents."

No time was lost in making purchases. In less than a year, the company not only exhausted its cash capital, but went heavily into debt. It did not buy outright, but "under contract sales." Thus, it contracted to buy for $400,000 cotton lands in Mississippi, "lately occupied by the Chickasaw Indians" and title was to be obtained "directly from the Indians," but "to be approved by the President." They also made a similar purchase for $250,000 of cotton lands in Arkansas. If the agents resold at a satisfactory price they were to get one-eighth of the profit. Lands were also purchased in Florida on the St. Johns River at $5 per acre. But the most significant purchases were made in town lots in Chicago, Toledo and elsewhere.

These additional investments in the northern field were believed to be equally as safe as those made in the southwest, since "they have been made through the agency of judicious and prudent men." The company's directors reported that "with the facts which are daily transpiring before our eyes in that portion of the United States, we have the surest guaranty that good land, well located, will continue a safe investment. The foreign and domestic emigration to the west is daily increasing—and in a short time, we shall see as dense a population covering the northern part of Ohio, Indiana and Illinois, as we now find in the western part of New York."[16]

It is quite evident that the American Land Company did a general land-jobbing business, so prevalent at this period. Though in its first annual report, there is the explicit statement that it was not the purpose "to speculate in urban lands," it bought and resold to James L. Curtis and Silas M. Stilwell (two heavy real estate "plungers" and town jobbers of the time), a tract in the "boom town" of Toledo. It gave $50,000 for this land, payable in one year, and resold it at $80,000, but payable in ten annual instalments at 7 per cent interest. The profit, of course, was on paper—as the New Yorkers never completed the required pay-

[16] *The Annual Report of the Trustees of the American Land Company* (1836), p. 25.

ments, though "the purchasers were said to be highly responsible." Yet, Stilwell, who was prominent in New York politics, had to refuse an offer in 1839 from President William Henry Harrison of a cabinet appointment, because the loss of his fortune in the 1837 Panic "did not permit him to bear the expense."[17]

A similar deal in Chicago real estate was made on the same basis. On an investment of $18,803 the company made within a few months a paper profit of $12,837. But they allowed the purchasers five years to complete payments. As will be shown, hardly a real estate sale on credit in Chicago at this time was consummated by the purchaser meeting all the required payments.

Probably the most spectacular purchase of the American Land Company was 2,525 acres in Orleans County of New York, for which it paid $22 per acre; meeting one-half the purchase price in cash. On this, they expected shortly to make an enormous profit. "The lowest estimate which is put upon it by judicious men is $35 per acre. . . . The trustees [of the company] have reason to believe that, after carrying out their plan of improvements, the property will yield a rent equal at least to the interest on the capital invested, and that within five years it may be sold at $50 per acre."[18] In five years, however, land and real estate in New York State were as difficult to sell as snowballs to the Eskimos.

The American Land Company made purchases through appointed local agents. Under this plan "the investing agent agrees to take entire care and charge of purchased property until sold." When sold, the agent is to get a percentage of the clear net profit; this percentage to be from one-fourth to one-third of the net gain. "If there are no net profits, then the Agent gets nothing for his services." Of course, "the trustees" in common with shareholders assumed the risk of investment, and "risk [they stated] is inseparable from enterprise." The company, moreover, did not propose to hold property. Its aim was to "sell quickly at a fair profit."

The foregoing details regarding the American Land Company's operations are given largely with a view to showing the methods, aims and principles of the land-jobbing concerns of the time.

[17] See Appleton's *Cyclopedia of American Biography*, Vol. V, p. 690.
[18] *Ibid.*, p. 22.

Numerous other and smaller companies operated in the same way. Nor did they all originate on American soil. Several were owned and financed by British and Scotch capitalists. George Smith, who later became a multimillionaire—not, however, through land speculation, but by issuing his "circulating notes"—came from Scotland to Chicago "as a prospector" in 1834. Greatly impressed with the immense possibilities of gain the country offered, he organized the "Scottish Illinois Land Investment Company" and acted as its agent. He also took on other agencies for both land companies and private bankers. Though he, personally, became a large real estate owner in Chicago and other sections of Illinois— probably through purchases made after the debacle in 1837—he was attracted to banking and note shaving, and during his stay in America until 1857, he waxed extremely wealthy. He is reported to have returned to Scotland with enough "dollars" to purchase a kingdom.[19] But his Scottish Illinois Land Investment Company appears to have "gone by the boards."

.   .   .   .   .

Of all the various fields of speculation just previous to the Panic of 1837, none were more flagrantly exploited than urban real estate and town jobbing. Due to currency inflation, real estate, of course, rose in value with all other forms of wealth and immense fortunes were being made in real estate transactions. This was to be expected in a period of buoyant optimism created by constantly expanding currency; a craze for public improvements; and a régime of liberal and cheap credit. But the amazing manner in which the whole explored territory of the United States was converted into "paper" cities, towns, ports and suburbs, during the period between 1830 and 1837, is unparalleled in history. There was hardly a county (East or West, North or South), in which new towns and new settlements were not laid out.

Speculative furor was most pronounced in the Northwest. Here raged the "Michigan fever," as land speculation in this territory was then called. All along the Ohio, Missouri and Mississippi rivers; all along the Great Lakes from Buffalo to Superior, and even beyond, were new towns or plans for new towns. Almost every nook, every bay on Lake Erie and Lake Michigan was

[19] Huston and Russell, *Banking in Illinois*, p. 107.

taken up for a town site. Town lots and more town lots! This was the commonest form of merchandise then in the country. As an English traveler remarked, "towns would be advertised and trumpeted forth in the moon" if there was a chance of selling lots.[20]

Here again, Hugh McCulloch, who in 1833 had removed from New England to Indiana, offers us a good contemporary description: "Hundreds of tracts," he wrote in 1890, "were laid off in town lots where the original forests were still standing. What took place under my own observation seems now to be too absurd to be real. On the Maumee River, from its mouth on Lake Erie, there were for miles a succession of towns; some of them like Maumee City, Perrysburg, Manhattan, and Toledo were realities, but most of them existed on paper only. In the spring of 1836, a young man whom I met in Maumee City, said to me that he had made a great deal of money in a few months buying and selling lots. "Maumee City," says he, "lies, as you know, at the foot of the Rapids; and is destined to be one of the great cities of the West; property is rising rapidly in value and I am buying and selling every day."[21]

When McCulloch asked him, "How did you raise the money to commence with?" he replied: "Oh, very little money is required in this business. I pay when I buy, and I require, when I sell a lot, a few dollars to bind the bargain; but nearly everything is done on credit.

McCulloch thus describes the system of the wild speculation in Toledo, in 1836, which may be taken as typical:

On my way from New York to Fort Wayne . . . I stopped overnight at a hotel in Toledo. After dinner, I noticed that there was a gathering of gentlemen in the parlor, and in the course of the evening, I was waited upon by one whom I knew, and invited to join it. "Our rule," he said, "is to admit no one to these meetings who is not worth $100,000. As you are a banker, you must be worth at least that" . . . I accepted the invitation. The company consisted of politicians, scholars, writers and one or two of them, authors of considerable renown, but not one was there whom I recognized as being

[20] William Oliver, *Eight Months in Illinois*, p. 41.
[21] Hugh McCulloch, *Addresses, Speeches, and Letters upon Various Subjects*, p. 384.

engaged in regular business pursuits. It was a sort of private exchange, at which the members made themselves rich by buying and selling to each other lands and town lots. There was at times a good deal of excitement, much like that which is witnessed in the New York Stock Exchange. When the meeting closed, everyone felt that he was richer than when it opened. In a few brief months, there was not one of these hundred-thousand-dollar-men who was worth a hundred thousand cents.[22]

The greatest "boom town" of this period was Chicago. It was a village in 1833, surrounding a frontier fort. In 1836, it was the fastest growing "metropolis" in all Christendom.

When the coastwise steamship lines ran special excursions to Florida during the "boom" in 1925-26 it was regarded as a novel experiment. But there was nothing new in it! Similar trips by lake steamers were made to Chicago and Milwaukee in the boom years of 1835 and 1836. Whole boatloads of speculators, infected with the "Michigan fever," flocked to the region.

So great was the demand for "lots" that almost all northeastern Illinois was laid out in towns. Chicago grew in population from 550 inhabitants in 1832 to over 5,000 in 1836, to say nothing of the perambulating speculators and real estate vendors. The value of taxable property rose in the same period from $19,560 to several millions. So utterly reckless had the city grown that the people "chased every bubble that floated on the speculative atmosphere." The more absurd the project, the more madly was it pursued." The government land office in the city was besieged from morning till night with eager speculators. Those who bought anywhere within hundreds of miles, even before seeing the plot, laid it out into city lots, "in the most approved rectangular position, emblazoned in glaring colors, and exhibiting the public spirit of the proprietor in the multitude of their public squares, church lots and school lot reservations." The whole Chicago area was infested with strangers, capitalists, clerks and even greedy clergymen. The hotels, inns and boarding houses also did "a land office business."[23]

[22] *Ibid.,* pp. 384, 385.
[23] See Moses and Kirkland, *History of Chicago,* Vol. I, p. 98.

The greatest excitement prevailed in 1836, when the Illinois Legislature ordered the Illinois and Michigan Canal trustees to sell the "canal lots." These constituted a part of the land gift of the federal government to foster the construction of an internal waterway between Lake Michigan and the Mississippi River. The sale was thought to be a wonderful success. Single lots brought from $9,000 to $21,400. Aggregate sales from June to September amounted to $1,359,465, but only $401,042 was received in cash. In nearly every instance the sales were never completed. In 1837 there was hardly one important purchaser who did not prefer to forfeit his lots, rather than complete the payments. After the crash, lots that had sold for more than $1,000 would not fetch $100 in specie.

The whole Chicago population was in the real estate business when the boom was on. There is a story that a prominent physician was busy selling "town lots," when a messenger informed him that a lady urgently required his professional services. He reluctantly left his office and made the call. He diagnosed the case hurriedly and made out a prescription, then proceeded to leave.

"Why, doctor," the lady called after him, "you don't state here how I shall take the medicine."

"Oh," he called back, over his shoulder, "Canal terms. One-quarter down, and the balance in one, two and three years."

He had "town lots" impressed on his brain, and even professional practice could not erase the usual terms of sale.

All sorts of advertising media and entertainment were employed by the town jobbers. No better description of this is afforded than that given by Harriet Martineau, in her delightful account of *Society in America*:

I never saw a busier place than Chicago was at the time of our arrival [in 1836]. There streets were crowded with land speculators hurrying from one sale to another. A negro dressed up in scarlet, bearing a scarlet flag and riding a white horse, with housings of scarlet, announced the times of sale. At every street corner, where he stopped, the crowd flocked around him; and it seemed as if some prevalent mania infected the whole people . . . As the gentlemen of our party walked the streets, storekeepers hailed them from their doors, with offers of farms and all manner of land-lots, advising them to speculate before the price of land rose higher. A young lawyer realized $500 per day by merely making out titles to land.

And the great English lady added prophetically: "Of course, this rapid money-making is a merely temporary evil. A bursting of the bubble must soon come. The absurdity is so striking, that the wonder is that the fever should have attained such height as I witnessed."[24]

And the bubble did burst! For it was ridiculous, as Miss Martineau remarked, that "wild land on the banks of a canal, not even yet marked out, should sell in Chicago for more than the rich land, well improved in the finest part of the Valley of the Mohawk."

When the bubble burst, and ruin was brought to almost every inhabitant and sojourner, the very mention of "town lots" exasperated the Chicago populace. It is stated on good authority that at a political meeting in 1837, which was urging upon the legislature the grant of a city charter to Chicago, one speaker "launched into the future and predicted that the place would one day have a population of 50,000." He was howled down with yells of "town lots, town lots," the audience suspecting that he had lots to sell them and was humbugging the people as to the town's future greatness, merely to help along his sales.

Chicago was but an exaggerated replica of what then happened in many other new western cities. The speculation craze also affected the more settled eastern regions. It was especially violent in New York City and in Buffalo. Philip Hone, noted in his diary, on February 23, 1836, that "Twenty lots in the 'burned district' of New York . . . were sold at auction this day . . . at most enormous prices, greater than they would have brought before the fire in 1835, when covered with valuable buildings."

On March 8, he again wrote: "I have this day sold my house in which I live, No. 255 Broadway . . . for $60,000. . . . I made a large profit, but the rage for speculation is at present so high that it will prove an excellent purchase."

Suburban lots in Manhattan and on Long Island rose enormously in value. "Lots two miles from City Hall," Hone noted,

[24] *Society in America*, Vol. II, pp. 259, 260.

"are worth $8,000 or $10,000. Even in the eleventh ward toward the East River, where they sold two or three years ago for $2,000 or $3,000, they are held now at $4,000 and $5,000. Everything is in the same proportion. The market is higher now than I have ever known it." Yet, about a year later (May 26, 1837), he remarks, facetiously: "Lots which a year ago were rough edge guineas, and brought any price for fear they might run away, stand now in the same places and do not look nearly so pleasant nor so valuable as they did then."

Mr. Guy H. Salisbury, Buffalo historian, states that by comparing the prices of lots in that city in 1836, as shown by the Buffalo Land Register, with what the same property would bring in 1863 (the year he was writing), "our prices at this time are less than one-half as high as they were then." The number of Buffalo real estate transactions during the boom was enormous. "As far as the records show," says Mr. Salisbury, "there were some twelve thousand deeds (in 1836) mostly for city property." The deeds do not cover contract sales, which were probably much more numerous. Following the 1837 collapse, lands in and around Buffalo "were a drug on the market and could hardly be disposed of at any price. Sales were made mostly for outer lots at from one-tenth to one-twentieth of the prices they bore in '36."[25]

Even in the secluded inland town of Auburn, N. Y., the craze was severely felt. William H. Seward, whose home was in Auburn, and who built up a larger fortune in land deals than in law practice or in politics, wrote on February 8, 1835: "A great rage for speculation in real estate has arisen here. Property has advanced about 25 per cent, and sells readily. This gives me reputation of increase of property. Whether I realize it or not will depend upon whether I sell while the fever is upon us."[26] Yet Seward, in 1835, was modest in his estimate of the rise in real estate values in his home town, for his son and collaborator mentions that the next year "houses and village lots advantageously located rose suddenly to seven times their former values," and that the town of Auburn was extended on paper to over four times its previous space.[27]

[25] *Buffalo Historical Society Publications*, Vol. IV, pp. 317-336.
[26] *Autobiography of Frederick W. Seward*, Vol. I, p. 251.
[27] *Ibid.*, p. 316.

Not all the "booming" was in town lots. Suburban developments also participated in the spectacular speculation of this period. J. L. & S. Joseph & Co. diversified their activities in land promotions. In addition to fostering deals in "Texas scrip," they, together with George A. Ward and other New Yorkers, in 1836, organized the "New Brighton Company." Its purpose was to develop an aristocratic suburban community on Staten Island. The proposition soon perished, however. The banks foreclosed a mortgage of $470,000 on the property, and it was sold for a song. The Stevens family, famous for engineering ingenuity, also made efforts to attract population to their lands in Hoboken near Castle Point, and in addition to spending large sums in improving this Jersey suburb, and lowering the ferry rates, made offers from time to time, of prizes for oratory and other contests of skill in order to popularize the resort. The Swartwouts, famous in New York City political annals, acquired a part of the Hackensack meadows from the Stevens family, and in imitation of their Dutch ancestors, made large outlays to reclaim the lands from salt water. "They made seven and a half miles of embankment. . . . They dug 120 miles of ditches. They reclaimed 1,300 acres. . . . It was expected that all the vegetables that would ever be needed in New York could grow upon these fields. They had reason to hope for success when they saw before them 4,000 acres of garden within sight of Trinity steeple."[28]

They conceived the idea that these swamps could be made into suburban plots as well as cattle grazing grounds and truck gardens. They organized a dairy company, and offered shareholders twenty-five gallons of milk a share annually, in lieu of dividends. They soon discovered, however, that mosquitoes drive away human beings, that cows can't swim, and vegetables don't thrive in salt marshes. They sought loans from the City of New York and in Holland without success, and before Samuel Swartwout ended his turbulent political career by abstracting funds belonging to the national till, the whole project floundered. A portion of the Swartwout swamps came into possession of the United States. It was held for a number of years, in the expectation that it would increase in value, but was finally disposed of.

[28] Walter Barrett, *The Old Merchants of New York* (1855), Vol. IV, p. 253.

Some of the suburban developments of this period met with fair success and still survive. Noteworthy among these is the Canton Company, of Baltimore. This concern, created in 1828, to develop an industrial and shipping section of the Monumental City, has attracted speculative interest for more than a century. Peter Cooper was early concerned in it, and when its success seemed doubtful, because the Baltimore and Ohio Railroad could not find a suitable means of propelling cars, the New York capitalist applied his inventive genius to the construction of the first genuine American locomotive—the Tom Thumb. Later, the Canton Company had its shares listed on the New York Stock Exchange, and in this way old "Uncle" Daniel Drew obtained an influential interest in its affairs. Its progress has been slow, however, and after a century of plodding, its property has been finally taken over by the Pennsylvania Railroad at the neat sum, according to reports, of $13,000,000.

The East Boston Company is another industrial suburban development, organized in 1835, which has also survived the changing conditions of a century and still is in existence. Its shareholders had a rocky road to travel, however, in the years immediately following the panic. In 1835, the shares of the East Boston Company were quoted at 185. In 1838, the price slumped to 7¾ and later reached as low as $4 per share.

It is not meant to create the impression that all who were concerned in the wild real estate and land schemes just prior to the Panic of 1837 met with misfortune. Many realized large profits, and were started on the road to further wealth. Charles Butler and William B. Ogden both came out ahead of the game, though their American Land Company went to pieces. Butler bought a plot in Chicago from Arthur Bronson (who paid $20,000 for it) for $100,000, and soon sold a one-third parcel of it in lots for the same amount. He also made other profitable sales before the crash. Gardner S. Hubbard, in 1834, purchased 80 acres near Chicago at $5,000. He then made it into an "addition" to the town, went to New York and sold one-half of it, which he had plotted into lots, at auction, for $80,000. Similar tales of fabulous gain may be told of others, but compared with the more numerous cases of lost fortunes, these successful "profiteers" are the exception rather than the rule.[29]

William B. Ogden, the "general agent," of the American Land Company, was not discouraged by the financial collapse which he personally witnessed at Chicago. At least, he did not abandon the place. Instead, he remained there, and became the first mayor of the "city" and its most prominent citizen. He continued to buy land and lots, and became the most progressive and active railroad promoter in the West. He subsequently was elected president of the Union Pacific Railroad, and this is the reason why its western terminal in Utah bears his name. Regarding his successful real estate operations after the 1837 debacle, Ogden's notebook states: "I purchased in 1845 property [in Chicago] for $15,000, which twenty years thereafter [in 1865] was worth ten millions of dollars. In 1844, I purchased for $8,000, what eight years thereafter sold for three millions of dollars, and these cases could be extended almost indefinitely."[30]

But, of course, all these purchases were made in a period when speculation had been crushed, and when the pendulum of property values swung an equal distance in the downward direction. It took almost a decade for the country to recover from the shock of the 1837 collapse. In the intervening period, convalescence was slow, and land speculators were so much disheartened that it required a new generation to prepare the stage for another boom period.

[29] Moses and Kirkland, *op. cit.*, p. 98.
[30] *William B. Ogden and Early Days in Chicago,* by Hon. Isaac N. Arnold, *Fergus Historical Series,* No. 17, p. 22.

(255)

CHAPTER XII

CALIFORNIA'S GOLDEN LAND GAMBLES

"In all the new states of the Union, land monopolization has gone on at an alarming rate," wrote Henry George, California philosopher and economist, in 1870, "but in none of them so fast as in California, and in none of them, perhaps, are the evil effects so manifest."[1]

Henry George, though a native of Philadelphia, spent the golden years of his life in California. Here he noted growth in land values in the progress of time. Here he witnessed land grabbing dating back to the Spanish period, and here he saw the evils—but ignored the benefits—of speculation. The ardent single taxer undoubtedly absorbed his economic philosophy from the landed property situation in the Golden State. Had he been reared in the midst of the violent land speculations of post-Revolutionary times, had he personally witnessed the loss of great fortunes, the utter collapse of great land schemes, and the fiascos of town-jobbing just prior to 1837, he might have adopted different views.

California occupies an exceptional situation as an episode in American land speculation. At the time of its occupation by American forces, the country was still suffering from the effects of the speculative debauches culminating in the Panic of 1837. Feverish enterprise was stifled. Moreover, the Pacific Coast was then too inaccessible to make the region a playground for land booms. There were places in Texas, Florida, Kansas, Iowa and the great Northwest, which were nearer home, and to which

[1] Henry George, *Our Land Policy, National and State*, p. 13.

settlers and immigrants could be attracted as a bait for the land shark.

But more than all this! Another sort of fever displaced that of land speculation in California, at the most opportune moment, i.e., when it became a new and frontier territory. It was the lure of gold—precious gold—actual, movable merchandise extracted from its soil, that almost obliterated all other gainful endeavors.

Gold was discovered in California, January 18, 1848. The reports of it reached the Atlantic States a short time thereafter. The rush of "Forty-Niners" then took place. "Land grants," land titles or patents, were not required. Or, if they were, they were ignored. The ruling passion was to dig out the yellow metal. "Squatter sovereignty," which under the national preëmption laws had already gained much headway in the frontier regions, was merely transferred to California. Who owned the soil from which gold was sifted or dug mattered little. The fortune seekers of all classes went there for it, and they insisted on their rights to take it. Anyone moving to California during the first two decades after the gold rush with the object of acquiring wealth through the purchase and sale of lands would have been regarded as insane.

Yet, more fortunes were made in California lands and real estate than in gold mining. And land grabbing became as prevalent in the Golden State as in the other new territories of the Federal Union. The old "Spanish grants," which had been a disturbing political factor and a serious legal problem in the Louisiana territory, became here also a source of speculation and legal controversy. The period was characterized by the same sorts of fraud, villainy and corruption as have already been described.

It is quite conceivable that, even if gold had not been discovered in California just after the American conquest, real estate and land speculation would have flourished in the territory. San Francisco was a scene of town-lot manipulation as early as 1847. General S. Watts Kearny, American military commander of California, issued, on March 10, 1847, a proclamation, granting to the municipality of San Francisco "the right and title of the Government of the United States, and of the new territory, to the beach and water-lots on the eastern part of the town." Within a week thereafter this property was ordered to be sold and the proceeds used by the town authorities. In that year, also, an important section of the town was laid out into streets by the public authorities and the vacant area converted into town lots.

A public sale of these lots took place. Speculators and investors bought altogether 450 lots at $12 per lot. Each purchaser was required to fence the lot, and erect a building thereon, within a year. At this time, the chief source of income of the city authorities was the receipts from the sales of public lots. Corruption prevailed, and it is reported that the choice sites were secured by speculators "under the old regulations" or by private agreements with the city officials.[2]

The next year (1848), another great public sale of town lots took place. Values had advanced, but owing to the best selections having already been engrossed, prices were disappointing. The price of lots ranged from $16 to $50, averaging about $22.50 each.

At this time, San Francisco was buzzing with the excitement of the gold discovery. A "boom" was on. The best locations had been snapped up by astute buyers, and they were demanding high prices on resale. In the meantime, immigration was rapidly adding to the population. "Squatting" became a general nuisance, both in the city and in the outlying districts. The "squatters" organized themselves into associations, and resisted efforts to oust them. In fact, "squatting" was the popular method of acquiring real estate even in the old Spanish days, and with "preëmption," the byword for settlers on the United States public domain, the newcomers from "the states" set up their tents or cabins wherever they found a suitable vacant plot and defied those who claimed title to the property to dispossess them.

But the sale of "city lots" in San Francisco continued with increasing vigor. Speculation and corruption became intensified. Members of the City Council, i.e., the *"Ayuntamiento,"* and other political favorites figured largely as buyers. Horace Hawes, the recently elected "prefect," i.e., mayor, protested that the best city lots were being taken by the speculators and politicians at

[2] Frank Soulé, John H. Gihon, and James Nisbet, *The Annals of San Francisco* (1855), pp. 180-184. Also Theodore H. Hittell, *A History of California,* Vol. III, p. 116.

ridiculously low prices. On his recommendation, the governor of the territory intervened and ordered the sales to stop. But the "*Ayuntamiento*" merely passed a formal resolution protesting that the governor had no legal right to interfere with the sale of city property. It then announced another sale of desirable "water lots" on March 15, 1850.[3]

Thus, the city for a while was bountifully supplied with revenue, and the land grabbers had a veritable feast. Among the "city councilors," who obtained choice parcels of real estate were Samuel Brannen and J. W. Osborn, business partners; William H. Davis, Gabriel B. Post, Talbert H. Green, and Rodman Price. "The names of some of this delectable lot," remarks a local historian, "are still perpetuated and honored by the people of San Francisco."[4]

The prefect's protests naturally angered the speculators. Their political influence, combined with the territorial governor's own personal interests in the matter, led to the prefect's suspension. He was accused of having corruptly granted land and having accepted fees illegally. But Horace Hawes, even after he was removed from office, continued to reiterate his accusation of fraud, in which he implicated the governor. He brought charges for impeachment, but the legislators threw out his petition. So the corruption in the sale of city lots proceeded undisturbed. Subsequent sales, however, brought increasing prices. In December, 1853, the city again offered the "water lots" it had received as a gift from the military representative of the national government. Some of these were far out in the bay and were covered with water. The size of individual lots was cut down one-half, but several brought as high as $16,000. "Four small size building blocks alone produced the enormous sum of $1,200,000."[5]

There were apparently good reasons in this period for the rapid rise in real estate values in San Francisco, though, of course, speculation carried it beyond prudent heights. The town was the only good port accessible to the gold regions. It became

[3] John P. Young, *San Francisco, A History of the Pacific Coast Metropolis,* Vol. I, pp. 186, 187.
[4] *Ibid.*
[5] Soulé, *op. cit.,* p. 182. See also Hittell, *History of California,* Vol. III, pp. 390, 391.

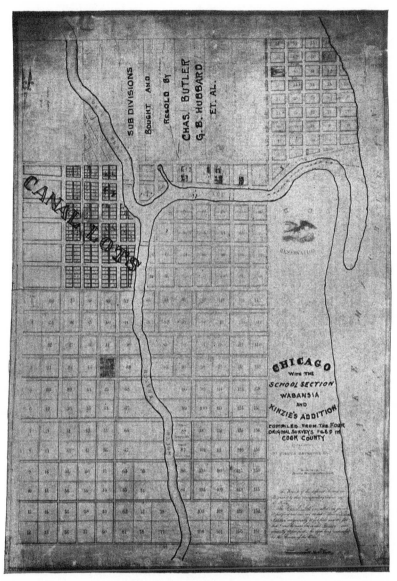

MAP OF CHICAGO, DATED 1836, SHOWING LOCATION OF THE "CANAL LOTS," AND
TRACTS BOUGHT AND RESOLD BY CHARLES BUTLER, G. B. HUBBARD, AND
ASSOCIATES

(See pp. 248-249)

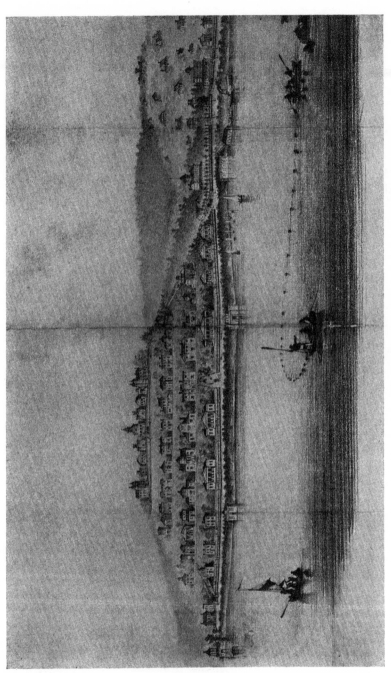

THE "PROPOSED" NEW BRIGHTON, STATEN ISLAND, DEVELOPMENT

(Reproduced from G. A. Ward's *Description of New Brighton on Staten Island, opposite the City of New York*, 1836)

(See pp. 251-252)

the landing place of thousands of fortune seekers. It was the chief emporium for an immense back country where real money was being sifted from the soil by the increasing hordes of prospectors. As a contemporary annalist noted: "In two years space, the financier doubled his capital, without risk to himself; and the accumulation went on in geometrical progression. But chiefly it was the holders of real estate that made the greatest fortunes. The possession of a small piece of building ground in and about the center of business was a fortune in itself. Those lucky people who held lots from times before the discovery of gold, or who shortly afterwards managed to secure them, were suddenly enriched beyond their most sanguine hopes. The enormous rents paid for the use of ground and temporary buildings in 1849 made all men covetous of real estate. By far, the greater part had originally belonged to the city, formerly the so-called *pueblo*, or village of Yerba Buena, but the guardians of its interests from the conquest downwards, liberally helped themselves and their friends to the choice lots."[6]

Retribution for this real estate mania—induced by the inflation of the gold rush—was soon to come. Hardly had the lot sale of 1853 ended, when real estate values collapsed. The market was glutted with the offerings of recent purchasers, who needed cash to complete their payments. The bottom seemed to have fallen out. The contemporary annalist thus describes the situation in March 1854:

Looking disinterestedly at the great extent of the ground around the city, still unbuilt upon, the number of empty stores, the acknowledged overdoing of commercial business, and, above all, the comparatively slow rate at which, of late, the population of the State and city is increasing, it appears to be highly probable that many years will pass before recent high prices will again be witnessed. Most likely, the present reduced prices for all kinds of real estate, but more particularly for unimproved lots, will continue for some months to fall lower. When the population of the State, and by consequence, that of its great Port, are materially increased, prices of real estate in San Francisco may be expected to rise far above the present, or even the recent high prices.[7]

[6] Soulé, *op. cit.*, pp. 498, 499.
[7] *Ibid.*, p. 520.

One of the most adventuresome spirits during the early Frisco boom, who was carried down by the crash, was "Harry" Meiggs. He was a New York lumber merchant, who came to California in the early gold days—and, incidentally—he was a relative of the Texas Austins. Soon after arriving in San Francisco, he started a lumber business at North Beach, a section of San Francisco. He caught the "land fever," and started a "development" there. He thought his title to the property secure, and began to buy and sell lots at one-fourth of the prevailing prices for lots in the central district. He argued that the city must grow toward North Beach, and as the water front lots along Yerba Buena Cove had made millions for those who bought them from the city, there was equally as good chance that his lots would prove as profitable purchases.

Accordingly Meiggs bought over 2,000 front feet of water lots at North Beach. Some of these he had no difficulty in selling. He had a pleasing manner, and a faculty for making friends. They called him "Honest Harry." Moreover, he was a member of the City Council. The fever for water front lots, however, greatly subsided in 1854, and Meiggs found himself loaded down with a large part of his lots, on which he owed an unpaid balance on the purchase price, as well as unpaid assessments and taxes. His cash ran out. In order to obtain funds, he purloined signed city treasury warrants from the City Hall, and offered them as collateral for loans. Other dishonest acts were ascribed to him. But before his fraudulent practices were discovered, he had loaded a schooner and at early dawn, on October 6, 1854, secretly sailed out the bay, never again to return to California.

He was next heard of in Chile, where he had become a successful building contractor. But his greatest service to humanity—if it can be called such—was as virtual dictator of Peru, and as the most enterprising railroad builder in the western hemisphere. Charles R. Flint, in his interesting *Memoirs of an Active Life*, thus describes Meiggs' remarkable career:

Don Enrique (as Meiggs was known in Peru) was a builder. He made millions, but it was the adventure and the power that lured him,—"el empresa," the undertaking, as he expressed it. As a railroad builder, I should say he was fully in Hill's class, *and as a financier, in a class in himself.* He remained an American, and although the money he was spending came from Europe, he bought most of his material for the railroads in the United States.

Meiggs died in 1877, and before his death, it is reported he "made good" many of his San Francisco forgeries, and paid those to whom he owed money when he absconded.

James Lick, another California pioneer and real estate magnate, furnished a good contrast to Meiggs. Instead of going from San Francisco as a bankrupt to Peru, Lick came to San Francisco from Peru, with considerable capital to invest. He was of Pennsylvania Dutch stock, and had left Lebanon County, Pa., to seek a livelihood in the piano business in South America. He arrived in San Francisco in 1847, and being "unlovable, eccentric, solitary, selfish and avaricious," soon made money. He had an abiding faith in the future growth of his adopted city, and bought its real estate in immense amounts. His first acquisition was the ugly sand dunes back of the straggly village of Yerba Buena. But his business acumen kept him from the snares of speculation. He did not buy when prices were high, but waited until distressed owners were forced to sell. Though no one knew the extent of his acquisitions, or the prices he paid, it may be assumed that his largest purchases were made following the collapse of the boom, in 1854. He held on to his properties. In his real estate deals, he encountered many resistances over titles, and, it is said, was "often obliged to enforce his rights against squatters with a leveled pistol."[8]

Lick did not confine his investments to city real estate, but purchased large tracts in the country around San Francisco. He did much to improve the city, however. He built the Lick House, for a time its largest and finest hotel. He also built, in the Santa Clara Valley, a "mahogany mill"—for no other purpose, it is said, than to carry out an oath that some day he would have a finer mill than his sweetheart's father, who had refused him a daughter in marriage because of his poverty. His monumental contribution to humanity, of course, is the Lick Observatory on Mount Hamilton, under the dome of which he is buried.

"James Lick was not a bad man, as bad men go, nowadays,"

[8] *Pennsylvania German Magazine,* Vol. 6, p. 155.

remarks Hubert Howe Bancroft. "He made his money honestly, kept no corruption fund, and left it decently when he died, left it with regret, not so much from love of it, as because it troubled him that any one should be benefited by it."[9] His fortune at his death in 1876 was estimated as seven millions, all of it acquired through judicious real estate transactions.

Peter Smith was another interesting character in the early "boom" days of San Francisco. He became land rich, not by buying lots from the city or from speculators in straitened circumstances, but by accumulating "city scrip." As in other boom towns, the corrupt local government of San Francisco went beyond its financial means in promoting public improvements. It could not meet its current indebtedness, and its warrants or "scrip" accordingly depreciated in value. In fact, the city's treasury was bankrupt in 1851.

Smith bought up large quantities of this "scrip." He subsequently used it to obtain, through execution of judgments, the unsold real estate still held by the city. In these operations, it is suspected that he was assisted by a "political ring" composed of municipal officials. The city property was sold at ridiculously low prices to satisfy the judgments. The transactions, popularly known as the "Peter Smith sales," naturally created a scandal, which involved a number of San Francisco's reputable citizens. Among these was David C. Broderick, United States Senator from California from 1857 to 1859. He bought, under judgment executions, sixteen beach-and-water lots, two south beach blocks and one "one-hundred *vara*" lot. These purchases and others bought in under the "Peter Smith" judgments, despite the political opposition and the outcry of "fraud," were validated by court decisions after several years of litigation. The acquisitions included, besides the beach-and-water lots, the public wharves and the city "underwater" lands not previously disposed of. Today their monetary value is enormous.[10]

·   ·   ·   ·   ·

Land speculation in early California was not confined to city lots and other real estate in San Francisco. The lure of the large

[9] Hubert Howe Bancroft, *Retrospection*, p. 457.
[10] Young, *op. cit.*, p. 192. See also Hittell, *History of California*, Vol. III, p. 400.

WILLIAM B. OGDEN, FIRST MAYOR OF CHICAGO, AND A LARGE REAL ESTATE
PROPRIETOR THERE

SAN FRANCISCO IN 1848

(From an old print)

estates obtained under Mexican grants also was the cause of considerable excitement. As happened previously in Texas, the Mexican Government and its appointees were exceedingly liberal in California in giving away parts of the public domain. It is estimated that prior to the American conquest, there were approximately 800 "grants" to individuals. These comprised a total of about 8,000,000 acres and embraced more than one-quarter of the cultivable area of the whole state. What a grand opportunity for land jobbers to acquire these "grants" from the reputed holders, and to resell at a profit!

Many of these grants were of a conditional nature, and legal titles in most instances were doubtful. Here again Congress was required to take a hand. The treaty of Guadaloupe Hidalgo, which ended hostilities between the United States and Mexico in 1848, provided that in the ceded territories all prior property rights should be upheld. The problem immediately arose as to how these rights were to be determined. As in Louisiana, a half century previous, Congress appointed a commission to investigate land titles. Owners of grants were called upon to prove their titles. This, many of them could not do. They had received no deeds or patents. Verbal "gifts" by governors, prefects and other officials had been quite common.

It was a wonderful harvest for lawyers, speculators and politicians! "The usual fee for securing to the occupant a title was half the land, while with a bill of extras he [the attorney] might easily sweep up the other half," says Hubert Howe Bancroft, the profuse historian of early California. "He was not much of a lawyer in those days," he adds, "who had not a Mexican grant in his pocket, the title to which his client had paid for."[11]

In order to simplify the problem of quieting the titles of "pueblo" and mission lands, and of Mexican grants, the archives of the villages, towns and missions were ordered sent to the United States Surveyor-General's office at San Francisco, and the land papers retained there. Three hundred bulky volumes which resulted from this gleaning and collating are an indication of the enormous task undertaken in validating California land titles. The work extended over many years, and there are cases

[11] *Retrospection,* p. 309.

still pending. Needless to say, there were many instances of gross fraud and deceit in the prosecution of the rights of alleged owners.

It would be exceedingly tiring to attempt to cover even a substantial portion of the schemes of villainy and speculation that prevailed in the settlement of titles to California lands. The field became a battleground for lawyers, adventurers and capitalists. A group of Philadelphia speculators are reported to have established headquarters in San Francisco for the purpose of gambling in the Mexican grant claims. Local politicians and financiers also attempted to increase their wealth by buying rights to grants, or by backing up claimants. The numerous reports submitted to Congress by the land office officials and the special commissioners appointed to investigate the claims contain frequent references to these fraudulent land-grabbing operations.

One of the most notorious of the fraudulent Mexican grants is known as the "Limantour Claim." Edwin M. Stanton, who was sent to California as special counsel of the United States in the land cases, calls it "the most stupendous fraud ever perpetrated since the beginning of the world." Limantour, a resident Mexican, claimed title to about 600,000 acres, part of which covered the present city of San Francisco. This and other grants, he averred, were given him for aid furnished the Mexican Government. The claim was at first upheld by the California land commission, and for this reason Limantour is said to have collected, during the years 1856 to 1858, about $300,000 from Frisco property owners to quiet their titles. Many prominent lawyers defended the Limantour claims, and many opposed them. The United States District Court declared them all fraudulent, and Limantour fled to Mexico, much to the chagrin of the property holders who had paid to buy him off.[12]

The "Santillan Grant" was another conspicuous forgery. This claim was acquired by a group of land grabbers, styling themselves the "Philadelphia Association." They succeeded, "by hook or by crook," in having the title confirmed by the California land commission, but in subsequent proceedings the "grant" was de-

[12] Hubert Howe Bancroft, *Works,* Vol. 23, p. 554. See also article "Limantour," by J. S. Hittell, *Overland Monthly,* February, 1869.

clared a forgery, and the association wasted its funds and the efforts in prosecuting it.

Santillan's claim, called the "Mission Dolores Grant" also covered "three leagues" within San Francisco. It was reputed to have been donated in 1846 to Santillan, "a poor parish priest on condition of paying the mission debt." The claim was finally rejected in 1859, by the United States Supreme Court, as a preposterous payment for the small sum owed by a mission. The Philadelphia Association, however, continued to petition Congress to ignore the court's decision, and even succeeded in 1878 in getting a favorable report from the House Committee on private land claims. The next year, however, when a bill was brought in to compensate the "Trustees of the San Francisco Association of Philadelphia" for the Santillan grant, it was defeated. There is no evidence that monetary compensation for the alleged grant was ever made.

A national interest attaches to one of the most widely known of California land claims. "General" John Sutter, was not a land speculator. Neither did he crave land for the purpose of gain. He was an "enterpriser"—a man of indomitable courage and skill in the execution of great undertakings. Until gold was discovered on his Sacramento property in 1848, he conducted a vast and prosperous colony, of which he alone was lord and master. But gold on his lands proved his undoing. The squatters overwhelmed him. In vain did he appeal to Congress year after year for just compensation. But compensation never was granted. His descendants are still pressing their claim for something like $50,000,000 as the rightful award to the enterprising pioneer and colonizer whose northern California empire was destroyed by the "Curse of Gold."

Though he was not primarily a land jobber, Sutter did not stand idly by and merely protest against the gold rush about him. Like others, he sought to exploit the situation. He organized the Sacramento Town Company, and surveyed a site into town lots in the autumn of 1848. The sales were rapid and at good prices. With the receipts, Sutter was enabled to pay off some pressing debts. But in the excitement of town-jobbing and land sales, he made conveyances of sections to which his title was doubtful, and as afterwards proven, worthless. Moreover, the squatters on his land began to resist ejection and organized a revolt. There was disorder and bloodshed. All this caused an abatement of Sacramento town lot sales. It caused also a collapse of real estate values and general financial embarrassment in the new northern California metropolis. Thereafter, Sutter was too busy defending the validity of his enormous land grants personally to engage in real estate transactions. The years he spent on the doorsteps of Congress cost him a vast sum. He died in Washington, on June 17, 1880, a poor, disheartened man. Justice by state and nation had been denied him.

Sutter's land in recent years has been the scene of another development similar to that first attempted by the original grantee. The fertile Feather River delta in the Sacramento Valley lay fallow for many years after Sutter was forced out of it. During the rainy season much of it was under water, and useless, but at other seasons it was covered with a luxuriant plant growth. An idea was conceived of diking the banks of the stream and thus making possible the cultivation of the rich surrounding lands. Through irrigation, and a favorable climate, these lands could be made to produce almost any crop.

The wealthy meat packer and grain plunger, J. Ogden Armour, became interested in the scheme. The Sutter Basin Company was incorporated in 1913, with $6,000,000 of capital stock. It also issued, in 1922, $7,500,000 of mortgage bonds. These bonds were personally endorsed by J. Ogden Armour, who guaranteed payment of interest and principal. He also expended something like $17,000,000 on the property. The project was not a success. The interest on the bonds was defaulted. Armour died bankrupt—and thus the region in California where gold was discovered was responsible for a second great financial disaster.

Another Mexican grant, for several years in the public eye, and which attracted the attention of even Wall Street for a while, was known as the "Mariposa Estate." When General John C. Frémont "conquered" California in 1847, with his small band of American scouts, he was not unmindful of the opportunities for acquiring vast personal wealth in this region. In his "pathfinding" activities, he was led into a highway, which was destined to hold out promises—but only promises—of great profits both to himself and to others. In February, 1847 (only a few months after the surrender of California), he purchased from the grantee, Alvalardo, for $3,000, a large tract of land, comprising ten leagues square, on Mariposa Creek, between the Sierra Nevada Mountains and the Joaquin River. As the land was mountainous, it was not highly regarded by the Mexicans, but, by a peculiar trick of fortune, it was the only large grant which was comprised in the region of the gold mines.

Frémont became a California resident and was elected United States Senator in December, 1851. According to Hubert Howe Bancroft, Frémont "was in a sense the representative of the Spanish grantees," and in this capacity he had the support, in the same Senate chamber, of his father-in-law, Thomas Hart Benton, of Missouri. Accordingly, as Bancroft points out, "there was a feeling among Senators that this Benton-Frémont-Jones combination might not be acting from disinterested motives."[13]

At least, Frémont proceeded to fix the boundaries of his ill-defined estate, swinging "it around in such a manner as to locate the auriferous mountain regions and the famous Pine Tree and Josephine mines."[14] Others who had been in quiet possession of these mining claims, protested—but Frémont persisted in demanding his rights, and succeeded, after some open warfare, in securing property in which others had invested.

Of course, all this brought political obloquy upon the famous explorer who was twice a presidential candidate. But it bade fair to make him one of America's wealthiest men. His personal resources were not sufficient for the exploitation of the mines, so he sought financial assistance in Europe. While his agent, David Hoffman, was in London organizing "mining companies," out of his estate, and offering the shares to British investors, Frémont gave Thomas D. Sargent an option on the whole grant for $1,000,000. Sargent then went to England and resold at an enormous advance.

In the meantime, however, Hoffman raised a "hue and cry" against the act of his principal. He published a pamphlet ad-

[13] *Ibid.*, p. 538.
[14] Theodore H. Hittell, *History of California*, Vol. III, p. 133.

dressed "to the British Public" in which he asserted that he alone had a power of attorney to sell or lease the Mariposa property, and that Sargent's purchasers were likely to have trouble.

Hoffman's protest was effective. The English refused to take over the grant. Moreover, legal complications about the grant developed, because the original conveyance did not specify that the grantee possessed the mining rights. As a result of all this, Frémont could not raise the money to pay his presidential campaign debts. At this time, he is reputed to have made the facetious remark: "When I came to California I was worth nothing— but now I owe two million dollars."[15] Judgments were obtained by his creditors against him. On September 9, 1859, the sheriff sold his Mariposa Estate. With this sale all the foreign companies holding leaseholds and mining rights in the property faded into thin air.

The "investing public," however, was to hear more of the "Pathfinder's" land grabbing venture. Frémont succeeded in obtaining a part interest in the property from his chief creditor, to whom it was assigned under a sheriff's deed. With the assistance of several New York capitalists, he organized the Mariposa Land and Mining Company, and, inasmuch as the United States Supreme Court had, in 1858, upheld the right to mine the land, it was expected that the new venture would be profitable. Nothing much ever came of it, however, although, after repeated "sell outs," the shares of the company were listed on the New York Stock Exchange. It did not prove a success.

Frémont lost his financial interest in the Mariposa property shortly after the organization of his stock company. All he obtained from it was worry, vexation and public hatred. The old Californians seemed to have shed no tears because of this. Bancroft, in his reminiscences, in commenting on Frémont and his "Mariposa mine," remarked that "when he was in Paris the man would have been sent to the Bastile as a royal fraud if preadventure that edifice had not been closed for repairs."[16]

During a half century following the American conquest of California, the United States Supreme Court's records were

[15] See Samuel Bowles, *Our New West*, p. 425.
[16] Bancroft, *Retrospection*, p. 234.

cluttered with the Mexican land grant claims. The foremost legal authorities in the country were employed in these cases. Some are still unsettled and every now and then Congress and the courts are called upon to decide on disputed titles or to unravel the frauds growing out of "original Mexican grants." In most cases, of course, the grantees or their heirs are not concerned in the controversies. As pointed out by Bancroft, "the estates have passed for the most part into the hands of speculators, who were shrewd enough or rich enough to keep them." "Land monopoly in California," he further remarks, "is due less to the original extent of the Mexican grants than to the iniquitous methods adopted by our government; and as to the fraudulent claims it is believed that the worst ones were concocted, or at least mainly fortified with supports of forgery and perjury, after the commission and the courts were fairly at work, and after the concocters learned by experience what supports were likely to prove effective."[17]

Moreover, the Mexican grants were not profitable propositions to those who were successful in defending them. "Very few of the old Californians, notwithstanding the principalities in the shape of lands, were enriched by them. As an illustration, it may be stated that though over 326,000 acres were confirmed to the De La Guerra family, they were miserably poor, and so were the brothers Pio and Andre Pico, to whom 532,000 acres were confirmed."[18]

Yet, California, according to Henry George and later investigators, has more large landed estates than any other state in the Union. From statistics furnished by the California Tax Commission in 1916, it appears that 310 landed proprietors owned over four million acres, "capable of intensive cultivation and of supporting a dense population." "One firm owns nearly a million acres; one railroad 500,000 acres. In Kern County four companies own over 1,000,000 acres or more than half the land held in private ownership. The Kern County Land Company alone owns 356,000 acres. In Mercer County, Miller and Lux own 250,000 acres. The evil of such ownership is each year becoming

[17] Bancroft, *Works*, Vol. 23, p. 578.
[18] Theodore H. Hittell, *History of California*, Vol. II, p. 753.

more apparent. We have at one end of the social scale a few rich men who as a rule do not live on their estates, and at the other end either a body of shifting laborers or farm tenantry."[19]

A number of the large California estates were acquired by wealthy capitalists, neither for speculative nor for development purposes, but largely for the glory of being great landed proprietors. Thus, Jerome O'Neil, James Irvine, William Randolph Hearst, E. L. Doheny, and several other millionaires acquired large single tracts. More often than otherwise, these "parks" are a financial burden. The lands, unless underlaid with oil or precious metals, cannot be made productive. Taxes and interest eat heavily into income from other sources. Rich Americans, as a whole, are not content to become "land poor." Occasionally, a ranch, a vineyard or an orchard is held as a pleasure ground or place or retreat, but this, as a rule, is expensive sport—and our millionaires, like the English, pay heavily for their sports and pastimes.

. . . . .

The story of jobbing in Mexican grants would not be complete without some reference to the land deals in California's twin-sister state, New Mexico. The grants in New Mexico, like those in California, generally covered large areas of vacant lands, and the boundaries were indifferently described. The grantees also, as a rule, claimed a larger acreage than the patents called for. The conveyances, moreover, were made much earlier than those west of the Sierras.

Following the cession of the Mexican territory to the United States, American speculators stepped in and acquired the most important claims. Thus, the Armendaris Grant of 4,000 acres lying on the west bank of the Rio Grande, in which the town of San Marcial is located, was deeded to Hugh N. Smith, and Thomas Biggs, Santa Fé traders, largely for aid in defending its validity. The property was subsequently sold to the San Marcial Land and Improvement Company. The title to the Canada de Cochiti Grant which dated back to 1728, was acquired by James G. and Joel P. Whitney, and the Sandoval Grant in Valencia County, was also bought by Joel P. Whitney, who conveyed a

---

[19] *Report* of the Commission on Land Colonization and Rural Credits of the State of California, 1916, p. 7.

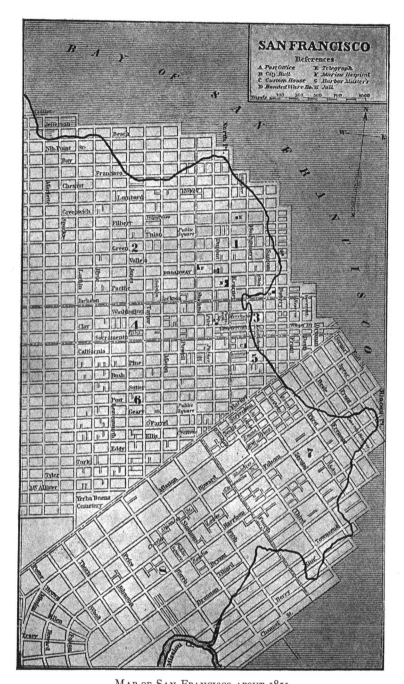

MAP OF SAN FRANCISCO ABOUT 1851

(The lots lying outside the black line, known as "the water lots," were the chief objects of speculation)

John Augustus Sutter, on Whose Estate Gold Was Discovered

half interest in it to Franklin H. Story. The valuable Oritz Mine grant, comprising about 70,000 acres, was also conveyed to Americans, and was finally acquired in 1864, through Charles E. Sherman, by the New Mexico Mining Company.[20]

The titles to these and other New Mexican land claims were as troublesome to settle as those in California. Congress, however, did not take up the problem until a decade or more after the California mess was attended to. The courts, moreover, were slow in adjusting New Mexico claims, and as late as 1890 there were still 107 claims pending, covering 8,704,785 acres. It was not until 1904 that most of these were settled.

Here, also, the lawyers found the land claim business highly lucrative. One, who became exceedingly wealthy, was Stephen B. Elkins, in later life a West Virginia millionaire, cabinet officer and United States Senator. Elkins went to New Mexico in 1863. He learned the Spanish language, entered politics, was then sent to the state legislature and later to Congress. His chief occupation in New Mexico, however, was in defending the titles to lands granted under the Mexican régime—and incidentally, he acquired a substantial financial interest in them.

George W. Julian, who in 1868 was appointed United States Surveyor-General of New Mexico, in a speech at Indianapolis on September 14, 1892, thus characterized the land dealings of Elkins:

Elkins' dealings were mainly in Spanish grants, which he bought for a small price. Elkins became a member of the land ring of the territory, and largely through his influence, the survey of these grants was made to contain hundreds of thousands of acres that did not belong to them. He thus became a great land holder, for through the manipulation of committees in Congress, grants thus illegally surveyed were confirmed with their fictitious titles. . . . By such methods as these, more than 10,000,000 acres of public domain in New Mexico became the spoil of land grabbers.[21]

As in the case of California, excessive claims were the rule rather than the exception in New Mexico. Although under the Mexican régime the maximum acreage granted to an individual

[20] See "History of New Mexico, Its Resources and People" (1907), Vol. I, pp. 170-178.
[21] *Ibid.*, p. 186.

was eleven leagues (about 50,000 acres), several claims embraced a much larger area. The Las Vegas grant comprised a million acre tract, and the so-called "Maxwell Grant" almost two million acres, i.e., about 3,000 square miles.

The Maxwell Grant was one of the most notorious of the New Mexico land claims, and in this Elkins "made himself particularly conspicuous as the hero." Lucien Benjamin Maxwell, a native of Kaskaskia, Ill., and one of the most striking early figures along the Rocky Mountain frontier, acquired it in 1864, from Carlos Beaubien and Guadelupe Miranda, the original grantees. It was adjacent to the Red River in northern New Mexico and contained almost the whole of the present Colfax County. In extent, it would make three states the size of Rhode Island. Here Maxwell, while living in barbaric splendor, attempted to found an American barony, but his principal business was raising sheep.

He probably would have continued as America's greatest sheep herder, had it not been for the discovery of gold on his domain. This gave him plenty of excitement. By disposition a gambler, he forthwith invested large sums in developing placer mining. The results were negative. Like Sutter in California, he was met by an army of squatters and free-lance miners, who refused to be ousted except by force. In order to save a remnant of his fortune, he sold his grant to an English syndicate for $1,250,000—one-half of which sum was paid to his sales agents.

The syndicate formed the Maxwell Land Grant and Railroad Company and tried to unload its obligations on the public. It did succeed in selling bonds to Dutch investors, who were undoubtedly influenced by the fact that the "Hon." Stephen B. Elkins was president of the company. All this was done before the validity of the grant was fully established. In the meantime, the finances of the company went from bad to worse, and by 1875 it was bankrupt. Its lands were sold for unpaid taxes, and its personal property disposed of at sheriff's sale to satisfy creditors.

After the Maxwell Land Grant failure, Stephen B. Elkins left for West Virginia, where he married the daughter of its wealthiest citizen and statesman, Senator Henry Gassaway Davis, and where he also became a United States Senator. Maxwell's subsequent career was less fortunate. He invested a large part of the proceeds from the sale of his land in the bonds of the Texas and Pacific Railroad. Through subsequent bankruptcy of the railroad, the bonds became almost worthless. He also essayed banking, and organized the First National Bank of Santa Fé. As its first president, he pictured himself on its notes with a cigar in his mouth. He died in comparative poverty, July 25, 1875. Sheep raising on his New Mexico property would have been more profitable to him and more beneficial to the country than the exploitation of its gold mines.

Another notorious New Mexico land claim which became a securities gamble, and which was, in 1895, adjudged a criminal forgery, was the so-called "Peralta-Reavis Grant." This fraudulent scheme to obtain title to about 1,300,000 acres under a supposed gift from the King of Spain dating back to 1748, was concocted by James Addison Reavis, a St. Louis real estate dealer. Reavis, in 1871, met George M. Willing, Jr., who represented himself as the proprietor of an immense tract of land on the borders of New Mexico and Arizona, that he had purchased from the heirs of Don Miguel de Peralta. Reavis visited the location with Willing, and while at the latter's home, it is charged, stole a deed to the property made out in blank and signed by Willing. Armed with this document, he proceeded, in 1883, to seek the validation of his land claim under the Act of Congress of July 22, 1854. In the meantime, he married a squaw, who, he claimed, was the direct heir and descendant of the original grantee. He then assumed the name of Addison Peralta-Reavis.

While awaiting the results of his petition, he proceeded to sell "releases" to the numerous "squatters" who had settled on the lands. He also organized a mining company, called the "Casa Grande Land and Improvement Company," which he incorporated under the laws of three states. For these three corporations he received $65,000. In addition, the Southern Pacific Railway Company paid him $50,000 for right of way through his mythical grant and the Silver King Mining Company paid him $25,000 for a release of title to their mining property. He received similar revenue from other sources, based on his supposed ownership of the land, and in this way waxed rich and financially influential. He is said to have had the backing of the wealthy promoters of the Southern Pacific Railroad, among whom was Collis P. Huntington.

But retribution was to come. In 1889 both the grant and the conveyances were declared by the Surveyor-General to be forgeries. Reavis, however, did not give up the fight. About 1890 he entered suit in the United States Court of Claims for $10,000,000 on account of injury he had suffered through the illegal disposition of his grant. He went to great expense and exercised great ingenuity in collecting documents in Spain and in Mexico to support his case, and presented numerous supposed transcripts to the court at Santa Fé. Discrepancies in these soon became apparent, however, with the result that Reavis was convicted for criminal forgery, spent two years in prison, and lost all his property. After his release, he settled in California, where, it is reported, his ingenuity as a litigant was further enhanced by the study of law.

Regarding the Reavis case, the United States Attorney, who opposed the claim, comments: "In all the annals of crime there is no parallel. This monstrous edifice of forgery, perjury and subornation was the work of one man. No plan was ever more ingeniously devised; none ever carried out with greater patience, industry, skill or effrontery."[22]

[22] See *Land of Sunshine, Los Angeles,* February and March, 1898. Also, *History of New Mexico* (Pacific States Publishing Co.), pp. 210-220.

CHAPTER XIII

RAILROAD LAND JOBBERY

THE peerless co-author of *The Gilded Age*, Mark Twain, was from Missouri. But he knew Yankee characteristics as well as those of his southern neighbors, and his description of Squire Hawkins', of Obedstown, great faith in his "Tennessee lands" was no more genuine than his characterization of Mr. Bigler's, the eastern contractor's ideas of railroad promotion:

Mr. Bigler's plan this time, about which he talked loudly . . . was the building of the Tunkhannock, Rattlesnake and Youngwomenstown railroad, which would not only be a great highway to the west, but would open to the market inexhaustible coal-fields and untold millions of lumber. The plan of operations was very simple.

"We'll buy the lands," explained he, "on long time, backed by the notes of good men; and then mortgage them for money enough to get the road well on. Then get the towns on the line to issue their bonds for stock . . . We can then sell the rest of the stock on the prospect of the business of the road, . . . *and also sell the lands at a big advance, on the strength of the road."*[1]

Note that Mr. Bigler's mind was on the rising real estate values. "On the strength of the road," he argued, "there would be a big advance." Land speculation was the lure of the railroad promoters. Land speculation and railroad construction went hand in hand.

When Congress, in 1833, gave Illinois the right to apply to railroad construction the national land that had been granted to

[1] *The Gilded Age, a Tale of Today,* by Mark Twain and Charles Dudley Warner (Harper & Brothers), pp. 167, 168. The italics are mine.—A. M. S.

it for the Illinois and Michigan Canal, it started something. Little was it realized then that this act was the beginning of land-jobbery promotion on a tremendous scale, and that, though resulting in economic benefit to the nation, it would carry in its wake speculation, town-site jobbing, political corruption and downright fraud.

During the fever of violent speculation which characterized the period of rapid western settlement from about 1820 to 1837, it was frequently suggested, and even importuned, that internal improvements be fostered by free gifts of public land. There was a craze for canals and turnpikes, for bridges and railroads. The land jobbers wanted these to enhance the value of their properties. The promoters of the improvements wanted land to reap the profit which they felt might not result from the public utilities they were creating. Land was the bait. Land was the quarry.

The use of the public lands to promote economic development was broadly advocated. No political party was strongly opposed to it, and no geographical section complained against it. As early as 1828, Daniel Webster, staunch "Old State" New Englander, advocated it. In a speech at Faneuil Hall, he said:

In most of the new States of the West, the United States are yet the proprietors of vast bodies of land. Through some of these States and through some of these same public lands, the local authorities have prepared to carry expensive canals for the general benefit of the country. Some of these undertakings have been attended with great expense, and have subjected the States . . . to large debts and heavy taxation. The lands of the United States, being exempted from all taxation, of course, bear no part of this burden. Looking at the United States, therefore, as a great landed proprietor, essentially benefited by these improvements, I have felt no difficulty in voting for appropriation of parts of these lands, as a reasonable contribution by the United States to these general objects.[2]

And with this reasoning, Webster and other statesmen of the time began to distribute, in modest quantities, parts of the national heritage of free land. River improvements, wagon roads, and canals received cessions of the public domain.

[2] *The Works of Daniel Webster*, Vol. I, p. 169.

Railroads came later, but the railroad rage soon took precedence over the canal craze. As already noted, real estate development and land booming went hand-in-hand with railroad construction. Rail highways were promoted in many cases, not with the main idea of profiting from their operation, but to increase town and rural land values. Large landowners were, therefore, concerned in early railroad projects. Soon after the organization of the Baltimore and Ohio Railroad in 1825, a group of capitalists, some of whom were among its promoters, formed the Canton Company in Baltimore. They acquired a large tract of land near the city. They expected the value to increase greatly because of its access to both the railroad and the harbor. Although the Canton Company and the railroad company remained separate corporations for over a century, their interests coincided. As already noted, the Canton Company's property only recently came under the control of the Pennsylvania Railroad, but not without the serious protest of the latter's rival—the Baltimore and Ohio.

The right to own real estate was regarded as a special advantage by the early railroads. The original prospectus of the "Mt. Carmel and New Albany Railroad," of Indiana, in 1838, takes note of this: "Were the company to purchase a million acres of the lands adjacent to the work, the increase alone in the price of the lands so purchased would, before the work is half completed, pay for the entire construction of the work. The bare location of the route would triple the price of every acre of land within two miles of it. All that is wanted is capital to invest in lands, and go on with the work for a short time without being compelled to make sale of them."[3]

In the same belief, individuals and corporations eagerly granted rights of way over their properties to railroads so as to enhance the value of the portions retained. Donations of land, both public and private, to transportation companies, as a speculation aid, thus became an established policy. Overbuilding of railroad facilities was the logical result.

Although Congress had previously granted lands to corporations and individuals for the purpose of creating and maintaining

[3] F. A. Cleveland and F. W. Powell, *Railroad Promotion and Capitalization in the United States*, p. 199.

public utilities of various kinds, the first substantial grant for a railroad enterprise was not made until 1850 when the Illinois Central Railroad was organized. As early as 1836, however, Congress was petitioned for a land grant for the same enterprise.[4] A similar measure was advocated by Senator Sidney Breese in 1844. He desired to secure to the proposed "Great Western Railroad of Illinois" the right of preëmption of public land along its lines. This meant that the railroad would pay the government price for the land, if it was acquired, but, of course, the lands would only be paid for as they were sold at an advance above the government price. Hence, it is quite evident that early railroad building, even in the new and unsettled areas, was closely interlaced with land speculation.

Congress had already made a gift of public land to Illinois in 1828, in aid of the proposed construction of a canal between Chicago and the Illinois River, in order to create a "Great Lakes to Gulf" waterway. The fever of speculation that was engendered by this project was described in a previous chapter. Before the canal was even marked out, lands, supposedly adjacent to it, rose to high values. William B. Ogden, who went to Chicago in the interests of the American Land Company, wrote on May 3, 1836, that he purchased nearly two thousand acres along the proposed canal, at $5 per acre. "It is considered a good investment at $10," he stated, "for it would not only be on the Canal, but near the flourishing town of Joliet." In Chicago, of course, the "canal lots" brought ridiculously high prices. But most of the sales were canceled because of default in payments following the crash in May, 1837.

As the canal was slow in building, and costly, and as railroads were demonstrating their superiority over other means of transportation, Illinois sought to apply the canal land grant to railroad construction. The panic, however, had caused a bankrupt state treasury. Even with land donations, there were insufficient public funds for internal improvements. Moreover, land was then a "drug" on the market. Accordingly, although Congress consented to the diversion from canal to railroad purposes in 1833, the grant was not used.

[4] See *American State Papers*, Public Lands, Vol. VIII, p. 593.

JOHN C. FRÉMONT

ROBERT RANTOUL, JR., WHO OBTAINED THE LAND GRANT FOR THE ILLINOIS CENTRAL RAILROAD

(From an engraving by Sartain)

In the meantime, Darius B. Holbrook, a town jobber, was eager for the success of his "Cairo City and Canal Company." This concern grew out of a town-site speculation started by Baltimore capitalists, as far back as 1818, in Illinois, at the confluence of the Ohio and Mississippi rivers. The project lingered in obscurity for several years because the "town" was seasonally under water. The Cairo City and Canal Company, however, endeavored to offset this inconvenience by constructing "dikes, canals, levees and embankments."

When Holbrook could not make a "go" of his town-jobbing venture, he conceived the idea of making the place a railroad terminal. In 1835, he promoted the "Illinois Central Railroad Company," an Illinois corporation, and it was this company which petitioned Congress for a land grant, but without success. This did not discourage Holbrook. About 1840, he obtained a new Illinois charter for a railroad and again sought Congressional assistance. His petition was opposed by Stephen Douglas, then Senator from Illinois, on the ground that Holbrook's railroad was "a stupendous private speculation to enable the Cairo Company to sell their chartered privileges in England."

Douglas then offered a substitute plan. Instead of granting land for railroad purposes to Holbrook's company, he proposed a grant directly to the State of Illinois, to be used in aid of private railroad construction. In the meantime, the crafty Holbrook induced the Illinois Legislature to pass an act, ceding to his proposed railroad all lands that might be granted the state by Congress. When Douglas learned of this trick, his ire was greatly stirred. He threatened to withdraw his bill for a land grant. To appease him, Holbrook was induced to release the state from the privilege given his company. Douglas regarded Holbrook and his associates as merely land grabbers and town jobbers, and he wished lands conveyed to an out-and-out railroad proposition.

Douglas' land grant bill was enacted by Congress, September 20, 1850. It did not convey a definite acreage. It granted an alternate section of land, extending six miles on each side of a railroad to be built as part of a line between Mobile and Chicago. As each alternate section was a square mile, speculators could not obtain directly from the railroad company large contiguous tracts.

Moreover, if the railroad's lands rose in value, the government's sections would rise proportionately. Thus, the government would participate equally with the railroad in the profits resulting from land ownership. This system—designed primarily to block monopolization of land along the railroad—was continued in all subsequent railroad land grants.

But who would build and own the railroad that was to get all that land? Surely, not the people of Illinois. They lacked the funds. This situation was undoubtedly well known to eastern capitalists, and particularly to the New England Congressmen who voted for the land donation. And they were not long in taking advantage of it! Daniel Webster was not a capitalist, but he had an eye for business and his legal services were in demand by the moneyed interests. Webster had a colleague in Congress, with whom he was friendly, even though they adhered to opposite political parties. This man was Robert Rantoul, Jr., a strong supporter of internal improvements. He was an able lawyer, a good business man, but not a successful politician. As a Democrat, he supported free trade and "state's rights," and accordingly was not in political harmony with Webster. Yet, it is stated on pretty good authority that Webster, almost immediately after Douglas' land grant bill was passed, advised Rantoul to go to Illinois in the interests of a group of capitalists and seek the railroad charter, and in this way get the conveyance of the land. In fact, it is said that Rantoul drew up the charter under Webster's supervision.

Rantoul went West, and arrived in Springfield, Ill., just in time to forestall the efforts of a young lawyer and politician—Abraham Lincoln by name—to obtain the railroad charter and the land for a group of western capitalists. Lincoln confirmed this in 1863 to Rantoul's son, while the latter was on a visit to the White House; and remarked with characteristic jocularity and a slap on his visitor's knee: "Your father beat me, your father beat me."[5]

Rantoul obtained, without much difficulty, a charter for the Illinois Central Railroad on February 10, 1851. As stated in the

[5] William K. Ackerman, *Historical Sketch of the Illinois Central Railroad,* p. 29.

Senate in 1870 by Senator James Warren Nye: "He spread out to the Legislature of Illinois the boundless advantages that would accrue from affording aid to this great enterprise. He laid that upon the altar of his country for its benefit, and the nation also was induced to extend its aid."[6]

Of course, it required some "extravagant figures" and an attractive bait in the form of participation in the railroad's revenue to induce the legislature to turn over the liberal land grant to a private corporation. But Rantoul was equal to the task. The newspapers of the time caricatured his figures for their extravagance; but he returned East with his grant. Prominent New York and Boston capitalists became his associates. These included Robert Schuyler, George Griswold, Gouverneur Morris, son of our old land agent, William H. Aspinwall, Jonathan Sturgis, George W. Ludlow, Henry Grinnell, and John F. A. Sanford, of New York, and David A. Neal and Franklin Haven, of Boston.

Rantoul was also a member of the first board of directors of the Illinois Central Railroad Company, but death took him on August 7, 1852, when the actual work of construction had barely begun. Just before his death he wrote enthusiastically regarding the "value of the public lands of Illinois." His sentiments were disclosed in a published letter to Robert Schuyler, the first president of the Illinois Central Railroad,—a letter, of course, designed to attract investors to the company's securities:

"It is plain," he said, "that all the land within fifteen miles of the Central Railroad is intrinsically worth, from its power of production, not only as much, but on average twice as high as that which we have assumed to be the selling price of Ohio lands. Such an average would be realized if the supply of such lands were not much greater than the demand for cultivation. It becomes then necessary to inquire how long will the supply exceed the demand, not for speculation, because that is too precarious and unsteady for our consideration, but the demand for actual cultivation?"[7]

The enthusiastic promoter had his answer to this question. The demand would soon increase beyond the supply should the popu-

---

[6] *Congressional Globe,* April 7, 1870, p. 2480.
[7] *Letter on the Value of the Public Lands of Illinois,* by Robert Rantoul, Jr., Boston, 1851.

lation of Illinois increase only as fast as that which actually took place between 1840 and 1850. The railroad, moreover, would bring a larger number of settlers. Hence, it was a safe prediction that the Illinois Central lands would, in ten years, rise to from $10 to $12 an acre.

He was not wrong. In scarcely ten years thereafter, the Illinois Central Railroad publicly announced that it had 1,100,000 acres, or less than one-half of its original grant, for sale, in forty-acre lots and upwards, at prices ranging from $5 to $25 per acre, whereas the national domain was offered at $1.25 per acre, with not many takers. Certain tracts immediately adjoining stations, or "for other causes" especially valuable, were offered at higher prices on the familiar "canal terms," i.e., one-fourth cash and the balance in three annual instalments, with interest. The ordinary tracts were sold on smaller cash payments, amounting usually to but one year's interest on the purchase price. The balance could be paid in six annual instalments, secured by notes, with interest at 6 per cent. There was, moreover, the general requirement— usually disregarded—that one-half of each plot purchased be fenced and placed under cultivation.

It can be readily assumed that the speculative interest early created in the Illinois Central Railroad was based upon its land grant. An English capitalist, reporting on the company in 1856, wrote: "This is not a railroad company, *it is a land company.*"[8] Anthony Trollope, the English novelist, who visited America during the Civil War, made a similar remark. "Railroad companies," he wrote, "were in fact companies combined for the purchase of land. They purchased land, looking to increase the value of it fivefold by the opening of the railroad. . . . It is in this way that the thousands of miles of railroads in America have been opened."[9]

The main activity of the Illinois Central Railroad promoters in this early period was to sell the lands. They advertised them extensively in alluring pamphlets both at home and abroad. Moreover, the company's credit was based chiefly upon its land holdings. It mortgaged its land (though, of course, it had legal

[8] Wm. K. Ackerman, *Early Illinois Railroads*, p. 75.
[9] Anthony Trollope, *North America*, Vol. I, p. 143.

title only to such sections along which its lines were already constructed) and issued bonds secured by this mortgage. A large part of the land profits was expected to come from the sale of town lots in places of its own creation. A station was established every ten miles, and the surrounding plots divided into lots which were offered at various prices according to location. Town jobbing and railroad building thus went along hand in hand.

Altogether, the Illinois Central Railroad Company received about 2,600,000 acres. In less than twenty years after obtaining the grant, all except about 450,000 acres had been sold. Congress was told in 1870 that the company "was holding its lands for advance in prices, instead of offering them to settlers." It was then offering them at the exorbitant prices of $25 and $30 per acre.

Naturally, the building of the Illinois Central and its liberal land grant stirred up a fever of land speculation in its territory. The alternate sections retained by the government were eagerly bought up by speculators. Young Grenville M. Dodge, afterwards builder of the Union Pacific, who went to Illinois as a surveyor, wrote back enthusiastically to his father: "I can double any amount of money you've got in six months. . . . To start with, buy a couple of Mexican [War] land warrants, send them out, and I'll locate them in places where land is selling at this minute for $2.50 an acre. The warrants for a quarter section each, can be bought back east for about a dollar. Now this is no gun game, but the truth. Don't tell anybody about it, but go to work." And, referring to his father's meager means of a livelihood, he added: "This will pay better than all the post offices and book stores in the kingdom."[10]

The records of the national land office in Illinois show heavy sales along the lines of the railroad to large and influential speculators at the fixed minimum price of $2.50 per acre or a little above it. Stephen A. Douglas, John Wentworth, John S. Wright and other prominent names appear among the purchasers. Not only did politicians and land boosters buy land in the neighborhood of the company's lines, but they sought to influence the location of the route. Jesse Fell, of Bloomington, Ill., a large

[10] J. R. Perkins, *Trails, Rails and War, the Life of General G. M. Dodge*, p. 13.

western land jobber, was instrumental in getting the Illinois Central to Clinton, Decatur, Bloomington and other towns in which he held real estate. All this fostered political "wire pulling" and corruption.

The land grant to the Illinois Central led to a host of similar projects. Congress was swamped with petitions. Every town-site promoter or landed nabob put in applications. The western Congressmen, in whose states were vast stretches of public domain, were kept busy backing up the claims of their constituencies for federal aid in railroad promotion. In these activities, corruption, bribery, log-rolling, and other questionable political practices flourished.

Horace Greeley, whose slogan "Go West, Young Men," placed him among the friends of the pioneer settlers, could see no need of "hiring or bribing capitalists to construct railroads." He advocated limited land "ownership" as an antidote to land speculation, and he even hinted his approbation of "squatter's rights." "The mischiefs already entailed on the industry and business of the country by land speculation," he wrote in his paper, the *New York Tribune,* "are incalculable. . . . Only those who have seen much, reflected much, have any full idea of them. Wheresover, upon a natural harbor, a bay, a head of navigation, or a water fall, a village begins or promises to spring up, there, the speculator or his agent are early on hand, and pounces upon the unoccupied land within a circuit of a mile or two. This he holds back for a price treble to sixty-fold that he paid for it."[11] By releasing capital tied up in vast tracts of unproductive land held by speculators, there would be money enough, Greeley thought, to construct railroads without the aid of land grants.

Greeley made a tour of the West in 1847, and while there, discovered the heavy traffic in military land warrants. The warrants were bought up in great wads, in both the East and the West, and the owners converted them into large tracts of vacant land of their own selection. They needed settlers to make the lands valuable, but settlers now followed railroads and canals instead of going ahead of them. Hence, the numerous railroad projects.

[11] *New York Weekly Tribune,* July 17, 1847.

Maps in emigrant guides to the western states, published in this
period, show veritable net works of "projected railroads," most
of which were never even surveyed. All the "projectors," however, had in mind possible land grants as a means of putting their
plans over. "By stimulating the building of roads, where they are
not wanted, and where the leading cause for building them is the
gift of public lands, we shall throw such discredit (when the
breakdown comes) on our western roads, that the building of
useful roads will be retarded or indefinitely postponed." Thus,
wrote John Murray Forbes to Charles Sumner, February 14,
1853. Forbes was then engaged in the construction of the Rock
Island Railroad entirely with private capital, and, of course, was
opposed to the encouragement given to rival lines with land
grants.[12]

Sober-minded statesmen realized that railroad operation in the
sparsely settled areas of the Great West was not a profitable
business proposition. It was different from the transportation
situation in the East. Here population centers were already sufficiently large and prosperous to furnish traffic immediately. But
in the new states, still in the process of pushing back the Indians
and in preparing the soil for human sustenance, rail traffic must
be developed. This requires a comparatively long period. Under
the circumstances, the prospects of dividends on capital invested
in western railroads were remote.

It was, therefore, not from choice but rather from necessity
that the railroads were proffered lands amounting in extent, in
some cases, to empires or principalities as a reward or a bait
for their construction. On the whole, prospective profits of operating railroads in most sections of the country had little influence
in inducing capital investment in these enterprises. The opportunities for making money in land speculation, in town-site
projects, in construction contracts and numerous other schemes
were more generally the lure than operating legitimate transportation facilities. In some cases, as, for instance, in the Illinois
Central, the proprietors of the railroad could have donated the
entire original cost of construction, and still have realized a capital gain from their land sales. The Illinois Central is reported

[12] See Henry G. Pearson, *An American Railroad Builder*, p. 189.

to have cleared about $25,000,000 from the disposal of its do-
main. Its success, however, is exceptional. The largest and most
richly endowed land grant railroads were financial failures. The
Union Pacific and Northern Pacific are outstanding examples.
The land-grabbing activities connected with these gigantic ventures will be next considered.

. . . . .

The first plan of a transcontinental railroad, to be supported
by a land grant, was proposed by Asa Whitney as early as 1843,
and was considered seriously by Congress and the nation at
large continuously for more than a decade. But the bickering
of sectional interests as to the most desirable route prevented
Congress from taking positive action to promote the enterprise.
It was not until the secession of the Southern States that the
opportunity was afforded to agree upon a proposed route. But even
prior to the Civil War, land speculators gambled on the anticipated route. Prospectors went West to search out probable terminals and town sites along the line. Others kept their ears to the
doors of Congress to get the earliest news of the location of the
lines. Congressmen themselves became financially interested in
what was likely to happen.

One of the shrewd Yankee engineers who had an eye out for
the "most feasible route" was Grenville M. Dodge. Dodge, a
native of Danvers, Mass., "went West" in 1851 to get work in
railroad construction. While engaged on the Chicago and Rock
Island line, he took up a "preëmption" claim to government land
on the banks of the Elkhorn River, in Iowa, twenty-five miles
east of Omaha. He also staked out claims in the same vicinity
for his father and brother. These soon came out to put up their
log cabins and make a pretense of plowing the virgin prairie soil.
In this way they could claim the land as "homesteaders" and pay
the government price for it. Their chief interest, however, was
to hold for a rise in value, in the expectation of the Pacific Railroad passing through their properties.

Dodge was encouraged in his selection by Frederick Lander,
an old friend and fellow engineer who had been appointed by
Jefferson Davis, then Secretary of War, to make one of the
seven or more surveys for a most feasible transcontinental route.

GEORGE FRANCIS TRAIN

(From a photograph taken about the time he was promoting the "Credit Foncier
of America")

LAYING THE TRACK OF THE PACIFIC RAILROAD. FROM BOWLES' *Our New West*

He was in charge of the Puget Sound-Missouri River location. While on his return, he stopped at Dodge's log cabin settlement on the Elkhorn. "The Pacific Railroad is bound to be built through this valley," he assured Dodge, "and if it doesn't run through your claim, I'll be badly mistaken."

"I've already figured that it will," Dodge replied. "How else could it go from the Missouri River if built this far north?"[13]

The South's secession caused an adoption of a northern route for the Pacific Railroad, though in order to connect with the Central Pacific of California, which had been incorporated in June, 1861, the Puget Sound terminus was abandoned. The eastern end was to be "on the hundredth meridian of longitude west from Greenwich, between the south margin of the Republican River, and the north margin of the Valley of the Platte River, at a point to be fixed by the President of the United States." The railroad was to have free right of way over government domain and, in addition, *was to be given ten miles on each side in alternate sections*. All this made an aggregate acreage of about 12,000,000 acres—a vast inland empire, the like of which had never been known before to be held in single private ownership.

But this was not all. The government was to furnish a construction loan in 6 per cent, thirty-year bonds, at the rate of $16,000 per mile of road through the prairies, $48,000 over the Rockies and $32,000 per mile between the Rockies and the Sierras, not to exceed, however, a total of $50,000,000.

Of course, there was opposition and cries of land grabbing. But these protests were unheeded, and the landless Atlantic States joined with the "land-poor" West in favoring the project. "I give no grudging vote in giving away either money or land," exclaimed the Massachusetts Senator, Henry Wilson. "I would sink $100,000,000 to build the road and do it most cheerfully, and think I had done a great thing for my country. What are $75,000,000 or a $100,000,000 in opening a railroad across regions of this Continent, that shall connect the people of the Atlantic and the Pacific, and bind us together? . . . Nothing! As to the lands, I don't begrudge them."

[13] See J. R. Perkins, *Trails, Rails and War, The Life of General G. M. Dodge*, p. 30.

Wilson was right! Why begrudge them the land? Twelve million acres was an ocean of territory that would require several decades to fill. It was offered at $2 to $10 per acre, and sold in forty-acre tracts and upward, with liberal terms of credit. But sales were exceedingly slow. A vast influx of population would have been required to have settled them during the period of construction. Moreover, the Homestead Act of 1862 made it possible to acquire government lands free of cost, and this competition was a serious handicap to the railroad company in disposing of its vast domain.

But it was not the vast stretches of vacant wild lands that attracted speculators. Mere acreage is not what the railroad promoters most desired. *It was the favored town sites, the terminals and the way-stations that were the chief objects of pecuniary exploitation.* Town jobbing and town-site planning began even before the work of actual railroad construction was under way.

One of the "nosy" schemers, who sought to exploit the choice lands and town sites, was the sophisticated and idiosyncratic celebrity, George Francis Train. He was a typical New England trader and adventurer. After having accumulated a fortune in the shipping business, and in trading in Australia during the gold rush there, he returned to America with great capitalistic ideas. He took a hand at railroad promotion, and represented Queen Maria Christina of Spain in furnishing capital for the construction of the Atlantic and Great Western Railway, extending from western New York to Cincinnati. When Congress passed the Pacific Railroad Bill in 1862, he took the first active steps to form a construction company. Having become fascinated, while residing in France, with the adventuresome financial methods of the brothers Emile and Isaac Perrère, he hit upon the idea of organizing finance companies similar to their two concerns: the "Crédit Mobilier" and the "Crédit Foncier." He proceeded to organize companies with the same names. The "Crédit Mobilier of America" was to construct the railroad, and the "Crédit Foncier of America" was to capture and exploit the choice real estate along the lines.

It is George Francis Train, therefore, who is responsible for one of the most notorious names in American financial history—

the Crédit Mobilier. The very term now smacks of corruption and scandal.

The enterprising Train sought the coöperation of capitalists, politicians and statesmen in the promotion of his finance companies, designed to reap the profits from the creation of a transcontinental link to the Pacific Coast. He first tried Boston, with indifferent success, putting up $150,000 of his own funds. This, he said, was "the pint of water that started the great wheel of the machinery." "I had offered," he continues, "an interest in the road to old and well-established merchants of New York and other cities—the Grays, the Goodhues, the Aspinwalls, the Howlands, the Grinnells, the Marshalls, and Davis Brooks & Company; and even to some of the new men, like Henry Clews— agreeing to put them in on the ground floor . . . But they were afraid. It was too big. Only two of them, William H. Macy and William H. Guion would take any stock."[14]

James A. Garfield was one of the politicians whom Train endeavored to have assist him in the promotion of the "Crédit Foncier." In the course of Garfield's testimony at one of the Congressional hearings relating to the Crédit Mobilier scandal,— which, as is generally well known, involved prominent Congressmen,—he testified:

George Francis Train called upon me in 1866 and said he was organizing a company to be known as the Crédit Mobilier of America, to be founded on the model of the Crédit Mobilier of France; That the object of the company was to purchase lands and build houses along the line of the Pacific Railroad at points where cities and villages were likely to spring up; that he had no doubt money thus would double or treble itself each year; that subscriptions were limited to $1,000 each, and he wished me to subscribe.[15]

Garfield probably confused Train's Crédit Foncier of America with the Crédit Mobilier. It was the Crédit Froncier and not the Crédit Mobilier that was to deal in town lots.

Train did not take a prominent part in the activities of the Crédit Mobilier—the construction company which undertook to build for the Union Pacific Railroad Company. His lack of re-

---

[14] George Francis Train, *My Life in Many States and in Foreign Lands*, p. 287.
[15] J. B. Crawford, *The Crédit Mobilier of America*, p. 134.

sources and his eccentricities handicapped him. He did, however, take active steps to reap the benefits of the railroad's location. As he himself expressed it: "I looked upon it [i.e., the railroad] only as the launching of a hundred other projects, which, if I had been able to carry them to completion, would have transformed the West in a few years, and anticipated its present state of wealth by more than a full generation. One of my plans was the creation of a chain of great towns across the Continent, connecting Boston with San Francisco by a magnificent highway of cities . . . Most of these plans were defeated by a financial panic; by the lack of coöperation on the part of the very people who were interested in their success. Some of them succeeded, however, and I was able to accomplish a great deal of work that has gone into the winning and making of the West."[16]

Surmising that Omaha, Neb., would be the eastern terminus of the Pacific railroad, he straightway engrossed a large part of its real estate. He is said to have personally acquired about five hundred acres in Omaha "which cost him only one hundred and seventy-five dollars an acre,—a most promising investment."[17] He also built a magnificent hotel there—the Cozzens Hotel— which, he said, "was more written about than almost any other hostelry ever built in the United States."

What became of Train's real estate speculations in Omaha is something of a mystery. He does not mention it in his memoirs —written after he had been adjudged insane—and certainly they could not have brought him great wealth, because he died comparatively poor. In fact, during the last years of his life, he was a resident of a workingman's hotel in New York, and his only associates in this period were "children in parks and streets."

Little also is known of Train's city building company, the Crédit Foncier of America, which was to develop towns along the railroad. This concern was incorporated under a special act of the Nebraska Legislature, and was publicly advertised as organized in connection with the Union Pacific Railroad to "own cities along the line." A printed prospectus, issued by John J.

[16] Train, op. cit., pp. 293, 294.
[17] See Albert D. Richardson, Beyond the Mississippi, p. 565.

Jay Cooke

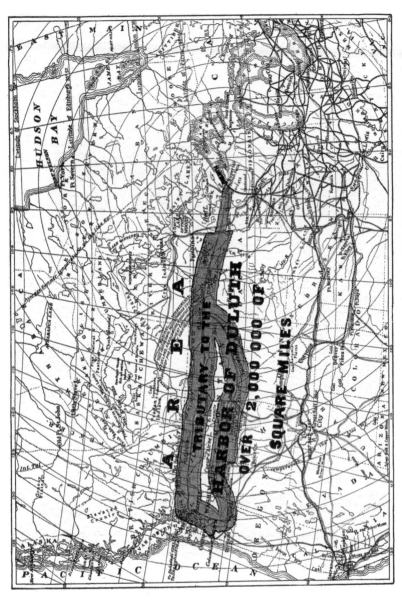

Map of Location of the Northern Pacific Land Grant, "Banana Belt," Which Inspired J. Proctor Knott's Famous Speech

Rings Indicate 100, 200, etc., Miles from Duluth

(From Oberholtzer's *Jay Cooke, Financier of the Civil War*)
(See pp. 304-305)

Cisco and Co., who were, for a while, the bankers of the Union Pacific Railroad, indicates that this organization made an attempt to "boom" the town of Columbus, Neb.

This prospectus contains some extravagant language.

"OMAHA ALREADY AN ACKNOWLEDGED FACT— COLUMBUS THE NEXT IMPORTANT CITY," ran the headlines.

Other captions were: *"A fifty dollar lot may prove a $5000 investment." "Paris to Pekin in thirty days." "Two Ocean Ferry Boats and a Continental Railway." "Passengers for China this way!" "Money is cheap—Our national credit sound. The nation prosperous." "The Rocky Mountain excursion of statesmen and capitalists pronounce the Pacific Railroad a great fact." "The Crédit Mobilier a national realty, the Crédit Foncier (owning cities along the line) an American institution."*

And by way of showing the high standing of the Crédit Foncier of America, it is remarked that "Most of the directors and subscribers of the Crédit Mobilier are shareholders of the Crédit Foncier of America."

Like many similar town-lot "booster circulars" issued before and since the creation of the Crédit Foncier, there was an accompanying sketch map showing the important geographical position of Columbus, Neb. It was "the natural point for an important station." It was "surrounded by the finest agricultural lands in the world." Moreover, "the Crédit Mobilier owns lands near the city; and some of the leading Generals and Statesmen are also property owners round about."

And by way of further inducement to make a town-lot investment in Columbus, it was pointed out that others have made fortunes by similar purchases:

Would you make money easy? Find, then, the site of a city and buy the farm it is to be built on! How many regret the non-purchase of that lot in New York; that block in Buffalo; that acre in Chicago, that quarter section in Omaha. Once these city properties could be bought for a song. Astor and Girard made their fortunes that way. The Crédit Foncier by owning the principal towns along the Pacific line to California, enriches its shareholders while distributing its profits by selling alternate lots at a nominal price to the public.

The authorship of the foregoing fantastic circular is not stated, but in view of the fact that George Francis Train, a few years after its publication, was legally adjudged insane, it may be assumed that it was written by him.

The Crédit Foncier of America, despite the enthusiasm and benevolence of its projector, undoubtedly had a short and unsuccessful career. Columbus, Neb., did not become "an important station" on the Union Pacific. Neither was it ever considered as the capital of the state. True, it is still on the map. But, after fifty years in which there have been opportunities to exploit its geographical and economic advantages, its population is less than 7,000, and its growth has been slow and uncertain. In the meantime, George Francis Train, its promoter and original "booster," has passed into the realm of celestial silence. The fire of his enthusiasm and the ring of his masterly oratory ceased thirty years before his demise. While living as a hermit at a Mills Hotel, at $3 per week rental, he saw the West grow up, and boasted that his predictions of the marvelous effect of the building of the transcontinental rail link had come true. He died in 1903.

Omaha, the chief center of Train's operation, likewise failed to realize the vast gains he anticipated. He and his associates did not make money from their speculations in its vicinity. This may have been due to a change of location of the eastern terminus of the Union Pacific from Omaha to Council Bluffs, on the other side of the Missouri River. According to General Dodge, this change was made because of "the aim of Congress and the intention of Lincoln." The martyred President, incidentally, owned a piece of land hard by the established terminus on the eastern side of the Missouri, and the critics of his railroad policy made capital of this. But if Lincoln selected Council Bluffs as the starting point of the Pacific Railroad merely to gain wealth from the rise in the value of his real estate there, the decision to follow his plan came rather late, for the new terminus was not selected by the directors of the railroad until ten years after his assassination.

Though the Crédit Foncier of America soon petered out as a money-making proposition, town-site jobbing along the lines of the Union Pacific persisted. Hardly a location in any way suitable as a station or a junction point that did not develop into a "mushroom city" because of the activity of land speculators.[18] As soon as the location of the railroad line was determined, "a town would be plotted, streets laid out and named for the heroes of the Civil War, and lots put on sale." The same may be said of the places along the Central Pacific in California, which, like the Union Pacific Railroad, received a similar grant of land in aid of construction. The Southern Pacific also came in for a handsome land bounty, and its promoters became deeply concerned in townsite and terminal land jobbing.[19] And so with the Northern Pacific, the story of which will be told in the next chapter.

From a financial viewpoint, the land subsidies of the first transcontinental railroads did not accomplish the results expected by the promoters. The lands had no value until the roads were completed, and, even after completion, the process of disposal was exceedingly slow and costly. Direct financial aid, through cash loans, was much more serviceable as a means of successful promotion, and even with this form of assistance the profitableness of the railroad enterprises only became established many years after the lines were completed and in full operation. Nevertheless, land was the lure for undertaking the construction by private interests, and it was the bait that led many capitalists to subscribe to the project.

[18] See *Building of the Pacific Railroad*, by Edwin L. Sabin.
[19] See Stuart Daggett, *Chapters on the History of the Southern Pacific.*

CHAPTER XIV

JAY COOKE'S "BANANA BELT"

WHEN Jay Cooke, "financier of the Civil War," in 1869 consented to furnish capital to rescue the Northern Pacific Railroad from the pangs of infantile weakness, he made the following stipulation:

A Company shall be organized for the purpose of purchasing lands, improvement of town sites, or other purposes, and the same shall be divided in the same proportion; that is, the original interests shall have one-half, and Jay Cooke & Company shall have one-half.

Thus, Jay Cooke, foremost private banker in America, looked upon the great enterprise to which he lent his fame and fortune, as a land gamble. More than this! He was led into the disastrous undertaking (for him) chiefly through his large personal investments in real estate in and about the frontier town of Duluth— "the Zenith City of the Unsalted Seas."

Having participated, as a shareholder, in the Philadelphia and Erie Land Company, a land improvement company owning property in towns along the line of the Philadelphia and Erie Railroad; and having invested with success in large tracts of real estate in Ohio and other states, Jay Cooke turned to the barren northwestern region at the head of the Great Lakes as a favorable field for fabulous wealth. He soon became one of the largest landowners in northern Minnesota. He took a share in the promotion and construction of the Lake Superior and Mississippi Railroad Company and, in this connection, he and his associates organized the Western Land Association, "to exploit Duluth and other town sites and land privileges of the proposed railroad from

St. Paul to Lake Superior." Thus, in various ways, the great
financier became pecuniarily interested in the much "blessed state
of Minnesota."[1]

Jay Cooke had no part in the original plan and promotion of
the Northern Pacific Railroad. This was the work of Josiah Perham, a Boston wool merchant who, on July 2, 1864, obtained
the charter from Congress. This charter granted, in addition to
free right of way, the *alternate sections of public land ten miles
on both sides of the tracks* "to aid in the construction of a railroad and telegraph line from Lake Superior to Puget Sound on
the Pacific Coast by the northern route." Perham, whose speculations in Maine timber lands have been spoken of, associated
with himself in the venture a number of prominent persons.
Among these were Senator Samuel S. Fessenden, of Maine, William Sears, George Opdyke, Chauncey Vibbard, General John
C. Frémont, William B. Ogden, Leonard Sweet, J. Edgar Thom-
son, and Henry D. Cooke, brother of Jay Cooke. They had the
statutory assurance of the government that patents to the contiguous land would be issued as each twenty-five miles was constructed, and that the even numbered sections, retained by the
United States, would not be sold at less than $2.50 per acre. Al-
together, the total grant was to be about 47,000,000 acres—an
astronomical acreage, almost beyond human comprehension.

This free donation of a domain larger than all New England
attracted little public attention, and passed without much opposition. "It was a faulty measure," wrote John Sherman afterwards,
"making excessive grants of public lands. . . . It was an act of
incorporation, with broad and general powers, carelessly defined,
and with scarcely any safeguards to protect the government in its
lavish grants of land. Some few amendments were made, but
mostly in the interest of the corporation, and the bill, finally,
passed the Senate without any vote by yeas and nays."[2]

Perham did not delay initiating the project. He incorporated
a company commonly known as "Josiah Perham's Peoples' Pacific
Railroad." Stock subscription books were opened in Boston and

[1] Ellis Paxson Oberholtzer, *Jay Cooke, Financier of the Civil War,* Vol. II,
p. III.
[2] *Forty Years in the House, Senate and Cabinet,* Vol. I, p. 325.

Portland, Me., almost immediately, and 20,000 shares were subscribed by November, 1864. Subscribers made a payment of only $10 per share on each $100 face value, and nothing like the $100,000,000 or more required for construction could be obtained. There was a time limit placed on the period of construction by Congress, and Perham was forced to petition repeatedly for its extension. Congress was liberal in this matter, but active construction had to be put off because of lack of capital.

Perham sought the financial aid of Jay Cooke as early as 1865, but the financier was then too busy with dealings in government bond issues to become interested. Sir Morton Peto, an English promoter, who lost millions for British capitalists in American railroad promotions, was also solicited, and it was believed for a while that he would finance the Northern Pacific Railroad. But European capital was timid about ventures in America then, and the collapse of Peto's Atlantic and Great Western resulted in still greater caution.

In the meantime, Jay Cooke became interested in the Lake Superior and Mississippi Railroad, which was to extend 140 miles from St. Paul in a northerly direction to Duluth, and thus connect Lake Superior with the Mississippi River. This railroad also had a Congressional grant of about 1,500,000 acres, nearly all of which was heavily timbered with pine, cedar and oak. Cooke became connected with this project following a trip to Duluth, during which he inspected the proposed route of the railroad. Directly and through agents, he bought large areas in this section jointly for himself and his partner, William G. Moorehead. He chose tracts covered with pine trees which, it was anticipated, would yield timber for the saw mills and be a valuable product for eastern lumber markets. While personally investigating his prospective purchases, he traveled for days in the woods, sprained his ankle, and "wore his feet out," but incidentally obtained, in addition to the pineries, several parcels of good farming land near Duluth. This site, he said, must "become an important point as a terminus of the road." Though he admitted that Duluth "may not equal Chicago, there must be a large town there within a few years after the road shall be in operation."[3]

³ Oberholtzer, *op. cit.*, Vol. II, p. 105.

Duluth, at this time, contained six or seven frame houses, a school and a land office. Superior, Wis., on the south side of the Bay, an older settlement, also presented a desolate and dilapidated appearance. John C. Breckinridge, of Kentucky, had attempted to found a resort of Southerners there after the repeal of the Missouri Compromise in 1854, believing that "it would become a watering place where they could be free to take their slaves with them, deserting Saratoga, Newport, and other northern resorts where such an accompaniment as a slave was not permitted." The project failed and, until Jay Cooke again set the works going, Superior was merely a name on the map.

Cooke undoubtedly knew that his large land purchases in and around Duluth would bring no return unless the place had rail connections with the interior. He, therefore, assumed the task of financing the Lake Superior and Mississippi Railroad. This was difficult, as the Civil War had absorbed home capital, and the impending rupture between Bismark and Napoleon III discouraged European bankers from placing investments in American securities. However, he had faith in the Minnesota country. He continued to instruct his agent at Duluth to buy lots in this "city," where prices were already advancing and where land, which a few years before was considered worthless, was then selling at $600 per acre. Altogether, Cooke and Moorehead became the owners of about 40,000 acres in and around Duluth. Rice Harper, his agent, in May, 1869, wrote him encouragingly: "Men are coming every day, some to purchase city lots, some to work on the railroad, and some mechanics to build the city. Every available place is filled with new shanties and houses are going up."[4]

He also received encouragement in his land speculation from other sources. General George B. Sargent, who had been a government surveyor in the Northwest, and who, in 1869, abandoned his brokerage business in New York, to engage in land jobbing in Duluth, wrote to him, after his arrival there: "I give it to you as my firm conviction that the terminus of your road on Lake Superior will attain a larger growth in five years than any city . . . , in twenty. With this belief I go there to build up a general

[4] *Ibid.,* Vol. II, p. 109.

land business . . . and to assist all in my power in every way in building up a city."[5]

Sargent offered his services in handling Cooke's Duluth real estate, which were accepted. The result was an agreement between them to carry on joint operations for a period of five years. This contract was soon to have a significant bearing on the relationship of Jay Cooke & Company with the Northern Pacific Railroad.

As already noted, one of the projects growing out of Jay Cooke's connection with the Lake Superior and Mississippi Railroad was the "Western Land Association of Minnesota." The purpose of this company was similar to George Francis Train's Crédit Foncier of America. It sought to exploit Duluth and the town sites and land privileges along the right of way of a projected railroad. The first published report of the Western Land Association was made in 1871. The company had received cash of $200,000 for its shares. Its receipts consisted of $97,321 for real estate sold and $21,166 in interest on deferred payments, and it paid out $182,390 for real estate purchases. But the most important item mentioned in the report is the stock interest acquired in the company by the Northern Pacific Railroad. In return for an agreement of the Northern Pacific to fix its eastern terminus at Duluth and to connect with the Lake Superior and Mississippi Railroad, the Western Land Association sold 2,000 shares of its stock for $120,000 to the "Lake Superior and Puget Sound Company," the real estate subsidiary of the Northern Pacific.

A still more interesting item in this first report is the announcement that its shares were sold at a tremendous premium. "The Management congratulates itself on having seen its stock sold at a premium of 750%," and "also upon the fact that the property that cost $102,270 in cash, is now, after deducting sales made, estimated by our agent, to have a cash value of $1,500,000." This vast increase in wealth could readily be passed on to the promoters, as in 1870, the Minnesota Legislature enacted a law permitting the company to partition its land holdings among the shareholders. The president of the company, Mr. Samuel M. Felton, recommended that such apportionment be made. For, he said, "the

[5] *Ibid.*, Vol. II, p. 110.

company will soon be attacked by the Press and in the Courts as a monopoly, and being the creature of the law, may be subject to continual and expensive annoyance." Moreover, "the Western Land Association has now accomplished, as a holder of a large number of town lots, the object for which it was organized, . . . and kept out of the hands of unprogressive speculators the property they would otherwise have held to the detriment of all large plans of improvement."

The shareholders followed the advice of their president. Accordingly, Jay Cooke, the Northern Pacific Company and a few other "insiders" received their ratable proportion of approximately 13,416 town lots, located mostly in Duluth. These lots, together with Cooke's other investments in Duluth and vicinity, were to stand him in good stead. He held on to them, and their sale was one of the chief means by which he succeeded in rehabilitating his fortune after the failure of his firm in 1873. Based upon the original cost to him, the profits from this Duluth real estate were enormous.

When Cooke, largely because of his engrossment of lands in Minnesota, became the banker for the Lake Superior and Mississippi Railroad, the next logical step was to acquire an interest in the Northern Pacific Railroad. This was a big proposition. But in May, 1869, he "had practically determined to take hold of it." His partners, however, insisted on expert advice in the matter. A group of engineers and bankers was engaged to make a trip covering the whole route. The country through which they were to pass was so wild and barren that a military escort was provided. The region was described by General Sherman "as bad as God ever made or anybody can scare up this side of Africa." After many difficulties, during which several of the exploring party deserted or were sent home, the remaining members returned. The engineers gave favorable reports. "The immense landed property of the company as a body in connection with valuable town sites and water powers will ultimately be worth more than the entire cost of the railroad," wrote Cooke's engineer, Mr. Milnor W. Roberts. Henry Cooke, Jay Cooke's brother, insisted that "if successful, the financing of the Northern Pacific would be the grandest achievement of our lives."

So Jay Cooke & Company, the leading banking house in America, became identified with the Northern Pacific. It employed all its influence to favor and forward the enterprise. Cooke personally was put in almost complete control, as the original stockholders, including Josiah Perham, sold out their interests to him. He began to offer publicly the Northern Pacific Railroad bonds, secured by mortgage on the prospective vast land grant. He used the same forceful methods that he had employed during the Civil War in selling United States bonds. He advertised extensively. He organized touring parties to go over the route. He published and widely distributed pamphlets describing in alluring and seductive language the wealth and possibilities of the great region to be traversed by the railroad. These pamphlets were embellished by a map of the proposed railroad route, set off by a wide border representing the donated lands. The picture extended from a point at Duluth to a point on Puget Sound. It resembled in shape a banana. The Northern Pacific thus became known popularly as *"Jay Cooke's Banana Belt."*

But the banker did not act alone in the venture. He formed a "pool" to which he invited a selected group. The "pool" was to subscribe $5,600,000, of which $5,000,000 was represented by mortgage bonds and $600,000 by capital stock. This amount was to be divided into twelve parts, to correspond with Jay Cooke & Company's twelve "interests" in the railroad company. Each part, therefore, represented $416,666.67 in bonds and $50,000 in stock. But the parts could be divided and subdivided to suit the various subscribers. Each subscriber was assigned a proportionate interest in the capital stock of the railroad company. This, to the amount of $40,000,000, was to be distributed as the construction work proceeded, each of the twelve "interests" ultimately to obtain $3,333,000 of capital stock.

The capital stock was really not the most important or alluring bonus to "pool" participants. Each member was to have, in addition, a share in the land company, to be organized in connection with the railroad, "to own and improve town sites, etc." Interest in this land concern was divided into twenty-four parts, "Jay Cooke & Company receiving twelve parts." This half interest owned by the banking house was thrown into the "pool"; the remainder went directly to the Northern Pacific Railroad Company. The land company was capitalized at $2,400,000, and the "pool" and the railroad company jointly were to supply the capital as needed. The land company was duly incorporated as the "Lake Superior and Puget Sound Company." As already shown, its first acquisition was the shares of Cooke's Western Land Association of Minnesota, thus assuring the fixing of the railroad's eastern terminus at Duluth.

Needless to say, the most prominent men of the country participated in the "pool." Politicians, financiers, clergymen and leading journalists were invited to become subscribers and participants. These hailed from all parts of the country. There were, among others: Dr. S. Weir Mitchell, novelist and nerve specialist; Hugh McCulloch, capitalist and cabinet officer; Thomas A. Scott, railroad president and real estate magnate; and Schuyler Colfax, Vice-President and Crédit Mobilier scandal victim.

Chief Justice Chase at first refused to participate because, as he remarked, "though the prospect of future profit is very inviting, it is rather too remote for one who does not expect to live longer than I do." The Chief Justice, of course, was very friendly with Cooke, whose services he had employed in raising national loans; and when Cooke offered to supply the cash required for the proffered subscription, he finally accepted "with thanks." Then, by way of encouragement to Cooke, he wrote while on a visit to Duluth: "Hurrah for the Northern Pacific. I wish I was able to take four times as much as has been assigned me. This is your greatest work. The world will be astonished by it."

The land grant was the bait that attracted many of the subscribers, and this fact was kept in mind by the locating engineers. John Gregory Smith, Governor of Vermont, who assumed the direction of construction work, wrote to Cooke on January 21, 1870, that "everything possible is being done to get the work started." Cooke then suggested to him that the locating engineers "should be accompanied by land prospectors."[6] There was difficulty, however, in following out the instruction because the snow in the woods "was too deep to make a thorough exploration of the country on each side of the line"; nevertheless, a few men

[6] *Ibid.*, Vol. II, p. 167.

who were accustomed to traveling on snowshoes, were employed as land prospectors to accompany the engineers.

There was great rejoicing among the real estate operators in Duluth. Jay Cooke's control of the Northern Pacific assured to them the eastern terminus of the line. But Chicago, and Superior, Wis., as well as other towns in Wisconsin and Minnesota, were not satisfied, and entered their political protests. Sectional jealousy, as well as town rivalry and town jobbing, was a serious handicap to the Northern transcontinental railroad in obtaining national financial aid for the project.

Moreover, strong opposition to the town-jobbing schemes developed in Congress. James Harlan, of Iowa, on April 7, 1870, exclaimed in the Senate chamber: "Is it not enough that you give them a vast quantity of public lands to be sold for agricultural purposes? Must they be permitted to monopolize all the town sites across half a continent in addition? It is quite doubtful to my mind whether the right even to locate their depots is a proper thing to be entrusted to these companies. . . . Companies not infrequently have located their depots in the new states just far enough away from a town to ruin the existing town in order to secure enhanced value to their lots that they sell at the new location." To this argument, Senator Stewart, of Nevada, rightfully answered that if the selection of town sites and depots were taken away from the railroad promoters "there would not be enough money realized from the whole land grant to locate their stations upon."[7]

In spite of Cooke's efforts to create a speculation fever, the countless acres of waste lands with occasional prospective town sites were not a lure to the general public as they had been to the Northern Pacific promoters. Jay Cooke & Company met with ill success, despite strenuous efforts to sell the railroad company's mortgage bonds. The efforts abroad were even more discouraging. The Franco-Prussian War made capital scarce in Europe, and there was none to spare for a gigantic speculative project overseas. The great banking house of Rothschilds in London refused a participation in the proposition because it involved a management as well as a financing problem to them. Hugh McCulloch,

[7] *Congressional Globe*, "Senate," April 7, 1870, p. 2491.

on resigning from the secretaryship of the Treasury, was sent by Jay Cooke to London to open a branch of his banking house there, in the effort to dispose of "Northern Pacific 7.30 Per Cents." He established the firm of "Jay Cooke, McCulloch & Co.," but success was lacking, and the London house barely escaped failure along with the other Cooke banking concerns.

Thwarted at home and abroad in the endeavor to finance the land-burdened transcontinental railroad, Jay Cooke & Company finally succumbed on September 18, 1873. Not long thereafter, the Northern Pacific was also in bankruptcy. But in the three years that Jay Cooke was the authority controlling the destinies of the railroad, steps had been taken to exploit the increase in land values and the favorable town-site locations along the proposed route. This was done through the independent land holding concern, the Lake Superior and Puget Sound Company, one-half interest in which, as already noted, was acquired by Jay Cooke and his associates in the "pool." The land company, under agreement with the railroad company, was entitled to purchase such lands within the Northern Pacific grant as it might apply for. As Cooke stated, in a letter dated September 12, 1872, to Thomas H. Canfield, president of the Lake Superior and Puget Sound Company, "I have always understood that the Puget Sound Company had purchased in their names, or had the refusal of properties at all points likely to be chosen by the Northern Pacific as its terminus."

When the desired lands were not within the railroad's grant, but came within the "even section" retained by the government, the land company found it expedient at times to use dummy entrymen fraudulently to acquire the property. This was occasionally done to keep off "the roughs who had earlier infested the lines of the Union Pacific."

In 1873 difference arose between the land company and the railroad company, "and the cleavage was so great that Mr. Cooke took steps to oust Mr. Canfield from the presidency of the land company." This led almost to the disruption of the land company, but it remained intact even during the Northern Pacific receivership. Shortly before the reorganization of the railroad in 1875, its share capital was acquired by the successor corporation by payment of $721,630 in the defaulted bonds of the old bankrupt company.

Thus, the land company became a direct subsidiary of the railroad company, and the interests of the two were then combined. Previously, the railroad company had only a 50 per cent participation in the real or prospective profits of the land company. Jay Cooke and his associates could claim the other 50 per cent. As the operations of the land company had barely begun when the railroad receivership halted construction activities, there was little opportunity for profit of any kind. It is definitely known that Jay Cooke and his associates never drew any dividends from this source.

The affairs of the land company were finally wound up in 1891. Its remaining lands and lots in Puget Sound were turned over to a local real estate concern for $72,000. Its other properties had been sold from time to time, and the proceeds invested in the securities of the railroad company. The final distribution of assets revealed little gain from the enterprise. On the whole, Jay Cooke's idea of engrossing favorable land sites did not work out any more successfully than George Francis Train's Crédit Foncier in connection with the Union Pacific. Cooke's personal investments in Duluth real estate, made prior to his connection with the Northern Pacific, however, "panned out" well. This real estate was gradually sold by him after the failure of his banking house, as a means of liquidating its indebtedness.

A query here naturally arises: What became of the vast Congressional grant to the Northern Pacific? And this is an interesting story:

Jay Cooke & Company, in their efforts to dispose of the Northern Pacific lands, drew much advertising material from the magnificent land grant. The fertility, climate and resources of the lands were painted in such glowing colors as to bring forth public ridicule. Even Dr. Ellis Paxson Oberholtzer—Jay Cooke's eulogistic biographer—felt the urge to point this out. "The people," he wrote, "were so full of isothermal lines, comparative latitudes, and glowing facts about climates, crops and distances from New York, Liverpool and Shanghai, of new cities set in concentric circles upon the map of the American Northwest, that they were ready to enjoy the satire of J. Proctor Knott. He held a seat in Congress from Kentucky, and rose, on January 27, 1871, during the debate on the St. Croix land bill, setting the House and the whole country in a roar of laughter by a speech which was remembered for many a day."[8]

Congressman Knott was well versed in English literature, for he applied to the "Banana Belt" Lord Byron's poem, adapted from Goethe, in which the romantic Orient is depicted:

> Know ye the land of the cedar and vine,
> Where the flowers ever blossom, and the beams ever shine,
> Where the light wings of Zephyr oppressed with perfume
> Wax faint o'er the gardens of Gul in her bloom.
> Where the citron and olive are fairest of fruit
> And the voice of the nightingale never is mute;
> Where the tints of the earth and the hues of the sky
> In color though varied, in beauty may vie?

Duluth was the butt of Congressman Knott's derision. It was a name, he said, "for which his soul panted for years as a hart panteth for the water brooks." But where was the place? "It is situated," he exclaimed, "somewhere near the western part of Lake Superior, but there is no dot or other mark indicating its location. I am unable to say whether it is confined to any particular spot, or whether it is just running around loose. . . . I cannot really tell whether it is one of those ethereal creations of intellectual frostwork, more intangible than the rose tinted clouds of a summer sunset; one of those airy exhalations of the speculators' brain, which I am told are ever flitting in the form of towns and cities along the lines of railroads with government subsidies" (Laughter).

Yet he was led to believe that wherever Duluth may be "the symmetry and perfection of our planetary system would be incomplete without it." "I see it represented on this map," he exclaimed, in exhibiting a chart of the "Banana Belt," "that Duluth is situated exactly half way between the latitudes of Paris and Venice, so that gentlemen who have inhaled the exhilarating airs of one, or basked in the golden sunlight of the other, may see at a glance that Duluth must be a place of untold delights, a

[8] Oberholtzer, *op. cit.*, Vol. II, p. 308.

terrestrial paradise, fanned by the balmy zephyrs of an eternal Spring, clothed in the gorgeous sheen of ever-blooming flowers, and vocal with the silver melody of the choice songsters" (Laughter).[9]

Newspaper editors reprinted these remarks with zest, much to the embarrassment of Cooke and other Northern Pacific "boosters." The difficulties of these gentlemen multiplied on an increasing scale. Despite their efforts to sell land, little was actually disposed of. Owners of the Northern Pacific 7.30 per cent bonds were given the right to convert at any time their holdings into the land of the company for $2.50 per acre, at 110 per cent of face value. But few took advantage of this proposition until after the financial collapse. Jay Cooke then publicly advised bondholders to make the exchange as a way out of a bad situation. He had more faith in the future value of the lands than in the profitableness of the railroad.

Several large holders of Northern Pacific bonds, feeling that it was better to own waste lands than a doubtful equity in a partially constructed railroad, the completion of which was problematical, engrossed large tracts in the Red River Valley, N. D. Here the virgin soil was in condition for cultivation, without the expense of clearing. It was demonstrated by homesteaders that wheat could be advantageously grown in this section. Hence, the bondholders became the owners of the "bonanza farms."

Some of these farms had acreages in excess of ten miles square. William Dalrymple was the pioneer "bonanza farm" manager. During the years 1876 to 1879, he reported yields of more than 20 bushels of wheat per acre. A homesteader, in 1874, rode into Fargo with 1,600 bushels of wheat raised on 40 acres. In this period, wheat prices were high, and net profits were made by Dalrymple of from $10 to $12 per acre. The cost of the land exchanged for bonds, even at their original offering price, was less than $2.00 per acre. At the depreciated value of the bonds, during the railroad receivership, the cost of the land was about 50 cents an acre.

General George W. Cass, B. P. Cheney, and several other officials and large investors in Northern Pacific before 1873, ex-

[9] *Congressional Globe*, Appendix, January 27, 1871, pp. 66-68.

Duluth, the "Zenith City of the Unsalted Seas," in 1871

(From Oberholtzer's *Jay Cooke, Financier of the Civil War*)

HARVESTING ON A BONANZA FARM

(From Thayer's *Marvels of the New West*)

changed their bonds for Red River lands. With additional sections purchased from homesteaders, they became the lords of the "bonanza farms." They employed managers to work them, and in a short time recovered the losses on their original investment. Corporations also engrossed the lands by buying up the bonds, so wheat-growing became a real business in Northern Pacific territory. The American and Sharon Land Company, the Baldwin Corporation and other concerns consolidated large tracts and worked them as a unit.

Reports of the enormous profits obtained from the soil in the region attracted speculators as well as farmers. As a result, lands that had been bought from homesteaders and from disgruntled

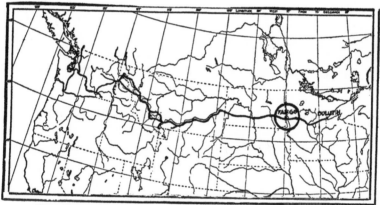

THE CIRCLE MARKS THE LOCATION OF THE "BONANZA FARMS"

Northern Pacific bondholders at from 50 cents to $3 per acre, were selling in the nineties at from $40 to $60 per acre. Gradually it became profitable to divide up large tracts for sale to individual farmers. In this way most of the "bonanza farms," which flourished from 1875 to 1900, have disappeared. Large ranches in the same area also have been broken up. A few still remain, and are held for "sport" purposes, but experience has demonstrated that small acreages give better satisfaction to the owners, both politically and economically.

Notwithstanding the beneficial effects of the policy of the Northern Pacific promoters in converting their defaulted bonds into cultivated areas, there was considerable contemporary complaint against the "bonanza farms." William Godwin Moody, a radical writer of the time, thus stated his objections in the *Atlantic Monthly*, of January, 1880:

> The owners of these large tracts have bonanzas, yielding great profits, not one dollar of which is expended in beautifying and permanently improving their vast estates, beyond that necessary for the care of stock and tools, nor in sustaining population. Their homes, their pleasures, their family ties are not upon the farms. Their wealth is flaunted in the gaieties and dissipations or expended in building and developing some distant city or country. But the owner and cultivator of the small farm in the neighborhood, upon which he has planted his rooftree, and around which are gathered all his hopes and ambitions, finds it impossible to pay his taxes, clothe and educate, or find any comfort for his wife and little ones. The case of the small farmer is steadily going from bad to worse. The two cannot exist together; the small farmer cannot compete with his gigantic neighbor under present conditions. He will inevitably be swallowed up. It is at best but a question of time.[10]

What a false prophecy—so far as the "bonanza farms" are concerned! Millionaires do not run large farms for profit or engage in the risky business of agricultural production, especially when they can sell the land for many times the sum they have paid for it.

When the Northern Pacific Railway was reorganized in 1875, it reacquired the magnificent grant which had been conditionally conveyed to its predecessor. The machinery of land colonization, which had been interrupted by the failure of Jay Cooke & Company, and the subsequent Panic of 1873, was again put in motion. The energetic land-selling campaigns which had been inaugurated by Cooke's agents at home and abroad were intensified. A rush of population into the region followed. Lands in Minnesota and Dakota rose rapidly in value. The railroad sold land not only to settlers, but also to speculators. In numerous instances, accordingly, the condition requiring purchasers to cultivate a certain proportion of the land was omitted from the sales contract or was disregarded. The Weyerhaeusers bought immense tracts to

[10] William Godwin Moody, *Land and Labor*, p. 58.

preserve for timbering. They thus became the lumber kings of America.

Others bought tracts with a view to holding for later developing, or for town-jobbing purposes. The eagerness of the railroad company to realize cash for its patented lands in order to prosecute the construction work as far as Puget Sound led it into making sales to speculators who, while retarding immigration and settlement, became later serious competitors to the company in disposing of its lands at advanced prices.

In the summer of 1881, control of the Northern Pacific passed to Henry Villard, former German newspaper correspondent and agent of German banking interests. Villard was already in charge of extensive railroad operations in the Pacific Northwest, particularly in the Puget Sound area. In connection with these activities, he had launched upon several town-jobbing schemes. The Northern Pacific, as early as 1873, had fixed upon Tacoma as its western terminus, and organized the Tacoma Land Company to do the town jobbing. This was one of the assets sought by Villard. Moreover, Villard, through his European connections, was a strong force in attracting foreign emigrants to the Northern Pacific lands, and while in charge of the company, he continued with increased vigor to dispose of the lands. Colonization projects were carried out on a scale not previously attempted. Land agents were employed in almost every country in Europe, and, with the coöperation of the transatlantic steamship companies, "assisted immigration" became so manifest as to lead to serious political opposition on both sides of the Atlantic. The extent of the colonization activities may be surmised from the statement in the Northern Pacific's annual report to stockholders, in 1882, that it employed 831 active local land agents in the United States and Europe.

Another means of rapidly disposing of Northern Pacific lands after the reorganization in 1875, was the creation by the railroad company of a preferred stock, exchangeable at par value for the company's lands. This was an attractive bait to speculators. The stock could be purchased at a depreciated value, making the cost of the land at from $1.00 to $1.25 per acre. If the lands rose in value above the minimum price of $2.50 per acre, at which price

the company was selling directly to the public, the preferred shareholders could thus realize a profit in making the exchange, since
they were entitled to land at the minimum price for their stock.
The continuous resale of lands obtained in this way by speculators created a serious competition against direct sales by the company, until the entire preferred stock issue was redeemed. Thus,
land gambling followed the Northern Pacific throughout most of
its history.

The vigorous land disposal policy was fruitful in its results.
It was reported to the Interstate Commerce Commission in 1917
that the gross receipts from land sales by the Northern Pacific
had amounted to $136,118,533, and there was a large acreage
still retained. The total cost of originally constructing the road
was estimated at $70,000,000.[11] Accordingly, the prophecy of
Mr. Milnor Roberts, Jay Cooke's engineer, was correct: "The
immense landed property of the company will be ultimately worth
more than the entire cost of construction."

But this is stating it mildly! The receipts reported by the company from its land sales constitute only a part—and probably a
minor part—of its gains from its donated domain. The land and
"improvement" companies, created as subsidiaries of the railroad
and owned by it, also made vast profits, which trickled into the
coffers of the company or its stockholders. These subsidiary companies, consisting of coal, mining and other enterprises, have
constituted the mysterious "hidden assets" of the Northern Pacific Railway Company, by means of which its shares were boosted
by stock manipulators.

The Northwestern Improvement Company has been an important land-holding subsidiary of the Northern Pacific. What business this company has been actually engaged in, or what it owns,
has been largely withheld from the public. Its operations, however,
have been profitable. In 1908 it declared a dividend from accumulated surplus directly to the stockholders of the Northern Pacific Railroad equal to 11.26 per cent on the capital stock of that
company. In recent years it has paid at times as much as $5,-
000,000 a year into the railroad company's treasury, and the

[11] See *Hearings before the Joint Congressional Committee on the Investigation of the Northern Pacific Land Grants* (March 18, 1925), p. 2020.

Northern Pacific still owns the Northwestern Improvement Company, so that more may be expected.

Certainly, Jay Cooke was not very wrong, after all, in his belief that, given free lands and engrossed town sites, the construction of the Northern Pacific would be a good business proposition. Though faith in this belief led to his financial ruin within three years after backing it, he lived to see his expectations realized. The remarkable growth of Duluth—his pet "Zenith City of the Unsalted Seas"—materialized when it was linked by rails with the Pacific Northwest. It then became an emporium of a vast inland empire. As previously told, this permitted Cooke to convert his real estate there into the cash which, in time, restored him to solvency. And the citizens of Duluth have acknowledged a debt of gratitude to its prime promoter, who was chiefly responsible for its remarkable growth, by erecting a suitable statue to him within its limits. Thus, future generations may gaze on the kindly countenance of the great financier whose bold and progressive spirit, in combination with human cupidity, helped to put down civil strife and to build up a united nation from coast to coast.

CHAPTER XV

"MAIN STREETS" AND "BROADWAYS"

THAT caustic commentator and caricaturist of American characteristics, Charles Dickens, when he visited the United States
in 1842 could not have failed to notice the prevalence of town
jobbing and "city building." Picturing himself as Martin Chuzzlewit, he is told, soon after landing, by Major Pawkins, "a most
distinguished genius for swindling, who could start a bank, or
negotiate a loan or form of land-jobbing company, (entailing
ruin, pestilence, and death on hundreds of families) with any
gifted creature of the Union":

"You have come to visit our country, sir, at a season of great commercial depression,"

to which the journalist, Mr. Jefferson Brick, added:

"at a period of unprecedented stagnation."

This was then undoubtedly true, and it is also true, as Dickens
pointed out, that in America, if "individual citizens, to a man,
are to be believed, it always *is* depressed, and always *is* stagnated,
and always *is* at an alarming crisis, and never was otherwise."

Certainly, at the period whereof Dickens describes the adventures of the naïve Martin Chuzzlewit in the Land of Liberty,
many individual citizens of the type of Major Pawkins could have
looked back just a few years earlier, when they accounted themselves millionaires and land magnates. But Americans, in their
business affairs; in their chase after the dollar; in their extravagant greed, which Dickens and other of his traveling compatriots
have caricatured to the pleasure and satisfaction of their own

countrymen, *always look ahead*. Things will get better! Prosperity is coming! The country will grow! Lands will rise in value! Buy now, and take advantage of low prices in the present depression, and get rich in the approaching days of prosperity!

Such was the feeling when the disastrous collapse of 1837 had run its course. Land jobbing and town-site booming were stifled, but they were not dead. Land speculation still remained as an American business, and though full recovery did not come until after a decade, it began to be manifested after only a few years of almost complete cessation.

That Martin Chuzzlewit should be made a victim of American optimism and faith in the rapid growth and development of an expanding territory is not a mere fictional concept of a successful satirist. Chuzzlewit invested in New Eden,—a boom *"city,"* mind you, not a town or a colony, as was wont to be the practice in the earlier period of land speculation. Eden was a *city project*. This surprised the credulous Martin:

"Why, I had no idea it was a city," he exclaimed, glancing at the map on the wall.

"Oh, it's a city," [answered the agent].

A flourishing city, too! [remarks Dickens, in his own language] An architectural city! There were [on the map] banks, churches, cathedrals, market places, factories, hotels, stores, mansions, wharves; an exchange, a theatre, public buildings of all kinds down to the office of the *Eden Stinger*, a daily journal,—all faithfully depicted in the view before them.

All this, of course, was put down for literary effect. But the hyperboles connected with real estate developments have persisted down to the present. And there is no necessary intention of fraud or deceit on the part of the many city boosters, past and present, who start out with great ideas of what they can accomplish in placing on the map a new metropolis, bearing usually their own names or those of old-world centers, and having their "Main Streets" and "Broadways."

Ambitious capitalists, imbued with optimism, have not only innocently plotted great emporiums on shallow creeks, rocky bays or country crossroads, but they have projected canals, railways, waterworks and other "internal improvements" in the fond belief that their ideas of future growth and prosperity were correct. "Internal improvements" were political bywords in the early days of the Republic. Though the phrase is rarely used in these modern times, projects of a similar nature, to be accomplished with public or private funds, are constantly on the American calendar. "Although," as Jefferson Brick remarked, "unprecedented stagnation exists," yet the speculative and adventuresome genius in American character always plans great and fantastic things.

. . . . .

Following the recuperative period produced as an aftermath of the '37 Panic, the Middle Southwest, now comprising Kansas, Oklahoma and Nebraska, took up the old mania with the old-time vigor. This territory had been neglected prior to 1850, for several reasons. Its settlement had been delayed because of the slavery controversy. Northerners would not go there because of their dislike for the institution. Southerners were not attracted because cotton did not thrive on its alluvial soil. They were not grain growers. The adherents of both parties were deterred by the presence of the large Indian tribes. These occupants kept the government from making the land available for settlers. But the rush began when the Indians were forced out and the section opened up for settlement. Then, the free-staters strove against the pro-slavery party for ascendancy in the disputed region. There followed a perfect mania for town sites among the first settlers.

"All wanted to get rich in town speculations," wrote H. Miles Moore, himself a *city* promoter in this region, "and every chap who had squatted upon a decent quarter section near a creek or a crossroad, turned it into a town site, and if he could only succeed in roping in a half dozen other fools, who had a little money or were like himself, town-crazy, they had a company formed, the town surveyed and laid off into blocks, lots, streets, alleys, public squares, etc., and several hundred lithographic maps struck off; and their pockets full of town shares of this great city in embryo, —they were happy." And he adds:

Of houses and improvements in the town,—that important part of the necessary and future success and prosperity of the town—never entered their heads, or if it did, they only reasoned that the suckers and gudgeons who bought their shares and lots, could build if they wanted to. These schemes generally lasted from three to six months, sometimes a little longer, depending somewhat upon how successful the proprietors had been in disposing of shares and lots to "greenies" from the other States.[1]

Albert D. Richardson, in his once famous book, *Beyond the Mississippi*, gave a similar description of the city building mania in Kansas about 1857:

When Themistocles at a feast was asked to play upon a musical instrument, he replied, "I cannot fiddle, but I know how to make a small town a great city!" Every Kansan thought himself a Themistocles . . . The genie of real estate speculation touched them with his wand . . . Young men, who never before owned fifty dollars at once, a few weeks after reaching Kansas, possessed full pockets, with town shares by the score.

On paper all these towns were magnificent. Their superbly lithographed maps adorned the walls of every place of resort. The stranger studying one of these fancied that New Babylon was surpassed only by its namesake of old. Its great parks, opera houses, churches, universities, railway depots and steamboat landing made New York and St. Louis insignificant in comparison. But if the new-comer had the unusual wisdom to visit the prophetic city before purchasing lots, he learned the difference between fact and fancy . . . In most cases he would find one or two rough cabins, with perhaps a tent and an Indian canoe in the river.[2]

It was under conditions such as are described by these contemporary observers that Leavenworth, Topeka, Lawrence and other towns or "cities" in Kansas were started. Leavenworth was laid out by the Leavenworth Association, a group of land jobbers who, in 1854, pooled their squatter claims. They surveyed and laid out the city, and then sold off the lots. By December 6, 1856, they had completed the sale and closed out the town-jobbing business. Like other similar town-site plans, they erected public buildings and set aside lots for educational and religious purposes.

In a similar way, Topeka, which later became the capital of Kansas, was founded in 1854. This city was partially the result

[1] H. Miles Moore, *Early History of Leavenworth*, p. 60.
[2] *Beyond the Mississippi*, p. 58. See the cuts showing New Babylon as planned and New Babylon as it really was on the following pages.

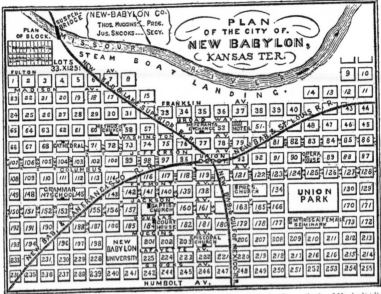

(From Richardson's *Beyond the Mississippi*)

THE CITY OF NEW BABYLON ON PAPER

of the efforts of the Emigrant Aid Society of Boston to flood Kansas with "free-staters." The society made it generally known that its purpose was not to foster land speculation. As Amos Lawrence, one of its philanthropic founders, remarked, "It did not propose to stand between the squatter and the government." But the "settlers" sent there through its financial assistance, soon contracted the land and town-jobbing fever.

The actual founder of Topeka was Cyrus K. Holliday, who came from Pennsylvania to Kansas in 1854 with $20,000, and began to speculate in town lots. He was later the promoter of the Santa Fé Railroad. He purchased a tract near Tecumseh, Kan., and secured it by a Wyandotte "float." This was a government warrant authorizing a Wyandotte Indian or his assigns to locate on a piece of unoccupied land wherever he might select it. He then formed the Topeka Town Association, and became its first president. "The selection of the site," according to Holliday's own story, "was not an accident; it offered every advantage of a town site. Here was a great river, plenty of water, and above all, two great trails of the continent, Fort Leavenworth and St. Joe

(From Richardson's *Beyond the Mississippi*)
THE CITY OF NEW BABYLON IN FACT

to Santa Fé, and Independence to California, crossed at this point."

Holliday had high ideas of city development. The shareholders of the Topeka Association provided that lots were to be sold only with the condition that "ornamental trees were to be planted in front, and that no liquor was to be sold on the premises." They were especially liberal in donating ground for educational and religious purposes. The Emigrant Aid Society obtained large holdings in the city as a reward for its colonizing efforts. Such colonization afforded prospective lot purchasers to the city promoters.

A road to California from the city was planned, and a charter was drawn up for a railroad line from the place to St. Joseph, Mo. This was the forerunner of the Atchison, Topeka and Santa Fé system. Moreover, Holliday, through his political influence with the free-staters, succeeded, in 1859, in establishing the territorial capital at Topeka. All this was done or planned in the short space of five years. Such was, and still is, the intense Yankee energy, when incited both by anti-slavery sentiments and by the lure of land speculation.

. . . . . .

City building thus became the standard form of real estate speculation in the middle of the nineteenth century. The nation was becoming mature. It began to clothe itself in an industrial garb. Agriculture was no longer the predominent occupation of its citizens. It was displaced by the use of mechanical power, the invention of machinery, the extraction of raw materials, the building of great factories, the construction of vast transportation systems, and by constantly broadening markets. All this required coöperation of large human aggregates, and a concentration of population within narrow limits. Vacant land speculation had gradually declined. City planning has taken its place. Martin Chuzzlewit, English architect, may have been deluded in the prospect of finding professional work in Eden in the early eighteen-forties, but he could have had many opportunities since that time, for "city builders" had much use for his services.

City building found its most fertile field in the Far West. A great deal of it was associated with railroad construction. Chicago, Milwaukee, Duluth, Omaha, Council Bluffs, Tacoma, Seattle, Spokane and a host of pioneer settlements took on a genuine urban aspect after railroad communication was acquired. Some had their periods of rapid advance culminating in a boom. Others expanded and developed gradually. Several have declined. Some are still in the ascendant—and still others await the rod of the real estate promoter and speculator to give them a conspicuous place on the map.

Following the rail movement westward, the "city builders" wended their way through the plains and deserts to the Rocky Mountains, and then beyond. Population centers in the Dakotas, Iowa, Nebraska, Kansas, Wyoming, Colorado, New Mexico, Arizona and all the "Great West" received at their births the title of "cities." When, through cuts in the mountain passes, the iron bands were carried beyond the Rockies and the Sierras, the city builders moved along with them. They reached the neighborhood of the Pacific Coast in the early eighties. The work of these "boomers" in and around Los Angeles may be taken as typical.

As early as 1868, the former "pueblo" of Los Angeles, in Southern California,—once the seat of a Spanish mission,—gave financial assistance towards the construction of the Los Angeles and San Pedro Railroad. When, shortly thereafter, the Southern Pacific was planning a railroad from San Francisco by a southerly route to the East, the citizens of Los Angeles were desirous of having this line pass through their town. The place, moreover, was a port and could be made a Pacific outlet for this new transcontinental venture. At this time, however, its total population was less than 6,000. The promoters of the Southern Pacific demanded a large payment for the privilege of bringing their tracks to the place. Collis P. Huntington, the company's promoter, insisted that the railroad be given 5 per cent of the assessed valuation of all Los Angeles County. To this proposition the citizens agreed. They passed over to the Southern Pacific $200,000 in stock of the Los Angeles and San Pedro Railroad, and about $377,000 in cash, acquired by an issue of the municipality's 7 per cent bonds. In addition, the city of Los Angeles donated 60 acres of ground for a depot. These donations amounted to more than $100 for each inhabitant of the place, but they were satisfied. The groundwork was laid for a real estate boom.

Then the Panic of 1873 came and caused a delay. Although the Southern Pacific was completed to Los Angeles before 1882, and the city had started "to grow" in consequence, it was not until five years thereafter that a veritable "boom" took place. In the meantime, the Atchison, Topeka and Santa Fé Railroad had stretched rival tracks across the Sierras and had also reached Los Angeles. A railroad war ensued. Tickets were sold from the Missouri River to the Pacific Coast from $1 to $15. The town jobbers thus found it convenient to transfer their operations from the Middle West to the Pacific Coast.

If these "developers" had any honest scruples in their dealings prior to their arrival in California, they certainly lost them before they crossed the Rockies. They mapped out new mushroom cities all over Los Angeles County. Within three months no less than thirteen town sites were plotted along the rails of the Santa Fé, in Los Angeles and San Bernardino counties in California— a distance of 136 miles. At the same time, almost as many new ones were marked off on the line of the Southern Pacific. The boundaries of each new "city" almost overlapped those of its neighbors. The wooden street markers and lot pegs gave the appearance of a battlefield cemetery. Lots were offered in large quantities and just as eagerly bought, both on the spot and at other places.

The founding of the "city" of Azusa may be taken as typical.

When the day was fixed for the first sale of the lots in this place, anxious buyers waited before the office of the real estate company all through the preceding night. The advance places in line were sold by those holding them at prices ranging from $300 to $1,000. The sale, of course, was a complete success to the promoters. But today the "City of Azusa," Cal., is a mere hamlet. "Like most others of these phantom cities, it soon faded almost from view." In many cases, within two years the white stakes that marked off the boulevards and avenues "have been buried by the plowshare or gnawed away by the teeth of time."[3]

The county recorder's office of Los Angeles furnishes evidence of the extent of the boom. Its files of subdivisions and resubdivisions of tracts and blocks, in addition to the cities and towns, for the single year of 1887, fill twenty large map books. In that year real estate transactions, as recorded by deeds in Los Angeles alone, approximated $100,000,000. This, however, does not tell half the story, since the bulk of the sales were merely contracts or options to buy. As is usual in land speculations, liberal terms of payment were granted, and when the collapse occurred in 1888, thousands of contracts were defaulted, and thus do not appear on the records of real estate transactions. Land which sold at $100 per acre in 1886, changed hands at $1,500 an acre the following year. City lots, which in 1886 brought $500, sold for $5,000 in 1887, and fell back again to the old price at the end of the following year. Between January 1, 1887, and July 1, 1889, sixty new towns and cities, covering about 80,000 acres, were laid out in Los Angeles County, and these at the end of the boom period had an aggregate population of less than 3,500.[4]

This Los Angeles boom, like so many others before and since, was carried on by professional town jobbers. It was not a native product. At this time, immigration into the region consisted of a few souls, but many "real estate operators." These, taking advantage of the tourist travel to Southern California induced by cheap railroad rates, advertised the section far and wide as a favorable health resort and a coming commercial emporium. Alluring lithographed posters were displayed in Los Angeles and other places,

[3] J. M. Guinn, *History of California, and an extended History of Los Angeles,* Vol. I, pp. 260, 261.
[4] *Ibid.,* p. 263.

and "land offices" were set up not only in the new "cities," but in distant towns. Charles Dickens' description of the Eden City office, in which Martin Chuzzlewit made his unfortunate real estate investment, is an ungarnished prototype of those which have been set up from that day to this. The furnishings of the offices may have been improved and the agents may have become more polished in behavior, but the purpose and the methods have always been the same.

And to show that Dickens' "Eden City," back in the forties, was not so much an exaggerated fictitious conception as patriotic Americans, who took offense at the English novelist's characterizations, have maintained, one merely has to refer to the operations of Simon Homberg, the most unprincipled speculator in the Los Angeles boom of 1887. Homberg bought from the government two separate quarter sections of land bordering on the Mojave Desert. One of these he correctly named "Border City," the other he called "Manchester."[5] Without going to the expense of having either site surveyed into lots and staked off, he plotted it in squares and blocks. He then offered the lots in various eastern cities whose inhabitants were ignorant of their barren nature, and sold about 4,000 of them. He had the deeds already printed, so that all that was necessary was the insertion of names, and the consideration. The lots cost Homberg about 10 cents each, but he sold them for as much as $250. "Border City" has disappeared from the map of California, and "Manchester" is today so small as to be almost unknown.

T. S. Van Dyke, the southern California author, seems to deride the idea that the Los Angeles boom of the eighties was "analogous to any South Sea Bubble, or oil or mining stock swindle." In his fanciful account of the speculation, he states: "The actors in this great game were not ignorant or poor people, and from end to end there was scarcely anything in it that could be called a swindle. With a few exceptions, the principal victims were men of means. Most of them, and certainly the most reckless of them, were men who in some branch of business had been successful . . . All had the amplest time to revise their judgments and investigate the conditions . . . Some of the silliest of the lot were

[5] *Ibid.*, Vol. I, pp. 262, 263.

men who, during the first three-fourths of the excitement kept carefully out of it, and did nothing but sneer at the folly of those who were in it."[6]

Of course, Los Angeles County is marked out by nature to be a wonderful country, and in the years subsequent to its first great boom it has taken its place in the sun. In fact, the county today is one large aggregation of cities and towns. But its rapid growth, though accompanied by real estate boosting and town jobbing, has been placed on a firm foundation. Tourist tales, moving picture progress and petroleum projects, together with a magnificent port development, have combined to make it the most populous portion of the Golden State. Unlike Florida, neither epidemics nor hurricanes have yet marred its marvelous rise in real estate values.

.   .   .   .   .

But the growth and grandeur of Los Angeles as a Pacific port, fostered by real estate booms, may be matched to some extent by the rival cities located on Puget Sound. As San Francisco has looked with jealous eyes on the preponderant material advance of the once inconspicuous "pueblo", six hundred miles to the south, so Tacoma, the original terminus and Pacific gateway of that stupendous railroad undertaking, the Northern Pacific, now looks upon Seattle, its neighbor, twenty-four miles up the Sound. These two constantly "boosted" ports have watched each other like opposing prize fighters in the ring. Real estate operators and "land companies" were largely responsible for this.

The Northern Pacific promoters, we have seen, were on the lookout for profits from town-site speculation. When Tacoma was selected as the western end of the transcontinental rail line, the Tacoma Land Company was forthwith organized and acquired 3,000 acres of tide lands in the town, and 13,000 acres of additional neighboring lands. Like the Lake Superior and Puget Sound Company, which engrossed valuable properties in Duluth, one-half of the capital stock of the Tacoma Land Company was retained by the Northern Pacific promoters and one-half taken by the railroad corporation. Town booming was begun

[6] T. S. Van Dyke, *Millionaires of a Day: The Inside History of the Great Southern California Boom*, pp. 2-3.

THE THRIVING CITY OF EDEN "IN FACT"

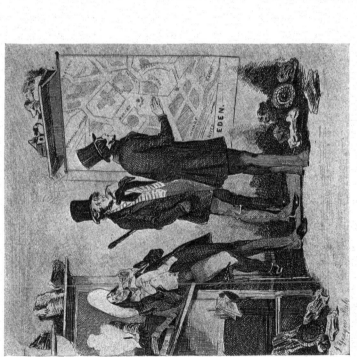

MARTIN CHUZZLEWIT SELECTS HIS LOT IN THE THRIVING
CITY OF EDEN

"PHIZ," THE DICKENS ILLUSTRATOR, DEPICTS AMERICAN TOWN JOBBING

MAKING MORE LAND IN FLORIDA TO MEET THE DEMAND OF SPECULATORS

THE DAVIS ISLAND COUNTRY CLUB BUILT ON LAND THAT A YEAR PREVIOUS
WAS UNDER WATER

by the company long before the rails reached the shores of Puget Sound. A magnificent hotel was built and the lots offered for sale.

There were no wild efforts, however, to dispose of the company's holdings. It pursued a conservative policy in its sales to newcomers, avoiding a strong semblance of excited town jobbing. Its operations were handicapped by the slow construction progress of the Northern Pacific. Before the lines of this railroad were extended to the coast, a rail connection was already made with the Columbia River, by which, with water navigation, the interior country could be reached. The slow growth of the city, and the gradual advance of its rival, Seattle, which became the terminus of Jim Hill's Great Northern Railroad, did not permit highly profitable real estate transactions.

Finally, in 1899, the Tacoma Land Company underwent a reorganization. It sold its water front lots to the Northern Pacific Railroad Company, but retained its real estate in and about Tacoma to the value of about $1,500,000. This property has been largely closed out, and the Tacoma Land Company is now inoperative.

While the original town-site concern was thus gradually going out of business, the City of Tacoma was in a stagnant situation. It was adversely affected by the business depression following 1893. The title to nearly all the real estate in the city had passed, under foreclosure proceedings, to eastern mortgagees. Its population dwindled. In the meantime, Seattle, its rival, was being pushed into a boom. The Great Northern came there in 1892, and Henry Villard—who had taken the Northern Pacific in tow in 1881—extended a branch line to the place. So Seattle had two rail lines to play against each other. Its real estate mongers could say to the Northern Pacific, "If you make improvements in Tacoma, we will give business to the Great Northern"; and to the Great Northern, "If you build to Tacoma, we will favor the Northern Pacific."

Thus, Seattle and Tacoma became deadly rivals. The opposing real estate boosters carried on a continuous warfare. Both had their Chambers of Commerce, and their "Booster Clubs," and both had developers of "subdivisions" and "suburbs." Large sums were expended in advertising. Industries were enticed to locate within the city limits of each. Their lots were widely offered on easy terms to all comers.

A boom for both cities came with the gold rush to Alaska in 1897. Their respective populations increased after that, and along with it the number of real estate agents. Visitors and prospective lot purchasers were urged to invest in Seattle, because that was the "Chicago of the Pacific"; and, if they chanced to cross over to Tacoma, why, there was the place to get rich with "lots" because (as the conspicuous sign over the town's harbor indicated) "you could just watch Tacoma grow." They certainly did some business, too, those real estators. Sales doubled, tripled and quadrupled during the years 1905, 1906 and 1907. Then came the financial panic. The "whooping up" of the cities continued, but sales of lots were at a standstill.

Lyman C. Smith, Syracuse, N. Y., typewriter manufacturer, was one of the eastern capitalists who was attracted to Seattle real estate soon after the Klondike gold discovery in 1897. Henry Whitcomb, an envelope manufacturer of Worcester, Mass., was another. Whitcomb is said to have invested $113,000 in city lots in Seattle. He soon sold at a handsome profit, then increased his investments and again sold off much of his holdings. He built a large office building in the city as a token of his interest in the locality.

Smith would not be outdone by Whitcomb. With the advice of his son, Burns Lyman Smith, he erected the tallest office structure outside of New York City—a sort of replica of the Woolworth Building in the nation's metropolis. It stands now like a central tombstone in a soldiers' cemetery—and looks as much out of place as a bay tree in a cabbage patch. But it is a lasting memorial of the great wealth which may be acquired in quiet and cautious real estate dealings in a boom town.

.   .   .   .   .

Not all the important speculative schemes of city building can be covered in this survey. Time and space would hardly suffice for that. Neither would it be worth while to list and describe fully the many land booms that have been, throughout almost a century, a common occurrence in American social and industrial evolution. A citation of a few of the conspicuous speculations of this nature will be given by way of illustration rather than attempt to cover the whole field.

One of the most interesting, if not the most successful, of "city building" ventures in recent times is that of Newport News, Va. The development of this important southern seaport and industrial center is largely the work of Collis P. Huntington, California pioneer millionaire and railroad builder. Huntington, after the successful completion of his western railroad ventures, came East and acquired control of the Chesapeake and Ohio Railroad Company. In order to obtain a satisfactory tidewater terminus for his railroad, he conceived the idea of building a port in Hampton Roads, Va., at a site having a harbor sufficiently deep to accommodate large ocean steamers. The place selected was given the name of "Newport News." It is reported that prior to the Civil War, Huntington, while traveling through Virginia, chanced to visit the site and at once realized its possibilities. A company, incorporated as the "Old Dominion Land Company," was organized in 1880 to acquire the site. A boom was started. Not only was the terminus of the Chesapeake and Ohio fixed at the place, but Huntington constructed one of the largest drydocks and shipbuilding plants on the Atlantic seaboard.

All this sounds unromantic, but the Sierra poet, Joaquin Miller, immortalized it in pleasing verse:

NEWPORT NEWS

The huge sea monster, the "Merrimac,"
The mad sea monster, the "Monitor,"
You may sweep the sea, peer forward and back,
But never a sign or a sound of war.
A vulture or two in the heavens blue,
A sweet town building, a boatsman call,
The far sea song of a pleasure crew
The sound of hammers. And that is all.

And where are the monsters that tore this main?
And where are the monsters that shook this shore?
The sea grew mad! And the shore shot flame!
The mad sea monsters they are no more.
The palm, and the pine, and the sea sands brown,
The far sea-songs of the pleasure crews;

> The air like balm in the building town—
> And that is a picture of Newport News.

The Old Dominion Land Company continued to operate Newport News until 1895, when a city charter was obtained from
the State of Virginia. The president of the company, in referring
to the change of municipal status, remarked in his annual report
that, in the interests of the company, the charter was "reasonable as to its nature, care having been taken to avoid the imposing
of extreme taxation or other burdens." At that time the company
still owned 156 lots in the city, and a thirty-acre farm. In addition, it owned the Newport News Lighting and Water Company.
Most of the company's lots had been sold on deferred payments,
so with high taxes they were likely to revert to the company; but
with a city charter, the expenses previously incurred by the land
company in keeping the streets of the town in order would be
borne by the taxpayers.

The Old Dominion Land Company, regarded in the light of
present-day high capitalization, would be considered a puny affair.
In 1896 its total capitalization was but $1,962,736. The cost of
its real estate was put down at $1,585,289, and its buildings,
including its hotel, cost but $1,118,564. Its other investments
hardly exceeded $500,000. Profits, moreover, were not large. Only
recently has it practically wound up its affairs. In 1930 the assessed valuation of taxable property in the city of Newport News
was about $35,000,000. Thus, real estate values there have in-
creased marvelously.

Elaborate suburban development is probably the most conspicuous phase of real estate speculation in recent times. And
there has been enough of it, too! So much, in fact, that no one
investigator can reasonably attempt to cover the whole story.
Every large city is encrusted with its "grand subdivisions" and
"suburban developments." Some have been successful. Some have
fared indifferently. But many have failed.

As a rule, these suburban developments have been the work of
a single capitalist, or of a small group of promoters. Occasionally,
they have been a means of stock speculation. The "Ocean View
Land Improvement Company" of Staten Island, incorporated

in New York in the early seventies, is an instance of a combination of land and stock speculation. Its capital was only $120,-000, but each of the 1,200 shares represented one lot of land. In order to attract purchasers of the shares, a lottery scheme was devised. "As soon as the stock is all taken," the pamphlet advertising the plan announced, "a distribution will be made among the stockholders *by lot* of the property of the company in a manner described by its laws. Immediately upon conclusion of such distribution, the stockholders, upon surrendering their certificates of stock, will be entitled to receive a warranty deed of the lot or lots to which they are entitled." The prize lot to be drawn in the lottery comprised the "late owner's homestead." The "late owner" agreed to pay $20,000 in cash to the person drawing it, or to lease it until May, 1872, at $1,500 per year. Thus, as stated in the pamphlet, "The temptation to speculate is very great," and in order to encourage those inclined towards speculation, an offer of free transportation to the location was made.

This, of course, is but one case, selected largely by way of illustration. There have been thousands similar to it, and the "prize lot" or "free lot" to the lucky ticket holder has been used as a bait innumerable times. Auctioning off city and suburban lots, accompanied by brass bands, oratorical and athletic contests, theatrical performances and the like, have been common occurrences in modern real estate operations. The appetite for town-lot speculation, like religious revivals and political propaganda, must be sharpened by sweetmeats and garnishments, or it is likely to vanish.

One of the largest real estate corporations in America, in recent times, which fostered elaborate suburban development schemes, was the American Real Estate Company. This concern was organized in 1888, with the insignificant capital of $100,000. Operating under this small capitalization, held by the "insiders," it gradually unloaded on the public millions of dollars of its "real estate bonds" and "certificates."

The American Real Estate Company adopted the so-called "thrift scheme" of obtaining funds, i.e., selling its bonds on instalment payments. In this way, the investing public bore practically the whole risk of its operations. It never built up reserves to cover contingencies or possible losses. In 1913, at the height of its prosperity, its total surplus was but $2,147,789; its capital (including $1,000,000 of 7 per cent preferred stock sold to "bond-holders and clients") was $1,100,000 and its bonded indebtedness $13,660,900. In addition to this indebtedness, all its real estate was mortgaged. At this time, against total assets consisting of real estate and improvements carried at about $26,000,000, its total indebtedness was almost $25,000,000. Its cash resources were generally below $1,000,000.

All went well with the company until 1914, when real estate values in and around New York began to slump. Without reserves and with large "developments" under way in Yonkers, in the Bronx, and in Queens, the concern was forced into bankruptcy in 1917. Soon after taking charge of the company's affairs, the receivers discovered underhanded transactions inuring to the benefit of the officers, and suits for recovery were instituted against them. Notwithstanding efforts at reorganization to preserve the equities of the bondholders, the affairs of the company underwent complete liquidation, a matter requiring more than a decade. Its security holders, of course, fared badly.

Although the American Real Estate Company's securities were sold throughout the country, it confined its real estate operations to New York and vicinity. Its most ambitious undertaking was a development in the city of Yonkers known as "Park Hill on the Hudson." A carefully edited pamphlet, undoubtedly written by a "literary expert," revealed the beauties and allurements of this splendid suburb. In bold letters on the first page, the reader is informed:

Without romance or exaggeration we have set forth herewith as simply and as briefly as possible some of the essential features of the "Suburb Beautiful." No words can adequately describe its charm. Our only hope is that the story which word and picture herein present may attract you to see and know it for yourself.

Yet, "word and picture" did not bring desired results. When the company failed, it still held more than 1,300 lots in Yonkers. In addition, it had purchased a tract comprising almost 3,000 lots in Astoria, on Long Island, opposite New York—few of which were sold. It also owned office buildings, apartment houses and vacant lots in New York City, all heavily mortgaged, and all acquired with funds received through high pressure salesmanship from "innocent investors."

No record of modern suburban real estate speculation in the United States would be complete without the story of the Van Sweringens' masterful creation of Shaker Heights, situated on a plateau just east of Cleveland, Ohio. It is said that, as poor newspaper boys, Oris P. and Mantis J. Van Sweringen were accustomed to tramp over the pasture country overlooking the busy city of Cleveland, where a Shaker community was once established. When "Oris P.," the elder of the two, reached the age of twenty-one, he became a free-lance real estate speculator, and took in his younger brother as a partner. They obtained control of a 1,500-acre tract on Shaker Heights which a syndicate of Buffalo capitalists had tried in vain for eighteen years to sell. They innovated the idea of reselling parts of this property in small blocks, with a guarantee to repurchase at a slightly higher price, if buyers were dissatisfied. Thus, the buyers helped to finance their deal. Through cash received from the sale of additional options and contracts, they expanded their holdings until they finally obtained the whole acreage of Shaker Heights.

They carried out vast development operations. They built broad boulevards; they laid out elaborate golf links; excavated lakes, and donated spacious plots for parks and playgrounds. All this was regarded as visionary by the old-fashioned real estate dealers of Cleveland. But the method of wholesaling lots by the Van Sweringens on a guaranteed repurchase basis seemed to work well. It accelerated sales and gave them funds to carry out further purchases, and as their customers soon resold at a profit, they again came back for more "blocks."

But the Van Sweringens lacked one important real estate factor to make their project a complete success. They needed cheap and rapid transportation to the heart of Cleveland. The city street railways would not extend their lines to Shaker Heights. The traffic from this suburb did not warrant the expense. The Van Sweringens, however, got the transportation facilities. They offered to donate the right of way through the section and to pay interest for a limited period on the cost of construction.

The offer was accepted. The railway construction was expensive, because grade crossings were eliminated, and excellent physical equipment installed, but it gave the residents high speed express transportation and attracted many working in Cleveland to make their homes on Shaker Heights.

As a suburban real estate development, the Van Sweringen venture is the outstanding success of its kind. In 1900 the land was appraised at $240,000. In 1924 it was valued, without buildings, at $30,000,000. Its projectors became nationally famous. They were greatly encouraged. They extended their real estate operations into the city of Cleveland. Here they encountered some competition. The Nickel Plate Railroad, in contemplation of the construction of a terminal, was buying up land in their neighborhood. And Cleveland needed a Union passenger station.

This gave the Van Sweringens an idea. Because the Interstate Commerce Commission had ordered the New York Central to part with the ownership of the Nickel Plate, the railroad could be bought. They offered to buy it. The bid was accepted, and partly with their own capital, and partly with borrowed funds, they graduated from real estate developers to railroad magnates. But they continued to buy up Cleveland real estate and construct magnificent buildings. What is more, they continued, on a still larger scale, to buy up and develop railroads. All this was well and good. Their names became bywords for successful railroad combinations. Wall Street gave them assistance and "Van Sweringen babies" were jerked up to high price levels among railroad shares. Moreover, their own securities, by means of which they financed their manifold railroad acquisitions, were eagerly absorbed by investors and speculators.

Then the 1929 crash came! It drastically shrunk the value of their real estate and their railroad shares.

The final outcome is still in the lap of the gods!

CHAPTER XVI

FLORIDA—THE LATEST PHASE

THE semi-tropical, semi-submerged State of Florida has ever been an inspirer of fantastic dreams. Ponce de León believed that he would find there the Fountain of Youth. Others who came after him believed that *there* the rainbow ends, and that merely to stake off a part of its soil would give them access to the fabulous pot of gold. Youth, health, wealth, and freedom from inheritance taxes have been the lures to the sunshine and everglades of this Riviera of America.

Yet, American speculators heard little of Florida until the Spanish king, in 1819, was induced to pass over to the control of the United States this half-sunken and troublesome peninsula. To him it was as worthless as the Sahara Desert. And his "governors" in the territory had granted away its soil with much the same feeling. Millions of acres had been donated under all sorts of pretexts. These "Spanish grants" were almost as troublesome to the United States Government as those in Louisiana and California, and the records of Congress and the courts have been cluttered with the claims to them. Some were upheld, others were denied. Whether legitimate or not, they attracted the land grabbers. Some were assigned to "companies" and "associations" and made the basis of vast land-jobbing enterprises.

One of the largest of the early land claims in Florida was known as the "Forbes Purchase." An English firm in St. Augustine, under the name of Panton, Leslie and Company, in 1806, acquired from the Creek Indians, with the consent of the Spanish Government, a tract of land east of the Apalachicola River, and bordering on the Gulf of Mexico, in West Florida. Its area in all comprised about 1,400,000 acres. The Indians had "committed depredations" against the firm, and by way of compensation deeded them the land. John Forbes, a member of the firm of Panton, Leslie and Company, succeeded to the claim. It was later acquired by Robert Mitchel and associates. The United States Supreme Court confirmed the title in 1835.[1] Soon thereafter the successful litigants organized the "Apalachicola Land Company of Florida," and founded the town of Apalachicola. In 1842 a patent to the property was received from the United States.

In the meantime, both Indians and squatters had settled on the lands. The latter were driven off by the company, but many settled near by, to start a rival town and a rival land boom. Apalachicola (I must apologize for the name) was developed into a "Gulf port," with streets, wharves and warehouses. Lots in the city and lands in the interior were offered for sale. Cotton could be grown on these lands and the Apalachicola River offered favorable means of transport. Both the lands and the lots were advertised in New York City. Altogether, there were about 1,800 dwelling lots, 521 business lots, and 43 wharf lots. Sales were extremely slow, however, and many who bought lots and lands on credit terms turned them back to the company. Handicaps to the proprietors were numerous. It was a period of business depression. Occasional storms, moreover, destroyed property of the company, and the neighboring Seminole Indians were from time to time on the war path. Finally, in 1845, the company, or its creditors, auctioned off parcels of its vast property in New York City.

In the meantime, the dispossessed former occupants of the Forbes Purchase were busy boosting their new city of "St. Joseph." Unlike the Apalachicola Land Company, they had the support of local interests. Various Florida banks became interested in the "Wimico and St. Joseph Land Company." Ben Charres, a banker and planter of Tallahassee, became its president. With this financial support, they built a short railroad, the first in Florida, from Lake Wimico to Apalachicola Bay. They established the Bank of St. Joseph with $1,000,000 capital; the

[1] See Mitchel, *et al, vs.* United States, 9 Peters 740.

St. Joseph Insurance Company was similarly capitalized. Other efforts were made to make St. Joseph a modern city and ocean port. The place grew in importance, as indicated by the fact that the first constitutional convention in Florida met there in 1838.

While all this was going on, lots in the town were being sold and resold. Local newspapers were issued as "boosting sheets." A regular advertising warfare was carried on with the rival town of Apalachicola. The result was that every newspaper of the period in Florida and the adjacent states was filled with material relating to the Wimico and St. Joseph Company. The *St. Joseph Times* was "the most quoted sheet in Florida." It had a close "follow-up" in the *Apalachicola Gazette*.

Conditions in the "boom town" soon began to resemble those of the recent Florida episode. Houses were insufficient to accommodate the increasing population. Rents were extortionate, wages extremely high. Everything might have continued favorable— but, Fate, then as in recent times, brought about a complete collapse. A West Indian hurricane swept over St. Joseph in the autumn of 1840, and almost completely ruined it. In 1841 an epidemic of yellow fever completed the destruction. The town was abandoned. Some of the inhabitants took their belongings and emigrated to Texas. "G.T.T." (Gone to Texas), a common phrase at the time, as previously noted, was posted on their deserted homes. The place today is as difficult to discover as the ruin of an Aztec temple.[2]

There were other Florida land companies in these early days, but it is not considered essential to our story to give details regarding them. The Apalachicola Land Company and its rival, the St. Joseph Company, are briefly described merely as evidence that "land booming" and "city building" are old affairs in this region. The Florida real estate promoter in recent years, therefore, did not engage in a pioneer occupation by taking his business to this state. Florida lands and lots in Florida towns and cities have been hawked about for over a century.

Yet, in some respects, the recent glaring episode of land speculation in Florida is a new phase. True, similar outbursts of specu-

[2] See *Quarterly of the Florida Historical Society*, April and July, 1927.

lative fever have occurred before. But the field of speculation, when confined to a single state, at no previous period has been conducted with such whole-hearted coöperation by all other sections of the country. From the Atlantic to the Pacific, from the Great Lakes to the Gulf, the people were infected with the Florida mania. Land in Florida—*anywhere in Florida*—attracted the attention of the whole country, to the almost complete exclusion of land booms, elsewhere. In this respect, the recent Florida land gamble is unique.

How did it start? No one can give a completely satisfactory answer. Yet its origin is not a mystery! For several decades Florida was the nation's winter playground. From millionaires down to farmers, all classes of the population made vacation visits there. The wheat growers of the West found it an opportune place to pass the idle and dreary months when their lands lay fallow. The capitalists of the North found it a convenient country in which to escape the rigors of severe winters, and to relax from business cares. Florida beaches and Florida camps thus became notable health resorts. The tropical vegetation, and the semi-tropical climate were alluring. It was something different from the environment of almost every other part of the nation.

What could be more natural, then, while passing hours of idleness in this national winter playground, than the purchase of a winter home or a large tract of land there? One becomes "an easy mark" during vacations, and is apt to spend more lavishly and purchase more liberally than when at home. Countless Florida tourists became Florida real estate proprietors. The millionaires bought large estates; the lesser rich bought town and beach lots.

Interest was thus accumulated in Florida real estate. Those who bought told others of their purchases. Millionaires would not be outdone by other millionaires. Rivalry and jealousy led to acquisitions of Florida "estates" and to the engrossment of large and favorably situated tracts. Moreover, the Florida waste and unoccupied lands could be bought relatively cheap, compared with land values in more settled industrial and farming sections. There were immense stretches of undeveloped coast lands and countless acres of untilled soil that were continually on the market. Much of this was held in large acreages by individual owners, and could be readily acquired at wholesale. Florida, in this respect, was "America's last frontier."

Because of these conditions, public attention was centered on Florida real estate. Just one large, well-advertised "promotion scheme" could set the pot of speculation boiling.

Another factor leading to the recent outburst of speculation in Florida was the creation of transportation facilities there. The Florida East Coast Railroad, a monumental enterprise conceived as a millionaire's hobby, was completed in 1900. It opened up for settlement a vast area, relatively unoccupied, in the southern part of the peninsula. As its traffic grew, it enlarged its equipment. Other railroad lines were constructed on both east and west coasts. In addition, new and improved highways were cut through. The Everglades were in process of being drained by state and local appropriations. Steamship lines also aided. Thus, the frontier character of the territory was changed. As in the western country, a "boom" followed the creation of transportation and communication facilities.

The boom was not a sudden outburst. There were rumblings for several years. Vast schemes of development were set on foot. The draining of the Everglades, the building of a canal and harbor at Lake Worth, the development of Palm Beach, the planning of Coral Gables and a hundred other projects gave a favorable setting. The year 1924 marks the beginning of the rush period. It followed the first mass invasion of real estate promoters and "developers," though many had arrived by means of peaceful penetration for several years previous. The climax was reached in 1925. In 1926 came the collapse.

Who were the instigators of the fiasco, and who were responsible for its execution?

The original promoters were all men of mark. There was Henry B. Plant, who came to Florida as early as 1861, and who built railroads and hotels there. He founded Plant City, a successful real estate development. Next, there is Henry M. Flagler, Standard Oil executive, who visited Florida in 1885. The possibilities of the state as a winter playground were revealed to him. He built at St. Augustine, the Ponce de León and the Alcazar hotels, dreams of massive architecture. His creative ambitions broadened.

He built the Florida East Coast Railroad—a marvelous, though foolhardy engineering feat—and adorned its lines with palatial hotels. He also bought heavily of Florida lands. "Flagler Street," the principal thoroughfare in Miami, and the headquarters of the late, though not lamented, real estate fraternity, is an adequate reminder of this master builder's benefactions to the Peninsula State. Then, there is Barron Collier, the advertising magnate, who developed a whole county that bears his name. This county was established in 1923 and embraces over 1,200,000 acres. When he acquired it, the land had never been touched by plowshare or other human tools.

Collier started to make his vast estate a garden spot, building roads, draining swamps and establishing a town. He invested his millions in these ventures and persuaded others to do the same by this proof of his faith in them. In speaking of the great future of Collier County, and its increasing population, he once remarked, poetically: "The light of the fireflies will be dimmed by the electric lights in happy homes, and the chirp of the katydids will be chorused by the laughter of happy children."

Many others contributed to Florida's expected greatness. The "Great Commoner" and perennial presidential candidate, William Jennings Bryan, made his residence there. Although his limited wealth prevented him from entering upon great development schemes, his contribution was equally effective, for his pen and his masterful voice gave extremely valuable aid and encouragement. Roger W. Babson, stock market forecaster and dispenser of voluminous statistics, also lent a hand. J. C. Penney, merchant and philanthropist, and John and Charles Ringling, circus operators, likewise contributed capital and enterprise, and raised their voices in praise of the Land of the Everglades. Others of this type, such as T. Coleman DuPont, August Heckscher and Jesse Livermore, could be mentioned, but it is not necessary to furnish a full list. When millionaires, statesmen and investment counselors—men of repute, foresight and discretion—added the weight of their influence to the persuasions of ordinary professional real estate promoters, then it was no wonder that the population went mad over the fabulous possibilities of pecuniary gain in the scrub lands and everglades of the Florida peninsula.

Thus encouraged by the aid of shrewd and enterprising capitalists, and by the nascent prosperity following in the wake of the post-war depression, the Florida people vigorously laid out the groundwork of the "boom." In March, 1925, there was convened at West Palm Beach a meeting of the representative business men from all parts of the state. Needless to say, the "real estaters" and "developers" were there in force. They organized themselves into the Florida Development Board and committed themselves to spend a million and a half dollars or more, if necessary, for publicity during the next five years. They began a series of boosting advertisements, art pamphlets, books and all other devices to attract the fortune seeker as well as the tourist to the confines of the state. Tourists and fortune seekers are almost indistinguishable. Tourists have surplus funds, otherwise they could not travel, and a goodly proportion of those who went to Florida merely for a holiday came back property owners and local taxpayers. One could hardly venture outside his hotel room in a Florida resort without stumbling over a half dozen high pressure real estate salesmen.

The advertising campaign of the Florida Development Board, assisted by the Florida land and real estate mortgage companies, brought to their aid the magazines and the press. Articles describing the allurements of the "American Riviera," the "Nation's Winter Playground," "America's Winter Paradise," as well as the immense agricultural, mineral and industrial resources of Florida, appeared in the leading literary and business periodicals. They occupied prominent positions in the Sunday editions and "travel numbers" of the newspapers. At the height of the excited boom, the *Saturday Evening Post*, the most widely read of American popular periodicals, began a Florida series by Thomas McMorrow and Kenneth Roberts, and continued them at almost regular intervals throughout the period of the boom.[3]

Even after the "crash" came, following the hurricane which swept away the paper fortunes of multitudes, the "boosting" continued. Florida would not only recover, but a new and greater

[3] Mr. Roberts' articles were subsequently published in a book entitled *Florida*, published by Harper & Brothers, 1926. It points out the pitfalls as well as the allurements. Mr. McMorrow, however, seems to have been infected with the "boom fever."

period of prosperity would be ushered in. "The suckers will not stop coming," one could almost read between the lines. "They have made only a beginning of buying into Florida. Those who lost their 'binders' may be discouraged, but there are others. Suckers are born every minute, and some can still be induced to put their savings in resurrected swamp lands and wind-swept beaches."

When the host of real estate promoters, gathered from all parts of the United States, concentrated in Florida, then the real boom was on. Most of these mongers were not "to the manor born." They were like the "carpetbaggers" of the South in post-Civil War days. They came to fill their pockets, not to make the country rich. They cared not whom they duped, nor what became of their projects when once they had unloaded them. The foolish mortals who hung around their "offices," and paid for "binders," "options" and "contracts," were merely fish in their nets. Nor were they, in many cases, merely "crooked dealers." As already noted, the vast "developments" engineered during the boom period had the backing of great names in present-day financial circles. There were among these men many who transferred their activities from stock market operations or legitimate real estate dealings in settled communities to a field where they saw opportunities of greater profit. When the collapse came, they withdrew and resumed their former occupations.

The methods of unloading lots and farms in the Florida gamble do not differ from those described in the discussion of previous episodes in land speculation throughout the country's history. Charles Dickens could have depicted Martin Chuzzlewit buying a lot in a Florida "development" in 1925, as readily and in the same language as he did eighty-five years earlier. Of course, every development in Florida was to be a "city," and the lots were sold before the project was even launched. This is well described by Mr. Walter C. Hill, vice-president of the Retail Credit Company of Atlanta:

Lots were bought from blue prints. They look better that way. Then the buyer gets the promoter's vision, can see the splendid curving boulevards, the yacht basin, the parks lined with leaning cocoanut trees, and flaming hibiscus. The salesmen can show the expected

Courtesy of the "Miami Herald"

SKYSCRAPERS RISING ON THE MIAMI WATERFRONT IN NOVEMBER, 1925

VISION

The Florida of Reality

THE Spanish *conquistadores* who discovered Florida and the Spanish *colonos* who followed them were over-eager in their quest for gold and quickly acquired riches.

They failed to realize the wealth in the soil they trod—in the balmy breezes that brushed their bronzed cheeks—in the beneficence of the blue dome overhead.

They sought advantage but missed opportunity because they lacked—VISION.

And yet it is a question whether Americans of today have even yet awakened to the tremendous powers of capital and energy now at work in Florida. Those who have informed themselves of her almost immeasurable resources of soil and climate know that they constitute America's most immediate and assured VISION OF OPPORTUNITY.

Thus, BOCA RATON now offers the test of VISION to the competence and culture of America. Just twenty-six miles south of Palm Beach, the Gulf Stream here sets in almost to the roots of the cocoa palms that march in stately procession along the golden beach. Blessed by sun and caressed by breeze, cosmopolitan society will find in BOCA RATON natural attractions of climate and situation unrivaled in any resort in the world.

BOCA RATON offers hitherto unavailable advantages as a place of residence, outdoor life and health benefits.

BOCA RATON assures soundness of investment as the most advantageous resort situation of a State inevitably destined to vast increase of wealth and population because of her natural resources—resources as yet unrealized by the vast majority and awaiting only VISION to yield assured returns.

Addison Mizner, the architectural genius of Palm Beach, has set himself to create in BOCA RATON the premier of cosmopolitan world resorts. The warrant of his ability to do so is found in the imposing estates, beautiful clubs and resplendent casinos of Palm Beach.

Every building of whatever sort to be erected in BOCA RATON must meet with his supervisory approval. Thus BOCA RATON shall ultimate in a municipal entity—a perfected architectural unity of enduring beauty

> Attach this advertisement to your contract for deed. It becomes a part thereof.

Board of Directors

U. S. SENATOR T. COLEMAN DUPONT, Delaware
JESSE L. LIVERMORE, Capitalist, New York
WARD A. WICKWIRE, President, Wickwire Spencer Steel Co., New York
ADDISON MIZNER, President, Mizner Development Corporation
STEPHEN WARNER, Secretary-Treasurer, Mizner Development Corporation
HON. GEORGE S. GRAHAM, L.L. Representative Pennsylvania
J. A. BLISS, Vice-President, DuPont Co., Pennsylvania
RODMAN B. CO., New York
H. J. MYERS, JR., Investment Banker, New York
ANDREW T. HURD, General Manager, Mizner Development Corporation
A. A. THOMPSON, Capitalist and Civil Engineer, Tuxedo, Pa.
WILLIAM A. WHITE, Real Estate, Palm Beach, Florida

Finance Committee

U. S. SENATOR T. COLEMAN DUPONT
H. S. SHERM JR.
ANDREW T. HURD
JESSE L. LIVERMORE
W. A. BLISS

Mizner Development Corporation
Developers of BOCA RATON Florida

Executive Office
Via MIZNER
PALM BEACH, FLORIDA

WASHINGTON OFFICE—Ground Floor, Munsey Building, 1329 E St., N. W
Phones: Main 8126—Main 7397

GEORGE FRYHOFER
General Sales Manager
S. H. WOLBERG
Manager Washington Office

lines of heavy travel and help select a double (two-lot) corner for business, or a quiet water-front retreat suitable for a winter home. To go see the lot—well,—it isn't done. Often it is not practicable, for most of the lots are sold "predevelopment." The boulevards are yet to be laid, the yacht basin must be pumped out, and the excavated dirt used to raise the proposed lots above water or bog level. Then they will be staked, the planning done, and the owner can find his lot.[4]

Whenever a new "development" was conceived, the promoters immediately advertised it in the newspapers and by handbills, giving descriptions of the location, extent, special features and the approximate prices of the lots. Reservations were made by depositing 10 per cent of the proposed price, and these reservations were taken up in the order received, and attended to before the regular sale of lots was opened. The holder of the reservation was thus permitted to select from a beautifully drawn plan, on which lots and prices were marked, the sites he desired. He then got a "binder," i.e., an option on the selected lot, which he could resell immediately. This gave him a thrill, for he felt that he was the owner of Florida real estate—even if actually in a swamp— and he hoped to transfer his "purchase" at a fabulous profit to an absentee or latecomer. This quick turnover was frequently a necessity to the "binder-boy" (i.e., the "option buyer") because he had not the cash required to make the first payment of one-fourth the purchase price within thirty days after the "binder" was issued to him. Speculation in "binders" was a leading occupation in Florida, and those who indulged in it were popularly termed "binder-boys."

During the height of the Florida boom, the sales of the new "developments" were markedly successful. Around Miami, the "subdivisions," with the exception of the very large ones like Coral Gables and Boca Raton, were often sold out on the first day of sale. The money values represented in such sales amounted, in many cases, to millions. Inside lots, existing on blue prints only, would sell from $8,000 to $20,000 each, and seashore sites ranged from $20,000 to $75,000. Prices were lower on the inland developments, unless they happened to be located on the Dixie

[4] Published by the Retail Credit Company of Atlanta, September, 1925.

Highway or some other favorite "trail"—then prices mounted again to a point approximating the Miami Beach "subdivisions." When lots were bought by dealers or local speculators, they were almost immediately offered for resale in the "real estate offices" of the city. Non-residents eventually became the lot owners. Possibly a few may still hold them. However, *they are relatively few,* since in a great majority of cases the "lot" speculators have defaulted on their purchase contracts. The "developers" have received back their properties, but the sheriff in most cases has made the final distribution; or the municipality or county becomes the ultimate owner through non-payment of the taxes levied upon them. Many tracts purchased for hundreds of thousands of dollars have been released from private ownership because of non-payment of a few hundred dollars in back taxes.

An enumeration of all the "developments" in Florida during the years 1924-26 would cover many pages. These stretched for hundreds of miles both north and south of Miami. They covered the west coast of the state from the southerly tip up to and beyond Cedar Keys. And fancy names they had, too! The Spanish language appears to have been quite an advertising asset to the "developers." Pasadena, Santa Monica, Buena Vista, Rio Vista, and other pleasant sounding appellations, so agreeable to Californians, were adopted, as well as names from Italy, such as Naples, Venice, Indrio, Riviera, and those of other famous Mediterranean resorts. Common Spanish terms were even adopted, such as "Los Gatos" (the Cats) and "Boca Raton" (Rat's Jaw), hideous in the vernacular but, of course, high sounding, since the real meaning was unknown to most of the speculators.

Every important city, town or "development" had its slogan. Miami was "The Magic City"; Orlando, "The City Beautiful"; Hollywood, "The Golden Gate of the South"; St. Petersburg, "The Sunshine City"; and Fort Lauderdale, "The Tropical Wonderland." Indrio, a development that never "panned out," was called "Florida's Newest and Most Beautiful," although it is still largely a wind-swept stretch of sand and scrub. And Hollywood, "Golden Gate of the South," leads to nowhere. Coral Gables, the largest of the projected "cities," was to be the "Venice of America." To make the slogan effective, its promoters are said to have actually imported Venice-built gondolas, and expert gondoliers were expressly ordered to complete the architectural *motif*.

One of the means of luring tourists and others into making "investments" was the free motor-bus trips. It was not necessary to hire taxis or use railroad trains to travel in Florida. One could have ridden almost over all the state by merely evincing an interest in real estate. This, of course, is an old "bait," employed by the real estate gentry of the nation for many years. Truly, the land business has long been on a low ethical plane.

As usual in excited periods of speculation, fraud, villainy and deceit prevailed in the Florida fiasco. The notorious crook, Charles Ponzi, went there to recoup the loss of his ill-gotten gains from his "get-rich-quick" scheme in Boston. He organized the "Charpon Land Syndicate" which claimed it had an option on an undeveloped tract of land "near Jacksonville" (though it was actually 65 miles from the place). He sought to obtain the capital required for "this purchase" by selling "unit certificates of indebtedness" at $310 per unit. He guaranteed a dividend of 200 per cent on each certificate within three months. His real estate activities, however, were cut short, as he was indicted and, on April 2, 1926, convicted for violating the trust laws of the State of Florida.

Another fraudulent undertaking was the "Florida Cities Finance Company," which promoted "Fulford by the Sea." Its founder was also apprehended and jailed, along with a number of other downright swindlers who were trailed through the efforts of the National Better Business Bureau and the United States Post Office Department. Both before and after the collapse of the boom, there were hundreds of arrests, convictions, suits and countersuits growing out of the frenzied real estate transactions of the period.

All this naturally could not go on without attracting public attention. The sober-minded element of the nation's business men looked upon it with amazement and scorn. Occasional and sporadic warnings were issued, and attempts were made to stem the tide of wild speculation. The Massachusetts Savings Bank League, in November, 1925, issued a statement cautioning depositors not to withdraw money to speculate in Florida real estate. The Investment Bankers Association set aside a whole session of their annual convention to consider means of checking the wildcat land gambles. Their members complained of loss of business due to customers placing funds in Florida lands and in buying Florida 8 per cent mortgage bonds, advertised with the slogan "where the security is a certainty."

To all this the Florida "boosters" naturally objected. When the secretary of the National Credit Association pointed out the danger of inflated Florida credits, the Florida Credit Association petitioned for his removal from office. The Better Business Bureau of New York City, late in 1925, began a thorough investigation of questionable Florida "developments," and its revelations were labeled by the Florida "boosters" as malicious and false propaganda.

Thus, the Florida real estate fraternity did not stand idly by when these warnings appeared in the press and other publications. They also had their defenders. By way of outside support there was organized in New York City, in 1925, a Florida defense association, composed of speculators and dealers in Florida real estate. W. W. Rose, the president of the Florida Real Estate Association, and his associates were "on deck" whenever a statement or an address, traducing the practices and motives of his constituency, appeared. They built up elaborate defenses. A sporadic break in security prices on the New York Stock Exchange in February and March, 1926, was seized upon by them as an object lesson. "Isn't it better," they pointed out, "for the public to invest in sound real estate values than in fluctuating and questionable securities?" A loss of four billion dollars in stock market values occurred in one month! Such a loss, they pointed out, could never occur in Florida real estate. There, "security was a certainty."

Special newspapers and magazines were published, and books were written and widely distributed, defending the "boom." Charles Donald Fox, in *The Truth About Florida*, published in

December, 1925, when the bubble had expanded to maximum proportions, (as stated by Mr. Meryle Stanley Rukeyser, who wrote
his "introduction"), endeavored to perform "a useful task in
making available ascertainable facts about climate, soil, other
natural resources and traffic conditions." Yet Mr. Fox boldly
stated in his text: *"I believe the so-called 'boom' will last forever,
for there can be no let-up to the development of a state which
offers so much to so many classes of people."*[5] And he added:
"Let me record once again. *There is no boom in Florida.* The
state is merely doing in a few years what it would ordinarily
take decades to do. It is doing all this on a permanent basis. It is
building for the future. It is turning the tables on the usual
development procedure—it is speeding up the future and making
it the present." Of course, Mr. Fox did not take into consideration hurricanes and financial panics, which retard the future and
agonizingly prolong the present.

No less extravagant is the language of another inspired volume,
entitled *Florida in the Making*, published less than a year later,
and written jointly by Frank Parker Stockbridge, a Florida real
estate operator, and John Holliday Perry, a journalist. In a
"Foreword," John W. Martin, then governor of Florida, pointed
out that the authors have not merely written a book, "they have
performed a public service, the value of which cannot be over-
estimated," and he adds: "No one can read 'Florida in the Making' without being convinced that all which has yet been done in
Florida is but a beginning towards what is to come."

The authors, however, did not, as Charles Donald Fox had
done, answer directly the question: "Will the Florida boom continue?" But they point out some pertinent facts, as follows:

The question which skeptics are asking everywhere is "When will
the Florida boom collapse?"

Men asked the same question in George Washington's day about
the Ohio country, when Cincinnati was as young as Miami is today.
They doubted in Lincoln's time whether Iowa land prices were not
too high. Forty years ago one could hear dire predictions of the
imminent collapse of a "boom" town on Lake Michigan, called Chi-

---

[5] *The Truth About Florida,* p. 12.

cago. Only recently similar forecasts were being broadcast of the ultimate fate of Los Angeles and all southern California.

Florida's boom differs only in detail from all the other land booms which, added together, comprise practically all there is of consequence in American history. Geography and topography are different; principles and methods are unchanged. The historical test serves, then, as the horoscope to resolve one's doubts withal. *Nobody who bought and held on in Ohio, in Iowa, in Los Angeles or Chicago, lost, all made profits. "Shoestring" speculators, investors who lost faith, lost out on the temporary setbacks which all the historical land booms have experienced.* Many more, those who acted on the time-honored Wall Street axiom that nobody ever went broke by taking profits, got in and got out on the successive upward waves, taking out more than they put in. But the solid backbone of every land development is the settler. Fluctuations in money value of his land do not affect him, if the land yields him the comfort of the livelihood he seeks.[6]

All this is very well! But land speculators do not care to wait a quarter century or more to bring real values up to the level of the inflated values which they themselves create in boom times. Fortunes have been lost, not made, by buying and paying for future values, without taking into consideration the accumulation of interest, taxes and other expenses that have only Death as a companion factor of certainty. Manhattan Island may have been worth more than the twenty-four dollars in merchandise the Dutch paid for it, but the shrewd Hollanders would never have been willing to look ahead a hundred years or so, and pay the Indians a price which it might then be worth.

The arguments of the peerless orator, William Jennings Bryan, and the renowned forecaster, Mr. Roger W. Babson, were not less convincing than those contained in the writings already mentioned. Mr. Bryan pointed out Florida's qualities as an earthly paradise and as a place of high moral and religious culture. Mr. Babson stressed especially Florida's wonderful economic possibilities: "Some feel that Florida is being overdone," wrote Mr. Babson in 1926, "but, based on the history of other sections of the country, I believe that the great movement in Florida has

[6] *Florida in the Making*, p. 286.

only started and that values in many sections will double, triple, and quadruple during the next eight years." Accordingly, he, in company with a host of other commentators, was firmly of the belief that the marvelous development of Florida in the boom years was "just a preliminary of the marvelous development that lies before it."[7]

Bryan's boosting talk was hardly less moderate. "The cities in Florida are friendly rivals," he wrote in a companion article to Mr. Babson's, "but they are united in the determination to make Florida one of the foremost states of the Union, and they are anxious for the State to be a leader in education and morals as they are that the State shall lead in material progress."

Undoubtedly, some instigators of the Florida boom, especially those who bought and resold early in the proceedings, realized handsome profits. Several "millionaire winter residents," who previously had bought estates merely for their personal enjoyment, later sold to "developers" with fabulous gains. On the other hand, others who contracted the speculation fever, and endeavored to undertake developments on their own account, lost heavily. But aside from individual gains and losses, the boom period was one of great prosperity in Florida. Its wealth, as measured in current values, increased in a short period of two years to tremendous proportions. From 1923 to 1926, the state's population (possibly, excluding the "immigrant" real estate salesmen) increased from 1,057,400 to 1,290,350, or 22 per cent, and bank deposits from $225,000,000 to $850,000,000. Assessed valuations rose in proportion, and building operations in two years quintupled. The transportation facilities were inadequate to handle the passengers and goods which poured into the state in the excited days of rising real estate values. The effect was a high cost of living, high rates of wages and inadequate living quarters.

When these obstructions to material progress were being seriously encountered, the clouds of recession began to gather on the horizon. The frenzied activities of the summer and fall of 1925 were carried over into 1926, but the eagerness of specula-

[7] See "Florida, Old and New," 1925-1926, p. xix et seq.

tors to bid up values began gradually to disappear. The "developers" and "boosters" endeavored in vain to maintain the speculative interest in their undertakings. The municipal authorities assisted, and large issues of public obligations were floated to carry out improvement plans. The borrowing "cities" were, however, soon unable to meet the interest burden on this new indebtedness.

These efforts were being strenuously put forth, when the same benign Nature which made Florida the "Land of Flowers" and "An Earthly Paradise," reversed the process. As in years past, on September 19, 1926, a terrific West Indian hurricane blew over the southern portion of the peninsula and interrupted the dreams of "easy money" which the very atmosphere seemed to have engendered during the preceding three years. The debacle was complete. The hordes of real estate developers, high pressure salesmen, feature writers and private "investors," which had invaded the territory "in Pullmans and Packards," were now confronted with desolation and despair. They hastily departed.

The banks were drawn on heavily, and their swollen deposits faded away. From a high level of $850,000,000 at the end of 1925, deposits in Florida banks dropped to $550,000,000 at the end of 1926, and reached still lower figures thereafter. An epidemic of bank failures was the result. Florida real estate mortgages, with "security a certainty," were a drug on the market. One "development" after another lapsed. Instalment payments on lots practically ceased. The bubble had burst!

There were a few attempts at resurrection. The state authorities even decried the publication of the extent of the hurricane damage, because of its discouraging effects on land values. An effort was made to turn away the Red Cross from its relief work. Newspapers and magazines were told that Florida's marvelous progress would continue. A typical statement was contained in the *Wall Street Journal*, October 8, 1926. It quoted Mr. Peter O. Knight, of Tampa, counsel of the Seaboard Air Line Railway, as saying: "The same Florida is still there with its magnificent resources, its wonderful climate, and its geographical position. It is the Riviera of America, and always will be, within twenty-four hours or less, of eighty millions of prosperous people, and the same causes which developed Florida so rapidly in the last few years, will cause a greater and more permanent Florida to be developed in the future."

. . . . .

Among the many magnificent schemes of modern city building, with real estate speculation as the prime motive, two projects stand out prominently in the recent Florida boom. These are "Coral Gables" and "Boca Raton." Both are remarkable for the magnificence and the tremendous enterprise with which they were developed. Both have failed in the execution of the original grandiose conception as outlined by the promoters.

Coral Gables is the older, and was nearer to completion when the collapse came. It was originated by George Edgar Merrick —a native Floridian, who as a boy dwelt on a farm not far from Miami. According to an inspired booklet, beautifully illustrated, and under the authorship of Rex Beach, the novelist (though it is copyrighted by Merrick himself), "the boy Merrick listened, and as he grew older, his dream took shape. He built *a city*. His city is set among pines and palms, and flaming poincianas, and he called it Coral Gables. It is indeed a city of coral gables, and of soft tinted coral walls. Upon the fields he used to till, the stones have blossomed; those ragged stubborn rocks he used to curse, he has called to bloom into an eternal flower."

Merrick, in his early development activities, received the financial support of local interests. His first idea was an exclusive inland suburb. As his plans developed, and as the oncoming boom caused a rapid growth of Miami,—"like a tropical weed,"—the project was expanded into a sea-front community, with forty miles of beach land. It was to be a "modified Mediterranean—a new Venice, with silent pools, canals and lagoons," *and even more beautiful*, since no lot purchaser was allowed to put up a dwelling or other structure in it that would destroy the harmony of the general design. And, above all, it was to be a *complete city*, with business zones, with workers' districts, and with favorite locations for the rich and well-to-do. The "development," therefore, broke away from Miami, and received a city charter.

Thus, Coral Gables "was worked out with pencil and ruler,"

and nourished with widespread publicity.[8] It became the show-place of Miami. It resembled, in one aspect, a real estate exchange, and in another, a great county fair. Entertainments, concerts, lectures, all the old-time "booming" accompaniments, were resorted to. The "Hon." William Jennings Bryan was employed to deliver his masterful orations there almost daily. In these he stressed the high moral and religious tone of Florida, along with its fine climate and its excellent resources. It was worth the price of a lot to hear him,—and if the urge to "buy at once" overtook any of his audience, the high pressure real estate salesman was near to take advantage of the psychological moment. The old "land office business" was revived in a new atmosphere. And Florida—"America's Last Frontier"—was bursting its seams. To make more room for expansion, the "underwater" acreage was also offered for sale and settlement, and magnificent islands created out of the ocean's depths.

George Merrick and his associates planned to spend "ten years of hard work and a hundred millions of hard money" to complete the enterprise. Every effort was made to conceal the commercial aspect by romantic and æsthetic surroundings. "Gondolas from old Venice had been ordered to this New Venice," remarks Rex Beach. A university built in antique mission style was planned. "Beauty draws more than oxen," exclaims (on paper) the inspired author. But he does not say that dollars are drawn in by Beauty.

When the Coral Gables enterprise expanded both in concept and in area, its promoters organized "Coral Gables Consolidated, Inc." to take over the enterprise, with Merrick as its president. This corporation went heavily into debt. When the fever of speculation began to wane in the spring of 1926, the concern experienced difficulty in disposing of lots. Then the cruel wind came. It blew through Coral Gables and swept away hopes and fortunes. The financial difficulties of Coral Gables Consolidated, Inc. increased. Its officials sold the street railways, the golf fields, the swimming pools and other attractions to the city which they had chartered for this purpose, and which the promoters continued

[8] For a description of the methods of the Publicity Department of Coral Gables, see T. H. Weigall, *Boom in Paradise*, especially Chap. IX.

to operate under the guise of "a city commission." Under its municipal charter, the city of Coral Gables was given the most liberal power to incur indebtedness of any similar body politic in the country. Its debt could equal 25 per cent of its assessed valuation. Accordingly, the "city" issued municipal bonds to pay for the "improvements" it acquired, and in this way supplied the promoters with cash. But the financial difficulties persisted. The promoters then threatened to compel the former lot purchasers, by judicial proceedings, to continue their payments. They preferred to have cash rather than the real estate, which they, but a short time before, had advertised as an investment of certain and ever-increasing value.

All this was of little avail. Bankruptcy was the outcome. Altogether, $150,000,000 is reported to have been expended on Coral Gables in building and development, about half by the development corporation and about half by private investors. The money lost by lot purchasers and speculators amounted probably to larger sums. And to these losses might be added the cash invested by the unfortunate purchasers of the Coral Gables municipal bonds.

No less magnificent in proposed splendor, in artistic conception, and in high ideals, was the second of the leading "developments"—"Boca Raton." An architect, who had lived in Spanish America as a boy and who was attracted by the harmonious designs of the rich dwellings there in relation to the tropical surroundings, established his business in Palm Beach in 1918. He was Addison Mizner. His plans for fine residences in this luxurious and exclusive pleasure resort soon gave him a national reputation as an architect. When Coral Gables, built upon "Mediterranean models," bid fair to become a successful and profitable undertaking, the architect and his associates conceived the idea of establishing a still more elaborate "development" twenty-four miles below Palm Beach. They organized the "Mizner Development Corporation." Its directors comprised names of high social and financial standing. Among them were ex-United States Senator T. Coleman DuPont, Jesse L. Livermore, capitalist, Hon. George S. Graham, United States Representative from Pennsylvania, Ward S. Wickwire, prominent steel manufacturer, and L. A. Bean, vice-president of Dwight P. Robinson & Co., New York realty operators. "World leaders in finance, society and arts, establish an international resort on the Florida East Coast," reads the headline of the first full-page newspaper display advertisement of the project. Another stated: "The public has demonstrated its faith in the men and women back of Boca Raton. Its confidence in the future is assured to Boca Raton by the social standing and financial solidarity of its sponsors . . . Your decision to invest now is justified by their investment hitherto. Act now and every day will justify your decision."

As to the architecture and beauty of the "development," why, it was to be entirely "mizneresque." "Boca Raton will surpass in exclusiveness any resort on Florida's East Coast. But the democracy of Addison Mizner has provided large and well selected bathing beaches, golf courses, and tennis courts, aviation field, polo ground and dock rights for the use of all. No existing world resort of wealth and fashion compares with Boca Raton, and never before has there been offered such opportunity of financial reward through early participation in a Florida enterprise." And so on, until the sad end.

The lots in Boca Raton were offered in May, 1925, when the whole affair was still on paper. Purchases, the first day, are reported to have amounted to $2,100,000. In the first fourteen weeks more than $14,000,000 in value was sold, says a full-page display advertisement. It was not necessary to go to Florida to buy. Elaborate offices were opened in the principal cities. In Washington, the Mizner Development Corporation occupied the whole ground floor of a prominent office building, and its offices remained open day and evening.

The Boca Raton plan proposed the construction of a Ritz-Carlton Hotel, costing $6,000,000. Only a small hotel was opened in 1926. There were to be lagoons and canals, and, as in the case of Coral Gables, gondolas and gondoliers were to be brought from Venice. Every structure in the development must conform to the uniform plan of the general architecture. It was not to be "a crowded commercial center" or "an addition, however worthy, to an already existing community. It *is* a cosmopolitan world community."

Difficulties, however, developed more rapidly than the building operations. In November, 1925, the Finance Committee of the Mizner Development Corporation, comprising leading capitalists, resigned. They objected to the "management." On January 22, 1926, application was made to put the company in receivership. This was dismissed by the court, but it was merely a short delay. The insolvency was admitted soon afterwards. Thus, another "Dream City" proved to be only a "dream."

Not all the speculation in the Florida boom was concerned with city development and beach and underwater lots. Owners of large tracts of hitherto waste lands took advantage of the opportunity to rid themselves, at tremendous profits, of their holdings. Everglade lands, which were not worth the tax payments on them, were eagerly bought up and divided and resold at from $5 to $100 or more an acre. Schemes were put on foot to encourage rural settlements in this "last American frontier." Mr. J. C. Penney laid open to immigrants—who were expected, however, to come in Pullmans instead of covered wagons—his "Penney Farms," located in Clay County, thirty miles from Jacksonville "in the heart of a rich agricultural district." His was not an ordinary land settlement scheme. "I came to believe," he stated in a public address in 1927, "that under the same principle [as conducted in his stores] men could be found to take up tracts of land, and given a certain amount of expert guidance, keep their farms up to a standard and made to succeed." He offered plots in 2½, 5 and 20 acres, cleared and plowed at least once, and placed all under the guidance of the J. C. Penney-Guvin Institute of Agricultural Science. He also established coöperative marketing.

Thus, philanthropy, as well as profit, was back of investments in Florida. Barron G. Collier, and also the retired circus proprietors, the Ringling Brothers, likewise carried on agricultural land development projects. The growing population of Florida, the rapid increase in the size of its cities and the improvement in transportation facilities, it was pointed out, would make

Florida agricultural lands of as great value as those surrounding the large population centers of the North and West. Needless to say, hundreds of land companies were born almost overnight to exploit this conception of increasing value of the soil. Many of these concerns were fraudulent or partially fraudulent in their operations. They sold everglade and waste lands which are practically worthless for immediate cultivation. Much of this soil has again become the resourceless property of the state authorities, since the private owners have been surrendering them one after another for tax arrearages.

Such is the story of the Florida Boom—the latest phase in a long series of cycles of land gambling and town jobbing, which has marked American business annals almost from the time of Columbus to the present day.

(353)

INDEX

INDEX

INDEX

Mitchel, Robert, 332
Mitchell, S. Weir, 301
Mizner, Addison, 349
Mizner Development Corporation, 350
Mobile Bay, 196
Mobile River, 131
Mohawk and Hudson Railroad, 243
Mohawk River, 25, 54
Mohawk Valley, 11, 27, 54
Monongahela River, 10
Monroe, La., 203
Montgomery County, Ga., 142, 144
Moody, William Godwin, 308
Moore, H. Miles, 314
Moore, Thomas, 163
Moorehead, William G., 296
Moreau, M., 196
Morehouse, Abraham, 201, 203
Morgan, George, 117
Morgan, John, 121
Morris, Gouverneur, 40, 166, 281
  districts interested in, 64, 66, 142
  early land deals, 42
  general land agent, 87-95
  land agent in Ohio, 170-171
  land sales in France, 48, 68
  New York land deals, 59
Morris, Mary, 190
Morris, Robert, 107
  Fauchet's opinion of, 51
  in the post-Revolutionary wild land mania, 34-37
  land jobbing, 11, 47, 48
  land peddling in Europe, 57, 58, 74
  military land warrant trading, 32
  New York land gambling, 42, 58-63
  pre-Revolutionary land interests, 20-22
  public office, 41
  sections interested in, 56, 64, 130, 132, 134, 141-149, 158-168
  use of land "scrip," 53
Morris, Robert, Jr., 60-62, 144
  New York land sales in Holland, 61
Morris, Mrs. Robert, 166
Morris, Roger, 189
Morris, Thomas, 58, 62, 63
Morrisania, 42, 166
Morrison, Robert, 183
Morrison, William, 182, 183
Morristown, N. J., 111
Morrisville, 35, 149
Morse, Jedidiah, 19, 134

Morton, Perez, 136
Moultrie, Alexander, 125
Mt. Carmel and New Albany Railroad, 277
Mount Hamilton, 261
Mount Vernon, 8, 9, 161
Murray, John, 20
Murray, William, 18-20
Muscle Shoals, Ala., 131
Muskingum Valley, 113
My Life in Many States and in Foreign Lands, George Francis Train, 289, *note*
Myra Clark Gaines Case, 204

Nacogdoches, Texas, 227
Napoleon I, Emperor, 200, 211
Nashville, Tenn., 131, 201, 229
  Texas excitement in, 220
Natchez, Miss., 126, 131
Natchitoches, La., 214
National Land System, The, Payson Jackson Treat, *notes,* 57, 106, 169
Navarro County, Texas, 230
Neal, David A., 281
Nebraska, land booms, 314
  terminal speculation in, 290
Necker, Jacques, 42, 48, 91, 93
Neville, Presley, 11
New Amsterdam (*see* Buffalo *and* New York State)
Newark, N. J., 178
New Babylon, Kansas, 316
New Brighton Company, 252
New England, in the post-Revolutionary mania, 39-46
  land grabbing, 22-25
New England Mississippi Land Company, 135
New Hampshire, conflict with New York, 26-28
New Harmony, 188
New Jersey, 15, 111, 116
  English grants in, 1
New Jersey Journal, 115
New London, Conn., 120
New Madrid, Mo., 197, 198, 207, 209, 213
New Mexico, cession to United States, 270
  Mexican grants, 270
  Spanish grants, 273
New Mexico Mining Co., 271
New Orleans, La., 127, 131, 194, 203-212